CITIZEN, SETTLER, SOLDIER, SCOUNDREL:

A SOCIAL HISTORY OF THE
MILITIA OF MANITOBA, 1870–1885

Citizen, Settler, Soldier, Scoundrel:

A Social History of the Militia of Manitoba, 1870–1885

David W. Grebstad

Library and Archives Canada Cataloguing in Publication
Grebstad, David W., author
Citizen, Settler, Soldier, Scoundrel / David W. Grebstad

Issued in print and electronic formats.
ISBN: 978-1-998501-25-0 (paperback)
ISBN: 978-1-998501-26-7 (ebook)

Editor: Marie-Jade Charest
Cover Design: Pablo Javier Herrera
Interior Design: Winston S. Prescott

Double Dagger Books Ltd.
Toronto, Ontario, Canada
www.doubledagger.ca

TABLE OF CONTENTS

PREFACE

Manitoba has a fascinating history. I developed my deep interest in Manitoba history only a short time ago and, ironically, long after I had moved away from Manitoba. I am a perennial supporter of underdogs and this, perhaps more than anything, is what drew me to the history of Manitoba. Not that Manitobans are underdogs, but I find that Canadian history is, to a large degree, dominated by the histories of Ontario and Quebec, and in many ways Canadian history can be considered the story of central Canada, with appendices added on for the other regions of the country. When I started reading about Manitoba history in detail, I was struck by how unique and diverse it was. Perhaps I am a hopeless romantic, but I find the story of an isolated land on the verge of civilization, surrounded by untouched wilderness and maintaining only the most tenuous of holds on survival in the face of what can be described as an adversarial climate, fascinating. Consequently, in recent years I have become enamoured of all things Manitoba — history, sports, news, and politics, even though my career keeps me away. I have become somewhat of a laughingstock amongst my friends and colleagues due to my inordinate affection for Manitoba, but it is something I wear as a badge of honour.

Where did this admiration for Manitoba come from? I grew up in Dryden, Ontario, so for me, although I was from Ontario, Winnipeg was THE city. My intent, like most teenagers considering where to attend university, was to move somewhere far away from my hometown in order to experience the wider world. I was accepted to Western University and had every plan to move to London, Ontario after I graduated from Dryden High School. The Ontario government intervened. My parents, a teacher and a mechanic, were too financially successful for me to qualify for Ontario School Assistance Payments, but not financially successful enough to afford to send me to Western — although as the years went by I think my mother may have deliberately over-estimated the cost of university in Southern Ontario in order to bolster her argument to keep me closer to home. My parents asked me to try the University of Manitoba and I grudgingly agreed – on the pretense that I would spend a year at U of M and then transfer to Western. I arrived in Winnipeg in 1991 and never looked back. I spent the next eight years in Winnipeg — five in university and another three working in various capacities in the city. In August of 1999, I transferred from the Canadian Army Primary Reserve, and after a year of French language training and completing a final qualification course as an Artillery Officer, I spent the next five years stationed in Shilo, Manitoba, before my career dictated that I move away.

I also have a deep and abiding love of military history, an affinity I started developing when my mother bought me my first GI Joe and, if I remember correctly, it came from the toy department of the Hudson's Bay Company department store in Winnipeg. This interest, some called it a fascination, during my adolescence, led me to join Army Cadets at the age of fifteen, enlist in the Army Reserve at seventeen, and transfer to the Regular Army at twenty-five. After I enrolled in the Army Reserve, I fought the pull to a full-time career thinking there must be something else for me to do. In the end, it was the right fit and looking back on it, I wouldn't change a thing.

An explanation for my affinity for Manitoba manifested itself in 2019. While I was deployed on a year-long peacekeeping mission in Egypt, my mother passed away unexpectedly. The staff at the Canadian Task Force headquarters in Sharm el Sheikh, Egypt went out of their way to coordinate my return home on compassionate leave to support my father, my brother, and celebrate the life of my mother. As I stayed in the home of my adolescence, seeing to my mother's affairs, and dealing with the grief of losing a parent, I sought out coping mechanisms. My mother had been the family historian, so I undertook to shoulder the burden of that title and began researching our family history to distract myself from the pall of sadness that had settled over the home. To my surprise, I began to find numerous references to relatives on my mother's side of the family who were First Nations or Métis. This came as something of a shock to me, but upon further investigation I learned that the roots of my heritage ran deep into the historical past of the Red River Settlement of what is now the Province of Manitoba. Following up the Métis heritage of my ancestors, I applied for citizenship with the Manitoba Métis Federation and, since 2019, I have been a proud Red River Métis citizen. Cognizant of living my life outside the Métis community, I was wary of becoming too involved too fast, but I have, since the arrival of my citizenship card, experienced nothing but support and acceptance from the Manitoba Métis Federation.

It turns out that my story is not unique. There are hundreds, perhaps thousands, of people whose ancestors deliberately hid their Métis heritage and, consequently, these people are sadly ignorant of this vibrant element of their personal heritage. Somewhere in my mother's past a relative decided they would at best downplay, at worst ignore, their own heritage. Now, as I try to make up for decades of missed opportunity, I am forced to wonder why my ancestors would have taken such an approach. As we will see later in this book, the racism, intolerance, bigotry, and abuse heaped on the Métis by settlers from Eastern Canada and Europe reveal why Métis hid their ancestry out of purse self-protection.

So, a confluence of a deep interest in both Manitoba history and military history, and a deep personal connection to the region through my Métis heritage has, over several years, bred in me a curiosity about a military history of early Manitoba. I have long been enamoured with the story of the Wolseley Expedition, the Anglo-Canadian military force sent to Fort Garry by the Canadian Government in response to the Red River Resistance of 1869–70, particularly the impressive obstacles the force had to overcome. When I learned of the garrison of permanent Militia that stayed in Winnipeg from 1871 to 1877 as a result of this expedition, I began to wonder what they did, and what impact they had on the settlement. After investigation, I realized that there was far more to the story of the Militia in Manitoba, specifically how the early citizen soldiers of Manitoba shaped the society they interacted with and helped to create the Manitoba we have today, for good and ill.

The aim of this book is to shine a light on the role the Militia played in the cultural evolution of Manitoba during the first fifteen years of the province's existence. The timeframe has been limited to fifteen years for several reasons, predominantly because the cultural transformation of Manitoba between 1870 and 1885 from a proto-industrial pluralistic society to an agriculture-based cultural clone of Ontario was complete by 1885. When the North-West Rebellion broke out in that year, Winnipeg became a springboard for the Canadian military response to emergency. In fact, one might even go so far as to call Winnipeg the forward logistical base for the North-West Field Force — the Canadian expeditionary force formed to suppress the rebellion. Winnipeg became the major point of departure for all elements of the North-West Field Force, whether it was the Militiamen from Ontario, Quebec, and the Maritimes who took the circuitous and laborious route around Lake Superior, or the early leadership who took advantage of the more expeditious but politically sensitive route through the United States and then north to Winnipeg. The symbolism of Winnipeg being the "jumping off point" for the military operation that would complete the consolidation of Dominion authority over the Canadian North-West makes it the perfect culminating point for this book: the point when Ontario-style society that was established in Manitoba was literally shipped out of Winnipeg into the Canadian North-West to establish the same society there.

Most resources used in this work are primary sources, predominantly from contemporary newspaper articles. Two resources assisted in this regard: the website *Manitobia* which has an impressive collection of digitized Manitoba newspapers from the nineteenth century onward, and *Newspaper Archive*, which also has a very impressive collection of digitized newspapers reaching back centuries. I relied heavily on these contemporary newspapers as they provided both the raw data pertaining to dates, places, and events, but also provided a degree of contextualization. The newspapers of the day were politically opinionated and their tone, in and of itself, is useful to understand the nuanced feelings of certain sections of the population. Of course, this presents its own challenges, and I endeavoured as much as possible to ensure that when referring to these opinions, they were not simply extrapolated to represent a monolithic opinion of the province — a rarity in the racial, political, and cultural mosaic of early Manitoba.

I also took advantage of some of the resources in Public Archives Manitoba, material concerning the Provisional Battalion of Infantry and Artillery found in the James Taylor collection. For this, I am deeply indebted to the assistance of research assistant Nathan Kramer. Library and Archives Canada also hold all the memoranda exchanged between Military District No. 10 headquarters in Winnipeg and Militia Headquarters in Ottawa which have provided very useful first-hand accounts of life amongst the Militia volunteers. Annual *Militia Reports* collated by the Department of Militia from each Military District have been digitized by the Directorate of History and Heritage at the Department of National Defence and proved invaluable. *Early Canadiana Online* provided access to a bevy of official government documents, and the *Canada Gazette* holdings of the Library and Archives Canada are a ready source of digitized copies of *Militia General Orders*. There are several first-hand accounts of the period in question available, too numerous to mention here but which can be found in the bibliography. Finally, one cannot separate post-Confederation Manitoba from pre-Confederation Red River. Many valuable works concerning Metis life before and after Manitoba's entry into Confederation can be found in the bibliography. Of note, I invite your attention to the *Virtual Museum* website of the Gabriel Dumont Institute of Native Studies and Applied Research, as well as the website *Provisional Government of Assiniboia*, both of which are a font of information about Metis culture in Red River.

I have endeavoured, wherever possible, to use direct quotations from primary sources to tell the story themselves, with only the minimum amount of contextualization required. Some historians have an aversion to this approach and prefer to paraphrase direct quotations while providing the appropriate citation. I find this method unsatisfying, and I am of the considered opinion that it is far better in historical terms to read the very words that were written rather than trust to the interpretation of a historian, and then dig up the reference to see if they got it right. The result of this approach is many direct quotations in the narrative, as well as several block quotations. Understandably, these may tend to interrupt the flow of the narrative, so I have attempted in every case to contextualize the quotation and transition to it as effortlessly as possible in order to maintain a smooth and appealingly consistent narrative.

Secondary sources were also helpful, but I tried to limit my use of them so that this book could be as much of a fresh account of the period as possible. While all these works are listed in the bibliography, two warrant special consideration here: Frederick Shore's unpublished doctoral thesis for the University of Manitoba, *The Canadians and the Métis: The Re-Creation of*

Manitoba, 1858-1872, and George F. Stanley's *Toil and Trouble*. The former is an incredibly in-depth account of the Militia in Manitoba with a wealth of statistical information that proved invaluable. It is, as well, an assessment of the use of violence by the Militia garrison to intimidate Métis in Fort Garry that is both accurate and disconcerting. The latter work is perhaps the only historical work that focuses solely on a military history of Manitoba. While *Toil and Trouble* is a useful operational history of the military in Manitoba, it makes almost no reference to the socio-cultural impact the Militia had on the evolving province.

This is not a military history of Manitoba, but a social history of the military in Manitoba. One that should fill an unfortunate gap in the extant historical narrative of Manitoba, the Western region, and Canada writ large.

INTRODUCTION

"the old Manitoba of 1870 had been engulfed in the New Manitoba of 1881. In one decade of swift change the province had seen the fur trade give way to the grain trade, the cart brigade to the railway train"
-W.L. Morton, "Manitoba: A History"[1]

"the traveller, on crossing the line at Emerson as he enters Manitoba from Minnesota, is reminded not only by the appearance of the Union Jack that he is again on British soil, but by many other things as well. The dress of the people is more English, [as are] their manners and custom and speech."
-George Bryce, "Manitoba, Its Infancy, Growth and Present Condition."[2]

"there were two epochs in the history of Winnipeg; the first was the time when our brave volunteers came to our town, which was then composed of but a few houses; and the second time was when [we] waited upon the Legislature to demand incorporation."
-Alfred Burrows, Mayoral Candidate for Winnipeg, political speech 1875.[3]

In late August of 1870, the first Canadian Militia soldier of the Red River Expeditionary Force arrived in Fort Garry. We don't know exactly who he was, what rank he held, what his age was or where, exactly, he came from. We can, however, infer some general details about him. He was a soldier of the 1st Ontario Rifles, an *ad hoc* militia battalion composed of volunteers from various Active Militia Corps in Ontario. He was, most likely, an Anglophone

Protestant, either born in Ontario or a recent immigrant from the British Isles. He arrived in a thirty-foot long, seven hundred-pound canoe, in which he was one of a crew of about ten or eleven men, comprised of eight or nine soldiers and two *voyageurs*, civilian men hired by the Dominion government to help guide and convey the expedition due to their experience as woodsmen or fur traders. He had just completed a herculean trek from Toronto, where he had gathered with his colleagues in mid-May. From there, he and his colleagues had travelled by rail, steamship, and canoe from Toronto to Fort Garry via Collingwood, Sault Ste. Marie, Thunder Bay, and Rat Portage (now known as Kenora). Since he departed Shebandowan Lake, west of Thunder Bay, he had travelled over six hundred miles by canoe, and carried hundreds of pounds of supplies, equipment, weapons, and stores, to say nothing of the boats themselves, from one lake to another, over forty-seven portages which totalled nearly fourteen kilometers. The distance of fourteen kilometers is deceptive — the actual cumulative distance of the portages was much greater as our militia volunteer was required to traverse each portage several times to get the whole of his equipment and supplies across. Through it all, he was tortured by unrelenting, merciless clouds of mosquitos that were completely undeterred by the bug-repelling oil the Dominion government had issued.

He was preceded at Fort Garry, by about two days, by soldiers from a battalion of British regulars supported by British artillery and engineers. They had landed on the shore of the Red River just north of the village of Winnipeg on August 24, formed into a battle formation, and marched on Fort Garry, the Hudson's Bay Company redoubt and headquarters at the confluence of the Red and Assiniboine Rivers. Hitherto, the fort had been used by Louis Riel and his supporters as the headquarters of the Provisional Government of Assiniboia — a political body born of a popular uprising that was opposed to the annexation-without-consultation of the North-West by the Dominion of Canada. Riel and the other members of the provisional government were possessed of a genuine fear that upon annexation to Canada, the Dominion would not respect their property and cultural rights. When the advance scouts of the British Regulars approached the fort, they found the southern gate open, and the fort itself to be empty.

When our volunteer arrived in Fort Garry, he found a small settlement of frame houses scattered across the prairie. These homes were congregated in several parishes that lay interspersed along the banks of the two rivers, most bearing the name of a saint. The largest was the Village of Winnipeg, which lay about a quarter of a mile north of Fort Garry. The settlement our volunteer found was a diverse mosaic of cultures: Canadian immigrants, Hudson's Bay officials, French and English Metis, the former more numerous than the latter, Scottish émigrés of the 1813 Selkirk settlement, and American traders, all living check by jowl along the banks of two serpentine, muddy, prairie rivers. Throughout the Red River Settlement, as the conglomeration of parishes around the forks was known, the air was tight with racial and ethnic tension. Some of the inhabitants welcomed him as a liberator, others looked at him askance, their eyes filled with mistrust and revulsion.

Several days later, our volunteer bade farewell to his British colleagues as they set off on a return journey to Toronto, and thence back to the United Kingdom — London had recalled her Legions and the British government had agreed to participate in this expedition only insofar as they would depart almost immediately upon arrival. As the British regulars rowed down the Red River, our Canadian Militia volunteer, who had agreed to serve one year's garrison duty in the North-West, settled down to rustic accommodations, poor food, long hours, a mundane daily routine, an absence of leisure activities, and inhospitable weather.

After fulfilling his initial service obligation of one year, if our volunteer agreed to extend his contract, he could very conceivably have spent the next seven years conducting garrison duty, initially at Fort Garry, and then from early 1874 in Fort Osborne, a military barracks built to house the militia garrison and erected where the Manitoba legislature now sits. He certainly would have many tales to tell. In 1871, he turned out in a rainstorm and marched south to meet an invading Fenian army, only to learn the United States Cavalry had beat him to the punch. He may have been present at three different treaty-signing ceremonies with local First Nations, providing security and acting as an overt physical manifestation symbolic of the Queen's authority. At various times, he most likely deployed to the streets of early Winnipeg to fight fires and subdue rioters — some of whom were probably his own brothers in arms. At some time, he likely stood guard over the city courthouse lest its inhabitants be liberated or lynched by unruly mobs. He may have marched with dozens of his colleagues to the Interlake Region, the long strip of land between Lakes Manitoba and Winnipeg lying to the north of the Red River Settlement, to establish a quarantine line to contain the spread of smallpox. He would have been called out several times to provide a guard of honor and add pomp and imperial authority to the opening and closing of the provincial legislature and upon the arrival of great personages such as the lieutenant-governor, the Governor General and, in one instance, the Commanding General of the United States Army. He certainly would have seen firsthand the construction Fort Osborne — in fact, he probably cleared much of the brush from the site himself if he had been detailed to 'fatigues.' He would have been witness to the augmentation of the militia force when local inhabitants became worried about foreign incursions or indigenous uprisings, his new colleagues including amongst their ranks a battery of artillery and a draft of soldiers from the Maritime Provinces.

And he was no angel. He likely over-imbibed in the local saloons, of which there were plenty. He probably got in fights, was found to be absent without leave, was summarily disciplined or outright prosecuted for transgressions that may have varied from something as innocuous as reporting late to duty to murder. He may have volunteered for military duty in the North-West motivated by a racist desire to "even the score" with the Métis after he heard of Louis Riel's execution of Thomas Scott. If he was so inclined, he likely joined like-minded colleagues in their off-duty hours to attack Métis, intimidate them, threaten to kill them, and perhaps even do so. He would have banded together with local Anglo-Protestant citizens to smash the printing presses of newspapers whose editorial slant was found to digress from full-throated support of Canadian annexation or set fire to buildings to make a political statement. Maybe he was one of the Militia volunteers who chased a Métis lieutenant of Louis Riel, Elezear Goulet, through the streets of Winnipeg and then threw rocks at him as he tried to swim the Red River to find solace in St. Boniface, knocking him unconscious and drowning him. If so, our volunteer never faced justice for his crime.

Regardless of his political stripe, he would have witnessed the slow reduction of the militia garrison after 1874, about the same time as the recently formed North-West Mounted Police, some of whom were formerly his Militia brothers, came into existence. He would have witnessed the disbandment of the permanent Militia garrison in Winnipeg in 1877. It is possible that he chose to settle in Manitoba after his service ended and took the quarter section, or one hundred sixty acres, of land that the government gave him for his service, and then either sold it to a land speculator or claimed it to farm himself. Having spent the last seven years in uniform, he may have enrolled in one of the part-time Active Militia corps that had been established in Manitoba.

If he remained enrolled in the Active Militia, and even if he didn't, it is possible that he took up arms again in 1885 on the outbreak of the North-West Rebellion, once again led by Louis Riel. He could have found himself exchanging gun fire in Frog Lake or charging Métis trenches in Batoche with a fixed bayonet. Upon Riel's capture and the collapse of the rebellion, our volunteer would have been whisked homeward on the Canadian Pacific Railway or sailed triumphantly home on a steamer across Lake Winnipeg to Selkirk and thence to Winnipeg. He would have been witness to a raucous victory celebration upon his return to the prairie city.

During this victory celebration, he would have marched along Main Street to the City Hall. He may have taken pause to reflect on the immense changes in the city and the region that he had both witnessed, and indeed been party to, over the previous fifteen years. He may have hearkened back to the words written by the indefatigable chronicler of early Winnipeg events, Andrew Begg, who observed in 1880 that ...

> a decade has all but elapsed – on paper – since this history of Winnipeg has commenced...We have followed her development from her village epoch, with 100 settlers, through numerous metamorphoses, up to the date of her blossoming into a city with 10,000 souls. To-day she boasts of a street extension of 83 miles. To-day nearly 1,000 dwelling houses stud the plain, where ten years since they could be counted upon the fingers of two hands. To-day the total value of her property is assessed at $3,415,065, and taxes $50,875.76; in 1869 the same was represented by as many hundreds.[4]

The "postage stamp" province of Manitoba that was carved out of Rupert's Land as part of the *Manitoba Act* had, since its inception, grown to the west, north and east, even leading to a farcical 'war' between Manitoba and Ontario authorities in Rat Portage. The months-long wait for mails in 1870 had succumbed to near instantaneous telegraphic communication in the 1880s. Where only the moon, stars and aurora borealis had once challenged the dark prairie nights, by the end of the North-West Rebellion, the hum and glow of electric street lights guided Winnipeg citizenry along their nocturnal way.

Perhaps what had changed most in the previous fifteen years was the ethnicity of the people cheering our volunteer as he marched the victory route — they were almost exclusively Anglophone Protestants of British extract. Certainly, some Métis still lived in the city, but most of them had long since departed. Indeed, it was against some of these former citizens that he had recently taken up arms. In 1870, when our volunteer alighted from his canoe, the population of the Red River Settlement was 12,228 souls, 50 percent of whom were Roman Catholic, comprised of 5,757 French Métis, 4,083 English Métis, and 1,565 Caucasians.[5] Shortly after our volunteer marched down Main Street in 1885 the population of Manitoba was 109,000 of which only 7 percent were French or English Métis, and Roman Catholics represented only one-eighth of the populace.[6] By 1885, the North-West in general, and Manitoba and Winnipeg in particular, had changed mightily. Politically, economically, materially, and culturally, Winnipeg and Manitoba of 1885 were completely dissimilar from Fort Garry and the Red River Settlement of 1870.

The historical narrative of the period in Manitoba between 1870 and 1885 is generally well-trod, but what is lamentably overlooked is just how much a role our volunteer played in the massive social-cultural change that happened therein. When he is considered at all, it is in very narrow form, restricted to a few military history books focussed almost exclusively on the Wolseley Expedition of 1870. More recent historical inquiries have penetrated deeper, however, and our volunteer's nefarious exploits at the expense of the Métis and French population of Winnipeg and Manitoba have come to the fore. That our volunteer and some, perhaps most, of his colleagues conducted themselves in a reprehensible manner is undeniable, but it is only one part of the story, and focussing on it alone omits far too much of the historical narrative. Our volunteer was anything but one-dimensional: he was a citizen, a settler, a soldier, and a scoundrel. As he trundled his way towards the North-West, he brought more than his arms and accoutrements along with him — he brought his mores, traditions, customs, and institutions, and implanted them in Canada's newly acquired province, often at the expense of his new neighbours. He was a major agent of cultural change in early Manitoba, whose impact on the history of the Canadian West has been sadly overlooked. It is not too bold to say that one cannot properly understand the history of Manitoba in its first few decades after joining Confederation, and by extension that of the entire North-West, without reference to the significant influence the volunteers of the Canadian Militia brought to the new province.

This book will demonstrate that, far from being faceless automatons, the Militia in Manitoba were influential agents of cultural change beyond the barracks and battlefields. Chapter 1 — *Strategy: Occupy, Possess and Mold* will discuss the grand strategy of the Dominion of Canada towards the North-West. It will illustrate how the political leaders of the late nineteenth century in Canada understood their role to be that of a vitally important element of the global British Imperial project, as a secure trade route from the United Kingdom to Asia. Chapter 2 — *Soldiers* will establish a foundation for the remainder of the book by illustrating what the Militia *was* in Victorian Canada. It will explain how a force of Canadian Militia came to be what was essentially a colonial outpost of the Canadian Dominion garrisoned in Manitoba for seven years, how it was organized, and what life in its ranks was like. It will also illustrate the establishment and growth of the part-time Active Militia volunteers who, after the disbandment of the full-time garrison in 1877, became the only Canadian military force in existence between the Great Lakes and the Rocky Mountains. Chapter 3 — *Security* will then describe how the Militia garrison in Manitoba was employed to maintain security in the region, serving as a deterrent to American expansionism in the region, as a reassurance to settlers wary of Indigenous violence, and as a force for the maintenance of law and order in the rough and tumble early North-West. Chapter 4 — *Symbolism* will describe how the influence of the Militia garrison went beyond the physical to the intangible. It will demonstrate that the Militia established a symbolic and psychological linkage with the Dominion and the British Empire as an overt manifestation of the power of the state in a land cloistered by the Precambrian Shield from the political and cultural metropole of Ontario. Chapter 5 — *Society* will demonstrate that the men of the Militia in early Manitoba helped to establish a society in the North-West that reflected the mores, traditions, and institutions of British Ontario in everything from the theatre to the sports field. Chapter 6 — *Skullduggery* will expose the very unsavory aspects of the Militia's actions in Manitoba, including its poor discipline, rampant drunkenness, and plentiful insubordination. Most importantly, this chapter will describe the ethnically-charged violence that the predominantly Anglo-protestant Militia volunteers employed to intimidate Métis and French citizens and drive them out of the new province. Finally, Chapter 7 — *Suppression* will describe how the Militia of Manitoba played an inordinately large role in fighting the North-West Rebellion against many of the disaffected Métis who had been driven out of Manitoba to safer surroundings in what is now Saskatchewan and Alberta, which culminated in the consolidation of Dominion authority over the whole of the North-West.

Although this is not a military history, it will nonetheless also contribute to a wider understanding of the history of the military in Canada, its role, its organization, and its socio-cultural impact on its local environment. It will open the military historical narrative which, all too often, is based on operational history and ignores how the citizen soldiers of early Canada interacted with the populace in which it operated. In many ways this book can be a springboard to a broader analysis of how the Militia shaped the cultural evolution of the North-West region and the emergence of the provinces of Saskatchewan and Alberta, and perhaps other regions of the Canadian Dominion.

For the dedicated military historian, little of the history of the Militia in Manitoba between the departure of the British Regulars of the Wolseley Expedition in 1870 and the outbreak of the North-West Rebellion in 1885 is written of or analyzed. It is, to a degree, an historical void overshadowed by far brighter stars, such as the continuing tensions between Métis and settlers, the abolition of the Legislative Council and the incorporation of the City of Winnipeg to name but a few. As such this will shed light on the evolution of the military in Manitoba and help to link the current citizen soldiers who serve in the various units of 38 Canadian Brigade Group, headquartered in Winnipeg, with their predecessors in early Manitoba. For Canadian military history enthusiasts, this book will present an in-depth historical analysis of the role, organization, employment, and challenges of the Militia in Manitoba. That said, this book is not a hagiography of Canada's citizen soldiers. This book will present the historical facts, of the Militia volunteers' actions, even the plentiful unsavoury ones.

1

STRATEGY: TO OCCUPY, POSSESS AND MOLD

Canada's future in 1869 was by no means clearly defined. She was physically isolated from her imperial mentor and protector Great Britain by the vast expanses of the North Atlantic, and psychologically isolated by the emergent "Little Britain" mentality amongst the British political leadership which envisaged a contraction of British imperial power. Perhaps even more dangerous, she was bounded to the south by an expansionist United States where the imperialistic concepts of Manifest Destiny and the Monroe Doctrine were very much in vogue. Was Canada to be a transcontinental federation and a key link in the global British Empire? Or was it to be hemmed into the North-East corner of North America by the ascending American Empire?

If nineteenth century Americans were guided by the doctrine of Manifest Destiny — the idea that they were destined to rule over the whole of the Northern American continent — contemporary Canadians likewise espoused their own expansionist doctrine focussed on the vast territories of British North America. Like their American cousins, nineteenth century Canadians believed they had a mission and a destiny to fulfill as an integral element of a global British Empire, and their bailiwick was the vast territories of British North America, from St. Johns to Victoria, and all points in between. The duties wrapped up in this heady responsibility were perhaps best articulated in the succinct and telling words with which the Emerson, Manitoba welcoming committee greeted the Governor General of Canada, Lord Dufferin, on his visit to the North-West in 1877. Dufferin, accompanied by his wife, daughter and a coterie of advisors and assistants, had made the laborious trek from Ottawa to the small town on the international border by train through the United States, and then steamship north along the serpentine Red River. Arriving at the pier in Emerson, the Governor General and his entourage stepped onto a platform they found bedecked with patriotic bunting and a band furnishing heart-moving patriotic airs in the prairie sunshine. The welcoming committee met the vice-regal visitor on a receiving platform where the chair of the committee delivered a stirring welcoming address. "We feel proud, Sir," the chair intoned "of the mission which, as Canadians and British subjects devolves upon us to *occupy, possess and mold* the future of this vast territory [emphasis added]." Continuing, he added "we feel assured that, in the task of *welding into a homogenous population these people from various countries of the world* that will here make their homes ... we shall always find in your Excellency, in whatever portion of the empire you may be, a warm sympathizer, and a ready helper. [emphasis added]"[1]

In a brief passage of only several sentences, the welcoming committee of Emerson Manitoba were able to encapsulate the zeitgeist of nineteenth century Canadians in the North-West: a nation that spanned the continent, provided a British counterweight to American republicanism in the North-West, and functioned as a critical link in the global British Empire. They were not content to be shut up in a corner of the new world and denied the natural bounty that lay in the vast expanses of the northern continental interior.

The idea of bringing the North-West into Confederation began, counter intuitively, before the four original provinces were joined into federation by the British North America Act of July 1, 1867. Curious of the natural resource potential in the North-West, in the 1850s the British government commissioned an expedition to survey the region and report on its suitability for settlement. Likewise, the government of the Province of Canada, which prior to Confederation consisted of what would become the Provinces of Ontario and Quebec, known prior to 1840 as Upper and Lower Canada respectively, also commissioned their own survey. While the British expedition's report at the potential in the region was lukewarm at best, the Canadian expedition determined that the lands of the North-West held significant potential for settlement and resource extraction, which initially piqued the interest of the

Fathers of Confederation to admitting the region to the new federation.

This initial interest was more formally expressed at the Quebec Conference of 1864. At this early meeting of the Fathers of Confederation, the shape and substance of the future Dominion of Canada was articulated in a series of seventy-two resolutions. Included in these resolutions was one clause which opened the door for the possible inclusion of the North-West into the new federation. Resolution 10 stated "The North-West Territory, British Columbia and Vancouver shall be admitted into the Union on such terms and conditions as the Parliament of the Federated Provinces shall deem equitable."[2] Two years later, when representatives of the Provinces of Canada, Nova Scotia, and New Brunswick met with Imperial authorities in Westminster Palace to further discuss the nature of a possible Canadian federation, the commitment to some future inclusion of the North-west into Confederation was maintained.[3] Likewise, the British North American Act, which created the Dominion of Canada, included a section devoted to the admission of other colonies, specifically section 146 which stated "It shall be lawful for the Queen, by and with the Advice of Her Majesty's Most Honourable Privy Council ... to admit Rupert's Land and the Northwestern Territory, or either of them, into the Union."[4]

Confederation established the legal existence of the Dominion of Canada through the medium of the *British North America Act*, but the process of nation-building, that is to say of constructing a common national spirit and identity, was challenged by extant religious, cultural and regional differences that permeated the young nation. One of the strategies employed to overcome these differences, and in many ways employed latently by the actors involved, was the promotion of an overarching cultural structure that manifested itself in the forms of British institutions, practices, mores, and traditions all of which aimed to bind the disparate regional cultural elements together.[5] There was very little common ground between the Anglo-Protestant Ontarian, the Franco-Catholic Quebecer, or the Maritimer other than they were all subjects of the same imperial crown which, its adherents believed, served as a unifying force to the multicultural population of British North America.

After Confederation, the annexation of the North-West and exploitation of its natural resources became a key policy of successive Dominion governments, regardless of their partisan stripe — both Conservative and Liberal administrations were equally committed to the idea of opening the North-West to settlement and the immediate installation of the social, cultural, and political institutions of the Dominion upon those lands.[6] While the assumed birthright of the North-West was evident in the Emerson committee's charge to occupy, possess and mold, the belief in the unifying force of British culture was expressed in the words that followed concerning the assumed task of *"welding into a homogenous population these people from various countries of the world."* This British connexion was felt strongest in the province of Ontario, which would, coincidentally, be the source from which emanated most of the settlers who ventured westward to eke out a new life in the north-west. Consequently, the new North-West of Canada was created by settlers who installed in their new homes the political, economic, religious, and social practices and institutions that they had left behind.[7]

During the first fifteen years of Manitoba's existence, the extant cultural foundations of the Red River Settlement were replaced by a new, dominant socio-cultural structure. The colonial hinterland of Assiniboia, dominated by the proto-industrial buffalo trade and peopled by Métis, fur traders, and the remnants of Scottish émigrés was replaced by an embryonic, agriculturally-based, English Protestant clone of Ontario.[8] To understand what the strategic goals of the Dominion of Canada were with respect to the North-West, we must begin with the question: what does it mean to be British?

THE BRITISH INVASION

The question of what and who constituted "the British", including the culture, mores, and traditions of the British people, is one of some detail and potential pitfalls, not least because of the evolving nature of its culture over time. Suffice to say, what may pass as 'British' in twenty-first century Canada is substantially different from that which defined the late nineteenth century idea of 'British.' The problem here is further exacerbated by the fact that while this cultural group differs in time, it also differs in space. Individuals have a symbiotic relationship with their physical environs — their cultural ecosystem. This results in an inevitable situation of cultural 'layering' of personal identities along with other loyalties based on local, colonial, and ethnic influences.[9] Inasmuch as what was considered British in Manitoba in the 1870s is markedly different from what is considered British in the twenty-first century, it was also different from what was considered British in the Toronto in 1870s. This creates some problems for historians from an analytical perspective — the concept of nineteenth century Canadian Britishness being somewhat Protean in nature, shifting and evolving over time and space.

While there are indisputably minor variations in the nineteenth century British-Canadian culture, there is nonetheless significant commonality to make the concept analytically useful. This is reinforced by the great influence placed on British culture that evolved in Manitoba between 1870 and 1885 due to the overwhelming number of settlers to Manitoba who originated in Ontario or the British Isles. It was this cultural group that transmitted the British culture to Manitoba after it joined Confederation. Although in broad terms one may speak of the British-Canadian culture as emanating from the established provinces of the Dominion prior to 1870, these too had their cultural vagaries. In truth, the idea of what was "Canadian" was very much regionally based and born in post-Confederation Ontario rather than being a pan-Dominion culture. Illustrative of the differences between the various cultures extant in Canada in the 1870s, Ontario emigrant and *Manitoba Free Press* and later *Nor'Wester* reporter Julius Galbraith, using the pseudonym Geoff Gee, recounts a personal experience in his memoir *A Sketch of Both Sides of Manitoba*. In 1873, when Galbraith moved to Fort Garry, he found himself sharing a stagecoach with an older traveller, a long-time resident of the North-West. He recounted in his memoir that "I have a fellow passenger, a comparatively old inhabitant, and the man is actually intelligent - another shock. He is evidently a Canadian — that is to say, he hails from Ontario. If he was from Quebec, we would call him a Quebecer; from Nova Scotia, a Nova Scotian, and so on."[10]

Galbraith's shock at the man's intelligence is tongue-in-cheek. Galbraith had a singular wit, and his memoir is replete with barbs directed against what he saw as the undeserved air of superiority and condescension exhibited by Ontarians towards the North-West frontier settler and inhabitant. Nonetheless, the story is indicative of the cultural outlook of the emergent British in Manitoba, which identified closely with the "Canadian" of Ontario, as compared to what is presumably the more parochial inhabitants of the other original provinces. Consequently, the characteristics of the British culture of Post-Confederation Manitoba and Ontario are similar enough to tolerate the minor differences caused by local geography and culture.

We turn, then, to a definition of the nineteenth century British in Manitoba. Fortunately for historians of nineteenth century British culture in Manitoba, the scholarship of Kurt Korneski is enlightening. Writing in the *Journal of Canadian Studies* in 2007, Korneski's article "Britishness, Canadianess, Class and Race: Winnipeg and the British World, 1880s-1910s" is a valuable survey of what it meant to be "British" in late nineteenth century Manitoba. Unsurprisingly, it is by no means an easy concept. Firstly, it was not a nationality as the term is commonly understood — indeed Korneski argued that the core of Britishness was "about politico-ethical principles rather than about the particulars of a geographical region."[11] These contingent cultural characteristics were broad. Britishness, as C.P. Champion observed in his book *The Strange Demise of British Canada. The Liberals and Canadian Nationalism 1964-1968,* included concepts such as the rule of law, representative government, patterns of living, and a liberal approach to economics and certain ethnic customs, such as language, clothing, and food to name a few.[12]

One cannot dismiss the more foundational ethnic characteristics that went into Britishness, which is best summarized in the largely pejorative term WASP — white, Anglo-Saxon, protestant. In the main, most of the British, and certainly its elite, fit this term closely, although both Korneski and Champion point out that this was not necessarily a pre-requisite to being British in the broadest sense. For example, Korneski suggested that it was advantageous for those of a different ethnic background to adopt British practices and mores to facilitate access to better paying jobs.[13] Of like mind, Champion observed that there existed a large group of sub-cultural categories within an overarching Britishness where one could find Scottish, Irish and Welsh elements, as well as other, mostly European, constituents who, through continued exposure, came to personify the general characteristics of Britishness despite having little or no actual British or English blood in their ancestry.[14]

This British cultural synergy extended to the men who formed Louis Riel's provisional government in Fort Garry, the Legislative Assembly of Assiniboia, in the spring of 1870. A review of the *Sessional Journal* of the Assembly relates an interesting debate during the first session of the legislature concerning a motion expressing the loyalty of the people of the North-West to the Crown of England. The debate centred mostly on the use of the term "British subjects" to describe the sufferings and abuse of rights which the people of the North-West had endured at the hands of the Dominion of Canada's expansionist policy in the North-West. Representatives such as Thomas Bunn and CJ Bird argued that the motion should state that the rights of the people of the North-

West as *British subjects* had been infringed, while others, namely William O'Donoghue, an Irish Catholic patriot who harboured extreme animosity towards the British, argued that the motion should state that it was their *rights as men* which had been infringed. Louis Riel, the President of the Assembly, seems to have walked a middle road, but throughout his statements there is a consistent acknowledgement of the people of the North-West being British subjects. The resolution that was finally passed seemed to cover all the bases: "notwithstanding the insults and sufferings borne by the people of the North-West heretofore — which sufferings they still endure — the loyalty of the people of the North-west towards the Crown of England remains the same, provided the 'rights, properties, usages, and customs of the people be respected — and we feel assured that, as British subjects, such rights, properties, usages and customs will undoubtedly be respected."[15] Louis Riel and his followers' identification of themselves as "British Subjects" is indicative of the nineteenth century understanding of Britishness being a concept that bound diverse cultural groups together based on certain commonalities, rather than being strictly based on place of birth.

Despite this rather inclusive definition, the British were indeed dominated by a core internal elite that was definitively Waspish. In particular, the British elite in nineteenth century Canada was culturally Anglo-Protestant Canadian who identified as both Canadian and British but, more importantly, considered the two terms to be synonymous. Moreover, as this book will demonstrate, while Louis Riel *et al.* may have considered themselves loyal British subjects, the Anglophone Protestants in Manitoba, particularly those who were recently arrived settlers from Ontario, did not share the view. Quite the contrary, in the opinion of many members of the Ontario Anglo-protestant community, Louis Riel and the Métis were representative of a Franco-Catholic culture which they perceived as being totally at odds with their imperial agenda — the Canadian Manifest Destiny.

CANADIAN MANIFEST DESTINY AS PART OF PAX BRITANNIA

The Anglo-protestant Canadians that transformed and then led early Manitoba, like their counterparts in other parts of the country and around the world, saw themselves as critical actors in the establishment and maintenance of a global British Empire in which Canada batwas an integral and an important part, what Korneski refers to as the "imperialist national project."[16] This notion, of Canadian nation-building as part of a global British network, was stated plainly even before Confederation. At a meeting of the Executive Council of the Province of Canada in late June 1866, the leaders of what would soon become the Provinces of Ontario and Quebec observed that "the future interests of Canada and all British North America [are] vitally concerned in the immediate establishment of a strong Government [in the North-West] *and in its settlement as a part of the British Colonial System* [emphasis added]."[17]

This ideological pursuit of a global British synergy was not unique to the Canadian North-West, in fact the entire Victorian zeitgeist is one that was suffused with multiple intertwined themes based on Protestant values, liberal democracy, and personal and national industriousness. Colonial settlers of British colonies in other corners of the Empire shared similar ideological motivations. Take for example the political leaders of the Cape Colony in South Africa. Writing in the *Journal of Imperial and Commonwealth History*, D. M. Schreuder observed that there, the colonial administrators drew from the "cultural and ideological milieu of Protestantism and Improvement ... [and] they often appear to have perceived a larger ideological purpose in their actions than merely sustaining public order on an inflammatory frontier ... they scarcely differentiated between the spread of the Gospel and the spread of the British Empire, or, at least, of white rule."[18] This confluence of imperial and religious zeal was also strongly reflected in the protestant missionaries who arrived in Red River in the first half of the nineteenth century and went about attempting to create what historian Fritz Pannekoek called "a little Britain in the Wilderness."[19]

This global synergy fueled both the public and private aspirations of the settlers in the North-West who regarded themselves as both Canadian and British subjects. Consequently, this ideology thoroughly penetrated the policies of the Dominion Government resulting in a worldview in which the embryonic Canadian government regarded itself as an important stone in the arch of the vast global British cultural network. In *Macdougall's Guide to Manitoba,* which was produced by W.B. MacDougall, a real estate agent, accountant, and publisher in Winnipeg, to lure prospective British settlers to the North-West, Macdougall included extracts from reports from British tenant farmers' delegates. The aim of these reports was to inform prospective émigrés to the Canadian North-West what they could expect upon their arrival in Manitoba. The message was clear to the émigrés of Great Britain that they would feel right at home, observing that "the farmer who migrates from the British Islands to any part of Canada does not change his flag; nor does he, except to a very slight degree, change his mode of life or his companionship. He goes among his own people, to *conditions of life and society, the same as those he leaves behind* [emphasis added]."[20] Consistent with the message delivered at Emerson of a mission to "occupy, possess and mold," the Macdougall guide also patriotically declared that "the farmer who migrates from these islands, moreover, has the satisfaction of feeling that he is assisting to build up a great British Empire."[21] A less prosaic and more forthright appreciation was offered by the editors of the *Volunteer Review*, a Victorian periodical that focused on military and political themes, who blandly stated, concerning immigration into the North-West, that "we do not wish or want the refuse population of continental Europe, [but] the Dominion of Canada is to be the *Greater Britain,* and we prefer its slow and steady growth by healthy accretion from the parent stocks of English and French to the mongrel population of every nation and tongue on the continent of Europe."[22]

To 'occupy, possess and mold' a vast region peopled, predominantly, with First Nations and Metis was a heady task indeed. The cultural bedrock of the region had been laid generations previous by the First Nations peoples and enhanced, particularly in the Red River area, by the Metis. This book will demonstrate that many of the Anglo-Protestant settlers who arrived in the North-West believed the only way to occupy, possess and mold the region into an integral part of the global British cultural network, was to impose the strictures of British culture on the region. This lamentably manifested itself in the unsavoury and oppressive aspects of the nation building effort: the suppression or eradication of extant cultures, and violence against the First Nations and Metis inhabitants.[23]

In the second half of the nineteenth century this was not a situation unique to Canada. Quite the contrary, post-Confederation Canadians were but one in a series of global actors through which the British empire was flexing his colonial muscle to impose British hegemony, a situation described by Geoff Read and Todd Webb in the *Canadian Historical Review* thusly: "just as the Americans had experienced Indigenous resistance as they pushed westward, the British Empire saw a series of conflicts on its fringes ... as the new imperialism gathered steam, such clashes on the imperial periphery only became more frequent. The Asante of the Gold Coast were taught a lesson in imperial power in 1872; the Amir of Afghanistan was deposed and British hegemony in the country upheld in 1878–80; Zulu independence was smashed in South Africa in 1879; and the Egyptians were brought to heel and occupied in 1882."[24] In order to achieve this, the installation of the physical and symbolic trappings of Eastern Canada in the North-West required agents of cultural transference, the preponderance of who were found in the throngs of British settlers who moved to Manitoba after it joined Confederation, and the soldiers who occupied the Dominion's newest colony. It is to the question of the culture of Canadian soldiers that we will now turn.

2

SOLDIERS: CANADA'S MILITIA

As this book deals with the impact of the Militia volunteers on the socio-cultural evolution of Manitoba, obviously a working understanding of what the Militia was is a critical prerequisite. This is doubly important because Canadians, being a predominantly *unmilitary* people, in the words of the great Canadian military historian George Stanley, have only a passing acquaintance with the culture, organization, and role of the modern Canadian military. They have an even weaker grasp of the Canadian Militia of nineteenth century, which was significantly different from the modern Canadian Army. This chapter will outline the basic historical evolution of the Militia system in the Dominion of Canada up until the late nineteenth century, and then survey the role and organization of the Canadian Militia when Manitoba joined the Canadian Confederation. It will give a brief overview of the Militia at the both the national and local levels to familiarize the reader with the unique structure and culture of the organization.

A NATIONAL PERSPECTIVE: ROLE AND ORGANIZATION

Militia is a term that defies precision and its broad use, both in the late nineteenth century and in modern discourse, makes its definition problematic. The Oxford Online Dictionary defines Militia simply as a military force that is raised from the civil population to supplement a regular army in an emergency.[1] The use of the term by disreputable right-wing paramilitary groups in the

United States lends it a nefarious connotation in modern usage which further muddies the water. Notwithstanding its use by the aforementioned addlepates, the term has a much more formal meaning in the Canadian context. It was, in fact, the official title of the Canadian Army for several years. Indeed, indicative of the formality of the term's use in Canada, the cabinet position of *Minister of Militia and Defence* existed until 1922 until it was merged with the *Minister of Naval Services* to form the cabinet post more familiar to modern Canadians, that being the *Minister of National Defence.*[2] As late as 2002, the Department of National Defence stated in its *Backgrounder* that the "Primary Reserve is divided into four elements: The Naval Reserve, the *Militia* or Army Reserve, the Air Reserve and the Communication Reserve [emphasis added]."[3] While the term "Army Reserve" is now used more often in official correspondence, the term Militia is still used interchangeably, particularly amongst the serving members of the Canadian Army Primary Reserve.

The responsibility for the defence of Canada fell to the Imperial Government in London until at least the 1930s, and to a degree even as late as the end of the Second World War. From the time of the Treaty of Ghent in 1763, when French possessions in North America were ceded to Great Britain, Regular battalions of the British standing army were stationed in British North America. After the American Revolution and the emergence of the United States, those battalions were stationed in the remaining territories of British North America, most of which would eventually become, after July 1, 1867, the Dominion of Canada. The number of British battalions that were stationed in British North America waxed and waned over time, dependent on the international situation, and usually in relation to improving or souring Anglo-American relations. At the time of Confederation, fifteen thousand British Regular soldiers were stationed in the Canadian provinces and formed the backbone of the defence of British North America. The role played by the Dominion of Canada in the joint scheme of defence, was limited to the provision of a Militia to augment the British Regulars through the process of a *levée en masse* — the mobilization of the citizenry in defence of the nation.[4]

The Canadian Militia system that existed in post-Confederation Canada, and which was subsequently exported to Manitoba upon the creation of the province in 1870, was the result of a Militia legacy in Canada that stretched back over two hundred years and was rooted in both French and British traditions. As early as 1651, a law in New France required the men of Trois-

Rivières to possess weapons, drill, and perform guard duty. In 1669, King Louis XIV ordered the creation of a Militia for New France, and by 1673 every parish in New France had a Militia company, some of the larger ones even having two. After the French capitulated at the end of the Seven Years War in 1763, the colonial governments in pre-Confederation Canada continued the Militia system started in New France under the French regime. Thereafter, the first British law concerning the Militia in Canada was passed in 1777, which continued the French tradition of a *levée en masse* in which every able-bodied man was liable for service in an emergency. For example, Canadian Militia forces were employed alongside British Regulars during the War of 1812, and the Upper and Lower Canada Rebellions of 1837–38.

The Canadian Militia system was enhanced in 1855 when the British Parliament passed the *Militia Act 1855* which allowed for the creation of an Active Militia in the Province of Canada, in which volunteers trained and paraded. Until this point, the Militia were "sedentary," that is to say untrained, and undrilled. The *Militia Act 1855* significantly upgraded the military force available to augment the British Regulars by providing for 5,000 volunteers who were armed and paid five shillings a day for ten days of training per year.[5]

Upon Confederation in 1867, the Militia system remained in vigor, but was upgraded shortly thereafter. The new federal structure of the country, coupled with the fear of American expansionism, reinvigorated interest in the defence of the Dominion. When the first federal cabinet was sworn in on July 1,1867, George Etienne Cartier, John A. Macdonald's Quebec lieutenant, assumed the position of the Minister of Militia and Defence and, although he was delayed by illness, Cartier eventually turned his attention to updating the *Militia Act 1855* to reflect the strategic realities of the new Dominion. On March 31, 1868, in the course of a five-hour speech to the House of Commons, Cartier introduced *An Act respecting the Militia and Defence of the Dominion of Canada* (hereafter the *Militia Act 1868*) in which he established the scope, organization, and role of the Militia in the defence of Canada. The *Militia Act 1868* became law on May 22, 1868.[6]

The strictures of the *Militia Act 1868* dictated that all the male inhabitants of the Dominion of Canada between the ages of eighteen and sixty were liable for service in the Militia. In 1870, Colonel Robertson-Ross, the officer administering the Canadian Militia, styled the adjutant-general, stated patriotically that this universal liability was "based upon the principle that every man owes it to his country to serve in its defence against its enemies."[7] There were exemptions to this universality of service: judges, clergy, university professors, penitentiary guards, the infirm, and the only sons of widows were all excused from the requirement to serve in the Militia. Those who were not able to earn an exemption were grouped into four 'classes.' The first class consisted of unmarried men, or widowers aged 18–30 and without children; the second class consisted of unmarried men, or widowers aged 31–45 and without children; the third class consisted of married men or widowers aged 18–45 with children; and finally, the fourth class consisted of all men, aged 45–60. Any mobilization of the Militia in time of emergency would occur in priority, with men of the first class called up for service first and followed by second class men and so on.[8]

Beyond the four classifications, the institution of the Canadian Militia was further organized into three divisions: the Active Militia, the Reserve Militia, and the Marine Militia. The first consisted of men who volunteered to join the Militia and drilled regularly, more closely approximating the modern Canadian Army Reserve. Those who volunteered to serve in the Active Militia agreed to a term of service of three years.[9] The Active Militia was organized into local Active Militia *corps* such as infantry companies, mounted rifle companies, artillery batteries, and cavalry troops or squadrons. Within the ranks of these corps were volunteer part-time soldiers who mustered, paraded, and trained during their spare time. In 1870, the Active Militia numbered 40,000 men. In general parlance, and in the newspapers, periodicals, and government publications of the late nineteenth century, the Militiamen were often referred to as *volunteers,* the term being interchangeable with other terms such as *soldier* or *Militiamen.* The Reserve Militia, conversely, consisted of the men of the country, not exempted from service, and classified as above, who were not members of the Active Militia and volunteered, or were balloted, to serve in the Reserve Militia.[10] Balloting consisted of a random draw of male citizens who, if selected, were compelled to serve two years in the Reserve Militia. Fortunately, once they had finished their two years of compelled service, they were guaranteed to be free from being 'balloted' again until all the men in the same area, and not exempted from service, had served a term.[11] They represented the country's population liable to service in a *levée en masse* in the event of emergency, estimated in 1870 to number 675,000 men.[12] The Marine Militia consisted of sailors engaged in "navigating Dominion waters."[13]

The head and Commander-in-Chief of the Canadian Militia was, and remains to this day, the Governor General as the Queen's representative in Canada while the responsibility to administer the Militia fell to the aforementioned Minister of Militia and Defence.[14] The adjutant-general, who worked at Militia Headquarters in Ottawa, was the senior military officer responsible to the minister for the administration of the whole of the Militia in the Dominion.[15] He was a professional field-grad officer of the British Regular Army ranked colonel and paid by the Dominion $3,000 a year.[16] In 1874, the Dominion Government realized that it would be advantageous to augment the purely administrative role of the adjutant-general with the creation of the position of the General Officer Commanding the Canadian Militia. After some rather terse negotiations with the British on who would best fill such a role, in 1875 General Sir Edward Selby-Smith was selected to be the first *GOC*, a post that remained in effect until 1904 when it was replaced by the position of Chief of the General Staff.[17]

The role of the General Officer Commanding the Canadian Militia was a curious one. Although in command of the Canadian Militia, for the first several decades the position was filled exclusively by British officers. Consequently, the man who commanded the Dominion's forces was foreign and usually unaccustomed to Canadian Militia culture and sensitivities. Moreover, there was absolutely no guarantee that the man selected was the best fit for the job, or if he had any interest in the job whatsoever. Once in the position, the individual, particularly in the last few decades of the nineteenth century, considered themselves far more of a representative of the British military rather than the commander of the Canadian Militia. This led to friction between the GOC and Dominion political leaders who may have considered themselves part of the British Empire, but nonetheless regarded themselves with a certain degree of independence. Despite the friction and loggerheads that beset the relationship, in some cases the GOC proved to be a worthy fit. The first, General Sir Edward Selby-Smith was one of the success stories: he maintained an excellent rapport with the ministerial leaders and the soldiers under him. Another, Major-General Frederick Middleton, who will be dealt with in more detail in Chapter 6, sought out the position and had a strong affinity for Canada and its soldiers.[18]

Administratively, the Militia was divided into *military districts*. In 1870, nine military districts existed — four in Ontario, three in Quebec, and one each in New Brunswick and Nova Scotia.[19] Each military district was commanded by a deputy adjutant-general, a lieutenant-colonel, who resided in the district and who was responsible for the administration of the entire Active and Reserve Militia in his district, duties for which he was paid $1,200 a year.[20] If large enough, districts were further sub-divided into Brigade Divisions, and they into Regimental Divisions which were in turn sub-divided into Company Divisions. The purpose of the Brigade/Regimental/Company division structure was to maintain an up-to-date nominal roll of the men in the district in order to facilitate the mobilization of the population in the event of an emergency and issue ballots to the unlucky few who were compelled to enroll in the Reserve Militia.[21] To maintain the reserve rolls, Regimental Divisions had appointed to them one lieutenant-colonel and two majors, all members of the Reserve Militia, while Company Divisions were appointed a Captain and two sub-officers of the Reserve Militia.

The officers of the early Canadian Militia were expected to furnish their own arms, clothing, and accoutrements, while the Dominion Government agreed to furnish the same for the enlisted men of the force.[22] Consequently, the officer class of the Militia necessarily came from the upper classes of Canadian society, being the only people with the disposable income and time necessary to be an officer in the force. As this book will demonstrate in Chapter 5, this led to membership in the officer corps of the Militia becoming a major social status symbol.

Pre-Confederation Military Forces in Manitoba

While the focus of this book is on the Militia that existed in Manitoba after the province was created in 1870, it is important to note that this was not the first military force to inhabit the area. Throughout the nineteenth century, several variations of Militia forces, and even British Regular forces, existed in what is now Manitoba.

The antagonistic relations between competing fur trading companies the Hudson's Bay Company and the North-West Company, the latter known as *Nor'Westers*, often led to conflict in the North-West. In 1816, amid increasing violence between pro-Nor'West Company Metis and pro-Hudson's Bay Company Scottish émigrés in the Selkirk Settlement, Lord Selkirk arranged for a force of one hundred retired Swiss mercenaries, eighty from the *Regiment de Meuron*, and another twenty from the *Regiment de Watteville*, to settle in

Red River as a Militia force capable of providing defence against threats from the Nor'Westers and First Nations. These were two Swiss mercenary regiments that had entered British service in the late eighteenth century and transferred to Canada to serve in the War of 1812. The regiments were disbanded after the war and the veterans were allocated tracts of land in Upper Canada before some were convinced to relocate to Red River with Selkirk. Later, in 1834–5, there was once again sufficient antagonism within the Red River Settlement, caused by racial tension between the Metis and the predominantly white leaders of the Hudson's Bay Company, that to maintain its authority the Company created a volunteer corps commanded by Alexander Ross, and including a sergeant major, four sergeants and fifty-four privates.[23]

The first deployment of British Regular forces to the Red River Settlement occurred ten years later, in 1846, in response to increasing American expansionism in the continental interior, and to provide a force for the maintenance of law and order amid ever-present religious and racial tensions in the Red River Settlement. The Imperial Government dispatched a force of 347 soldiers of the 6th Regiment of Foot, the Royal Warwickshires, to garrison the Hudson's Bay Company fort situated near present day Selkirk, Manitoba and known colloquially as the Lower or Stone Fort, the latter due the use of local limestone in its construction.[24] This Royal Warwickshires' expedition to the Red River Settlement was under the command of Lieutenant-Colonel John Ffolliot Crofton and comprised 291 men of the regiment supported by 26 men of the Royal Artillery and 12 engineers.[25] The force departed from Cork, Ireland on June 26, 1846 aboard Her Majesty's ships *Blenheim* a 74-gun Vengeur-class ship of the line, and *Crocodile,* a twenty-eight-gun Atholl-class corvette. The two warships were joined by two supply ships from the Orkney Islands. The expedition's North Atlantic passage was generally calm, but when the convoy arrived in the Hudson Bay straits, they were met with several ice flows that were light, but nonetheless posed a hindrance to their advance. Consequently, the ships were separated and rejoined each other at their designated rendezvous, Resolution Island, which lay off the south tip of Baffin Island in the entrance to the Hudson Strait. The *Blenheim* arrived off York Factory, the Hudson's Bay trading post situated where the Hayes River drains into Hudson's Bay, on August 11, 1846. The Captain of the *Blenheim* was compelled to drop anchor twenty miles offshore on account of shoals and a sand bar that prevented his entrance to the river mouth. The *Crocodile* arrived two days later. The men were landed in four parties, between the 17th and 23rd of August, one officer stating it took sixteen hours to get ashore from the boat.[26] The soldiers also had to unload the three hundred tons of stores they had brought along with them with the help of a small schooner and two boats form the factory. So far off the coast were they that it required three tides to make a single trip to the fort.[27]

Eventually the Warwickshires and their supporting elements moved off in boat brigades, each consisting of six craft, and climbed the Hayes River southward. The lead brigade arrived in Lower Fort Garry on September 10, followed by another two brigades on September 17. Two other brigades were sent further south to Fort Garry at the confluence of the Red and Assiniboine Rivers, arriving on September 18, 1846. The grueling expedition from Cork to the Red River Settlement surprisingly produced only two casualties: one man became ill on the crossing and had to return to England on board the *Crocodile,* while another drowned in the Hayes River on August 24, 1846.[28]

The Royal Warwickshires passed a generally quiet year in the settlement until the Commander- in-Chief of the British Army, Arthur Wellesley, 1st Duke of Wellington — yes THAT Duke of Wellington of Waterloo fame — ordered the regiment withdrawn. In their place, a Militia of fifty-six pensioners, along with forty-two women and fifty-seven children were convinced to settle in the region by the Hudson's Bay Company with the offer of free plots of land.

The plan to conduct a military colonization of the territory followed after a similar attempt in New Zealand. Calls for volunteers went out in the spring of 1848 and the Secretary of War issued the requirements. The pensioners were to be no more than forty-five years old, and a minimum of five foot six inches in height with a robust health and confirmed medically sound by a physician. They were to be enrolled for seven years, and upon arrival in Fort Garry they were provided quarters near the fort, and a plot of land ranging in size from twenty acres for a private and forty acres for a sergeant. Each pensioner was liable for three days work per month for the Hudson's Bay Company during the first year, and six days a month in the second year, during which they could be employed in public works or in instructing the local militia. Additionally, they were expected to attend a twelve-day, unpaid, military exercise every year.[29] Unfortunately, the pensioners were unaccustomed to farming and many left not long after arriving.

More robust efforts to garrison Red River occurred a further ten years later in 1856 when, in response to the arrival of United States Cavalry near Pembina, the Imperial Government once again felt the impetus to make a display of British resolve and authority in the North-West. Interestingly, the real concern was first articulated by the Hudson's Bay Company, no doubt fearing that any encroachment of American authority might threaten its economic monopoly in Rupert's Land. The Governor of the Company, John Sheppard, wrote to the Foreign Minister in London to recommend the dispatch of a force of regular soldiers to Red River where, he reminded him, there was ample accommodation for the force and that the canons brought out in 1846 had been left there to assist in the defence of the colony. More to the point, the Company even agreed to pay the expenses to transport 100–120 men and provide them with free rations during their deployment.[30] Consequently, the Imperial Government dispatched to Fort Garry 120 soldiers from the Royal Canadian Rifles, a British Regular regiment raised in Canada, via Hudson's Bay. The detachment, under the command of Major George Seton, embarked on the ship *Great Britain* in Montreal on June 24, 1857, and arrived at York Factory on August 28, 1857. Sixteen boats were hired for the voyage to Fort Garry, the advance party arriving at Lower Fort Garry in October.

The Rifles occupied the Lower Fort for three years, passing a generally quiet time. Life was likely peaceful yet mundane. The soldiers were able to enjoy a garrison library, provided by the Hudson's Bay Company, grow fresh produce, and enjoy fresh milk and beef from twenty-four cows and one bull also provided by the Company. In the summer of 1860, many of the terms of service of the men at Fort Garry were set to expire in the very near future. Of the 120 men garrisoning the colony, forty-eight wished to rejoin the regiment in Canada, while eighteen desired to proceed to England. Given the logistical challenges of reinforcing Fort Garry and, having determined that the Imperial Government had made a significant enough statement of resolve, the Colonial Department decided to withdraw the force. The inhabitants of Red River were leery to lose their military protection and petitioned the Imperial Government to dispatch another force to the region. Their pleas fell on deaf ears, and the government informed the inhabitants that if they wanted defence, they would have to provide it themselves in the form of a Militia. On August 6, 1861, the detachment of the Royal Canadian Rifles began the arduous trek north to York Factory, embarking there on August 30, 1861, and arriving in St. John's in mid-November. No Regular military force would return to Red River until 1870 when Imperial and Dominion authorities dispatched a joint expedition of British Regular and Canadian Militia to Fort Garry in response to the Red River Resistance.[31]

THE RED RIVER RESISTANCE ERUPTS

The Red River Resistance led by Louis Riel between December 1869 and June 1870 was a seminal event in Canadian and Manitoba history. It has been investigated by a myriad of historians in the years since Manitoba's entry into Confederation and never fails to elicit strong emotions amongst not only historians but the public as well. Its leading figure, Louis Riel, is a lightning rod of conflicting narratives, heightened emotions, and intense debate. It is fair to say that, until recently, the Canadian historical narrative has accepted him as, variously, a traitor, a lunatic, a megalomaniac, and a murderer. In recent years, however, Canadians' understanding of Riel's nature has undergone a long-overdue revision. His leadership, intelligence, kindness, and devotion to the Metis people have fortunately come to light.

The renaissance of Louis Riel's legacy began in 1992 when the Government of Canada passed a resolution that recognized Louis Riel as the founder of Manitoba. Several years later, the statue of Louis Riel which had stood on the grounds of the Manitoba Legislative Assembly since 1970, depicting him naked, his wrists bound behind him and enclosed in two curved walls which gave the impression of captivity, was replaced. In its stead was erected a more dignified statue reflecting his statesmanship as leader of the Metis people and depicting him dressed in a suit, with a Metis sash around his waist, holding in one hand the Bill of Rights that led to the Manitoba Act. More recently, in the winter of 2024, he was named the honorary first premier of Manitoba as the first act passed by the newly elected Manitoba Government of Premier Wab Kinew, the first First Nations premier of any province in Canada. Truly, Riel is a nuanced and layered character, reflective of the heterogeneity of human nature. Whether one considers him a saint or a sinner cannot change the fact that he was the single biggest catalyst to the eruption of the Red River Resistance and the dispatch of Imperial and Dominion forces to the region.

By the second half of the nineteenth century, Great Britain was looking to divest herself of elements of her vast empire. Canada was interested in the North-West, and Great Britain seemed to be interested in being rid of it. In

December of 1867, only five months after Confederation, the Canadian Senate and the House of Commons sent a joint address to the British government recommending the surrender of Rupert's Land and the North-West Territory to Canada.[32] In September of 1868, the Dominion Government sent to London Sir George Etienne Cartier, Prime Minister Sir John A. Macdonald's Quebec lieutenant, and William McDougall, a Conservative minister from Nova Scotia, to represent Canada in tripartite discussions with the Imperial Government and the Hudson's Bay Company to negotiate the surrender of Rupert's Land and the North-West Territory to Canada. The Hudson's Bay Company dragged their heels and fussed, but eventually the three parties came to agreement: the Canadian government would pay £300,000 to the Hudson's Bay Company, via Great Britain, who would in turn surrender all its territory, except for some small tracts of land that they required to maintain their installations, to the Dominion. The deal was written up, hands were shaken, and all seemed a *fait accompli*. Lamentably, nobody bothered to inform the inhabitants of the North-West, let alone seek their input, as they were, for all intents and purposes, transferred like chattel from the Hudson's Bay Company to the Dominion of Canada.

Whilst the act to surrender the North-West to Canada navigated the halls of Westminster *en route* to Her Majesty's inbox, Cartier and McDougall returned triumphantly to Ottawa, submitting their report to the Canadian Parliament in May 1869. For his efforts, McDougall was named the first lieutenant-governor of the North-West.

Assuming a successful outcome in the British Parliament, in June 1869 the Governor General of Canada, Lord Monck, sought and received permission from the Hudson's Bay Company, through the Secretary of State for the Colonies in London, to dispatch survey teams to the Red River Settlement as soon as possible in order to take advantage of the season.[33] Shortly thereafter, Dominion Survey teams arrived in the Settlement and began to lay out future plots of land in accordance with an Ontario-style grid pattern — in some cases over top of established long and narrow river-front plots. Red River farms followed the *Seigneurial* system of land allocation, which featured homesteads with a short frontage of ten chains (220 yards) on a river, extending away from the water in two-mile-long, narrow strips of land, thereby giving equitable access to the water supply. Beyond the two-mile length was a further two-mile strip of 'hay privilege', which was uncultivated land used by the owner to provide hay for his animals.[34]

The reaction by local inhabitants, particularly the Metis, to the arrival of the survey teams and their casual disregard for established property rights, was understandably frosty. Much of the animosity arose from the perception that the surveying parties were securing the best lands for themselves as they went about their duties, dividing and sub-dividing the land as they saw fit.[35] Alexander Begg, a contemporary and prolific *raconteur* of Settlement history recalled that "it began to look as if no man's property was safe; ... there was nothing to prevent anyone from laying claim to [land] by simply running a furrow round it and planting stakes here and there — an easy way it must be admitted to become a landed proprietor."[36]

Concern amongst the Metis of Red River regarding the intentions of the Dominion representative and contractors had been escalating for some time. News of the impending annexation by Canada understandably created friction among the populace. A fear emerged amongst the Red River inhabitants that not only would they not have an opportunity to offer their opinions on the matter of the annexation, but it also seemed like once the transfer was done, they would have no voice in the way the territory was administered. Moreover, it became apparent that the envisioned administrative council, which was to replace the Council of Assiniboia as the governing body of the region, was to have some representation from local inhabitants, but a large portion was to be comprised of friends and supporters of McDougall who, it was assumed, would fill the most influential and powerful positions.[37]

As a result, several of the inhabitants of the settlement held a regular series of meetings in which they discussed the situation and considered their possible courses of action in response to the proposed annexation. The result of these discussions was a determination amongst the inhabitants to stop McDougall's entrance into the territory until some sort of reassurance could be provided that the rights and interests of the people of Red River would be respected.[38] Additionally, it was decided to put a stop to the activities of the survey parties. On October 11, 1869, a survey party had their progress stopped by a band of some eighteen Metis led by Louis Riel. The Metis were unarmed but "by standing on the chain and using threats of violence if the Survey [sic] was persisted in, it became evident that to go on with the Survey [sic] would probably have led to a collision."[39]

About a week thereafter, men started to gather at a Roman Catholic church near the La Salle River in St. Norbert, a parish lying about fifteen kilometers south of Fort Garry. Here, the Metis formed a council, *The Métis National Council*, with the intent of stopping McDougall's entrance to the region. They elected John Bruce as the president and established a headquarters in a small house adjoining the Roman Catholic Church near where the La Salle River empties into the Red River. A force of about forty mounted soldiers erected a barrier across the cart trail that ran from Fort Pembina to Fort Garry, and then they ensconced themselves in the area to await the unsuspecting McDougall's arrival.[40]

Towards the end of October 1869, McDougall arrived in the region, travelling via the United States and Fort Dear, a United States Army installation near modern day Emerson, Manitoba, to assume his gubernatorial duties. As he slowly made his way towards Fort Garry to the ear-splitting squeal of a Red River cart, he received reports of the goings-on in Red River and was informed, by reports of travelers recently departed from the location, about the heightened tensions within the Settlement. When he arrived at the Hudson's Bay Company post at Fort Pembina on October 30, 1869, he found a Metis gentleman waiting for him who presented to him the following, rather forthright note:

Monsieur,
Le Comité National des Métis de la Rivière Rouge intime à Monsieur Wm McDougall l'ordre de ne pas entrer sur le territoire du Nord-Ouest sans une permission spéciale de ce Comité.

Par ordre du Président John Bruce
Louis Riel, Secrétaire.[41]

What followed was a series of dramatic events that has become known to Canadian history as the Red River Resistance. Louis Riel and his followers established a provisional government and seized Fort Garry as its capital. Racial tensions escalated, a counter-revolutionary force was created — Colonel Dennis' unsuccessful militia — and were eventually suppressed. Members of a pro-Canada faction, known as the *Canada Party* led by an immigrant from Ontario named Dr. John Schultz, were arrested and incarcerated in Fort Garry by Riel and his followers. Eventually one of their number, a bellicose alleged Orangeman named Thomas Scott, was condemned to death and executed.

Thomas Scott, had come to the region as a laborer working on the Dominion Road that was meant to link the North West Angle of Lake of the Woods and Fort Garry, and upon the outbreak of the Red River Resistance, he threw his lot in with the adherents of the Canada Party. After his capture, he was sentenced to death at what Riel called a 'court martial' for his constant haranguing of guards and disrespectful language towards Riel and his Provisional Government.

On March 4, 1870 Scott was publicly executed by firing squad outside the eastern wall of Fort Garry. The death of Scott has become enmeshed in conflicting narratives despite the many witnesses to the event. It is generally agreed that the initial volley from the firing party failed to kill Scott, and some witnesses claim he was then dispatched with a revolver. Others witnesses reported hearing moans emanating from Scott's coffin several hours after the event as it lay in Fort Garry until the *coup de grace* was delivered, perhaps even by Riel himself, using a knife. Complicating matters, his remains were never found although Riel claimed that his men had buried him inside the walls of Fort Gary. When the grave was disinterred four years later, the rough box was found to be empty. His remains have never been found and many believe his body was sunk in the Red River.[42]

Faced with the eruption of the Resistance, the Dominion, under Sir John A. Macdonald, pursued a comprehensive approach to resolving the issue, using all the tools available to achieve its strategic goal of securing the North-West for Canada. These include diplomatic efforts which were undertaken by sending representatives of the Dominion Government to parley with Riel and other leaders of the Provisional Government. These Canadian emissaries included Vicar-General Jean-Baptiste Thibault, a Catholic priest and missionary who had spent extensive time in the North-West amongst the Metis and First Nations, Donald A. Smith, the Commissioner of the Montreal Department of the Hudson's Bay Company, Lieutenant-Colonel Charles-Rene-Leonidas D'Irumberry de Salaberry, a French Canadian Militia officer who had participated in the Canadian exploratory mission to the North West in 1857, and Bishop Alexandre-Antonin Taché, Bishop of St. Boniface who had been proselytizing throughout the North-West for the previous twenty-five years.

Louis Riel and the other leaders of the Provisional Government undertook diplomatic efforts themselves. In late March of 1870, the Provisional

Government dispatched to Ottawa three emissaries of their own, chosen from amongst their number: Judge John Black, Reverend Ritchot, and Mr. Alfred Scott, to negotiate the entrance of the North-West into the Canadian Dominion. The emissaries were armed with a list of conditions and terms demanded by the Provisional Government for admission to Confederation covering diverse subjects such as the region's level of representation in parliament, financial terms, and citizen's property rights. Upon their arrival in Ottawa, the delegates were granted an audience with the Prime Minister Sir John A. Macdonald and, when the prime minister fell ill, George Etienne Cartier, to present their grievances and negotiate a settlement to the uprising.

The negotiations between the Dominion Government and the Red River emissaries were successful, and Macdonald's decision to accede to all of Riel's demands resulted in the diplomatic resolution of the resistance. In May 1870, the Dominion Government passed the *Manitoba Act*, which addressed the concerns of the Red River inhabitants and created the Province of Manitoba and the North-West Territory out of Rupert's Land. The emissaries returned to Red River with a copy of the statute, and Riel's Provisional Government unanimously ratified the Act in June of 1870 and the bill received royal assent on July 31, 1870. Thereafter, for all intents and purposes, the North-West peacefully entered the Canadian Confederation. Interestingly, while the Provisional Government was not a *de jure* government, the fact the Dominion Government accepted its representatives, negotiated with them, and passed a statute addressing their grievances indicates that the Dominion Government nonetheless recognized it as the *de facto* popular representation of the people of the region. Diplomacy between the Dominion and Provisional Governments, however, did not forestall military action. Even as the Red River emissaries and Dominion officials negotiated the terms of the North-West's annexation, preparations to assemble and dispatch a military force continued in parallel.

THE FIRST RED RIVER EXPEDITIONARY FORCE

The idea of sending a military force to Red River came early into the strategic reckoning, although both the Imperial and the Dominion governments were loath to annex the North-West by force, notwithstanding the jingoistic approach many of the members of the force would take once it was underway.[43] The execution of Thomas Scott had engendered intense animosity amongst the predominantly Anglo-Protestant political and societal leaders in Ontario.

Scott's death became a *cassus belli* that rendered a military response nearly inevitable. When news of his execution reached the eastern provinces, 'indignation' meetings were convened in Toronto, Montreal, and Ottawa, the three largest cities in the Dominion at the time, each chaired by their respective mayors. The *Canadian Illustrated News* reported that each "adopted emphatic, but well and temperately expressed resolutions, characterising in fitting terms the atrocious conduct of the Riel faction, and calling upon the authorities to take prompt and efficient measures for bringing the guilty to justice."[44] In fact, when the Provisional Government's emissaries arrived in Ontario *en route* to Ottawa, they were arrested by local authorities and remanded while charges of complicity in what many in Ontario saw as the *murder* of Thomas Scott were brought before the court. Fortunately, wiser minds prevailed, and the emissaries were ordered released by a magistrate.[45]

That some sort of military force was required was an easy question to the Dominion leadership — the real delicacy lay in what the composition of the force should be. Certainly, some Canadian Militia were required — this was Canada after all — but Macdonald also felt, vehemently, that British participation was essential. On March 24, 1870, the War Office wrote to the General Officer Commanding British forces in Canada, Lieutenant-General James Lindsay, to inform him that he may be required to dispatch a force of approximately two hundred regular soldiers, accompanied by a larger body of Canadians, to "maintain order in [Red River] during the process of its annexation to Canada."[46]

By the start of April, Macdonald and his ministers were being grilled by the opposition in the House of Commons about rumors appearing in both the Canadian and British press concerning a planned military expedition to the North-West. Macdonald refused to divulge details, saying only the Dominion and Imperial governments were working together to resolve the situation. After several days of opposition hectoring, on April 6, he conceded that "the two Governments are quite in accord as to the policy [to be] pursued, and that policy is one of action."[47] One commenter in the *Volunteer Review,* a periodical dedicated to Canadian military matters, observed that "The Volunteers here [in Montreal] are very anxious for the march to Red River; an announcement to get ready would cause the greatest enthusiasm. Every regiment thinks and hopes it may be favored, and many hundreds would volunteer to remain as settlers after peace has been restored to the country."[48] As we will see in later chapters, this verve amongst the soldiers to settle in the North-West turned out to be far less emphatic than the writer in the *Volunteer Review* predicted it would be.

The issue of who was to command the operation was addressed shortly thereafter. On April 11, 1870, Lindsay issued a memorandum providing his operational guidance for the formation of the force. He stated that the expedition should consist of 1,000 men, of which 25 percent should be British Regulars supported by artillery and engineers. The remaining 75 percent of the force, or about 700–800 men, should be Canadian militia volunteers and, Lindsay added, they should be assembled as soon as possible to commence training and develop some degree of team cohesion before departure. He advised that the Militia officers should be experienced, particularly because the British Regulars would depart shortly after their arrival in Fort Garry, leaving the Militia officers to command the garrison in the North-West.[49]

Of critical importance, Lindsay stressed that preparations for the expedition should be directed by him, and him alone. He wrote that "it is indispensable that the organization of the Expeditionary Force should be at once entrusted solely to me." In particular "all purchases of stores … for this Expedition by the Dominion Government, [is] to cease from this date, except for such articles as I may consider, and deem it advisable for the public service." Additionally, he recommended that the Dominion Government should avail itself of the use of the Royal Canadian Rifles to fill the Canadian portion of the force as it was destined to be disbanded soon.

The importance of selecting the proper officer for such a delicate and important task was underlined by the Colonial Office who observed that much may depend on the designated officer's firmness, prudence, and judgment, especially if "the Canadian Government should desire him to act as the first Civil Lieutenant-Governor of the district."[50] History has bequeathed upon Garnet Wolseley a great man's status. Born in County Dublin, Ireland, Wolseley joined the British Army in the 12th Regiment of Foot at the age of nineteen, later transferring to the 80th Regiment of Foot and serving with that regiment in India. He was injured in Burma, and again during the siege of Sevastopol during the Crimean War, the latter resulting in the loss of vision in his right eye. His martial talents were obvious even at this early stage of his career when he was awarded the *Legion d'honneur* and was recommended for the Victoria Cross. In 1861, as a lieutenant-colonel, he was transferred to

Canada where he became the assistant Quartermaster General of the Canadian Militia. He was called back to Britain in 1867, but then returned to Canada only months later to assume the duties of the deputy Quartermaster General. At thirty-four, he was the youngest staff officer to assume such a senior post in Canadian history. He was eventually chosen to command the Red River Expeditionary Force, and afterward enjoyed an extremely successful career, rising to the rank of Field Marshal and being named as Commander-in-Chief of the British Army. He developed a cultural following in the British military where the term "all Sir Garnet" became slang for something very well planned and executed. Even Gilbert and Sullivan celebrated him, and he was easily recognizable as the "very model of the modern major general" from *The Pirates of Penzance*. In 1900, Wolseley retired from the military but continued to write, although his health and mental faculty were failing him. He died in 1913.

Wolseley's selection as the force commander merits some consideration. That the leader would have to be an Imperial officer was no question: no British politician would have accepted the idea of British Regular forces falling under the command of an officer of a Colonial Militia. As a colonel, he held the appropriate rank for the size of the force the authorities were contemplating dispatching, so there would be no disagreement over who was in charge amongst he and the three lieutenant-colonels commanding the battalions. His experience as the deputy Quartermaster General indicated that he had the requisite skills for logistical preparations that would be necessary for such a long and arduous journey, through isolated terrain where resupply was all but impossible. His aptitude for such planning was on full display in a March 28, 1870 report he prepared, in his capacity as Deputy Quartermaster General, entitled "Outline of Plan for Sending an Armed Force to Red River" in which he articulates, in painstaking detail, his recommendation on the size, organization, equipping, and sustainment necessary for a successful expedition to Fort Garry.[51] His hard work must have paid off as less than two weeks later, on April 11, 1870, Lindsay selected Wolseley to command the expeditionary force, news which the Deputy Minister of Militia, Geoff Futvoye, reported that the Government of Canada received "with much satisfaction." [52]

About the same time, the adjutant-general wrote to the Minister of Militia and Defence to recommend that two battalions of riflemen with a strength of 350 men per unit, should be raised in Ontario and Quebec for service in the North-West for a period of one year. Specifically, he suggested that the recruits should be men "between the ages of 18–45 years, of good character, sober habits, and physically fit for the service" and that the force should be concentrated as soon as possible.[53] In order to have a balance between Quebec and Ontario forces, he envisioned the following quotas for the seven military districts of the two provinces, divided as follows:

District 1 (London) 100.
District 2 (Toronto) 100.
District 3 (Kingston) 100.
District 4 (Ottawa) 50.
District 5 (Montreal) 100.
District 6 (St. Jean) 100.
District 7 (Quebec City) 150.[54]

By mid-April, the rumors of a possible military expedition had grown exponentially, so much so that the *Canadian Illustrated News* assumed that the decision to dispatch a military force was a *fait accompli,* with only the composition of the force left to be decided.[55]

On April 19, Lindsay received word from the Department of Militia and Defence that the Dominion Government had agreed to send their portion of the force, as stipulated by Lindsay in his April 11 memorandum. Quizzically, the Dominion Government declined General Lindsay's offer of the Royal Canadian Rifles, made some time earlier. And finally, providing some intimation of the role of the Militia force in the North-West after its arrival, the government also announced that that "a mounted police force of fifty men is to be sent for service in the Red River territory. It will be commanded by Captain Cameron, R.A., with instructions to increase the force to 200 men from the people at Red River. Captain Cameron is on service in the Artillery at Halifax and was seconded at the request of the Canadian Government, at the Horse Guards, for the purpose of his proceeding, care will be taken that the suggestions therein made be duly carried out."[56]

It may have seemed that the dispatch of a military force to the North-West was inevitable by this point, but there was still much dithering to be done by the Dominion Government, all of which led to increased consternation on the part of General Lindsay. Only four days after the Dominion Government committed to the mutually agreed composition of the force, Lindsay wrote to the Governor General to express his misgivings about the venture. Lindsay expressed his concern that, on top of the arduous nature of the route, there was a real possibility of opposition by Metis, First Nations, or Fenians along the way. He realized that a force larger than originally considered was necessary considering a perceived requirement to leave garrisons at strategic points along the route, known as the line of communication, which connected the force with eastern Canada. Lindsay therefore requested permission to increase the size of the Regular portion of the force. On April 23, Lindsay wrote:

> I cannot say that I feel satisfied with the arrangements as they at present exist with respect to the efficiency of the force to be employed, and considering the moral effect of a body of trained soldiers … it would be desirable to obtain the sanction of the Imperial Government to increase the number of the 1st Battalion 60th Rifles to be employed from 200 to 400 rank and file. This measure would augment the confidence of the loyal settler, decrease that of the insurgents, and give greater security for success.[57]

The Governor General supported his recommendation and sought the concurrence of the Dominion Government for such an increase. Although the final decision would be made by the Imperial Government, given that the Dominion Government would play such a large role in financing the overall force its approval in this matter, Macdonald's support was necessary. On April 26, the Deputy Minister of Militia and Defence agreed to the suggested increase in the regular portion of the force.[58] Two days later Lindsay made the request to increase the Regular Component from 200 to 350 — why he did not request the 400 he mentioned to the Governor General is not known — to the War Office.[59] He justified his request stating the increase was "for military reasons, and to leave garrisons at Fort Francis and Fort William."[60] Oddly, the garrisons that were left at these two locations were provided by the Canadian Militia battalions, not the Regular component.

As all this this played out behind-the-scenes no public mention of a military expedition was made. Despite the advanced state of planning and preparations, Macdonald and his ministry played their cards close to their chest. On April 26, the Leader of the Government in the Senate, Sir Alexander

Campbell, reminded the upper chamber that "it should not be assumed that because the expedition had been spoken of in newspapers and elsewhere that the Government had decided upon the same." He asked for patience and stated that the Government policy towards Red River would be released in the next several days.[61] And indeed it was. On May 2, Macdonald rose in the House to share the initial details of the *Manitoba Act*, which had been arrived at after negotiations with Riel's emissaries, and announce that "an arrangement ... has been made between Her Majesty's Government and the Government of Canada for the dispatch of an expedition. That expedition will be a mixed one, comprised partly of Her Majesty's regular troops, and partly of Canadian Militia ... commanded by an officer of Her Majesty's service, under Her Majesty's sanction."[62] The worst-kept secret in Ottawa was now official policy.[63]

Although many historians have assigned Wolseley's name to the expedition of 1870, the official name of the force was the *Red River Expeditionary Force*. As agreed between the Dominion and Imperial authorities, the force was a cobbled-together mish-mash of British Regulars and Canadian Militia — the regular component consisted of soldiers from the 1st Battalion of the British 60th Rifles Regiment, with supporting detachments from the Royal Engineers, Royal Medical Services, and the Royal Artillery, the latter armed with four bronze nine-pounder mountain howitzers while the Canadian volunteer component consisted of two Canadian Militia *ad hoc* infantry battalions composed of volunteers from Active Militia corps in Ontario and Quebec, named the 1st Ontario Rifles and 2nd Quebec Rifles.[64]

The orders for the creation of the force were not published in *Militia General Orders* until May 10, 1870, however these were mere formalities that did not pre-empt concurrent activity.[65] The districts were told specifically to look for men "between eighteen and forty-five years [old], of good character, and as the service upon which they were about to be employed required more than ordinary physical strength and power of endurance, a strict medical examination was necessary."[66] The volunteers were enrolled for one years' service with a liability for a further year of service at the discretion of the government.[67]

In the creation of the Ontario and Quebec Battalions, the Dominion Government attempted to create a force culturally balanced between Anglophone and Francophone elements. In Quebec, however, the appetite to volunteer was less robust than it was in Ontario, thus the majority of the Canadian volunteers originated from Active Militia corps in Ontario and were predominantly Anglophone Protestants.[68] Lindsay wrote the War Office and bemoaned that "of the 292 men in [the Quebec battalion's ranks] not more than one-fourth at most are French Canadian."[69] Five days later those numbers had grown only to 298 men of the 400 necessary.[70] Lindsay tried to help fill out the ranks of the Quebec battalion by lending Staff Sergeants from the Royal Canadian Rifles, and also by expediting the discharge of men from the Royal Canadian Rifles so that they could enlist in the Quebec battalion.[71] One correspondent from Montreal wrote to the *Volunteer Review* that "able-bodied men have been slow in coming forward for the Red River Expedition ... there are still vacancies and recruiting is being pushed on briskly, temptations of all sorts being held out, and it is asserted that bounty money is freely lavished. I cannot say there has been much enthusiasm displayed in the matter."[72] Despite these efforts, 85 percent of the volunteers in the Quebec battalion were Anglophones from Ontario.[73] This cultural and ethnic makeup of the Canadian volunteer force was to become a key element of the less savory efforts to culturally transform Manitoba in later years.

Another question that emerged during the planning of the expedition concerned the route to be taken. A railway link between Winnipeg and the Eastern Canada wasn't established until 1885, thus there were only three practical routes from Eastern Canada to Manitoba: through the United States, by ship and boat via the Hudson's Bay and Hayes River system, or the "amphibious" Canadian route.

The American route was perhaps the most expeditious as it allowed one to take advantage of train transportation for most of the trip, arriving in modern North Dakota where a cart trail led north to Winnipeg. This route would be used by senior officers several times before the completion of the transcontinental railway in Canada, particularly when travelling in small groups, usually incognito. For political reasons, the Americans were loath to allow large bodies of uniformed British and Canadian troops to travel through their country, consequently the American route was generally not a viable option for moving the expedition. The Hudson's Bay route allowed forces to be transported by sea to Churchill and then follow the traditional fur trade river highway of the Nelson and Hayes River systems to Winnipeg, as the Royal Warwickshires had done in 1846 and the Royal Canadian Rifles in

1856. Churchill's location near the arctic circle meant that the window of opportunity to make such a trek was short, and in the end, the time taken to transport forces from a point on the St. Lawrence, around the Ungava peninsula and into Hudson's Bay, followed by a canoe trip up the Nelson River System, didn't make this route any more expeditious. The only politically acceptable and practical route from Eastern Canada to Manitoba thus lay through the rugged Canadian Shield. The "Canadian route" was challenging, and it should be noted that the force that was dispatched was not composed of rugged soldiers who were immune to such hardships through experience, but Militiamen who spent at most sixteen days a year in training, and when not in uniform were clerks, farmers, or general labourers.

The political and military authorities obviously arrived at this decision early in the planning, but not easily. Many political and military leaders thought the route was impractical, and the risks to the force were insurmountable. Simon Dawson, of the Dominion Public Works Department, was tasked to attend to the logistical needs of the force after Thunder Bay, and recalled in his report to the Dominion Government how he had convinced the powers that be to use the fur trade route:

> the route for a distance of two hundred miles, had never been traversed by any vessel larger or stronger than a bark canoe, and the chief officers of the Hudson's Bay Company, who were supposed to be well acquainted with the country, had declared it to be impracticable to their boats ... so general was this opinion as to the character of the route, by Lake Superior, and so firmly fixed had it become, that the Imperial Government on two occasions sent troops by way of Hudson's Bay to Fort Garry ... having traversed the route by Lake Superior frequently, I was in a position to explain to the Government that the reports as to its impracticability were exaggerated, that it had been for many years the high-way of the North-West Company of Canada, and that, after the mountainous country, on the borders of Lake Superior was passed, there would be no difficulty whatever in sending forward a force of considerable numbers by means of boats.[74]

The Government accepted Dawson's recommendation and settled on using the Canadian route. Although the Dominion and Imperial Governments did not settle on dispatching a military force until the early spring, that there was at least some consideration of doing so much earlier is reflected in that fact that as early as January 1870, Dawson was instructed to increase the workforce he had in Thunder Bay which was improving the road inland from Thunder Bay with the hopes of making the route passable for a possible expedition.[75] Moreover, understanding that much of the route, particularly the most challenging portion from Thunder Bay to Fort Garry, ran through indigenous lands, the government realized that a successful expedition would require the acquiescence of local First Nations. To this end, the Dominion government undertook efforts ensure a safe passage through the region by deploying emissaries amongst the indigenous peoples to communicate "the beneficent intentions of the Canadian Government" and to "disabuse the minds of the people of the misrepresentations made by designing foreigners."[76] These emissaries included Catholic priest the Very Reverend Jean-Baptiste Thibault, who had worked as a missionary amongst the indigenous people of the region for nearly forty years, and Colonel Charles-Rene-Leonidas D'Irumberry de Salaberry, a Canadian Militia officer and explorer who had become familiar with the people of the area when he accompanied Henry Youle Hind, George Gladman, and Dawson on an exploratory expedition to the Red River Settlement commissioned by the government of the Province of Canada.[77] In support of these diplomatic overtures, in January 1870, Dawson, now in Thunder Bay, ordered an agent of his in Thunder Bay to proceed to Fort Frances to enter into discussions with the indigenous leaders and inform them of the peaceful nature of the expedition that would follow.[78]

By the second week of May 1870, the Militia component had assembled at the Crystal Palace exhibition hall in Toronto, designed along the lines of the Crystal Palace in London, England where medical inspections, training, and the issuance of the uniforms of a rifle regiment took place. On the evening of May 12, 1870, Wolseley finally received authority from Ottawa to proceed.[79] He dispatched the first elements of his force two days later sending two companies of the 1st Ontario Rifles to establish the Sault Ste. Marie portage route.[80] On May 21, the vanguard of the expedition departed from Toronto, followed over the next several days by the remainder of the force. The expedition's planned route of advance was by rail to the port of Collingwood on Georgian Bay of Lake Huron, and then by steamship to Thunder Bay via the straits at Sault Ste. Marie. At this latter locale, Canadian and American territory are separated by a narrow river impassable to steamships due its rapids. In 1870, a series of locks on American territory were the only means for ships to pass through the channel between Lake Huron and Lake Superior, however the American government insisted that no warlike stores were to be transported through the American locks. Consequently, Wolseley was compelled to have his men offload combat stores on the Canadian shore of Lake Huron, portage them three miles around the rapids to the Lake Superior shore, and then re-embark them for transport to Thunder Bay.[81] To expedite matters, one of the steamships passed through the locks, and thereafter ferried cargo from Sault Ste. Marie to Thunder Bay, while another did similar service between Collingwood and Sault Ste. Marie.

After crossing Lake Superior, the force came ashore near Thunder Bay in an inlet that Wolseley christened Prince Arthur's Landing in honor of Queen Victoria's son, who was then on service in Canada. Here, a stores depot and a wooden redoubt were established near the Hudson's Bay Company fort to serve as a forward logistical base. To protect this vital link on the force's line of communication, Wolseley detailed a company from the 2nd Quebec Rifles to garrison the site.[82]

Thereafter, the remainder of the force executed a herculean task over corduroy road (tree trunks laid lengthways to form a road) — much of which was built by the force itself — canoe and portage to Fort Garry via Rainy River and Rat Portage.[83] The force traversed six hundred miles of rock, river, and swamp, over forty-seven portages comprising a cumulative total distance of almost nine miles. There was no hope of resupply, reinforcement, or rescue as there was no habitation for hundreds of miles around, and thus the force had to be completely self-sustaining. Consequently, the weight and number of supplies and equipment that needed to be ferried across the portages on the backs of the soldiers necessitated each man to traverse the forty-seven portages several times over. The cumulative distance of nine miles is therefore deceptively unrepresentative of the total distance each soldier had to travel, which is likely much greater. While doing so, they were burdened, in at least one direction, with their arms, accoutrements and supplies some of which, such as barrels of pork, weighed upwards of two hundred pounds. [84] Wolseley recorded that each boat carried "sixty days' provisions for all embarked, consisting of salt pork, beans, preserved potatoes, flour, biscuit, pepper, salt, tea and sugar ... ammunition, intrenching tools [sic], camp equipment, cooking utensils, waterproof sheets, blankets, &c., &c."[85] The men were issued long leather straps which formed a loop and allowed them to carry their burdens by passing one end across their forehead and the other around the lower part of the box or barrel they were carrying, which then rested on their lower back. Moving the boats was no mean task either. Rather than lightly skinned canoes they were thirty-foot-long vessels weighing seven hundred-pounds built to carry a crew of ten or eleven men, comprised of eight or nine soldiers and two *voyageurs*, civilian fur traders, and woodsmen hired to handle the vessels.

Eventually the force descended the Winnipeg River into Lake Winnipeg, from whence it began the southerly ascent up the Red River towards Fort Garry. Due to the nature of the terrain, the expedition did not travel in a single body, but rather was strung out along the route of advance. [86]

Wolseley's vanguard consisted entirely of the regular component of the 60th Regiment, the Militia battalions being, in some cases, several days behind him. Wolseley had intended to march on the fort commencing much further down river, but the torrential rains of the previous several days obliged him to keep his force in boats as he approached Fort Garry, until the last possible moment. The force arrived at Point Douglas, a promontory of land within a meander of the Red River that lays about two miles north of the Fort, disembarked, and formed into open column of companies. Wolseley dispatched a line of skirmishers four hundred yards in front of the column and marched south-westerly with the infantry leading, followed by the engineers and artillery who limbered their guns behind some prairie carts that had been pressed into service from local farms. A company of the 60th Rifles was left in the rear as a guard. The force advanced on the fort through ankle-deep mud caused by several days of intense rainfall, swung around the village of Winnipeg and approached their objective from the west. The *Official Journal of Operations* captures the scene as follows:

> No flag was flying from the flagstaff in the Fort, and there was no sign of life visible; everything looked grim and frowning, and the gun mounted over the gateway that commanded the village and the prairie over which the troops were advancing, was expected momentarily to open fire. But the hopes of the troops were doomed to disappointment. On nearing the Fort some of the mounted men were sent forward to ascertain the state of affairs; they were followed by three of the Staff ... the

Fort was found to be emptied of its late defenders.[87]

The reconnaissance element dispatched by Wolseley discovered the southern gate was open, and they observed several men running away southwards across the bridge spanning the Assiniboine River — assumed to be Riel and his lieutenants. Upon entering the empty fort, they discovered Riel's breakfast sitting warm and uneaten on the table of his headquarters. The battalion took possession of the fort without a shot, raised the Union Jack, fired a royal salute, and gave three cheers for the Queen.[88]

Perhaps Wolseley can be excused his cautious approach to Fort Garry as the warm welcome the troops experienced was by no means assumed by the soldiers of the expedition. Quite the contrary, rumors were rife throughout North America that Riel and his supporters were planning on to resist the force upon their arrival. For example, the *Boston Globe* carried news from Minnesota that Riel had gathered a force of 3,000 men to confront Wolseley unless a complete amnesty was issued to him and his supporters.[89] The *Buffalo Express,* under the byline "The Winnipeg War" reported that Riel's supporters were not happy with the *Manitoba Act* and planned on resisting the troops upon their arrival.[90] The *Fort Wayne Daily Gazette* reported that "intelligence has been received from Fort Garry that a large meeting of French settlers was held at White Horse plains, when fighting and resistance to the Red river expedition [sic] was unanimously favored."[91] Obviously Wolseley would not have been exposed to these editorials, isolated as he was on his advance through the wilderness, but they are nonetheless indicative of the broader understanding of the conflict, and the widely held belief that a peaceful occupation of the settlement by the Wolseley Expedition — by either party — was by no means pre-ordained.

Interestingly, several weeks previous while the lead elements of the force were still making their way across Lake of the Woods, Wolseley had sent forward a communique to the inhabitants of the settlement stressing the peaceful nature of his mission and his openness to all elements of the populace. The distinctly tactical arrangement of the force upon its approach to the fort seems to be distinctly at odds with these pacific overtones, and one is left to wonder how genuine Wolseley was in the language he used.

Notwithstanding the fact that the *Manitoba Act* had been negotiated and signed, and the resistance had ended, Riel wisely withdrew from the region upon the arrival of Wolseley's aggressively arrayed column. Wolseley's force invested the Fort and surrounding settlement and became, in effect, a permanent military garrison stationed at Red River. The British Regular component of the force was not long to remain, however. A criterion insisted upon by the Imperial Government during its negotiations with the Dominion Government on the size and composition of the expedition was that the British Regular forces were to withdraw from the area immediately, and return to the east where they would commence their redeployment to Great Britain.[92] This was part of a general re-organization of the British Army from a global colonial police force comprised of regular, professional soldiers, to a smaller, centralized Army based on a small body of regular troops supported by a larger number of reservists liable for duty in time of emergency.

The British Government was determined to reduce its global military footprint, and consequently the Secretary of State for War, Lord Cardwell, entertained no arguments for maintaining large British forces abroad and set his sights on reducing the number of British colonial garrison soldiers from 50,000 to 26,000 men. Under his intransigent guidance the British treasury realized a decrease in defence expenditures from £3,000,000 in 1868–69 to £2,237,000 in 1869–70, a reduction in part achieved through the reduction in the British garrison in North America from 16,185 to 6,249 men for 1869–70.[93] With this philosophy as strategic guidance, within only a few days of their arrival the British Regulars departed Fort Garry to return to Ontario and thence to the United Kingdom, leaving the 862 Canadian Militia volunteers under the command of Lieutenant-Colonel S.P. Jarvis, the senior of the Canadian militia officers, to garrison the new province.[94]

The Canadian volunteers who remained in Fort Garry maintained the original organization of two volunteer infantry battalions, the 1st Ontario and 2nd Quebec Rifles, which were further subdivided into a total of sixteen companies.[95] Fort Garry was not able to accommodate the entire force, thus the Ontario Rifles were quartered in three long buildings along the west side of the fort, each of two stories and capable of accommodating one hundred men, while some others were forced to live in tents outside the fort. One company of the Ontario Rifles under Captain Cook was detailed to garrison the Hudson's Bay Company Post at Fort Pembina, and initially the Quebec Rifles were quartered in Lower Fort Garry.[96] Thus disposed, the volunteer force settled in and passed a generally quiet year in Fort Garry, although tensions amongst the force and local Métis were substantial and often led to violence, a question that will be dealt with in greater detail in Chapter 5.[97]

AFTER WOLSELEY

The volunteers had agreed to a term of service of one year, and thus their commitment was due to terminate on May 1, 1871. The adjutant-general in Ottawa, Robertson-Ross, determined that it was advisable to reduce the size of the force, noting the imminent termination of their terms of service, and that "the necessity … for maintaining, under arms, so large a force in that Province no longer exists (the peaceful solution of all difficulties there having [as expected] been happily realized,) the reduction on 1st May next of the greater portion of these battalions has been decided on."[98]

Consequently, the Red River Expeditionary Force was reduced in size from 862 to 89 soldiers — four officers and eighty-five men, under the command of Major Acheson G. Irvine.[99] In addition to his decision to reduce the force, Robertson-Ross made a number of other recommendations to the Minister of Militia concerning the defence of Manitoba, the most important being his suggestion that "the Province of Manitoba be formed into a Military District numbered No. 10." His recommendation to create a new military district was subsequently approved by an order in council of January 19, 1871.[100] Despite the early approval of his recommendation, orders from Militia Headquarters to create Military District No. 10 were not published until October 1871.

After the decision to reduce the garrison of permanent Militia on service in Manitoba was taken, general orders to that effect were produced. The remaining companies were to be retained for at least six months, with the possibility of extending the terms for another six months as determined by the Commanding Officer. The companies were manned by volunteers from the original force who wished to stay on, while those desirous of discharge were offered a grant of land or transported back to the military district of their enrolment.[101] The plans for the creation of a volunteer local Active Militia Corps in the new province, pursuant to the decision to create Military District No. 10 mentioned above, were also enacted. The discharge of volunteers from the permanent force began in earnest in May 1871 and culminated in June 1871.[102] As the volunteers trundled down the Dawson Road that linked Fort Garry with the North-West Angle of Lake of the Woods and thence to the eastern provinces from where they came, or took possession of their land grant, and settled down in the North-West, foreboding martial clouds started to gather. In 1871, word of a possible Fenian incursion into Manitoba reached authorities in Ottawa, where actions to prepare for the defence of the new province were put in motion.

Chapter 3 will more fully explore the local response to the Fenian incursion into Manitoba during the fall of 1871. At this juncture, it is sufficient to mention that in response to the emergent Fenian threat, a cavalry troop and four infantry companies were gazetted into the Active Militia in Manitoba in September 1871. Moreover, the Order in Council that authorized the creation of Military District No. 10 of January 1871 was finally enforced in *Militia General Orders (23)* of October 16, 1871 which stated that "the Province of Manitoba be henceforth called and known as Military District Number Ten" with Lieutenant-Colonel William Osborne Smith, deputy adjutant-general of Military District No. 5 (Montreal, Quebec) named the new deputy adjutant-general of Military District No. 10.

As the civic leadership of Manitoba raised a defensive force of civilian volunteers in response to the Fenian threat, plans were pursued in Ottawa to dispatch a second Red River Expeditionary Force. In an encrypted telegram sent to Lieutenant-Governor Archibald from Sir John A. Macdonald, the prime minister advised that he intended to send at least another two hundred soldiers to Fort Garry.[103] The same issue of *General Orders* that had designated Osborne Smith as the new deputy adjutant-general in Manitoba also called for "an additional force of Militia being about to proceed immediately for service in Manitoba" to augment the remnants of the Red River Expeditionary Force under Major Irvine.[104] This force was under the command of Captain Thomas Scott, and consisted of 275 officers and men, drawn again from Ontario and Quebec Active Militia corps.[105]

The Fenian threat manifested itself in October 1871 and sputtered out quickly. The Scott, or Second, Red River Expedition has received less historical inquiry than the much more famous Wolseley Expedition but is interesting. Like its predecessor, the Second Expedition overcame numerous toils and hazards to deploy to Fort Garry. It's accomplishments, and what they meant for the Canadian Militia's independence caused by the withdrawal of Imperial battalions, were praised by the adjutant-general of the Canadian Militia in his annual report stating: "the expedition of 1871, composed entirely of Canadian Militia, commanded by a Canadian officer, and so promptly carried out, will one be remembered with feelings of pride by every Canadian as one of the most successful and remarkable marches of the kind."[106] Indeed, Scott and his troops accomplished quite a feat, for which they have not received sufficient historical attention. Only a month and four days after the Dominion Government issued the order to dispatch a second expedition to Fort Garry in response to the perceived Fenian threat, and only twenty-one days after the force was concentrated in Collingwood, it arrived in Red River "a thousand toilsome miles away."[107]

The response to the request for volunteers was intense — far more Militiamen put their names forward than there were positions available in the force. Those tentatively selected were subject to a medical examination, and were then forwarded by their District Headquarters, under the supervision of a Staff Officer, to Collingwood. At Collingwood, the volunteers were once again submitted to a medical examination. In consequence of the advanced season and the onset of winter, the authorities concluded only the most resilient participants would be accepted, consequently the minimum health standard was increased at this juncture to ensure that only the most robust men were admitted to the ranks of the force. Eight men were rejected in Collingwood and their places filled by other volunteers. The force received its full issue of uniforms and accoutrements, a large portion of its supplies, and sailed out of the Georgian Bay harbour only weeks after the call had gone out for reinforcements.[108]

In many ways the Scott expedition paralleled the Wolseley Expedition, at least in consideration of the route taken. While Wolseley's force congregated at Toronto and then moved forward to Collingwood to proceed to Fort Garry, Scott *et al* mustered directly in Collingwood. From this idyllic shipping town on the coast of Georgian Bay, lying in the shadow of the Blue Mountain, both expeditions traversed the Great Lakes by steamer to Price Arthur landing, and thence to Lake of the Woods via the Dawson Road and a series of lake and river crossings combined with arduous portages in-between. Scott had some advantages over his predecessor, however. The Dawson Road was mostly complete to Shebandowan Lake, whereas Wolseley and his men had to construct it as they marched along. In the intervening year, several steam tugs had been placed on the various lakes along the route which Scott and his men took advantage of to tow their canoes, saving the laborious process of paddling. Unfortunately, it seemed to Scott, just as many were out of service as were operational. Perhaps the biggest single difference between the two excursions was that thanks to the completion of the Dawson Road between Fort Garry and the North-West Angle of Lake of the Woods, completed with the labour of some discharged Wolseley Expedition men and hired on by Dawson, Scott avoided the descent of the Winnipeg River to Lake Winnipeg, and instead made use of the road. Scott and his men arrived at the Fort on November 18, long after the Fenian threat had ended.[109]

Ironically, Lieutenant-Colonel Osborne Smith observed, the whole of the officers of the Second Expedition, with the exception of one, were veterans of the First Expedition who had been discharged and sent home not long before and unlike the First Expedition, there were no British Regulars amongst the ranks of this force, as it was wholly composed of Canadian Militia officers and men.[110] The Second Expedition merged with the remnants of the First and formed what was thereafter referred to as the *Provisional Battalion of Infantry*.[111] The Second Expedition's voyage was completed a mere one month and four days after the mobilization order was issued. The importance of this accomplishment was noted by Robertson Ross, who stated: 'the expedition of 1871, composed entirely of Canadian Militia, commanded by a Canadian officer, and so promptly carried out, will be one remembered with feelings of pride by every Canadian as one of the most successful and remarkable marches of the kind.'[112]

While Scott and his charges may have made their journey quickly, it was by no means free of hardships. In particular, the Second Expedition was compelled to conduct its march in winter whereas Wolseley and his men had the advantage of deploying through the late spring and summer. In his memoir, *From Toronto to Fort Garry an account of the Second Expedition to Red River. Diary of a Private Solider,* the author Justus Griffin recounted one episode in which the weary Militiamen set up camp next to what seemed a well-provisioned farm in Manitoba writing that "there was an air of comfort and plenty which was quite charming to wearied, half-frozen and hungry soldiers, who have the prospect of spending the bitter and stormy night with no protection but damp, poorly pitched tents."[113] Griffin also recounted that upon arrival at this particular camp, when the roll was called several men were found to be missing, and the strongest and least fatigued of the party were required to go and search for them. Fortunately the missing men were found, although Griffin contemplated a different outcome: "Being successful in performing their mission, [they] brought in some poor stragglers, who, in all probability, would otherwise have slept their last sleep to-night on a softer bed than they have occupied during the past few weeks, and have had the pure white snow for winding-sheets; and where the only requiem over their lonely resting-place would have been the howling of the fierce northern wind as it sweeps over the broad prairie." [114]

As they moved through northwestern Ontario, the Second Expedition was met at the North-West Angle of Lake of the Woods by their new deputy adjutant-general, Osborne Smith, who escorted them to Fort Garry along the Dawson Road. In the *dramatis personae* of the story of the Militia in Manitoba during its first fifteen years, few others played quite as significant a role as Osborne Smith. Born in Ireland, he served in the British Army in the 39th Regiment of Foot and served in the Crimean War. After that conflict, he was deployed to Canada with his regiment, and upon the British government's subsequent decision to transfer the regiment to Bermuda, he sold his commission and chose to remain in Canada. He joined the Canadian Active Militia and raised an infantry corps, the Victoria Rifles, in Montreal. As the Commanding Officer of the Victoria Rifles, he participated in defensive operations during the Fenian Raids along the Canada-US boundary south of Montreal, and he was knighted a Commander of the Most Distinguished Order of St. Michael and St. George (CMG) for his efforts. He was the deputy adjutant-general of Military District No. 5 in Montreal in 1871 when he was selected to assume the position of deputy adjutant-general for Military District No. 10 in Winnipeg. He held that position from its inception in 1871 until 1881 when he resigned and handed control of the district to Lieutenant-Colonel Charles Frederic Houghton who had been acting as the deputy adjutant-general for Military District No. 11 in British Columbia since 1873. Osborne Smith remained in Manitoba after his resignation and raised the Winnipeg Light Infantry in 1885 in response to the North-West Rebellion in which he played a prominent role, which will be described in chapter six. Osborne Smith died in 1887 during a visit to Wales and his legacy remains etched on Winnipeg where Osborne Street, and its attendant trendy urban village, still carry his name.[115]

The permanent force of Active Militia that remained on full-time service in Winnipeg remained until 1877 and over those six years their number and composition fluctuated. In the spring of 1872, the terms of service of the men who had stayed on in Fort Garry, and those who had come out under Thomas Scott in response to the Fenian threat, were coming to an end. Osborne Smith was authorized by the adjutant-general to allow the discharges of the men whose terms of service were expiring, but only insofar as he could maintain the size of the force in Manitoba, based on recruiting local men. He was also informed that, should he be unable to do so, reinforcements from the eastern provinces may be required.[116]

In Red River, there was found to be an insufficient number of local recruits willing to join the ranks of the volunteers. Consequently, on September 6, 1872, the adjutant-general of Militia issued orders to the military districts to recruit volunteers for service in Manitoba. The quotas for the various districts were as follows: District 1 (London) 25, District 2 (Toronto) 35, District 3 (Kingston) 20, District 4 (Ottawa) 20, Districts 5 and 6 (Montreal and St. Jean) 66, and District 7 (Quebec City) 34. [117] Additionally, District 7 was tasked to provide one officer, one sergeant and twenty-four gunners from B Battery School of Gunnery at the Citadel in Quebec City, along with two seven-pounder muzzle-loading rifled guns ceded by the La Beauce Mountain Battery in Quebec.[118] 'B' Battery, along with 'A' Battery in Kingston, were two permanent corps of Active Militia units, created in the fall of 1871 to maintain the fortresses of Quebec and Kingston on the withdrawal of the British Regular forces. In his annual report for 1873, Robertson Ross noted that although the call went out for twenty-four artillery volunteers from 'B' Battery, thirty-nine men put their names forward for service. The fifteen gunners who were not selected to serve the guns were sent as infantry. Robertson Ross remarked that the B Battery volunteers were "a remarkable fine body of intelligent and trained soldiers including many artificers."[119] On October 11, 1872, Major J. Ernest M. Taschereau was gazetted as First Lieutenant to command the gunners who would make their way to Fort Garry.[120]

The inclusion of a detachment of artillery in this expedition raises some interesting questions. The original Wolseley Expedition included a small detachment of Royal Artillery to provide some firepower in the event of Fenian interference or resistance from Louis Riel and his followers. In the fall of 1872, Military District No. 10 had an Active Militia battery in the form of the Winnipeg Field Battery but to this point, the composition of the Militia columns sent to Fort Garry were exclusively infantry. What changed in 1872 that demanded the inclusion of additional firepower in the form of a detachment of artillerymen? There is no explicit evidence explaining why artillery was sent to Fort Garry in this particular instance, however, an increase in the apprehension of indigenous violence in 1872, and of course the ever present fear of Fenian incursion — both issues that will be delved into in more detail in a later chapter of this book — were doubtless key factors considered by the Militia authorities when they decided to dispatch artillerymen with the Third Expedition. Whatever the motivation, the Militia firepower in Manitoba was increased exponentially upon the arrival of the Third Expedition.

The Third Red River Expedition, consisting of 209 men and bolstered by gunners in their midst, arrived in Fort Garry on October 23, 1872.[121] In a departure from previous terms of service, which were usually six months of enrolment with a liability for a further six months at the discretion of the Commanding Officer, for the Third Red River Expedition, the terms of service were extended to one year with a liability for a further period of service not exceeding two years, at the discretion of the Commanding Officer.[122] This seems to indicate that the powers that be in Ottawa were growing weary of constantly dispatching reinforcements every six months and contemplated that a requirement for permanent forces in Manitoba would remain for the foreseeable future. The Third Expedition had as toilsome an adventure as the two proceeding it: Joseph Ford Arel recounted in his memoir entitled *Montreal to Fort Garry. Journal of a Private in the Third Expedition* that his feet had swollen so badly from the marching, when he was ordered to mount a guard when the force stopped to camp, he had to do so in stocking feet as he could not physically put his boots on.[123] As well, it seems that during Arel's march, discipline was an issue amongst the volunteers, and he recounts at one point there were at least nine "prisoners" under guard in the force. These prisoners were likely under guard only for some minor infraction of military discipline as they were summarily tried by an officer somewhere on the prairie south-east of Fort Garry, and all but two were released.[124]

Ottawa's determination to keep men in service in Manitoba for a prolonged period is further evidenced by the Militia Department's rather disingenuousness with regards to the terms of service of the men of the third expedition. An anonymous author, writing in the *Manitoban* of March 1892, recalled that upon mustering in Toronto the volunteers of the Third Expedition were informed that there would be no doubt of the men receiving their discharge after one year. After a year of service in the North-

West, several men demanded their discharge but were refused, the Militia authorities maintaining no such guarantee was ever offered. Consequently, the men of the Third Expedition were forced to remain in Manitoba for the full three years if they wanted their grant of land, the only other options being desertion or the purchase of a discharge by obtaining a substitute, that is, another volunteer to fill their place.[125] The government's increase in the minimum terms of service, and intransigence towards early releases, confirms that the Dominion authorities were exasperated at constantly dispatching reinforcements to Manitoba and had decided that Canada should maintain a long-term, permanent force in Manitoba.

In May of 1873, mere months after the arrival of this third expedition, Militia Headquarters in Ottawa advertised for a further 156 volunteers to proceed to Manitoba. The plans for this, the Fourth Red River Expedition, coming so hard on the heels of the arrival of the third Red River Expedition, is doubtless related to the fear of an indigenous uprising that was pervasive in Manitoba in the spring of 1873, a question that will be dealt with in greater detail in Chapter 2. Uniquely, whereas previous volunteers were drawn from Ontario and Quebec Active Militia Corps, this draft of replacements came from the Maritime Provinces — fifty men each from New Brunswick and Nova Scotia. Additionally, fifty-six more gunners from 'A' and 'B' Batteries were requested to bolster the Militia fire power in Winnipeg. Moreover, a week after the call for volunteers went out, the Dominion also announced that the increased force of artillerymen in Winnipeg would be outfitted with four new Armstrong 9-pounder field guns and stores, acquired by the Canadian Militia, as soon as they could be shipped to the North-West.[126] The combined Provisional Battalion of Infantry and the composite Artillery Battery, which was known simply as the *Dominion Artillery* in order to differentiate it from the local Active Militia Corps the Winnipeg Field Battery, became known collectively as the *Dominion Forces on Service in Manitoba*. As an enticement to volunteer and potentially settle in the region, volunteers to this expedition were offered a grant of land equal to a quarter-section (160 acres) upon completion of their period of service.[127] In fact, the government was up front about their ulterior motives in the selection of volunteers for the Fourth Expedition. The call for volunteers, published in *Militia General Orders* (10) No. 1 of May 16, 1873, not only stated that aspiring volunteers had to demonstrate "respectability of character," but also that preference would be given to farmers and skilled mechanics who are "desirous of settling in Manitoba."[128] Clearly, the government was attempting to sow future Active Militia members in Military District No. 10 after the Dominion Forces were inevitably withdrawn. The reinforcements arrived in July 1873 via the same toilsome route as the two preceding expeditions, referred to as the *Canadian Route* by *Militia General Orders,* and, sardonically, the "amphibious" route by the *Manitoba Free Press*.[129] As they marched into Fort Garry, the reporters at the *Manitoba Free Press* observed that the reinforcements "look a little seedy, but new raiment and a little rest will fix things."[130]

A nation-wide reduction of the Active Militia from 40,000 to 30,000 men occurred in 1874 and had a significant impact on the Militia in Manitoba. In June 1874, Militia Headquarters in Ottawa issued orders to strike the Winnipeg Rifle Company, and the Headingly Rifle Company from the list of Active Militia Corps in Manitoba.[131] Additionally, in fall 1874, Lieutenant-Colonel Osborne Smith received orders to reduce the size of the Dominion Forces in Manitoba as well — the recently-created North-West Mounted Police were considered a sufficient force to provide security in the North-West.[132] Osborne Smith was authorized to offer discharging soldiers a gratuity of two months' pay and a sum of money equivalent to the cost of transport to the volunteer's Military District of origin. This led to a doubling of the number of men seeking discharge, and Osborne Smith was compelled to prioritize them based on their length of service and conduct.[133] In his annual reports for the district in 1873 and 1874, Lieutenant-Colonel Osborne Smith reported that the number of Dominion Forces under his command had reduced from 344 to 200 personnel respectively.[134]

Generally, the size and organization of the Militia in Manitoba remained consistent for the next two years, with only slight variations in the number of men parading in the Active Militia or the size of the Dominion Forces. June 1876 saw another reduction of the size of the Dominion Forces in Manitoba, although unfortunately for the recently liberated soldiers, the land warrants for their promised quarter-section of land were not prepared at the time of their release. This led at least one ex-sergeant of the force to complain "we are obliged to hang 'round Winnipeg at our personal expense waiting for the Government to do us justice."[135]

It seems the process for the discharge of volunteers was never particularly well administered. The bungling was enough to force Private John Howman of No. 4 Company, Ontario Rifles to write to the *Manitoba Newsletter* in May of 1871, on behalf of himself and three colleagues, to bemoan a situation of bureaucratic bafflegab that could have been drawn straight out of Joseph Heller's 1961 novel *Catch-22*. Howman complained about the fact that, despite being discharged on May 6, 1871, he and his colleagues had not received any pay since April 30, 1871. Howman goes on to describe that, despite being nominally discharged, they would not be officially discharged until they paid for the rations they received since May 1 — despite not having received any pay to do so! As if that were not sufficiently ridiculous, two of his colleagues were compelled to serve several tours of duty because they had not been officially discharged ... but they would not receive pay for these periods of duty because they had been nominally discharged! Private Howman felt sufficiently aggrieved to openly ask "the *Volunteer Review* [or] Sir Geo. Cartier [the Minister of Militia] or someone else well up in Military Jurisprudence if this is all correct."[136] It is no wonder that so many of the volunteers were eager to turn their back to Fort Garry and the North-West.

Despite the allure of free land for settling, it was estimated that less than ten percent of the men released in 1876 chose to remain in the area.[137] The clear majority took their land warrants home with them upon discharge, hoping to realize a greater profit in Southern Ontario, given that speculators in Manitoba were offering much lower prices for the land warrants.[138] The local Active Militia Corps also felt the sting of reduction due to ineffective parade states. In the *Militia General Orders* of October 1876, both the Mapleton and Poplar Point Rifle Companies were struck from the list of Active Militia corps due to insufficient personnel.[139]

These reductions, particularly in the Dominion Forces, were the initial death throes of the permanent volunteer force in Manitoba. In May of 1877, the editors of the *Manitoba Free Press* lamented to their readers that "they will be sorry to learn there is some foundation for the rumour which prevailed yesterday that the garrison of Canadian regular Militia hitherto maintained here, and which has been looked upon as one of the institutions of the place, is likely to be abolished in the course of a few weeks."[140] Indeed, there was plenty of sorrow amongst both the populace and the political leadership of the province. When it was learned that the Militia Department was contemplating the elimination of the force in Manitoba, on June 11, 1877, the Lieutenant-Governor, Alexander Morris, forwarded to the Secretary of State in Ottawa, an extract of the minutes of a meeting of the Provincial Executive Council. In this extract, the Executive Council stated that in consideration of the contemplated disbandment of the Militia in Manitoba they "deem it their duty, to represent that such a measure will tend to spread amongst the people of the Province an idea of insecurity highly detrimental to the best interests of this young country." The Executive Council reminded the Secretary that the province was exposed and isolated from the remainder of the country for six months of the year and was thus liable to a *coup de main* at any time during its period of isolation by the "Fenians of the United States or the lawless part of the floating population of Railway working men." In conclusion, the Council stated, "they feel compelled by a strong sense of responsibility of their position and their information on the subject to enter respectfully, but most energetically their protest against such measures."[141] The Militia garrison in Manitoba served to provide security for the province and assist in its settlement from the eastern provinces and Great Britain by providing at least some degree of reassurance to those potential settlers. The remonstrations of the Executive Council to the news of the disbandment of the Active Militia is a perfect example this. The energetic protest of the Council fell on deaf ears, and the decision was taken in Ottawa to disband the Militia. There was surprisingly little delay between the official announcement of the disbandment of the regular garrison in May and the act itself, which occurred in August 1877.

The void created by the departure of the permanent garrison was filled, to an extent, by the Active Militia. In 1877, infantry companies were gazetted in Emerson and Winnipeg, followed in 1878 with a troop of cavalry in Winnipeg and an infantry company in Saint-Jean-Baptiste in 1879, although the South St. Andrews Infantry Company, one of the original infantry companies gazetted in early 1871, was struck from the rolls as ineffective in 1878. In 1880, the precepts of the *Militia Act 1868* were extended to the North-West Territories and Keewatin districts (modern Saskatchewan and post-expansion Manitoba), and military authority for the region was delegated to the deputy adjutant-general of Military District 10, who remained Lieutenant-Colonel Osborne Smith. The extension of Osborne Smith's area of responsibility resulted in a significant increase in the number of Active Militia corps belonging to Military District No. 10, including mounted rifle companies in Prince Albert and Duck Lake, as well as infantry companies in Prince Albert, Battleford, and St. Boniface.

The beginning of the 1880s did not improve life very much for the Active Militia in the province. Despite the honours of having the Governor General visit in 1881, and the Minister of Militia in 1882, Military District No. 10 had trouble keeping the ranks of the Militia full. In 1881, Osborne Smith, long a mainstay of military life in Winnipeg, decided to withdraw from official life, and handed the reins of the District to Lieutenant-Colonel Houghton. In his annual report for 1882, Houghton complained to the General Officer Commanding the Militia in Canada that the press of business in the North-West, combined with the high salaries that came with the economic boom meant that interest in the Militia could not be maintained. He did strike an optimistic tone however, and expressed his firm belief that should a drill shed and armoury be erected in a central location in Winnipeg, due to the impressive martial stock in the populace of Manitoba, an effective six-company battalion could be maintained because, he felt "there is no finer material in any portion of the Dominion that is to be found at the present time in the city and the North-West generally."[142]

This time, the deputy adjutant-general's advice was heeded and on November 9, 1882, the 90th Battalion, Winnipeg Rifles was gazetted into existence. This six-company battalion absorbed the Winnipeg Infantry Company and, Houghton observed "infused new life into Military circles here, and [promised] to engender a wholesome spirit of emulation most beneficial to the welfare of the force."[143] The city and province continued to grow, and eventually the long hoped-for drill shed was built in 1884, as was the magazine. The organization of the 90th Battalion proved to be a continuous success in the city.

A Soldier's Life on the Frontier

Life as a soldier in the Provisional Battalion was substantially different from the civilian life the Militiamen had left behind. The Canadian volunteers that made up the Provisional Battalion were citizen-soldiers of the Active Militia when they enrolled, and thus their only military experience, with the exception of those who had served in the British Army, centered on the Active Militia's annual drill which encompassed about twelve to sixteen days during the summer, and any voluntary drill taken on at company headquarters during the remainder of the year. Permanent full-time service was new to most of them, and after the toilsome trek from Toronto to Fort Garry, once they arrived in the new province, they found garrison life monotonous.

Griffin gave an account of what a typical day was like for a soldier of the Provisional Battalion in his memoir. The troops awoke at 5:30 in the summer, 6:30 in the winter, and cleaned their personal spaces. Twenty minutes after reveille, the Regimental Orderly Sergeant walked through to inspect their quarters, and at 7:45 a.m. breakfast was announced, with the men sitting to eat at eight o'clock. The ill reported to the Battalion Surgeon at nine o'clock for 'sick call' while at the same time, those soldiers detailed as members of a work party would report for 'fatigues' thereafter being employed in whatever little maintenance jobs were required — everything from emptying latrines, to clearing brush, to building huts. The remainder prepared for inspection, and at 10:30 a.m. the adjutant, the commanding officer's principal staff officer, inspected the troops. An hour or two of drill followed inspection, after which lunch was served at one o'clock. More drill followed in the afternoon, followed by tea at five o'clock. Last post was played at 9:30 in winter and 10:00 in summer, with lights out enforced fifteen minutes thereafter.

The afternoon drills were carried out in marching order, which was an order of dress, incorporating not only uniform and rifle, but also a backpack and ammunition, the whole of which weighed approximately seventy pounds.[144] Sam Steele, who came out to Fort Garry on the First Expedition recounted that such a weight would normally have been a severe test, but thanks to the hard work experienced by the soldiers on the portages *en route* to the North-West, they "had contempt for any load less than the weight of a barrel of pork."[145] The volunteers conducted manoeuvres and drills during these parades at the double-quick time, akin to a light jog, as was the custom in rifle regiments. After about two and a half hours of this practice, a march-past behind the regimental band concluded the affair to "the intense satisfaction of a bevy of fair damsels and their mothers who sat on the balcony on the north side of the parade ground." Because of these unique spectators the volunteers dubbed the afternoon manoeuvres "Ladies' Parades."[146]

If they were unlucky, an overly eager officer would decide to practice the battalion's ability to respond to an emergency in the middle of the night and carry out a practice drill. On the evening of October 24, 1870, at one o'clock in the morning, the bugle call to assemble was made to test the reaction of the soldiers. The result of the nocturnal alert was recorded by the *Manitoban and North-West Herald*:

Within three minutes after the call to arms, the men of No. 2 Company had rallied at the gate, fronting the Assiniboine and deployed as skirmishers along the river bank, with Companies No. 3 and 4 in reserve, and acting as supports to the Garrison Artillery. The latter planted their cannon at the rear portal and fired several rounds of shell, grape and canister. Meantime the remaining Companies had manned the ramparts and northeast and North-West bastions, the front portal being held by one Company ... [the Commanding Officer] complemented the men very highly and said he had never seen old soldiers get into position and turn out in better style than they did.[147]

The Commanding Officer who heaped praise on the performance of the soldiers was one Lieutenant-Colonel Cassault, whose personal military experience lent credibility to his words. Cassault, who had commanded the 2nd Quebec Rifles in the First Expedition, had previously served in the French Army, and had participated in the Crimean War. He later joined the British Army, serving in England, Gibraltar, and Malta. Upon his retirement from the British Army, he moved to Canada and joined the Canadian Militia, eventually rising to the rank of lieutenant-colonel and employment in the position of deputy adjutant-general for Militia District No. 7 in Quebec City. It was from this post that he volunteered to join the first expedition. Upon arrival in Fort Garry, Cassault decided to remain in the North-West.

The speedy turn out of the soldiers is explained by the fact that the drill occurred only a few months after the arrival of the force, when tensions in the area remained high. The late-night alert was no doubt justified by the battalion leadership's genuine desire to keep their men in fighting form, their martial spirit still sharp from the recent 'victory' over Riel and his followers. That said, it is doubtful the local populace was much appreciative of the force blindly firing off artillery ordnance into the prairie in the middle of the night. These nocturnal barrages drew at least one complaint from a local citizen who was moved to write the editors of the *Manitoban and North-West Herald*. The author of the letter observed that "the only appreciable result of this military *manoeuvre* is to disturb all the animals of the feline species when the [cannon] goes off" and recommended that the Commanding Officer either eliminate such a procedure or at least fire it at the same time every night.[148] Three years later, another such drill, this time described by the *Free Press*, seems to have lacked the enthusiasm displayed in 1870 and is no doubt reflective of the complacency that comes with monotonous garrison duty:

> the shrill notes of the bugle at Fort Garry sounding the 'Assembly' and with much wondering, more grumbling, and a great deal of praying the force of sleepy warriors mustered in the Barrack Square, every man being at his post exactly eight minutes after the first call sounded. High were the hopes in many a martial bosom, that at last something in the shape of action was to be seen, and many a kestrel eye flashed in the expected conflict. Sad! Sad!! That such military ardor should be damped, but so it was.[149]

On top of the monotonous routine, the soldiers found, as many modern Manitobans understand, that winter in the North-West was oppressive. Unaccustomed to the chill, soldiers on duty, particularly on guard duty — *sentry-go* in the vernacular of the soldiers — were susceptible to frostbite in winter. The normal routine for soldiers was to serve two hours on guard duty, followed by a respite of four hours until they were once again on duty. Their only protection from the elements was a rickety sentry box, which Private John Kerr called a "poor affair" fitted with "a small stick stuck cornerwise" upon which to sit.[150] Steele recounts, however, that in time of extreme cold guard duties were restricted to only an hour.[151]

Kerr recounts one way he found to keep warm on guard duty. He recalled that when he was on sentry-go on the evening of his twentieth birthday he was joined in his duty by two mongrel dogs who lived in and around the fort. They accompanied him as he walked up and down the fort wall to stay warm, and when he snuck into the sentry box to rest, the two dogs curled up and fell asleep atop his feet, which were very shortly thereafter thoroughly warmed through. Perhaps he became too comfortable as he accidentally drifted off to sleep as well. He was fortunately awakened by the growling of the dogs and when he leapt to action to demand *"Halt, who goes there!?"* he was surprised to find it was the sentry coming to relieve him. The attentive dogs' warning allowed him to avoid being found asleep at his post and thus suffer the disciplinary action that would doubtless ensue.[152]

No cold-weather gear had been brought along with the First Expedition, although some was later shipped out from Toronto, but it did not arrive until November. As the *Manitoba News-Letter* observed, "our volunteers are suffering very much from want of their winter clothing ... it is far from pleasant to stand for two hours exposed to the searching winds that blow over the plains these cold nights."[153] Kerr recalled that he witnessed "men get their ears badly frozen while going from the barracks to the parade grounds — a distance of from two hundred to two hundred and fifty feet."[154] Private Driver of the Battalion had his hands frozen, necessitating the amputation of all his fingers at the metacarpal bones, a procedure performed by the two battalion surgeons, Dr's Codd and Turner.[155] A similar misadventure befell Private Walters of No. 1 Company, 1st Ontario Rifles whilst he and his company were stationed near the Hudson's Bay Company Post at the Pembina border crossing in the winter of 1870–71, only in the case of the unfortunate Walters, several toes were lost to frostbite.[156] Additionally, in 1873, Captain GFD Gagnier died from inflammatory rheumatism brought on by "indiscrete exposure during the past winter."[157]

Perhaps the most perplexing of cold-related injuries to occur was that in the case of Private Maloney of the 1st Ontario Rifles. One day, Maloney, at the time stationed in Fort Garry, simply appeared unexpectedly at the Hudson's Bay Company Post at Pembina, where a company of his colleagues were stationed, unable to explain why he was there, only that he was lost. His colleagues noticed that he was suffering from a mental health crisis but thought him harmless and did not place him under arrest or supervision for his own safety. Later that night, as the men were in their barrack room preparing to retire, amid the normal jokes and banter that occurs amongst a group of young men, Maloney awoke from his reverie on a cot, loaded a rifle and fired into a crowd of soldiers. The bullet miraculously passed through the crowd with no misadventure, penetrated the wall, passed through the sergeant's quarters next door where it also managed to miss all the occupants, and then lodged itself in the outer wall. Maloney was immediately arrested and sent back to Fort Garry under guard where he was placed in hospital. He subsequently escaped into the snowy landscape with hardly any clothing on and wandered some distance. When the hospital attendants finally caught up to him, he had frozen to death.[158]

If the cold didn't prove fatal, the tempestuous prairie storms could end a man's life. Gunner Cameron of the artillery was killed by a bolt of lightning in July 1874, when he and a colleague went to a tent outside the walls to collect the wife and children of a fellow soldier during an intense prairie storm. The lady's husband was absent on duty, and Gunner Cameron thought it prudent that the family move into quarters in the Fort rather than let them suffer under canvas. As he walked into the tent, he put his hand on the tent-pole which was shortly thereafter struck by lightning. Witnesses reported that the clothing on his right arm, which was holding the pole, was ripped from his body and the heels of both boots were torn from the soles.[159]

The accommodations at Fort Garry had never been intended to house an entire battalion of infantry and were thus completely inadequate. Colonel Robertson Ross paid a visit to the force during his reconnaissance of the North-West in the summer of 1872. He found that Fort Garry was "very inadequate, unsuitable, and generally unfit for permanent military occupation."[160] Sam Steele recounted that four long buildings ran along the west side of the fort, each two stories in height, built of logs and shingled with heavy oak shingles fastened to oak sheeting with hand-made nails. Each had a large door in the middle of the building facing West to the square in the middle of the fort. Inside, the door opened to a vestibule with a large barn-like room on either side, with similar rooms on the second floor. Cots lined the walls of the room for the men to sleep on, oriented with the head of the bed touching the wall and the foot of the bunk stretching inwards. In the centre were tables and benches for use of the soldiers. Each soldier was assigned a cot and was given a bed in the form of an empty sack which he had to fill with straw. Three of these buildings, each able to house one hundred men, were used to accommodate soldiers of the 1st Ontario Rifles, while the 2nd Quebec Rifles were sent to the Lower Fort, and a company of the Ontario Rifles was detailed to garrison Fort Pembina near the international boundary. Despite sounding comfortable, Robertson Ross reported that they were simply "wooden sheds, some of them mere shells" and he considered them unfit for occupation in winter.[161] The spaces available in the huts in Fort Garry were insufficient for all the soldiers so several found themselves housed in tents and temporary huts outside the fort, even during the worst of the prairie winter.[162]

Joseph Tenant recalled that the company detailed to Fort Pembina were housed in tents until as late as mid-November. He described the conditions as living "in tents without stoves, below zero, huddled together ten or twelve in a bunch for heat," adding sarcastically that "a tent collapsing in a snowstorm kept the boys in good humour."[163] Osborne Smith bemoaned the lack of a proper barracks to protect his men from the elements early on in his tenure. Not only was Fort Garry insufficient to house and protect the soldiers from the winter chill, but the proximity to the civil employees of the Hudson's Bay Company strained discipline, a situation Osborne Smith considered "very inconvenient and unsatisfactory."[164]

A cyclical lifestyle in a small town on the extreme verges of settled civilization was no doubt painfully monotonous. Griffin recalled that his life became "the same dreary round of duties and few changes of scenery and few incidents to interest and occupy the mind, the arrival of mails from home being the only interesting event perhaps for weeks."[165] Griffin also observed that once he and his colleagues began to experience the complete boredom of frontier garrison duties, they realized that "the hard work, danger and excitement incident to the march from Thunder Bay to [Fort Garry] was enjoyed by many more than the quiet, dreary and monotonous state of existence passed in barracks during the winter months."[166] Rations were spare, and Steele found them to be insufficient for young, strong soldiers who worked long hours on fatigue duty and drilling. He dreaded coming back to his quarters after guard duty or drill because "it was not encouraging to our ravenous appetites to return to a cheerless barrack-room and make our evening meal off a bucket of cold tea and the attenuated remains of the morning loaf of bread."[167] Consequently, many of the volunteers spent a fair amount of their wages at Devlin's bakery just outside the walls of the Fort.[168]

The volunteers were, at least for the first few years, allowed to leave the Fort in the evenings if they were not on the list of defaulters (those being punished) or the sick list. Soldiers could attend dances, enjoy newspapers in reading rooms, craft letters home, or purchase bread to supplement their meagre rations. The last post was sounded at 9:30 p.m. in winter and 10:00 p.m. in summer, at which time any man who was absent without pass was arrested on his return.[169] One enterprising soul, Private Bob Woods of Chatham, Ontario, found an industrious way to pass the long hours. When he learned several soldiers wanted to learn French, and he, being fluently bilingual, began giving French lessons to his colleagues in No. 1 Company, 1st Ontario Rifles while they were deployed at the Hudson's Bay Post in Pembina during the winter of 1870–71.[170]

For those of the 1st Ontario Rifles deployed to Pembina, there was the possibility of visiting Pembina, Dakota for a few hours should they be able to secure a pass. Some of them were even able to visit their American counterparts in the new US Army fort built nearby shortly after the First Red River Expedition arrived in Fort Garry. Tennant recalled that the Canadian soldiers were well treated by their American neighbors, except for a few of the populace who were diehard American expansionists or refugees from Riel's Provisional Government who had settled there. [171]

If no entertainment could be found outside the barracks, some minor distractions were available within the walls of Fort Garry. At the very least, there was an odd menagerie of animals that the volunteers had collected and kept as pets. Griffin recounted that the force had acquired a black bear, a wolf, two foxes, several cats, and about forty dogs. At the time of writing his memoirs, he recorded that he and his colleagues were "on the look-out for a moose, a deer, and a badger, when we think that our collection will be about complete."[172] The bear was a popular attraction and even figured as a mascot. Griffin recalls one instance when the battalion was marching to training camp in June of 1872 near Colony Creek where Osborne Bridge stands today, that "on the march the battalion was headed by the excellent band, and in advance the tame black bear marched along as if his trade were to lead a regiment."[173]

These distractions aside, the tedious existence was too much to take for some of the soldiers of the garrison. In 1874, Sergeant-Major Morrisette, of the Dominion Artillery stationed at Winnipeg, committed suicide during what the *Manitoban and North-West Herald* called "a fit of temporary insanity."[174] Fortunately, garrison life did not have as drastic an effect on others as it may have had on the unfortunate Sergeant-Major, but it certainly cured many volunteers of the impetus to settle in Manitoba after their terms of service had expired. In fact, the vast majority were inclined to return home to their districts of enrolment despite the lure of land grants in Manitoba.[175] Soldiers' whose terms of service were completed were free to return home and each man was provided cash in the equivalent of the cost of his transportation and maintenance to the Military District he had enrolled in.[176]

After the initial downsizing and subsequent reinforcement of October 1871, the Militia authorities tried to keep the strength of the force in Manitoba at the same level, and to that end, inducements were offered to discharging men intended to lure them to renew their terms of service for another period of duty. In May of 1873, the Adjutant-General of Militia authorized the payment of a five-dollar "bounty" and a free issue of kit to "such men of good character, proper physical health and strength, and who are between the ages of 18 and 30 years and may be desirous of re-engaging for a period of twelve months' service and accepting the liability of a further period of twelve months."[177] This was not sufficiently attractive an offer to many of the discharging men. To give an idea of how happy some soldiers were to receive their discharge, the *Free Press* entitled a column about the discharge of seventy-five members of the Battalion in 1873 "Emancipation" and referred to the discharge of soldiers intending to remain in the North-West as "manumission" — the release of slaves. In this instance, thirty-seven took their discharge with the intent of settling in Manitoba, a small number re-enlisted, and the balance returned home at government expense. For those who chose to stay in the North-West, an impressive little ceremony was organized by the chain of command. The battalion was formed up in a square, and the soon-to-be-discharged soldiers that were remaining in Manitoba were formed in the middle, whereupon they were treated to a complementary valediction by Osborne Smith. He went as far to say that "In the course of a long experience in connection with military matters it has never been my fortune to see a greater proportion of good characters." When the ceremony ended, the former soldiers collected their discharge papers and began boisterous celebration.[178]

FORT OSBORNE

Fortunately, some respite from the lack of accommodations for those who remained in uniform occurred in 1874. After his sojourn through the west, Robertson Ross reported to the Minister of Militia, in the most emphatic terms, that the accommodations for the force in Fort Garry were inadequate and unsatisfactory, and recommended "no further time be lost in taking the necessary steps to supply the Military Force required with proper Barrack accommodation." To drive the point home, he recounted that in his interviews with the men on the occasion of his visit, each stated they were happy with their rate of pay and the leadership of their officers, but "invariably, in the most respectful manner complained of the wretched Barrack [sic] accommodation."[179] Robertson Ross's report was submitted in March of 1873, and his observations were echoed only a month later in a memorandum sent to John A. Macdonald by Gilbert McMicken, who since 1871 had been acting as the Dominion Lands Agent for Manitoba, the assistant Receiver General, the Dominion Auditor and the manager of the

Dominion Government Savings Bank. McMicken warned Macdonald that he considered it likely there would be an increase in the number of desertions amongst the soldiers who remained members in the garrison after the terms of service of many of their colleagues expired on May 1, 1873, particularly given the mundane nature of their employ. To counteract this, he suggested that the soldiers could be used to help build the barracks, thus keeping them busy and also allowing them to receive a small stipend of "working pay" on top of their military salaries.[180]   That summer, the federal government voted a large sum of money for the construction of federal buildings in Winnipeg and of this sum, $15,000 was appropriated for the construction of permanent barracks for the housing of the Dominion Forces.

In September of that year, the *Free Press* happily reported that "we understand that Lieut. Col. Osborne Smith has received instructions to look over the ground intended for the erection of the new barracks and procure its survey, with a view to the immediate commencement of the buildings."[181] Osborne Smith conducted a survey of the area and settled on a stretch of prairie to the west of Fort Garry for the site of the new barracks, a site the Militia had used several times previously to conduct training camps. The chosen location for the barracks was the north-west corner of the present legislative grounds.

Construction of the barracks began in late September 1873 after the local construction company, W.J. Macaulay & Co, was awarded the contract. Not long after, Militia volunteers assigned to fatigues were found clearing the bush from the site while Macaulay's workers began framing the buildings.[182] Work was completed in January 1874, although the soldiers began moving into their new accommodations on November 5, 1873, as their quarters were the first buildings to be erected.[183]

After completion of the barracks, a board of survey was ordered in Militia General Orders of December 1874. The board comprised of Osborne Smith as the president with the battalion's supply officer, Major Peebles, and Captain MacDonald of the Provisional Battalion as members, convened on January 29, 1875, and completed their report on February 19, 1875. Their report, submitted in the annual Militia Report, is a fascinating snapshot of the infrastructure footprint of the Militia in early Winnipeg. The original barracks consisted of twenty-two buildings, including large stables and a bakery. The board found that due to the hurried construction of the barracks, and the use of untreated wood, the condition of the buildings was less than satisfactory, and at the time the board estimated the cost to bring them into order was between $3,000 and $3,500. Surprisingly, the barracks were constructed with no adequate magazine to safely house the high explosive ordnance of the artillery, nor was a fence or barricade erected to enclose the barracks. [184] Additionally, despite being built specifically to house a large body of soldiers, no well was sunk on the grounds to provide fresh drinking water for the Militia volunteers. Later, one anonymous soldier remarked in a letter to the editor of the *Free Press* "it is necessary all through the year — even when the thermometer is forty degrees below zero — for a fatigue party to bring all the water used by the garrison from the river by ox-team."[185]

It is beyond the scope of this book to summarize all the holdings listed by the board of survey — most articles enumerated are the standard holdings of any military force, such as the sixty-five pickaxes categorized as camp equipment, or the six night-caps held as military clothing. Some items are, however, more interesting. It seems the Militia was certainly well armed. The armoury held 298 long-barrelled Snider Rifles, 502 short-barrelled Snider Rifles, 50 cavalry carbines, 244 Peabody rifles and one, lonely Spencer rifle. The artillery possessed the four seven-pounder mountain howitzers that had come west with the Red River Expeditionary Force and several nine-pounder Armstrong guns. For ammunition, the garrison's gunners had access to 114 case shot, 404 common shell, and 538 shrapnel shells for the seven-pounders, while for the nine-pounders 15 case shot, 173 common shell and 313 shrapnel shells were available. Given how many explosive shells were housed there, the wisdom of overlooking the creation of a proper magazine certainly comes into question. Osborne Smith's constant hectoring for a proper magazine fell on deaf ears and the powers that be were not moved to meet his demands prior to his decision to retire from the Militia. His successor, Lieutenant-Colonel C.F. Houghton, faced similar reticence from his superiors. As the city of Winnipeg grew, the threat posed by an accidental explosion grew as well. Houghton stated in his annual report for 1881 that "the property in the vicinity of the magazine is now of immense value, and handsome buildings are being erected on either side, so that an explosion of a ton or of two of powder would now, or more particularly in the near future, be attended with far different results from what it would have been even a few short months ago."[186]

Despite being completed in 1874, the Fort went nameless for the first year of its existence. It wasn't until March 1875 that Osborne Smith sent a letter to the adjutant-general suggesting that a name be given to the establishment. On April 26, 1875, the Minister of Militia decided that the name would be Fort Osborne. The erection of Fort Osborne on this location has resulted in an enduring legacy of which most modern inhabitants of Winnipeg are probably unaware. The location of Fort Osborne, situated at the corner of Broadway and Osborne Street, explains why Osborne Street and Osborne Village bear the name of the province's first deputy adjutant-general, and why the Winnipeg Blue Bombers played football in Osborne Stadium, located where the current Great-West Life building is currently situated, from 1935–52.[187]

The Fort became a center of social activity, despite its relative isolation from Fort Garry and the City of Winnipeg which, by the mid-1870s, were still sparsely populated. This removal from the hustle and bustle of the growing village was likely one of the reasons that the site was selected by Osborne in the first place. As the city grew, Fort Osborne became an integral part of the infrastructure of the city. It even merited attention in J.C. Hamilton's account of the North-West in his 1876 book *The Prairie Province; Sketches of Travel from Lake Ontario to Lake Winnipeg.* In it, Hamilton takes the reader on a walking tour of the young city, recounting from his personal visit, and he paints a picture of Fort Osborne as a quaint, lively, and generally enjoyable place. Meandering towards Fort Osborne, he recorded that "following, as the sun is setting, the strains of music, pass to Fort Osborne, on the banks of the Assiniboine, we find that the strains proceed from a band of some fifteen performers, regimentaled [sic] in the uniform of the Canadian Militia, standing in the parade ground of the enclosure, in which we see a sergeant putting his squad through evening drill, and a lot of jolly fellows playing football, and [we] are kindly welcomed by some young Canadian officers."[188] This scenario seems idyllic, and while life in the North-West wasn't always so whimsical, Hamilton's observations at least indicate that the Fort was active and not perennially dour, notwithstanding the many disagreeable aspects of being stationed so far from home.

As immigration to the North-West increased over the years, and the permanent force on service was disbanded, in 1877 a large portion of Fort Osborne was handed over to the Department of Immigration and Agriculture for the housing of immigrants. A portion of the buildings remained for the use of the Militia which were fenced off from the portion allocated to support immigration.[189]

Fort Osborne remained in use until it was demolished to make way for the construction of the current Legislative Buildings. Prior to its demolition, Fort Osborne was a key location for the recruitment and training of elements of the Canadian Expeditionary Force during the First World War. Upon its demolition, new barracks were found in the Tuxedo neighbourhood of Winnipeg at the University of Manitoba's Agriculture College, and the name "Fort Osborne" barracks moved to the new site. The building that inherited the title remains standing to this day as a part of the Izzy Asper School of Business. Upon the creation of the modern military barracks, at the corner of Grant Avenue and Kenaston Boulevard, the name was once again transferred to the new site. It was finally retired when Fort Osborne Barracks was renamed Kapyong Barracks in 1973 in honour of the valour displayed at the Battle of Kapyong during the Korean War by the 2nd Battalion, Princess Patricia's Canadian Light Infantry, who were the final occupant of the barracks.[190] Kapyong Barracks was closed in 2004 after the 2nd Battalion was relocated to Canadian Forces Base Shilo, situated about twenty five kilometers east of Brandon, Manitoba.

LIFE IN THE RANKS - THE LOCAL MILITIA CORPS

While the Provisional Battalion were Active Militia soldiers who had enlisted for a period of permanent, full-time service in what were referred to as *service companies,* the soldiers of the local Militia corps also fell within the purview of the Active Militia but trained and paraded on a part-time basis. In fact, they spent very little time actually training at all. The *Militia Act 1868* authorized a maximum of sixteen days of paid training per year for Active Militia soldiers, all of which occurred during the "annual training" exercise normally held during the summer. For financial reasons, the government reserved the right to restrict which corps would conduct their annual drill, the length of the training, or to dispense with training altogether.[191] Obviously, such a small amount of training was only barely effective. Local corps conducted volunteer drill and training, however. To illustrate, the Winnipeg Field Battery met every Thursday night at their armoury to practice gun drill.

Time spent on annual drill was similarly rote as that described by the garrison troops in Fort Garry. A correspondent of the *Manitoba Free Press* dutifully recorded the annual drill of the Winnipeg Field Battery in 1876 in a series of columns. He reported the Gunner's daily routine as follows: reveille at 5:30, drill from 6:30 to7.30, breakfast at 8:00, hospital call at 9:00, guard mounting at 9:45, orderly room at 9:30, drill from10:00 a.m. to12:00 p.m., dinner at 1:00, drill from 2:30 to 4:00, tea at 5:00 p.m., retreat at sunset, and first post at 9:00.[192] The Battery's camp drew a number of spectators, and many couples made a point of attending the training camp to observe the Militiamen going through their drills. Providing an engaging spectacle was not the lot of the Gunners alone — the Kildonan Infantry similarly found themselves the subject of much admiration amongst the city's commentariat. Again, the *Manitoba Free Press* reported that "the Kildonan Infantry Company are putting in their annual drill, exercising for three hours per day, and doing very well."[193]

Whereas most, if not all, of the training conducted outside of the annual summer training camp was voluntary, attendance at summer training camps was rewarded with pay. In 1877, daily pay rates were as follows: officers $1, non-commissioned officers and men, $0.50. The Militia did not have enough of their own horses, and consequently had to hire them from local owners for the duration of the training camps. Hired horses earned their owners $0.75 per day.[194]

The local Militia corps were chronically under-equipped, exacerbated no doubt by Manitoba's distance from supply depots and the preponderance of the Canadian population which was situated in Ontario and Quebec. An editorial of the *Manitoba Free Press* of July 24, 1875 bemoaned the lack of equipment for the Winnipeg Field Battery, stating that "the equipment and uniforms of the organization were in a state of incompleteness, and consequent uselessness." [195] In a later letter to the editor, a writer lamented the woeful equipage of the battery stating the unit's guns remained fitted with mountain carriages and had "no limbers, no wagon, [and] no harness of any kind."[196] While Manitoba's isolation may have contributed in some degree to the lack of equipment and uniforms, at least in this vein they shared some of the challenges of their Eastern Canadian counterparts. The equipage problem was so ubiquitously prevalent in the early 1870s, at least one Commanding Officer of a Canadian Active Militia Corps, a Lieutenant-Colonel Davis, was compelled to add the following observation to his 1873 book *The Canadian Militia! Its Organization and present condition*:

> Surely the Government makes some concession or grants
> some privilege to men who [serve their country] ... Far from
> it. There is nothing provided for the men even when they are
> on duty, but a forage cap, that helps the sun to peel the skin
> off their faces, a pair of serge trowsers [sic] and a uniform
> coat. Everything in the shape of underclothing — boots, socks
> and all the necessary articles for personal cleanliness — have
> to be provided by the man himself at his own expense. The
> consequence is that as there is no uniformity in what the men
> procure, not one man out of every twenty has a pair of boots
> fit to march in.[197]

While the members of the local Militia corps did not require housing, being citizens of the local community, like their colleagues in the Provisional Battalion they were constantly in search of proper locations to conduct drill and to situate the company headquarters, thus they were dependent on the largesse of local proprietors to find space. The Winnipeg Field Battery, to illustrate, had to make use of Snyder & Anderson's Hall, where the Century Plaza on Main Street currently stands, as an armory. The Emerson Infantry Company occupied Wiltse's store to conduct their volunteer drill and the No. 1 Winnipeg Infantry Company was able to make use of Dufferin Hall, currently the Woodbine Hotel on Main Street.[198] In 1881, the recently formed St. Boniface Infantry Company was fortunate enough to obtain a drill hall through the kindness of His Grace Archbishop Taché, who allowed Captain Prud'homme and his company to use a classroom in St. Boniface College as a drill hall and another room in the college as an armory and company store.[199] In 1883, a company of the 90th Battalion used Wesley Hall on the corner of Portage and Main as a drill hall. When not set aside for military preparations, the upstairs of Wesley Hall were the offices of Dr. Young, while the main floor was a Methodist Church.[200] Other companies of the 90th had to make use of the City Skating Rink for its drill.[201] Eventually, the Emerson Infantry company was lucky enough to have an armory to drill in, but only due to the assistance of the company's commanding officer who built it adjoining his home. In 1878, the armory, and the commanding officer's house, burned to the ground. The dedicated commanding officer, Captain Nash, however, was in the process of building a new armory along with a new home — a level of dedication that earned him the following commendation from Osborne

Smith in his annual report: "officers who display such public spirit are the mainstay of the Volunteer Militia Organization."[202]

The absence of proper drill sheds even drove Osborne Smith to try to shame municipal authorities into paying for one's construction. In a speech to the Winnipeg Field Battery after an inspection he discussed such support in other areas of the Dominion and wondered aloud "have our civic authorities here in Winnipeg done the same? I see no vote, as in other places in Canada, for a grant in aid of a drill shed" and went on to browbeat the city council for support in the provision of prizes and band funds.[203]

The city leaders turned a collective deaf ear — while in the main the local populace was effusively supportive of the Militia volunteers in the province, there were practicalities that had to be respected. The Winnipeg Field Battery, in one instance, had used the city hall as a temporary drill shed, a practice that was ended in May 1877 when it was feared the marching and drilling might cause damage to the foundation of the building. One commenter from the *Free Press* observed, sardonically, that some of the aldermen thought that "the Field Battery in sword exercise recently while marching in the hall caused our $60,000 pile of brick and mortar to tremble to its foundations."[204] This obviously contributed to Osborne Smith's sharp tone. Several weeks after Osborne Smith's November address to the Field Battery, Alderman Conklin moved at a December 1877 City Council meeting that the officer commanding the battery be allowed to use the city hall every Saturday night as long as he was willing to cover the expenses of caretaker, light and fuel. Alderman More did not concur and repeated the concern about the impact of marching troops on the foundation of the building. Alderman Dunlop argued that the impact of the drill and marching would be no more dangerous than that of several dancing couples, but the two third majority required to pass the motion was not met, the motion being defeated four yeas to three nays.[205]

The poor state of the local corps drove their own officers to address the issue. On March 22, 1878, Lieutenant-Colonel W.N. Kennedy chaired a conference of all the officers of the district corps to discuss "the obstacles to maintaining efficiency arising from the want of drill sheds, armouries, rifle ranges, etc." A memorandum consisting of the proceedings of the conference was forwarded to no less than the Minister of Agriculture to forward to the Minister of Militia for consideration, an act that would today represent gross insubordination, but in the politically nebulous world of the nineteenth century, led to no negative consequences, but also no immediate improvement to the situation.[206]

It is worthwhile to pause here to review the content of the letter sent to the Minister of Agriculture. In it, Kennedy *et al* share a fairly long list of equipment and infrastructure shortages that were plaguing the Militia Corps of Manitoba in the latter years of the 1870s. Moreover, Kennedy notes in several instances some of the desired kit, such as mitts and fur caps suitable for use in the winter, were not issued to the Active Militia Corps although he was certain that they were available in storage at Fort Osborne.

Kennedy begins his letter by highlighting the issues confronting the Winnipeg Field Battery, the corps he commanded at the time. He notes that while the Militia Department allocated $150 per annum for the rental of a gun shed, due to the young nature of the city and the lack of infrastructure, the only shed he could find was too small and the ceiling too low to allow the gunners to practice gun drill — the drills associated with aiming, loading and firing the cannon — while standing up. For other training and parades, Kennedy rented out the Temperance Hall for $3 per night, one night a week, to allow the Winnipeg Field Battery to conduct squad drill and manual exercise. Unfortunately, there was no resource available for an armoury, so the rifles were given to the men to keep at their homes! The state of the battery's equipment was so poor that the officers volunteered to outfit the battery at their own expense with the new pattern helmet, each of which cost $4.50. Kennedy also noted that the battery had been called out twice in the preceding winter to fire a gun salute, but his applications for fur caps and mitts were denied each time.

The Winnipeg Infantry Company did not seem to enjoy very better circumstances. Kennedy reported that, fortunately, the company had been allowed to use the porch of an old building, formerly a church, as an armoury although the area measured only eight feet by eight feet. Unlike the Winnipeg Field Battery, the officer commanding the Winnipeg Infantry Company did not receive any funds from the Militia department for the rental of a drill hall, and consequently no drill had been carried out by the company since the annual drill in the summer of 1877. Like the battery, the Winnipeg Infantry Company were called out to furnish guards of honour in January and February and no requests for winter gear were approved, leading four men to freeze their ears, one of who was under medical treatment for several weeks thereafter "in consequence of an attack of neuralgia."[207] The Winnipeg Infantry Company's colleagues in the Kildonan Infantry Company were likewise disadvantaged. The officer commanding in Kildonan paid $25 a year out of his own pocket to rent an armoury and "by the liberality of the local church authorities, [was] permitted the use of the school room (gratis)" as a drill shed.[208] Likewise, the officer commanding the infantry company in Emerson was forced to establish an armoury at his own residence which was situated a mile from the town.[209]

Life on service in Manitoba was challenging for both the permanent force soldiers who formed the Dominion Forces on Service in Manitoba from 1870–77, as well as the Active Militia soldiers of local corps. Despite these challenges, both the permanent volunteers and the members of the local corps played critically important roles in enabling the growth and evolution of Manitoba. As we have seen with the local political authorities' concerns with the elimination of the permanent force garrison in 1877, the societal leaders felt the soldiers provided a degree of security for the growing province, a question we will now turn our attention to.

3

SECURITY: THE DOMINION'S IMPERIAL OUTPOST IN THE NORTH-WEST

It may be counter-intuitive to consider Canada an imperial power, but when the Dominion of Canada annexed the North-West in 1870, it acquired a peripheral colony to be exploited by the economic, political and cultural metropole of Central Canada.[1] As the introductory chapter to this book demonstrated, the Dominion of Canada had a strategic goal in annexing the North-West, well-articulated as an intent to "occupy, possess and mold" the region into a North American transcontinental dominion of the British Empire. Provision of a security force for its defence and to contribute to the establishment and maintenance of law and order was a necessary pre-requisite to achieve this goal.

Even before the Dominion government annexed the North-West the political leadership realized there was a requirement to deploy a military force in the North-West to secure the region. Discussing the creation and organization of the North-West Mounted Police, St. Mary's University historian Greg Marquis observed that "The West was to be Canada's colony and a firm policy was needed. In 1869 [Sir John A. Macdonald] envisaged a police force with 'the military bearing of the Irish Constabulary' for securing the North-West Territories."[2] Although Marquis was specifically investigating the provenance of the North-West Mounted Police, this observation is relevant to the question at hand in that it demonstrates that a key strategic element in successfully settling the North-West was the establishment of security. Moreover, in the creation of the para-military North-West Mounted Police — Macdonald originally envisioned the name North-West Mounted Rifles, which only further reinforces the original military nature of the force — was really the evolution of the Militia in Manitoba.

The Dominion's need to establish military security on its colonial frontier was not unlike similar military-strategic demands experienced by the British Imperial Government across its vast nineteenth century global empire. To do so, the Victorian authorities deployed a broad network of garrisons to protect and police its colonies. Historian Peter Burroughs produced an admirable academic investigation into the use of these colonial garrison in his article "Imperial Defence and the Victorian Army" which appeared in the *Journal of Imperial and Commonwealth History*. Burroughs highlighted the importance of colonial security to the culture and organization of the British Army by stating that "throughout the Victorian period the justification for an island like Britain maintaining a substantial army, ranging between 87,000 and 204,000 men in peacetime, lay in the heavy demands of defending an extensive, scattered and expanding empire. This shaped the whole pattern and operations of the British Army."[3] It would be folly to draw too close a correlation with British colonial garrisons and the Dominion Government's maintenance of a Militia garrison in Manitoba from 1870–77. Clearly there is an ocean of difference between deploying thousands of regular soldiers around the globe and deploying several hundred in a single colonial outpost in the North-West of Canada. That notwithstanding, there is common ground between the two, particularly concerning the military effect the presence of the force was meant to achieve. Consequently, Burroughs' article is instructive for the purposes of this present study in order to understand the military roles undertaken by colonial garrisons in the Victorian era. Specifically, Burroughs identifies the specific military security objectives of Victorian colonial garrisons as pre-empting external aggression by foreign powers, bringing order to unstable or lawless frontiers, and providing internal or policing duties.[4]

Security may seem an odd word to use as the title of this chapter, but it is apt. In current discussions of matters pertaining to national defence, the term security has been used as an overarching term that encompasses all manners of governmental efforts at the national, regional, and local level, to ensure the safety of the population from threats ranging from war to natural disasters.

The term security thus connotes more than simply defending the country against external threats. Consequently, borrowing from Burroughs' analysis, this chapter will demonstrate how the militia in Manitoba contributed to the national strategic goal by pre-empting external threats, bringing order to the frontier, and providing internal policing duties.

PRE-EMPTING EXTERNAL THREATS: DEFENCE OF THE DOMINION

The greatest perceived threat to the Canadian annexation of the North-West was the ever-expanding American Empire, although in the end this threat was more bark than bite. As the introductory chapter illustrated, Victorian Canadians saw Canada as a stone in the arch of the global British Empire, and in many ways British interests and culture were juxtaposed with American republicanism. Take for example the January 1871 editorial in the *Volunteer Review* that complained of the dovish British approach to the United States, lamenting that "of all the great Colonies of the [British] Empire, Canada occupies strategically the most important position, overlapping the flank and rear of that power created by the imbecility of English statesmen, combined with the treason and treachery of the English Whigs, whose existence is a standing menace to the integrity of her Empire."[5]

American interest in annexing British North America was a constant theme in American political thought, beginning even at the end of the Revolutionary War, although the vigour with which American statesmen pursued the idea waxed and waned.[6] Regardless of the level of interest American leaders had in annexing British North America, the assumption amongst Canadians both pre- and post-Confederation was that American annexation was a constant threat. Indeed, until the early twentieth century, fear of American interests in acquiring Canada were the predominant strategic consideration for Canadian leaders. George Stanley captured the essence of this enduring concern when he wrote in *Canada's Soldiers*:

> Canadians could not forget that defence measures in Canada hitherto had meant but one thing, the protection of their country from invasion from the south. It was from this direction that the threat to Canada had come during the Ancien Regime; it was from this direction that invasions

had come since 1763; it was from the south that Amherst's redcoats, Arnold's tattered provincials, Harrison's Kentuckians and O'Neill's Irishmen had come. All the fortifications and the defence measures of the nineteenth century had been devoted solely to the protection of the Canadian frontier against the menace of invasion from the United States. The threat of invasion had admittedly become less pronounced since the Treaty of Washington in 1871; but Canadians could not afford to shut their eyes to the policies and activities of their southern neighbours.[7]

The destinies of the American Republic and the Canadian Dominion collided to the west of the Great Lakes in the latter half of the nineteenth century. American influence in the continental interior grew exponentially during this period. As an illustration, in 1849 the territory of Minnesota was home to only 5,000 people. By 1860, that number had grown to 172,000.[8] The surging growth of the American mid-west, particularly the state of Minnesota, led to a concordant increase in America's economic influence in the continental North-West.

In the months following Confederation, inhabitants of the Red River Settlement were already feeling the pinch of American encroachment, and those who envisioned a Canadian Dominion stretching across the northern half of the continent feared that increasing American settlement, combined with lackadaisical Hudson's Bay Company governance, would drive local inhabitants to embrace the idea of American annexation. The Nor'Wester on October 5, 1867 carried a column warning of the dangers of American growth in the North-West. "The matter is becoming urgent...." they warned "the Americans are pushing up to the boundary line rapidly. Nay, Yankee traders have actually entered the hitherto sacred preserve of the company and buy furs before their eyes in Red River. American miners have squatted on the banks of the Saskatchewan ... in most significant relation to this view of the question are the facts that the settlers of Red River, discontented with the partial government of the company, are half inclined to look favorably on any prospect of annexation to the United States."[9]

Indicative of the expanding economic reach of the American Republic in the region was the increasing use of Minnesota and North Dakota as a hub through which to transport North-West goods. For example, in 1859 the first steamboat, the *Anson Northrup*, steamed from Grand Forks down the Red River to Fort Garry, establishing a tenuous steamship trade along the serpentine prairie river.[10] Shortly thereafter the Hudson's Bay Company began shipping its goods south from Fort Garry via the United States instead of using the Nelson-Hayes river system to Hudson's Bay, the traditional fur trade route used by the Company for centuries.[11] Railway had reached St. Paul, so to use the expeditious Minnesota route rather than the laborious York Factory route only made fiscal sense to the Company's bottom line. Additionally, immigration from the western regions of the United States into the North-West increased substantially and many American settlers openly agitated for annexation by the United States.[12] These influential changes in both the economic and demographic make-up of the North-West and the subsequent burgeoning influence of Minnesota and the American West threatened to pull the North-West into the American Republic.

America's optimistic outlook of the late nineteenth century is central to the contemporary zeitgeist which envisioned an American destiny to dominate the whole of the continent. Take for example this interesting interpretation which is found in journalist J. Wesley Bond's 1854 memoir *Minnesota and its resources; to which are appended camp-fire sketches or notes of a trip from St. Paul to Pembina and Selkirk settlement on the Red River of the North*. In it, Bond provides a history and topography of the Minnesota area which focussed on its suitability for settlement and its inevitable future to dominate the interior of the continent culturally and economically as part of a transcontinental American Republic. Of interest is his conclusion, which he writes as a "vision" of the future set twenty-five years after the publication of his book in which Minnesota is a thriving economic hub of the continental interior. It is written in the style of the Book of Revelation, using all the same metaphorical and allegorical devices to describe what can only be called a new Jerusalem erected in the American mid-west, indicative of the manifest destiny embraced by many mid-nineteenth century Americans.

In his mind's eye, Bond envisioned himself "stood upon the lofty bluffs, overlooking the great and populous city of St. Paul. Beneath and around me, on every side, a hundred lofty spires glittered in the morning sunlight." His scenario finds him in St. Paul on the Fourth of July, 1876 where, to celebrate the centennial of American independence and the completion of the trans-American railway, had gathered "representatives from the several old

Mississippi valley states, from Nebraska, and the other new states and territories extending westward to the Rocky mountains; the people from the North, too, *from Pembina, and the old Selkirk settlement, formerly so called — now the state of Assiniboin (pronounced Assin-i-bwaw), and ever from old Fort York, on Hudson Bay* [emphasis added]."[13] In his scenario, he depicts the arrival of the first train, bedecked with bands, vases, columns, altars, virginal women, and banners festooned with patriotic words and phrases such as *freedom, justice, equality, The Union, The Constitution,* and *E Pluribus Unum* amongst others. It arrives in St. Paul to rapturous applause. In fact, he observed that "never in all her history, save at the incorporation of the 'Republic of Mexico' into the American Union, some ten years previous, *or the annexation of 'Canada and Cuba,'* which happened some five years before, St. Paul had never seen such a day of rejoicing."[14]

Certainly, this is the lucid dream of but one man. While it may not be a perfect representation of the whole of the American Republic, it is nonetheless indicative of the feelings of a large segment of the population, particularly that part in the American Midwest. It is important to note that this work was produced in 1854, long before the first shots of the US Civil War was fired. Bond's Revelation-like description of 1876 leans heavily on motifs of American unity and cohesiveness, blissfully unaware of the gathering storm that would burst upon the nation in 1861.

Perhaps, had the Civil War not occurred, Bond's prescience might have been accurate. Fortunately for Canada, the eruption of the Civil War and the catastrophic destruction that ensued, distracted American interest in the North-West, if for only a few years. When the war finally ended, American interest in the North-West resumed, emanating primarily from Minnesota. One of the most outspoken post-Civil War proponents of American expansion was a Senator for Minnesota, Alexander Ramsey. To Senator Ramsey, the Red River Settlement was a springboard to the North-West, the resources of which he envisioned providing a massive economic boon to his state.[15] Senator Ramsey was not alone, however. If Ramsey was the dominant expansionist force in Minnesota, no less than Charles Sumner, the chair of the Senate Foreign Relations Committee, was his equal in Washington. Sumner was extremely vocal in his support of the removal of British authority from North America.[16] To illustrate, when the United States purchased Alaska in 1867, Sumner urged ratification of the purchase as he felt it was a crucial step to occupation of the whole of the North American continent.[17]

While a small group of American policy makers were supportive of annexation, the movement lacked broad political support. Except for peak periods of animosity, such as the War of 1812, Canada never figured prominently in the minds of most American political leaders. When it did, the consensus was that time and inertia would inevitably draw Canada into the Republic.[18] If interest in American expansion into British North America was lukewarm in the United States, the same could not be said of the anxiety over American expansionism amongst Canadian political leaders. The young Dominion Government was gripped with fear over American expansionism even if threat of American annexation was only tepid. Canadian politician Thomas D'Arcy McGee articulated the concern that many Canadians felt after the end of the Civil War in a speech to Parliament on February 9, 1865:

> the policy of our neighbours to the south of us has always been aggressive. There has always been a desire amongst them for the acquisition of new territory…. They coveted Florida, and seized it; they coveted Louisiana and purchased it, they coveted Texas, and stole it; and then they picked a quarrel with Mexico, which ended by their getting California. They sometimes pretend to despise those colonies as prizes beneath their ambition; but had we not had the strong arm of England over us, we should not now have had a separate existence. The acquisition of Canada was the first ambition of the American Confederacy, and never ceased to be so, when her troops were a handful and her navy scarce a squadron. Is it likely to be stopped now, when she counts her guns afloat by the thousands and her troops by hundreds of thousands?[19]

Canada's fears of American expansionism were not wholly without merit. American land purchases, annexations and outright conquests in Texas, Mexico and Alaska demonstrated the voracious appetite of the burgeoning American republic. Likewise, a series of Anglo-American treaties indicated Great Britain's appeasement of American interests in the face of potential conflict. The 1842 Webster-Ashburton Treaty, a political compromise between the United States and Great Britain in which Canadian interests were used by the latter as a bargaining chip, ceded a large part of the border between Maine and New Brunswick to the United States. The 1846 Oregon Treaty equally confirmed the willingness of the British Government to relinquish potential Canadian territory to the United States to avoid confrontation.[20] In each case, potential future Canadian territory was handed over to the US in order to avoid Anglo-American conflict. These fears prompted the Canadian Government to enter negotiations to purchase Rupert's Land in hopes of pre-empting the loss of the North-West to the US.

It is for these reasons that the Red River Resistance of 1869–70 caused fits of concern amongst Canadian political leaders, particularly concerning the possibility of the United States exploiting the situation to their benefit. Consequently, although the Dominion Government was initially reluctant to send a military force to the Red River Settlement, the fear engendered by reports from Fort Garry that the resistance was taking a pro-American bias increased the government's taste for an expeditionary force.

In the case of the Red River Resistance, there was some foundation to the fears of the Dominion. The *New York Herald* dispatched a correspondent to Fort Garry during the resistance who dutifully recorded the goings on in Fort Garry. In late July the correspondent reported that at the outbreak of the Resistance "the President [Riel] … the Catholic clergy and a large majority of settlers talked annexation to the United States." He attributes Riel's later change of heart from American annexation to Canadian confederation not to patriotism, but to a fear that aligning with the United States would invite violence from local Sioux who had found asylum in the North-West, fleeing American violence. Nonetheless the *Herald* reported optimistically that the "annexation of the country is but a question of time, and a few years will, in all probability, see the American flag waving over Winnipeg."[21]

Meanwhile in Ottawa, during a Cabinet meeting of February 11, 1870, the leadership of the Dominion Government realized that, as negotiators from Red River were planning to come to the capital, they should be received kindly, and that any discussion of annexation to the United States was to be avoided. Understanding that Canada's military power was less-than-impressive, and that the United States military, although demobilized after the Civil War, was large, well-armed and battle hardened, Macdonald realized that British involvement was a necessity for any sort of legitimate dissuasive effect to be realized.[22] He stated this outright in a letter to the Governor General on January 26, 1870 writing of the nature of the expedition that "it is of great importance that some of the force should be Regular Troops as it will convince the United States Government and people that Her Majesty's Government has no intention of abandoning this continent."[23] Thus, from a military perspective, the joint Anglo-Canadian expedition was necessary to the realization of Canadian strategic goals, not only to potentially subdue the insurgents, but also to pre-empt the danger of American interference. [24]

Perhaps this was the secret reason why the Dominion Government did not avail itself of the services of the Royal Canadian Rifles but insisted on a regular British battalion to participate in the expedition, both for the dissuasive effect, and as a forcing function to keep British forces in Canada. If this was the case, the gambit did not work and as we've seen, the 1st Battalion, 60th Rifles left Fort Garry shortly after their arrival, leaving the two volunteer Militia battalions as the only military footprint in the region. Although the size, strength, and experience of the Canadian Militia in Fort Garry was insufficient to defeat any concerted American invasion, it nonetheless existed as an overt symbol of Dominion authority in the region, a question we will return to later.

In the first decade of Manitoba's existence, the Militia was only once called out in martial form to face an external threat to Manitoba. It occurred early in the province's history, and in the end very much was made of what in retrospect reveals to be but a trifling threat to Canadian sovereignty. In fact, the Militia in Manitoba played rather no role at all in the defence of their native soil when the Fenians attacked in 1871.

Seeing an opportunity to exploit the simmering dissatisfaction amongst the Métis in the new province, "General" John O' Neill, one of the leaders of the 1870 Fenian incursion into Canada near Eccles Hill on the Vermont border, supported by William O'Donoghue, late one of the principal actors of the Red River Resistance at Fort Garry, attempted to 'invade' Canada, via Manitoba, with a band of about forty Fenians, in October 1871. The memories of the Fenian Invasions of Ontario and Quebec were still quite fresh in the minds of the political leaders of early Manitoba, and quite a panic was got up at the prospect of the 'invasion.'

The growth of the local Militia in response to the Fenian invasion was touched on in Chapter 1, but a more detailed survey is warranted here. Plans to raise a Militia were expedited, and a number of Active Militia corps were gazetted in *Militia General Orders* of September 1, 1871, including a troop of cavalry at St. Boniface — actually a force of Métis scouts under Joseph Royal that eventually included Louis Riel among its number — and rifle companies in Mapleton, South St. Andrews, Poplar Point, and Winnipeg.[25] A month later, an artillery battery in Winnipeg, and rifle companies in Portage La Prairie, Kildonan, St. Boniface, and St. Charles were added to the Active Militia rolls.[26] Years later, the deputy adjutant-general of Military District No. 10 would complain that the mobilization plan in response to the Fenian crisis was conducted too hastily and resulted in a Militia organization that required significant restructuring in order to be efficient.[27]

Learning that the Fenians had gathered around Pembina and were preparing for an incursion into Manitoba, Lieutenant-Governor Archibald rallied the men of the province in a proclamation issued in early October, calling on the settlements of Manitoba to raise companies of Militia to fight the apprehended invasion, and in response a hasty defence force was thrown together on October 3, 1871 to repel the invaders. Major Irvine assiduously recorded the strength of the force, which totaled 942 men in twenty-three companies — four of which were *gazetted* infantry companies of the Active Militia mentioned above.[28]

Fortunately, the Fenian 'invasion' was more farce than a genuine threat. One correspondent to the *Volunteer Review,* claiming to be a former Colour Sergeant of the 2nd Quebec Rifles and present at the incident recounted the "assault" on the Hudson's Bay Company Fort at Pembina. He reported that at five o'clock in the morning the invading Fenian force took possession of the post, making prisoners of the inhabitants, including a Mr. Watt, an officer of the Company, a Mr. Webster, a former Pay-Sergeant of the 2nd Quebec Rifles, and a Mr. Coutoure, a former Colour-Sergeant of the 2nd Quebec Rifles. The Fenians pilfered the Hudson's Bay Post taking clothing and provisions and, while reveling in the spoils of victory, were soon set upon by United States Cavalry thereabouts under the command of a Colonel Wheaton, and arrested, described by the correspondent thusly: "All at once the United States troops came down on them; they fled in all directions leaving two carts full of arms and cartridges. The United States troops pursued them, fired some shots but none were wounded; the United States troops succeeded in capturing 14 of them ... they were taken by the United States authorities ... 60 rifles were taken, some revolvers, General O'Neil's sword and 8000 rounds of ammunition."[29]

The threat to Manitoba posed by the Fenians, therefore, fizzled out before it really began.[30] This, of course, did not stop some of Manitoba's early citizens from taking full credit for the defence of the realm. One citizen wrote to the

Manitoba Liberal to lament the state of the volunteer Militia in the province, observing that upon the emergence of the Fenian threat and the dispatch of Captain Scott's expedition, that "happily ere those volunteers could reach Manitoba the inhabitants were able to repulse the insolent foe and prove to the world that the Manitobans do not lack the patriotism, the love of liberty and the undaunted courage of which older countries are justly proud."[31] Of course, no member of the hurriedly assembled defensive Militia even laid eyes on a Fenian, let alone "repulse" them, but the author was not about to let that little inconvenience sully what was the perfect opportunity for hyperbolic patriotism.

There remained, however, a latent fear of future incursions by Fenians that pervaded the settlement for years. Rumours of another Fenian invasion were rife in January 1872, mere months after the initial abortive attempted invasion of Manitoba, prompting several letters to the editor of the *Manitoba Liberal* to express concern. One writer, going by the pseudonym "Correspondent" asked "how long may we command the services of the brave Volunteers who now protect us? In a short time their term of service will expire, and we will be in as piteous a condition as ever, looking to another Colonel Wheaton [the US Cavalry officer who arrested the Fenian invaders] for protection — hoping and trembling."[32] "Correspondent" went on to suggest the appropriate size and constitution of a volunteer Militia for the province, with a focus on a cavalry force composed of "sixty or seventy dashing young fellows" capable of rapidly deploying to meet interlopers from the south and thus "save our families from destruction by ragamuffin bands, or, what would still be more terrible, the desecrating hand of the religious fanatic."[33] It seems that to the Protestant Anglo-Canadian settlers of Manitoba the Fenian spectre was a two-headed beast: one head representing the scourge of American republicanism, the other the menace of Catholicism.

Nineteenth century Canadians were apt to see Fenians lurking behind every corner, and suspected Fenian fingers in every conspiracy. This afforded an opportunity for clever merchants to exploit the commercial potential of the ever-present Fenian apprehension. In a series of advertisements running in the *Manitoba Free Press* in 1877, the grocers at M.J. Alcock & Company exercised a practice well known to many modern users of social media where they are lured by shocking headlines to select a link to another website, which has nothing to do with the original headline, and which often attempts to sell some product. No doubt understanding the continued concern about Fenian incursions amongst the readers of Manitoba newspapers, the merchants at Alcock & Co. produced advertisements that resembled proclamation columns not unlike that issued by Lieutenant-Governor Archibald when the actual Fenian invasion looked likely in October 1871. "Proclamation" the advertisement would read, followed by the terror-inducing alert "**Fenians! Fenians! Fenians!**" in bold type, after which the purveyors announced in a tone worthy of late night infomercials "100,000 volunteers called to the front to buy the new, cheap and well selected stock of dry goods, groceries and provisions at the Melbourne House, High Bluff."[34] This clever use of the pervasive fear of Fenians is indicative of the perpetuating mood amongst the young province when it came to a sense of security.

As settlers moved into the region and worked to create an affluent and productive society modeled economically, social, and culturally on Ontario, the political and economic leadership of the province realized that to draw settlers, one must ensure the area to be settled was sufficiently secure from violence — even apprehended violence — to lure those settlers to the region. Thus, bringing order to the frontier to facilitate its settlement and exploitation became a key military objective to the Militia in Manitoba.

BRINGING ORDER TO THE FRONTIER

Colonel Robertson-Ross assumed the duties of the adjutant-general in 1872, and shortly thereafter undertook a tour and inspection of the North-West. His visit occurred at a time when the political and military leadership was considering the practicality of maintaining the Provisional Battalion in Fort Garry. His reconnaissance, as he described it, took him to Fort Garry via Lake Superior, and thence through the Saskatchewan Valley and mainland British Columbia, arriving eventually in Vancouver Island after having travelled nearly the whole distance from Fort Garry to the Pacific Coast on horseback.[35] In his subsequent report to the Minister of Militia, he pointedly observed that "no doubt whatever exists in my mind as to the propriety of [maintaining a force in Manitoba], in view of the presence of many bands of Indians, considering the primitive state of the Province, the strong political party feeling which exists, and the fact that on both sides of the International Boundary Line restless and reckless characters among both white men and Indians abound."[36]

Robertson-Ross' observations epitomize the security concerns that were pervasive amongst the local and federal political leadership and newly settled citizenry. Internal political strife, criminals, and ne'er do wells traversing the plains, as well as the perceived threat from local First Nations, all contributed to a sense of discomfort amongst the settlers and deterred potential immigrants to the region. Security was thus a principal concern for the political leadership who wanted to lure settlers to the region, and the Militia played an important role in providing that security, even if their presence served more as salve for the consternations of the settlers than any genuine deterrent.

Inasmuch as the late nineteenth century Canadian political leaders had an abiding fear that American expansionism would rob them of their birth rite in the North-West, equally prevalent amongst both the settler population of the North-West and the politicians in Ottawa was a fear of Indigenous unrest. In retrospect, there was never any real physical threat to the settlers in Manitoba posed by the local First Nations during the latter half of the nineteenth century. For the most part, in the latter half of the nineteenth century, the First Nations of the North-West co-existed peacefully with the settlers, with the unique exception of several bands that rose up with Louis Riel during the North-West Rebellion in 1885 (see Chapter 7). Nonetheless, the fear amongst settlers and political leaders of an Indigenous uprising was palpable and it was a key factor in keeping a Militia force in the North-West.

The very presence of First Nations and their proximity to colonial settlements caused disquiet among the settlers. In his report filed after his inspection of the North-West, Robertson-Ross took note of the paradoxical nature of settler life in what is now Western Manitoba, which at the time lay within the North-West Territories, and the cooperation and anxiety produced by the proximity of a band of Sioux. He remarked:

> between Fort Garry and Portage du Prairie [sic] three large Camps of the Sioux tribe were visited — a portion of the same band who in 1862 massacred some American settlers in Minnesota, U.S., in retaliation for the many wrongs and outrages committed in the first instance on them by American citizens. Ever since that event this band has sought refuge in Dominion Territory. These Sioux Indians live quietly enough apparently among our people, and occasionally assist the farmers at harvest time. The presence, however, of such wild and warlike looking Band in the settlement frequently causes

no small apprehension amongst the settlers dwelling near Portage du Prairie.[37]

A similar case in point is the concern raised in the winter and spring of 1873. Intelligence was received in Fort Garry, and confirmed by an emissary from the Indian Department, that a band of Sioux led by a man named Little Knife living on the Little Missouri River, which is located north-west of Bismarck, North Dakota, intended to raid some part of the province in the spring which caused acute concern amongst the settlers of what is now Western Manitoba. In February 1873, Archibald MacDonald, the chief trader at the Hudson's Bay Post in Fort Ellice which sat near the junction of the Assiniboine and Qu'Appelle Rivers, wrote to Donald A. Smith, the Member of Parliament for Selkirk and Commissioner of the Montreal Department of the Hudson's Bay Company, and suggested that "it will be for the benefit of both the Company and the Government that troops be sent up here before the end of March."[38] Additionally, in March of 1873, the people of Palestine, now known as Gladstone, located about sixty kilometres north-west of Portage la Prairie, sent a petition to Lieutenant-Governor Morris in which they expressed their concern at the aforementioned intelligence and pleaded with Morris to furnish protection, in the form of one hundred soldiers, in order to "protect our settlement from being ravaged." Illustrating the impact of such fears on the growth of the region, an anonymous author, representing the citizens of Palestine, confided in a letter to the editors of the *Free Press* "I do not understand the policy of the present Dominion Government in regard to immigration, but *I do not think many immigrants will be induced to go farther west unless they can see some chance of their lives and property being protected* [emphasis added]."[39] The author's appeal to the Dominion Government, based on the negative repercussions to settlement caused by fear of Indigenous violence, is illustrative of the general belief that security and settlement went hand in hand, a sentiment shared in the official halls of Ottawa.

In response to the worries in western Manitoba, Robertson-Ross wrote to Henry Langevin, the Acting Minister of Militia and Defence, and recommended that a military force should be dispatched to the west of the province to provide some sense of security to the settlers there. In his letter, he echoed the concerns of the *Free Press* and stated that "with a view to give confidence to settlers residing on the outskirts of the Province of Manitoba it is very desirable to organize such settlers as companies of active Militia and arm and equip them."[40] In a later letter, Robertson-Ross recommended that Thomas Carney, a recently arrived émigré from Brantford County, Pennsylvania, should be authorized to create a company of Active Militia volunteers in Palestine.[41]

The fear of an Indigenous uprising in 1873 was founded in an irrational anxiety of Indigenous violence, sadly stoked by certain elements of Manitoba society who stood to benefit financially should the federal government take steps to assuage settler concerns. In fact, there were opinions loudly shared in some newspaper columns and amongst some of the political leadership of the day, that the rumours of First Nations being on the war path were created by the Hudson's Bay Company to prompt the Dominion Government to deploy soldiers to reassure the settlers — soldiers who would require sustainment from the only source of resupply in the region, the Hudson's Bay Company.[42] If this was indeed what occurred, the Company nevertheless exploited an already existing latent fear amongst the population — a ruse that succeeded. In response to growing concern and tension amongst the settlers in Manitoba, Robertson-Ross was authorized to deploy a force of soldiers to the west of modern-day Manitoba to stiffen the resolve of the settlers there. Consequently, on April 30, 1873, Robertson-Ross dispatched a letter to Donald A. Smith in which he informed him that he had been instructed by the government to dispatch a military force to Fort Ellice with as little delay as possible, and that he was authorized to communicate with the Hudson's Bay Company to expedite matters of sustainment. He wrote "will you be so kind as to inform me if the Hudson's Bay Company will undertake the transport and provisioning of the detachment on the journey, and at Fort Ellice for such time as may be required?"[43] Of course anything was possible, for a price.

The editors of the *Free Press* considered the threat of an Indigenous uprising overblown, even referring to the situation as the "Indian Humbug." The editors reported sardonically that "the alarm at Ottawa is something most remarkable. Our telegraphic dispatches indicate that the Lieut. Governor has started on his return to this country, in anticipation of Indian troubles; and, besides, that the military force in this country is to be reinforced [referring to the fourth Red River Expedition that was in the process of organizing, see Chapter 2]."[44] While the editors at the *Free Press* may have dismissed the fears of Indigenous violence as a contrivance, their colleagues at the *Manitoban and*

North-West Herald were more than happy to stoke the fires of fear amongst the populace. Two weeks after the *Free Press* printed their column on the "Indian Humbug" the *Herald* published an editorial that listed the large size of US forces garrisoning the west and asked "who will say that this array and distribution of force is unnecessary in the presence of 60,000 Indians who are impressed with the belief that the advancing settlements of whites will disperse the herds of buffalo and antelope and appropriate their hunting grounds? With such a prospect it is folly not to expect that collisions will not occur, and without great prudence and precaution, the inevitable antagonism may lead to indescribable horrors of Indian massacre."[45] The threat of Indigenous violence — real or perceived — was sufficient to justify the dispatch of fifty Militiamen to Fort Ellice to reassure the local population.[46]

While the 1873 scare was more rumour than fact, actual clashes with First Nations on both sides of the border exacerbated the concerns of the settlers in Manitoba. Word of the defeat of General Terry's United States Army column during the Great Sioux War of 1876, which included the 7th Cavalry under Colonel George Custer, immortalized by their defeat at Little Big Horn, reached Winnipeg at approximately the same time as news of the decision to reduce the number of soldiers in Winnipeg became public knowledge.[47] Such an unhappy confluence of events led the editors of the *Free Press,* previously so astute to dismiss unwarranted fear of Indigenous violence, to observe that "the disaster which has befallen Gen. Terry's expedition against the rebellious Sioux has engendered a doubt as to the possibility of the U.S. Government now accomplishing their subjection during the present season, and caused a feeling of some anxiety to be exhibited in Canada as to the degree in which the North-West Territories may be affected by the course of future events ... *To deal with [the Sioux], or to be prepared to deal with them, it is absolutely necessary that the strength of the Dominion forces in the North-West should be augmented* [emphasis added.]"[48]

In 1877, further reports of a Sioux war band of up to 350 Indigenous warriors reached Winnipeg and aroused consternation amongst the inhabitants, and even into the Canadian Senate. While discussing the public accounts of 1876–77 in late March of 1877, Senator Alex Campbell of the Conservative Party, then in opposition, stood in the upper chamber to make note of the disbandment of the garrison in Winnipeg, and remarked: "there is a decrease [in expenses] in the item of 'Military forces in Manitoba.' If that is partly caused by withdrawing the troops from Fort Osborne, Winnipeg, I think it is a very dangerous saving. We have between Winnipeg and the Rocky Mountains, 25,000 Indians of our own, besides the band of Sitting Bull and the Sioux. It is true no trouble with them has yet arisen, *but we know how exactly they are excited, and we never can tell the time when a military force may be required in the North-West* [emphasis added]."[49]

In July of that year, Osborne Smith sent a memorandum to the General Officer Commanding the Militia, at the time Lieutenant-General Sir Edward Selby-Smyth, informing him of reports of these Sioux, and relaying the story of a local trader whose brother was kidnapped. At first, Osborne Smith was reluctant to accept the veracity of the reports, but after conducting some cursory investigations, he thought there might be truth to the stories. On July 12, 1877, he wrote again to Selby-Smyth stating: "I may report that the feeling now is very uneasy as to these outlying bands of the Sioux being encamped close to, if not actually within, this province, and with no adequate military force for protection." It is important to recall at this juncture that the garrison of permanent soldiers had been disbanded only a few months previous. The very next day Osborne Smith telegraphed Selby-Smyth asking for reinforcements, which were never authorized. In the end, the kidnapped trader was released, and the perceived threat dissipated as the Sioux moved back south.[50]

Later, the hunger amongst the First Nations occasioned by the disappearance of buffalo, the result of encroaching white settlement, and the harsh winter of 1878 made local settler authorities wary of possible Indigenous marauding. To assuage the concerns of the outlying settlements, Smyth directed that several companies of local Militia be authorized.[51]

Even as late as 1883, concern about a rising of First Nations persisted. In his annual District Report in 1883, the new Deputy Adjutant-General of Military District No. 10, Lieutenant-Colonel Houghton, recorded that:

> Bounded, as Manitoba is, upon the west by the still powerful, though yet peaceful tribes of Indians, *the tenure of whose friendship is now more than ever likely to become a matter of uncertainty in the immediate future;* and on the south by the disaffected tribes of Indians of the United States, *from whom we are at any time liable to be obliged to defend our herds and granaries (to say nothing of our homes and families)* would it

not be prudent to take every precaution to fortify ourselves against possible contingencies, by taking advantage of the voluntary offers of the bone and sinew of the country to enroll themselves in the ranks of its defenders? [emphasis added][52]

In 1884, the *Portage la Prairie Weekly Tribune* reported that the citizens of the town of Prince Albert in modern-day Saskatchewan, which although lying in the North-West Territory still lay within the boundaries of Military District No. 10, agitated for the government to raise a battalion of Militia for their defence. The authors of the article observed sarcastically that they thought the "precaution necessary to the safety of their scalps."[53]

History demonstrated the threat to settlement posed by First Nations never really approximated the level of fear and unease their presence created. This fear, however unreasonable, translated into a deterrent to the settlement of British émigrés in Manitoba and the North-West which was the key strategic goal of the Dominion Government. Consequently, the Militia, both the permanent and local corps, became strategic tools to provide a military deterrent to the perceived Indigenous threat, while also serving as an expressive reassurance to prospective settlers contemplating life in the North-West. A far more tangible impact on Manitoba society can be found in the Militia's role in ensuring peace, order, and good government by providing non-defence assistance to local and provincial authorities.

ASSISTING CIVIL AUTHORITIES

Although the Militia stood as a military deterrent or, more specifically, a reassuring agent to settlers on the frontier, they were far more active in assisting civil authorities to maintain law and order, while also assisting during times of emergency such as conflagration and epidemic in what is known as 'Aid to Civil Power.' Such activities were conducted with a goal of establishing a safe and secure environment to facilitate settlement of the region.

Aid to Civil Power is a specific type of mission performed by military forces in support of local authorities for the maintenance of peace, order, and good government. It is an enduring element of the Canadian national mythos that the Canadian North-West was settled in an orderly and peaceful manner, a view deliberately at odds with the slapdash, land-grabbing, ethnic-cleansing, six-gun-shooting miscreants of the Western United States. To an extent this is true, although lamentably much of the credit for the orderly settlement of the Canadian North-West is granted solely to the North-West Mounted Police. Notwithstanding the very important role the Mounties played in the maintenance of law and order, the role played by the Militia in Manitoba in establishing a lawful, orderly, and settler-friendly society is little known. In early Manitoba the Militia was an embryonic police and civil defence force that set the conditions for settlement and growth.

The authority for local Militia forces to act in such measure was articulated in the *Militia Act 1868* which contained the following provision: "The Active Militia shall be liable to be called out with their arms and ammunition in Aid of the Civil Power in case of riot or other emergency requiring such services … the Officers and men, when so called out, shall … be special constables, and shall be considered to act as such so long as they remain so called out."[54] The use of the Militia to maintain law and order in the late nineteenth century was widespread throughout the Dominion, and commonplace in the larger cities of the country, particularly where there existed the conditions that would lead to racial, ethnic or class-based violence. Militia were, in many corners of the Dominion, the only public security force available to civic leadership to maintain law and order in the face of such manifestations. Military historian Desmond Morton has chronicled the use of the Militia in the Aid to Civil Power role in his article for the *Canadian Historical Review* entitled "Aid to the Civil Power: The Canadian Militia in Support of Social Order." Reflecting on the diverse number of threats to public order, Morton observed that "in the absence of effective local or provincial police forces, the Militia were frequently the only available support for magistrates confronted by rioting Orangemen or defiant strikers." [55] Today, the use of the Canadian military in a law enforcement role is an extreme rarity, but it was considered a routine task for the Militiamen of the nineteenth century. Manitoba was no exception, in fact Osborne Smith addressed the Winnipeg Field Battery in 1877 and stated that Militiamen train not only to prepare for war but "for those emergencies which even in the highest state of civilization, occasionally necessitate the strong arm of military force in aid of civil power"[56] Throughout Canada, both pre- and post-confederation, the military, both British Regulars and Canadian Militia were used to assist in maintaining social order. Manitoba was no exception.

Benjamin Sulte, who worked as a civil servant in the *Militia Department* in the 1870s and 1880s, recorded in his 1898 history of the French-Canadian Militia the surprising number of times the Canadian Militia was called out in aid of civil power between 1870 and 1885. For example, in 1875 local authorities in Montreal, expecting an uprising at the interment of Joseph Guibord in holy ground despite his being excommunicated seven years previous, called out 1,100 Militiamen to ensure the court-ordered burial took place without interference from a large group of protesters. In 1876, in the face of a riot in Saint-Jean, New Brunswick, eighty-five Militiamen were called out. The same year saw a revolt amongst the employees of the Grand-Trunk Railway in Belleville, Ontario causing 240 soldiers to be called out for three days to maintain order. Two years later, a riot of dockworkers in Quebec City resulted in the deployment of 1,300 Militiamen over three days, and a month later during Orangeman's Day celebrations that turned violent, 3,000 Militia were called out for a week. That same summer, riots against the Ottawa and Western Railway required 239 soldiers to deploy for four days. In 1879, Saint Andrews, New Brunswick looked about ready to riot for which eighty-five soldiers mustered, and that summer the dockworkers in Quebec once again got their backs up, resulting in the mobilization of eight hundred militia volunteers for three days. In 1880, the Militia was called out twice in Norfolk County, Ontario to provide security for boxing matches. A miner's strike in Cape Breton in 1883 was contained by one hundred militia volunteers. The year 1884 saw two railway worker strikes requiring Militia attention, the first in Aylmer, Ontario resulted in eighty-five volunteers being called out for a day, and three months later in response to strike demonstrations in Tamworth, Ontario another eighty-five volunteers were mobilized for a day.[57]

In the years immediately after being admitted to Confederation, Manitoba was a rough country, and the simmering ethno-racial tensions, fueled in many ways by the actions of the Militia garrison, only exacerbated the problem. Lieutenant George Lightfoot Huyshe, a British Regular officer who chronicled his participation in the Wolseley Expedition in his book *The Red River Expedition*, recorded that during the short time that the British Regulars were in Fort Garry "the place seemed turned into a very Pandemonium — Indians, half-breeds, and whites, in all stages of intoxication, fighting and quarreling in the streets with drawn knives"[58] A settler society could not be built on so shaky a foundation, so the use of the Militia in the Aid to Civil Power role began early in the province's history. Considering the general lack of an external threat, notwithstanding the ever-present spectre of American expansionism and Fenian incursions, the Militia in Manitoba became agents of social order far more than bulwarks of national defence.[59]

The province's first Lieutenant-Governor, Adams Archibald, arrived in the Red River Settlement to assume his gubernatorial duties on 2 September 1870. It was thereafter only a matter of days, on September 20, before Archibald reached out to the Militia for assistance in maintaining law and order. He wrote to garrison commander, Lieutenant-Colonel Samuel Jarvis, that:

> From information which has come to me from various quarters and on the accuracy of which I feel I can rely, I have reason to believe that a few lawless men belonging to this settlement propose to intercept some flat boats now on the way here from Abercrombie [North Dakota] by the Red River and to take possession of the goods in them. I learn also that there is a considerable quantity of Government Stores and property, besides private property en route, which is shortly expected at Pembina and which is liable to risk. Under these circumstances feeling the urgent necessity of preserving the Peace, and of preventing any Robbery or attempt at Robbery, I think it highly desirable that a company of troops should be despatched to the neighbourhood of the Hudson's Bay Fort of Pembina to be at hand in case of the civil authorities requiring assistance.[60]

Fort Pembina lay near the international boundary with the United States, although at the time the actual location of the international boundary along the 49th parallel was not agreed upon. In response to Jarvis' decision to provide the requested soldiers, Donald Smith of the Hudson's Bay Company was kind enough to put the company's river steamer *International* at the disposal of the troops. Jarvis detailed A Company, 1st Ontario Rifles under the command of Captain Cook, comprising a total of three officers, three sergeants and forty rank, and file to deploy to Fort Pembina. The company was despatched the morning of September 21, 1870, the soldiers doubtless happy to make use of the steam powered water vessel after their recent toilsome trek through the waterways of the Canadian Shield.

Jarvis was very detailed in his orders to Captain Cook, stating that he was to "exercise the utmost vigilance to protect all property public and private that may be in course of transport." To do so, Cook was directed to encamp his company within half a mile of the international boundary line, at least where British authorities felt it lay, within view of the river and with scouts deployed to monitor traffic thereupon. Jarvis stressed that Cook was to be careful not to allow any of his men to cross the boundary line itself, lest an international incident ensue.[61]

In his request for assistance, Archibald reinforced that the real authority lay with the constables who had been sent by the provincial government to secure the goods on the flat boats and the militia were to support of those officers in the execution of their duties. This is a key tenet of the provision of aid to the Civil Power in modern democracies. The British population had, in the nineteenth century, a pervasive fear of standing armies and firmly believed in a separation of the roles of civil and military authorities. To this end, Jarvis made it very clear to Cook that he was to "avoid taking any measures of a forcible character until appealed to for assistance by the Senior Civil Constable on the spot."[62] In the end, no attempt was made on the flat boats, but the originally envisioned ten-day duty of A Company at Fort Pembina was greatly extended. Indeed, a full company was maintained thereabouts until Robertson Ross' visit in the summer of 1873 when he directed that the force be reduced to one sergeant, one corporal, and twelve soldiers, the remainder being moved to Fort Garry.[63]

Politically-inspired violence often led to the employment of the Militia in aid of the civil power. One of the first instances came during the provincial elections of November 20, 1870. Sam Steele recounts in his memoir *Forty Years in Canada* that he was on duty when rioting began in the town of Winnipeg and help from the garrison was called for. The Militia guard sprinted to the scene of the riot, followed shortly by Steele who was sprinting to catch up to his colleagues as his quarters lay outside the fort. He recounted that as he ran to catch the remainder of the guard, he "was met by three hostiles who tried to stop me; but I clubbed my rifle and easily brushed them aside; they were not prepared to try conclusions in that way." The situation deteriorated to the point that Steele admits the officer in charge of the guard ordered his men to load their rifles with live ammunition. Steele thought "it seemed at one time that we might have to fire; but, fortunately, the disturbance was quelled without it, though there were many broken heads."[64]

Political violence reared its ugly head again during the provincial election of September 19, 1872, when a mob assembled, worked into fervour by inflammatory rhetoric from the hustings. A requisition signed by three magistrates for a force of seventy-five soldiers was immediately filled by the acting deputy adjutant-general, Major Acheson Irvine, Osborne Smith being absent on leave in Eastern Canada. The mob grew violent and was intent on burning the Dominion Savings Bank to the ground, and while they were able to smash a few windows, the Militia guard arrived in time to prevent the mob from setting the bank alight. Local printing shops, particularly those who had been supportive of the provisional government of Louis Riel, did not fare so well and many were severely damaged, their printers smashed. As the mob became emboldened by drink, another attempt was made to assault the Dominion Savings Bank where a small guard was maintained by the Militia after the initial confrontation earlier in the day. Happily, the diarist of the battalion recorded, in response to the advancing mob, the orders "*Guard turn out* and *fix bayonets* proved too great a barrier."[65]

In 1873, the provincial legislature was prorogued in some disarray after an attempt to incorporate the City of Winnipeg was stymied by what some considered the interference of the Hudson's Bay Company who, it was presumed amongst the aggrieved, feared the impact of municipal taxes that would accompany incorporation. Such ill will emerged from the incident that the speaker of the Legislature, Dr. Curtis James Bird, was "decoyed from his residence on the pretence of being called to see a patient, and when near Point Douglas he was taken forcibly from his cutter, and a pail of hot tar thrown over his face, head and shoulders.[66] In response to this and in order to "frustrate the carrying into execution threats freely circulated by citizens to set fire to the buildings" the Provisional Battalion was requested to post a guard of fourteen soldiers on the parliament buildings, while a force of soldiers was maintained at the ready in Fort Garry, should they be required at short notice.[67]

Later in 1873, the Militia was requested to send a detachment of soldiers to White Horse Plains where a quizzical confrontation between Mennonites, teamsters, and Métis had turned violent. As the story is related in the *Free Press*, a group of Mennonites were traveling in carts across the prairie near White Horse Plains, which lay about fifteen kilometers west of the Forks. A Métis horseman passed nearby and struck one of the horses. In retaliation, one of the teamsters driving the cart struck the Métis with his whip. Tempers flared and the Métis returned with a pistol but was fortunately pre-empted from violence by some of his colleagues. Nonetheless, the Mennonites and their teamsters stopped in at a local hotel for respite. Shortly thereafter, the same Métis gentleman arrived and the argument began anew, after which the same teamster roughed up the Métis. This did not aid in calming the situation, and soon a large group of the Métis gentleman's colleagues arrived at the hotel, armed and in a foul mood. Tempers flared to the point that the pacifistic Mennonites holed themselves up on the second floor of the hotel, and a request was expedited to Fort Garry for assistance. A detachment of fifty soldiers was dispatched from Fort Garry, accompanied by the Judge of the Queen's Bench and the Attorney General of the Province, to arrest the Métis.[68] The soldiers arrested a party of five Métis and marched them back to prison while escorting the Mennonites into Winnipeg.

Protecting the local prison became a routine task for the Militia on station in Winnipeg. In July of 1873, Osborne Smith furnished another force of soldiers to retain a party of men from the United States, Messrs. Hoy and Keegan, who had been incarcerated and were awaiting trial on serious criminal charges, namely the kidnapping of a notorious character who went by the unique name Lord Gordon Gordon. This man was a confidence trickster who had defrauded some business associates in New York and then fled, eventually to Winnipeg, where he was found out. When he was spied on Main Street in Winnipeg, word was dispatched to his aggrieved former partners, who received the tenuous legal advice that a warrant for arrest issued in the United States would be in vigour in the Dominion of Canada as well. Two police officers from Minneapolis — Hoy and Keegan — were despatched to Winnipeg to apprehend the man but were arrested for kidnapping and arraigned. There was indignation and tension on both sides of the border — Canadians insulted that Americans thought their warrants enjoyed authority in Canada and Americans were incensed that two American police officials, and several Minnesota businessmen with whom they were in league, were incarcerated. In the two weeks it took for the court case to reach a conclusion, there was legitimate concern about either flight of the accused, or rescue by their confederates, and thus a guard of Militia were detailed to secure the prisoners in Fort Garry.[69]

Later, in 1874, Ambrose Lepine, alleged murderer of Thomas Scott during the era of the provisional government of Assiniboia under Louis Riel, was also incarcerated in Fort Garry and the Militia were asked to provide a force to both retain him in custody and prevent locals from taking the law into their own hands. The incident is recorded in the Battalion's *Journal* thusly: "On one or two occasions threats were made in the presence of the guard to lynch the prisoner, the mob displaying ropes, but cold steel had a wonderful effect in dispersing the crowd, as the guard merely fixed swords [bayonets] and remained steady."[70]

Local disturbances were not the only disruption to good order that required Militia intervention. As the railway made its way through Manitoba, striking rail workers presented a threat to the maintenance of the capitalist social order, and as in other corners of the Dominion, the military were a tool that supported capital against labour.[71] In 1879, a strike of navvies working on Section 15 of the Canadian Pacific Railway line, near Cross Lake which sits about sixty kilometers west of Kenora, Ontario, caused considerable excitement, and reports arrived that over 1,500 workers had gone on strike and seized the rolling stock and stores. The Militia, by now only the local Militia as the Provisional Battalion had been disbanded and the members either settled locally or returned to their homes, dispatched a force of about eighty soldiers — cavalry, infantry, and artillery, under the command of Osborne Smith between May 7 and 13, 1879.[72] Alexander Begg reported that "owing to the firm attitude of the troops, no collision occurred: the ring leaders were arrested and the breach between the [contractor] and his men was satisfactorily healed."[73] This incident seemed to reinforce in the mind of Osborne Smith the importance of maintaining a strong military force in the region to deal with just these types of issues. He reported as much to the adjutant-general in Ottawa who observed that "[Osborne Smith] points out the necessity of increased forces, in consideration of the influx of foreign labour, in view of the large works of railway construction now in progress. This is a very reasonable suggestion, as experience has shown that this may, at any time, be a very disturbing element."[74]

The fall of 1884 saw one of the more peculiar examples of the use of the Militia to enforce law and order when the 90th Battalion was called out in response to near riotous conditions caused by the flogging of a man named John McCormick. McCormick had been imprisoned for stealing jewelry from a prostitute and was working in the prison yard when he made an escape. He was subsequently recaptured, but there had been several prison breaks in the recent past, so the prison authorities thought that this particular case warranted some degree of general deterrence to future runaways. Consequently, the provincial Attorney General, James Andrew Miller, ordered that McCormick be flogged.

Thus, on October 30, 1884, in a scene reminiscent of some eighteenth-century Royal Navy flogging parade, all prisoners of the jail, twenty-five in number, were mustered in the yard, joined by the Attorney General, his deputy Dr. Wilson, Sheriff Inkster, Dr. Benson the jail's physician, and about a dozen court officers.

News of the flogging spread rapidly. The details were published in the *Free Press* in grotesque — and completely false — detail. The reporter from the *Free Press* exaggerated the proceedings and in certain cases, made false observations, such as suggesting that McCormick fainted during the administration of the lashes, and was revived with snow rubbed in his face so that the punishment might continue, and that salt was applied to his wounds, and that he lay in agony on the floor of his cell afterward. [75]

The wholly inaccurate reports of the cruelty demonstrated by the prison authorities enraged the populace. Dr. Benson, the attendant physician, was compelled to write an open letter to the general public to clarify that McCormick did not faint, salt was not poured in the wounds but rather a salt poultice was applied in order to speed healing, and he did not collapse on the floor of his cell but sat up and ate a hearty meal.[76]

Dr. Benson's explanation came too late — the public's blood was up. The night after the flogging, Halloween 1884, a call went out throughout the city to gather and burn the provincial Attorney General Miller in effigy. By 8:30 PM the *Free Press* estimated that at least four thousand people had gathered in front of the Queen's Hotel on Portage Avenue, chanting, shouting and clamoring for justice for McCormick. Moving towards Trinity Hall, an effigy of the Attorney General was strung up from a telegraph pole and set alight. The crowd, which could not be accurately called a mob as it seems that the leading elements of it were committed to keeping the protest as peaceful as possible, moved from there to Fort Rouge and then along to the Provincial Jail and finally to the Government Buildings where they were addressed by the Premier, John Norquay.[77]

At some point a request was made to Lieutenant-Colonel Houghton for assistance from the Militia. He reported, rather proudly, in his annual report for 1884 that in two hours he was able to produce, in response to the request for assistance from the civic authorities, a force of 136 officers and men of the 90th Battalion, fully equipped, with some elements of the Winnipeg Field Battery and Cavalry Troop as well. He also noted in his report that he was able to do so without the use of the bugle to muster the men, its use being forbidden in this circumstance, presumably so as to not further excite the crowd.[78]

The *Free Press* corroborated Houghton's account and noted that the response of the crowd to the presence of the Militia was not very respectful. As the crowd meandered the streets of Winnipeg, it proceeded down Broadway Avenue where it happened upon the detachment of the 90th Battalion that was marching, with bayonets fixed, towards the Government Buildings. The crowd was not overawed by the sight of the soldiers, quite the contrary, the *Free Press* reported that the crowd "hooted" at the detachment as the two bodies passed each other, but fortunately no violence ensued, and the soldiers continued on their way. [79]

The troops arrived at the Government Buildings and erected a piquet line of sentries around the building. The *Free Press* reported that "the Government buildings were brilliantly illuminated and sentries marched back and forth in front of the north entrance … the lonely soldiers marched about in the blinding snow, listening to the monotonous music of the cruel winds."[80] A smaller detachment was dispatched to the jail house where together with the thirteen members of the city's mounted police, they erected a guard. One officer stood sentry outside the jail while the "remainder of the guard were quartered within the walls of that institution, armed to the teeth and ready for action."[81] The night passed quietly and in the grey light of dawn, the soldiers were marched back to Fort Osborne. Of particular interest, before being dismissed back to barracks, the soldiers were thanked in person by the Premier and the Attorney General, the latter stating "he considered he had done his duty when he sanctioned the punishment of McCormick, and knew that he would have the protection of the military."[82]

When not being called out *en masse* to protect government property and institutions, Militia members contributed in large numbers to the provision of law and order as individuals as well. In fact, in the early days of Winnipeg, it was from the ranks of the Militia that a very large segment of the embryonic police force emerged. Begg and Nursey reported in *Ten Years in Winnipeg* that upon the arrival of the Wolseley Expedition, there was but one police officer in

Fort Garry. The first robust, mounted police force in Winnipeg emerged after the arrival of the Red River Expeditionary Force and was drawn exclusively from the ranks of the Militia, the civic authorities having no luck in finding civilian volunteers. Captain Villiers of the Quebec Rifles organized the first mounted police force which consisted of nineteen soldiers of the Militia. Begg and Nursey recorded that "almost every day [Villiers] could be seen drilling his recruits in front of the Davis House."[83] Villiers was succeeded by another volunteer from the Militia, Louis Fasse de Plainval, who even went to the lengths of travelling to Montreal to interview Police Force authorities there and learn practices that might work well in Winnipeg.[84] Likewise, Portage la Prairie, long a bastion of English settlement in Manitoba, was able to secure the services of Gardiner Greenlay, a soldier of the first expedition, to act as one of the first police officers of that community.[85] Additionally, in 1872, Captain Edward Armstrong, who came to Fort Garry as the Quarter Master of the 1st Ontario Rifles, and later served as the Quartermaster of the Provisional Battalion, was appointed as Sherriff of the Province of Manitoba, a post he held until 1876. Although Armstrong requested to stay on strength with the Battalion, the adjutant-general declined his request stating that "it would be contrary to all military rules for a civil officer to fill a military position in time of active service."[86]

While several civilian police officers in early Winnipeg originated in the Provisional Battalion that was by no means a guarantor of success. The Militiamen were not professional soldiers and they had only received a minimum amount of training. At the very least, the soldiers chosen for the Wolseley Expedition had the opportunity to conduct some preparatory drill and training in Toronto before departure, so that their level of experience was somewhat better than the average Militiamen who only trained twelve to sixteen days per year. Nonetheless, their professionalism was, in some circumstances, wanting.

Take for instance the unfortunate example of Constable Dupont, late of the Provisional Battalion, who had volunteered to join the embryonic city police Winnipeg. The police force being unarmed, he purchased a revolver from a local store for personal protection. One evening in December of 1873, the young man visited Fort Garry to chat with some of his old colleagues. He met up with Private Vogt and shared a short chat — later depositions revealed that witnesses thought Dupont had been drinking but nonetheless seemed relatively sober. Private Vogt asked if the police were still hiring, and Dupont responded that the police were always looking for new men. After this, Dupont pulled the revolver out and pointed it at Vogt asking him if he were afraid of bullets. When Vogt answered yes, Dupont pulled the trigger and shot him in the right temple, killing the unfortunate private immediately. Witnesses deposed that Dupont looked surprised at the report of the pistol. Later, Dupont admitted he had been firing the pistol earlier to practice and thought the chamber was empty, claiming that he was only joking. Curiously, the jury acquitted Dupont on a charge of murder, but found him guilty of common assault. His casual disregard, or ignorance of, basic weapons safety is indicative of his low state of training and professionalism.[87]

While the Militia may have contributed to the creation of the embryonic police force in Winnipeg, their effectiveness was somewhat wanting. The pandemonic scene remarked upon by Lieutenant Huyshe did not readily correct itself, and in some cases the police were found to be ineffectual. One editor of the *Manitoba Liberal* observed in July of 1871 that in the previous twenty-four hours, six fights had erupted on the streets of Winnipeg, a scene so commonplace that he thought "it would be a new thing for a day to pass over without somebody getting his head broken." He went on to lament the scarcity of police presence in Winnipeg stating that "policemen on the streets of Winnipeg are as scarce as asses' funerals" and wondered what service the $18,000 bill for a police force was providing.[88] Notwithstanding this particularly damning epistle of police incompetence, the creation of a force of law and order in the new province, albeit one in need of refinement and professionalization, was due in no small part to the presence of Militia volunteers.

Beyond its contributions to the establishment of local policing in early Winnipeg, the Militia garrison also made substantial contributions to the establishment of that quintessentially Canadian organization, the North-West Mounted Police (known since 1920 as the Royal Canadian Mounted Police). Upon the creation of the force in 1874, current and former members of the Militia in Manitoba, such as Major A.G. Irvine and Captain Herchmer, were to be found in its ranks.[89] Even the venerable seven-pounder mountain howitzers, carried from Toronto to Fort Garry with the first expedition, and hauled out in a cart to face the Fenian invaders in 1871, were transferred to the North-West Mounted Police for service in the Cypress Hills detachment in 1876.[90]

Moreover, as Lower Fort Garry was to be the initial home base of the embryonic North-West Mounted Police, the local Active Militia played a prominent role in setting the conditions for the successful creation of the force, even if it meant — ironically — the eventual disbandment of the Dominion Forces on Service in Manitoba. Mounted Police recruits were instructed to report to Osborne Smith who exercised temporary command of the force in the early days. In fact, in an 1896 history of the force written by Captain Ernest Chambers entitled *The Royal North-West Mounted Police. A Corps History*, Osborne Smith is listed as having the temporary assignment of Commissioner of the North-West Mounted Police effective October 16, 1873.[91] Curiously, however, the *Victoria Daily British Colonist* reported that the assignment was only temporary because Osborne Smith resigned. It reported that "Lieut.-Col [sic] French, of Kingston, will probably receive the appointment of Superintendent of the Mounted Police in the North-west, *vice* Osborne Smith, resigned." This indicates that at some point it was at least contemplated by the authorities to make Osborne Smith the inaugural head of the North-West Mounted Police.[92] Perhaps he was approached by the Dominion authorities to be the first Commissioner of the Mounted Police, but did not accept the appointment as he admits in a letter to a Mr. W.E. Parker, Esq., who wrote him concerning his son in the force, that he only accepted the office of Commissioner of Police on a temporary basis, there being some implication in the phrasing that a more permanent option was on the table.[93]

It must be said that as the temporary Commissioner, he demonstrated sound judgement in executing his duties, being careful not to overstep his interim authority. In December of 1873, the North-West Council, the political body exercising authority over the North-West Territory, contacted him to request the deployment of Mounted Police to address illegal liquor trafficking on Lake Winnipeg. Osborne Smith responded that his duties were "confined to [the Mounted Police's] organization, and not [it's] employment" and declined to dispatch the officers.[94]

Credit is due Osborne Smith for the work he did in establishing the force. A review of the *Commissioner's Office Letter Box* in Archives Canada which contains his correspondence as the interim Commissioner between October and December 1873 reflects the herculean efforts that Osborne Smith undertook to ensure the successful establishment of what would become Canada's national police force. His correspondence deals with all the mundane but necessary administrative and logistical requirements for the establishment of such an organization: contracting for horses, repairs, and upgrades to barracks at Lower Fort Garry, issuing uniforms and accoutrements, training of the force and the like. His work in this regard is doubly impressive when it is considered that much of it was done at a distance, as throughout this period Osborne Smith remained in his headquarters at Fort Garry where he still exercised his duty as the Officer Commanding Dominion Forces in Manitoba. From time to time, he visited the Stone Fort, but his duties in Military District No. 10 did not abate while acting as the Mountie's interim Commissioner. Any success enjoyed by Lieutenant-Colonel G.A. French, the first substantive Commissioner of the force, is due in no small way to the efforts of Osborne Smith to establish the Mounted Police on such firm footing. Osborne Smith's important role in the establishment of the force has been lamentably overlooked by historians.[95]

While early Manitoba was a rough and tumble environment crying out for order and governance, political violence and riots were not the only dangers faced by the early citizens. One of the other threats to the lives and property of the growing city was that of conflagration, a threat exacerbated by the frame construction that typified the buildings of the era. Beyond acting as a *de facto* police force, the Militia also provided a readily accessible workforce when fires broke out.

The parish of St. Boniface lay on the eastern bank of the Red River where a Roman Catholic mission had existed since the early nineteenth century. In 1871, the Metropolitan Archdiocese of Saint-Boniface was created under the guiding hand of Archbishop Alexandre-Antonin Taché. In March of 1873, a fire broke out in the bakery behind the archbishop's palace. Alerted to the emergency, the troops of the Provisional Battalion rushed to the area to assist in fighting the fire, but they were unsuccessful in saving the bakery, although they were able to keep the fire from spreading to adjacent buildings. The building burnt to the ground with an estimated loss of $1,500 in property and $500 in flour. The loss of the archbishop's bakery was particularly painful as the archbishop provided bread for two hundred underprivileged individuals each day.[96]

Only ten months later, in December of 1873, by cause of a defective stove pipe, a great fire broke out in the Manitoba provincial parliament buildings, described by Alexander Begg and Nursey as the first great fire in Winnipeg.[97] Begg and Nursey reported that the citizens of Winnipeg turned out to fight the flames *en masse*, but the first people to respond, no doubt due to their proximity and familiarity with late-night turn-outs, were soldiers of the Provisional Battalion at Fort Garry who raced to the scene, dragging a fire engine along with them. The soldiers took the lead in battling the blaze, the *Manitoban and North-West Herald* reported that "the soldier boys worked with a will, under the command of several of their officers, and while one party undertook the charge of guarding the furniture and goods piled on the streets, the balance manned the engine … While the greater portion of the people worked with a will, there were many idlers who looked on and did nothing, and at one time when the soldiers were tired out with working at the engine there was some difficulty in procuring men to take their place."[98] There was a fear the fire would spread to the nearby stores of A.G.B. Bannatyne, but the efforts of the soldiers and citizens ensured that the fire was contained.

In mid-January 1874, another fire broke out, this time in Fort Garry. Once again the Militia were on the front line in fighting the conflagration, although curt orders from Osborne Smith, including an order to incarcerate a civilian he presumed was usurping his authority, contributed to some ill will between the citizens and the military.[99] Osborne Smith ordered that only military personnel would fight the fire when it was observed that several of the civilians, presumably with a grudge against the Hudson's Bay Company who still used the fort for storage and business, were actively erecting obstacles to impair the efforts of those trying to fight the fire.[100] The fire was contained to the bakery alone, although at times it threatened to spread to the Hudson's Bay Company stores in the fort and, far more alarmingly, to the twenty tons of gunpowder that were stored therein.[101] The Militiamen's efforts earned them effusive praise from J.H. McTavish, Factor of the Hudson's Bay Post in Fort Garry who wrote to Osborne Smith and stated "I estimate to the fullest extent the fact that owing solely to your own cool judgement, and the noble manner in which you were assisted throughout by your officers and men … we are indebted today for the existence of Fort Garry."[102]

No doubt these events gave rise to the demand for a fire brigade in Winnipeg, although one wasn't incorporated until September 1874 and even then, it did not receive its equipment until November of that year.[103] Unsurprisingly, when the roll of the first members of the fire brigade is examined, one can note several familiar names of Militia officers amongst the original members, including William Nassau Kennedy and Stewart Mulvey. Even when the fire brigade was finally in service, Osborne Smith communicated to the mayor that the troops at Fort Garry would always be available to assist during a fire.[104]

The spectrum of these tasks went beyond these rather traditional provisions of aid to the civil power and the Militia also found itself assisting local civic authorities during health crises. The first such occurrence came about very shortly after the establishment of the Provisional Battalion in 1870. Smallpox ravaged the Indigenous populace west of Manitoba particularly in the areas of Forts Pitt, Carleton, and Edmonton.[105] The ravages of the smallpox were fierce, and its impact on the local Indigenous population was calamitous. Its effects were recorded by Father Albert Lacombe, at the time a Roman Catholic missionary to the Plains Cree, in a letter he wrote to Archbishop Taché:

> the patient is at first very feverish. The skin becomes red, and covered with pimples, these blotches in a few days form scabs filled with infectious matter. Then the flesh begins to decompose and falls off in fragments. Inflammation of the throat impedes all passage for meat or drink. While enduring the torments of this cruel agony, the sufferer ceases to breathe — alone in a poor shed, with no other assistance than what I can afford. The hideous corpse must be burned, a grave must be dug and the body carried to the burial ground. All this devolves upon me and I am alone with Indians disheartened and terrified to such a degree that they hardly dare approach even their own relatives.[106]

In the face of grave reports such as this, the Lieutenant-Governor of Manitoba, Adams Archibald, dispatched to the region of the outbreak Lieutenant William F. Butler, a British army officer in Fort Garry, to report on the situation. His observations were shocking. In his report to Archibald, he painted a bleak picture of the situation that echoed the distressing news shared by Father Lacombe. He wrote that "it is difficult to imagine a state of pestilence more terrible than that which kept pace with these moving parties of Cree during the summer months of 1870. By streams and lakes, in willow copses, and upon bare hillsides, often shelterless from the fierce rays of the summer sun, and exposed to the rains and dews of night, the poor plague-stricken wretches lay down to die."[107]

Obviously, something had to be done. In response, the relatively new civic authorities in Manitoba established a board of health chaired by Lieutenant-Governor Archibald with the stated goals of providing some assistance to the suffering indigenous community and ensuring the epidemic did not spread into the province. The composition of the board included the Lord Bishop of Rupert's Land Robert Machray, Archbishop Taché, Reverend Geoff Young, Reverend John Black, Alfred Boyd, Marc Amable Girard, and the Commanding Officers of the two Militia battalions: Major Wainwright of the 1st Ontario Rifles, and Lieutenant-Colonel Cassault of the 2nd Quebec Rifles, as well as Dr. Schultz, Dr. O'Donnell, and Dr. Beddome.[108] The inclusion of representatives of the Militia indicates that the civic authorities thought some use, perhaps in quarantine, of the Militia may have been required. In mid-October 1870, the Board proposed to send a doctor to the west to pre-empt further spread of the disease, and the surgeon of the Ontario Rifles, Captain A.R. MacDonald, volunteered his services for just such a task. Initially, Captain MacDonald's offer of service was rebuffed by Lieutenant-Colonel Cassault, acting at the time in the capacity of the senior officer of the Active Militia in Fort Garry. Cassault based his decision on the concern that Captain MacDonald's departure might negatively affect the general health of the battalion.[109] MacDonald, a medical practitioner with substantial experience with smallpox, was the Board's first choice — not only had he volunteered his services to the province, but he was the only possible medical practitioner who the authorities could afford. Archibald wrote to the Secretary of State for the provinces, Joseph Howe, to inform him that after Cassault had turned down the request to second Captain MacDonald to the Board of Health, the search for another doctor to head to Saskatchewan was unsuccessful "except under terms that were perfectly exorbitant."[110] In response, Howe informed Archibald that he would enlist the assistance of no less than the Governor General to speak to the Minister of Militia and ensure the availability of Captain MacDonald. Even the Secretary of State for the Colonies in the United Kingdom, the Earl of Kimberley, was briefed on the situation with Captain MacDonald. Unsurprisingly, two weeks later, Cassault's order was rescinded, and Captain MacDonald was granted authority to proceed westward to Fort Edmonton to assist with the outbreak.[111]

In 1870, the despatch of Captain MacDonald to Fort Edmonton amounted to the whole of the Manitoba Militia's support to the civil authorities to combat the smallpox epidemic, but such was not the case six years later. In the late fall of 1876, another outbreak of small pox occurred in the Icelandic settlements of the Interlake region that devastated the colony: of a population of 1,441 people, 189 of the Icelandic settlers perished, the majority amongst the youth of the colony — 136 of the deceased were under twelve years of age.[112] Dr. W.A. Baldwin, who was one of four doctors sent to deal with the issue, recorded the tragedy he witnessed as follows "when I went to some of the houses I would find perhaps some six or eight sick, some that had only a few hours to live. You would see old men and women, young men and girls, and poor little infants that would make the hardest heart ache for them, and to see them in their mother's arms, and perhaps the next time I came round, their little bodies would be put outside till they had time to make a rough box to bury them in."[113]

The outbreak was identified in November 1876, and when it was realized that the situation was much worse than originally appreciated, the Dominion Government created a "Council of Keewatin" to address the issue which included Osborne Smith, Dr. Jacques, Dr. Codd (the battalion surgeon), Gilbert McMicken, J.A.N. Provencher, and William Hespeler.[114] In late November, Osborne Smith received the requisition from the local authorities to provide a quarantine force in an attempt to contain the spread of the epidemic. In early December, he left to conduct a reconnaissance of the area and determine the size of the force required to accomplish his mission, which was to cut off all communication between southern Manitoba and Gimli. He returned after a day's reconnoitring and the first detachment under Ensign Street was dispatched the very next day.[115] This task eventually required the deployment of 20 percent of the garrison to the Interlake region to enforce, leaving the remaining forces in Winnipeg stretched thin.[116] Certainly the quarantine task must have been equally monotonous to the daily routine in garrison, as Osborne Smith highlighted that their "duties mainly consist of patrolling and watching certain roads, and these they perform unremittingly, with an inadequate force, through days and nights, in which the thermometer has ranged down to 35 [degrees Celsius] below zero."[117] Seven months after deploying to the quarantine line, the force redeployed to Fort Garry by steamer. The *Free Press* was lavish in its praise of the great work done by the military quarantine force and took a moment to inform its readership of the privations the soldiers had endured. It recounted that "their duties were often exceedingly onerous, and they received no extra pay though performing civil functions. While detaining persons who had to be disinfected, they had occasionally to divide their rations with their involuntary prisoners."[118]

The duty may have been onerous, but it wasn't particularly dangerous, except in the case of Private Morris. The unfortunate soldier had gone on a chicken-shooting expedition, and upon returning to his temporary barracks, he laid his still-loaded firearm across a table while endeavouring to remove his snowshoes. A young lad ran by and knocked the rifle to the floor where it discharged, sending the bullet through Private Morris' wrist and into his leg. This unfortunate example notwithstanding, the beleaguered quarantine force returned safely to Winnipeg.[119] As unique as the quarantine task may have been, the gold standard for unique, if not comic, aid to the civil power must be the Rat Portage War of 1883.

The Rat Portage War

The political leaders of Manitoba in the 1880s can be excused their presumption that the land laying to the east between them and what would eventually become the city of Thunder Bay would eventually become part of the province. After all, the administration of the North-West Territory had initially been placed under the authority of the Lieutenant-Governor of Manitoba, when the territory of Rupert's Land was admitted to Confederation. Even when in 1876 the resultant North-West Territory was divided up to create the District of Keewatin, the area which is now known as North-Western Ontario, the act stipulated that "the Lieutenant Governor of the Province of Manitoba, or the person acting as such, shall ex-officio be Lieutenant Governor of the said District of Keewatin."[120] Despite the political authority for these tracts of land being centred in Winnipeg, Ontario's politicians in Toronto were casting covetous glances north-west.

Ontario's political leaders argued that former treaties, going as far back as the Treaty of Paris 1763, dictated the territory of the District of Keewatin should be part of the Province of Ontario. What followed was a series of contending claims between Manitoba and Ontario that were exacerbated by undulating federal government administrations switching between a

Manitoba-friendly Conservative Sir John A. Macdonald, followed by an Ontario-friendly Liberal Prime Minister Alexander Mackenzie, and then back to Macdonald. When Macdonald returned to power, his government passed *An Act to Provide for the Extension of the Boundaries of the Province of Manitoba,* which directed that Manitoba's eastern boundary be defined as "a line drawn due north from where the westerly boundary of the Province of Ontario intersects the boundary dividing Canada from the United States." This was ambiguous enough to allow the government of Manitoba to believe her eastern boundary lay near Thundery Bay, while Ontario, who considered its western boundary to lie near Lake of the Woods, believed the District of Keewatin fell under its authority. A farcical series of events, which eventually included the deployment of the Militia, thereafter ensued.

Manitoba began to appoint civic authorities in Rat Portage, now named Kenora, in the summer of 1881. It eventually repealed a prohibition on intoxicating liquors that had been in force in the district, although it is important to note that a federal statute still prohibited the sale of intoxicants at or near any federal public work.[121] Anyone who has visited Kenora will attest to the fact that federal public works, of which the railroad was one, occupy a conspicuous portion of the city. A Manitoba Constable, Patrick O'Keefe, seized four barrels of illicit liquor and brought them to his quarters for safe keeping. His rooms fell within the jurisdiction of a federal public work, and he was therefore arrested by a member of the Dominion Police for possessing liquor in a proscribed area. O'Keefe was paraded before a Dominion magistrate and fined. Upon paying his fine, he waited patiently for the magistrate to leave the bench, and promptly placed the magistrate under arrest for being in possession of the confiscated liquor without a (Manitoba) provincial permit! The Dominion magistrate was thereafter brought before a Manitoba provincial magistrate and fined $100.

Although O'Keefe was relieved of his duties for his actions, this did not salve the fury in the Ontario Legislature. Ontario Premier Oliver Mowat's words in response resemble a *cri-de-coeur* worthy of a war time leader. He fumed "It is absolutely necessary that we should go and take possession [of the district], that we should assume the duty of enforcing the laws there ... if the people of Ontario have been asleep, I venture to say that they are aroused now and that they will be asleep no more."[122]

Despite the thunderous rhetoric from Queen's Park, Manitoba's resolve did not waver. In July 1882, Rat Portage was incorporated as a municipality under the laws of the Province of Manitoba. Notwithstanding Premier Mowat's strong words, Ontario did not actively attempt to pre-empt the exercise of Manitoba authority in Keewatin until, that is, the summer of 1883 when Manitoba announced it would be calling a by-election in the area for a seat in the Manitoba Legislature. Two days later, the Government of Ontario announced that it was placing six Ontario constables in Rat Portage and by mid-July began issuing business licences in the town. Shortly thereafter, the Ontario constables proceeded to arrest anyone operating a business under a Manitoba licence, and the Manitoba constables began to do the same to businesses operating under Ontario licences. Prisoners arrested by Manitobans were broken out of prison by pro-Ontario inhabitants and vice versa; Rat Portage was incorporated by the Province of Ontario; and like Manitoba, Ontario announced a by-election for the Ontario Legislature.

The entire affair took on an air of absolute ridiculousness, and things seemed to be on the verge of violence as the two competing provincial elections approached. It was at this juncture that the military became involved. In September of 1883, in response to a requisition from the Manitoba-recognized Mayor and Manitoba-recognized Magistrate of Rat Portage, Houghton dispatched a force of two officers and forty men of the Winnipeg Field Battery to Rat Portage during the local elections.[123] In response to this unique provision of an Aid of Civil Power, the Ontario Premier thundered that "acts such as these would, as between independent states, have been a declaration of war!"[124] After a final fracas of Manitoba constables arresting Ontario constables — only to be arrested themselves by other Ontario constables — the two Premiers realized things had come to a head, and in a heretofore unknown sense of cooperation, both agreed to suspend the competing municipal and provincial elections and allow a municipal board to guide Rat Portage as the federal government referred the boundary question to the Queen's Privy Council. To the chagrin of political authorities in Winnipeg, and to a degree in Ottawa as well, in August of 1884 the Queen's Privy Council concluded that the boundary of Ontario did indeed lie where it currently sits.

When Manitoba was admitted to Confederation, it was still a rough and tumble place with very little in the way of civic resources to ensure law and order and protect the population from fire and disease. Moreover, the perceived ever-present threat of American expansionism, Fenian incursions and indigenous uprising contributed to an unease amongst both newly arrived and potential settlers, although in hindsight none of these were really viable threats. To evolve into modern Manitoba a degree of security from external and internal threats was required. It was amongst the ranks of the Militia garrison that this security was found. They provided a deterrent to American expansion, even if only an expressive one, a resource to instil peace, order, and good government in the face of riots and violence, and a pool of manpower for embryonic police and fire fighting services. These were all tangible representations of Dominion and Provincial authority that helped to set the conditions for the growth of Manitoba. In addition to these very real tasks, the Militia provided a symbolic representation of Dominion and Imperial authority that linked the new province with the Canadian nation and the British Empire.

4

SYMBOLISM: THE INTANGIBLE MADE MANIFEST

The symbols of the state surround us constantly. National and provincial flags, licence plates, even government infrastructure such as buildings, bridges, roads, and parks are all physical representations of the state. From the purely symbolic, to the everyday practical, these symbols serve to make manifest the intangible presence of the nation. They serve, whether intended to do so or not, to bind and unite the population. As political theorist Michael Walzer, observed in *Political Science Quarterly*, "the state is invisible; it must be personified before it can be seen, symbolized before it can be loved."[1]

Military forces played a key role in establishing a binding national symbolism. Take for example the observation provided by Lieutenant-Colonel Henry Charles Fletcher of the Scots Fusilier Guards. A British officer, he came to Canada with his regiment in 1861 in response to increasing tensions between Britain the United States during the Civil War as a result of the *Trent* incident, when the United States Navy seized two British diplomats from a Confederate vessel in 1861. He became a well-known writer and military theorist, even penning a report on the power of the American armies for the General Officer Commanding British forces in North America. His report was subsequently shared with the Duke of Cambridge, the British Commander in Chief, at Horse Guards in London. He returned to Britain, but he would once more move to Canada a decade later as the private secretary to the Governor

General Lord Dufferin where he produced a report on professional military education based on a visit to the US Military Academy at West Point which was well received in both Ottawa and London. An astute officer with a great deal of experience, he produced *A Memorandum on the Militia System in Canada* in 1872 wherein he argued that a nation's military force has a number of important tasks, namely to defend the country, maintain the power of law and, although of lesser importance, "to be a symbol of the state which pertains to all nations aspiring to rank as such among their compeers."[2] To Fletcher's well-travelled mind, the military was not only a manifestation of state authority, but also symbolic of the nation's status internationally.

This culturally binding process is particularly important in culturally diverse nations such as the early Dominion of Canada. In 1867, the embryonic nation was cobbled together from relatively disparate regions of Ontario, Quebec, New Brunswick, and Nova Scotia and its initial success can, in many ways, be attributed to the already established overarching cultural tie of membership in the British Empire, although admittedly that was still problematic, particularly in Quebec. Moreover, there were only limited ties to an overarching Canadian Dominion. The years immediately following Confederation are replete with tensions and acrimony in almost all the original four provinces concerning the wisdom of remaining in the federation.

The situation was exacerbated in Manitoba, where the new province's population was substantially more diverse and removed from the cultural commonality of its older, more established provinces in the east. Manitoba did not grow into the Canadian Confederation as much as it was purchased and thereafter admitted. Consequently, the bond between the population and the nation was tenuous at best, save for the vociferous and belligerent minority of the population that were vehement pro-Canada agents, more on them in Chapter 7. The symbolic role played by the Militia garrison in early Manitoba in helping to establish in the new Province of Manitoba that linkage with the Dominion and the Empire has been largely ignored. This chapter will demonstrate how the Militia in Manitoba was a crucial symbolic tool to establish this cognitive linkage.

TRAPPINGS OF EMPIRE AND DOMINION

The symbolism inherent in the British Monarchy underwent significant change in the latter half of the nineteenth century. It was during this timeframe that the United Kingdom, bolstered by colonial acquisitions around the world adopted its imperial persona — a global British cultural network characterized by British justice, political processes, and societal norms. Atop this hierarchical and self-professed benevolent imperium sat Queen Victoria who, over time, assumed a symbolic aura of semi-divinity.[3]

This symbolism pervaded public ceremonies in both Great Britain and Canada during events such as the opening of parliaments and legislatures, the sovereign's birthday, and Dominion Day, the forerunner of the modern Canada Day celebration. By the closing decades of the nineteenth century, all such public manifestations carried with them the regalia, pomp, and circumstance of the British Empire and the role Canada played within that empire.[4] This symbolism wasn't just hyper-patriotism, it was employed to smooth out regional differences and create a unified ideology. The Canadian Militia contributed mightily to this — every military honour guard, gun salute, parade, or procession became a patriotic pageant meant to establish order in a diverse environment through an overt, unifying expression of public ritual.[5]

The militia provided a direct link to the British Empire. As detailed in Chapter 2, the commander-in-chief of the Canadian Militia in 1870 was the Governor General, the sovereign's representative in Canada. The importance of this linkage must be noted. Although in the Westminster constitutional model, then and now, Parliament is the true authority that issues orders to the military and, most importantly, pays the bills, the symbolic linkage to the sovereign provides an overarching unity of purpose. The military represents the crown, not the political party of the day. All the embedded symbols of the nineteenth century militia, from the red serge uniforms to the regimental standards they bore, served to reinforce this symbolic linkage.

An excellent example is found in the presentation of regimental colours to the Provisional Battalion. In the fall of 1874, the Provisional Battalion was granted a stand of Regimental Colours, purchased by the Sherriff of Manitoba, Edward Armstrong, himself a veteran of the 1870 Red River Expedition, and presented to the battalion by the lieutenant-governor. The stand of colours consisted of two flags, the Queen's Colour, which was the Union Flag, also known as the Union Jack, and the Regimental Colour, which was made of white silk, with the red cross of St. George dividing the flag into four squares, with small Union Jack in the upper corner.[6]

The importance of these two flags, from a symbolic perspective, cannot be overstated. In the definitive work on customs and traditions of the Canadian Armed Forces E.C. Russel, an historian with the Directorate of History and Heritage, explained that the Queen's Colour symbolizes the unit's loyalty to the Crown. Authorization to carry a Queen's Colour can only be granted by the reigning sovereign and may only be presented by the sovereign or her representative.[7] Likewise, the Regimental Colours are "probably the most cherished possession of a fighting force. This is because it embodies a whole spectrum of ideas, beliefs, and emotions which together may be characterized as the 'spirit of the regiment.' The regimental colour symbolizes in a very visible way the pride a man feels in serving in a unit whose reason for being is one of worth, the proud heritage of those of the regiment who have gone before, and the record of achievement of the regiment."[8] The granting of these colours thus symbolically linked the Provisional Battalion with the Queen, and Imperial and Dominion authority.

What is more important for our present study is how this stand of colours was presented to the regiment. The presentation occurred in a ceremony replete with symbolic linkages to the British Empire and references to the travails of the Wolseley Expedition. First, the colours were consecrated by the Anglican Bishop of Rupert's Land, Robert Machray, and afterwards, the wife of Lieutenant-Governor Morris, along with other ladies from the civic leadership of the province, produced a congratulatory address for the occasion which was read to the Battalion by Mr. Justice Louis Betourney of the Court of Queen's Bench of Manitoba.[9] The symbolic linkage of the presentation of the regimental colours — the first to be bestowed in Western Canada — was reinforced by the hyper-patriotic address of Mrs. Morris and her colleagues. In a rhetorical flourish of pan-Britannic synergy, the address invoked the memory of the Militia volunteers from Eastern Canada of the Wolseley Expedition, linking them to their British forebears. Justice Betourney stated, on behalf of Mrs. Morris et al, that "although these sister provinces are so far apart from each other the gallant sons of Canada … have the same spirit of hardihood, courage and chivalry that throbbed in the breasts of their forefathers in their island homes across the ocean — the same spirit and daring that won the fields of Agincourt, Waterloo, the Alma, and Queenston Heights … your marches through the wilderness, and your services for the past four years assures us that the ancient fire of British chivalry has not been quenched and that a Briton once is a Briton still."[10] The message was clear: the soldiers had inherited the imperial grandeur of their British confreres and were as British and the British themselves. That they were being honoured by the societal and political leaders of early Manitoba reflected the latter's endorsement and acceptance of their place in the global British network. A week later the *Free Press* reported that "The infantry marched out Monday afternoon and created an imposing spectacle as they paraded Garry Street, with the colors flying, the capital band of the battalion in advance, and the men in heavy marching order."[11]

Interestingly, these regimental colours have a checkered history. When the Provisional Battalion was disbanded in 1877, the colours were retired as well and were meant to be kept in government storage until such time as a regiment of Active Militia could be formed in Manitoba who could adopt the colours. Shortly thereafter, Osborne Smith wrote to the adjutant-general complaining that Indian Agent Allan MacDonald, had "surreptitiously" removed the colours and placed them in his office at the Indian Agency. MacDonald had come west with the first Red River Expedition as one of the Captains in the Ontario Rifles, and remained in Manitoba, later taking a position as an Indian Agent in the Department of the Interior. Osborne Smith petitioned the Adjutant-General to secure the intercession of the Minister of Militia and Defence with the Minister of the Department of the Interior in order to effect the return of the colours, a request that was denied, the minister stating he did not want to get involved.[12] Cooler heads must have prevailed, because the colours were eventually returned and found their way to storage in Holy Trinity Church.[13] Recent correspondence with the staff at Holy Trinity Church revealed that, sadly, the colours cannot be found in the church and no record exists as to where they may have been transferred.[14]

Once the North-West entered Confederation, it became crucial that Dominion authority be established throughout the region, indeed, doing so was a strategic priority. The importance ascribed to ensuring that Dominion authority was felt throughout the region can be gleaned from the praise received by Lieutenant-Governor Morris, the *ex officio* governor of the North-West, from the Minister of the Interior, for accomplishing just that. Writing in his annual report in 1880, the minister observed that the exertions of Morris and his team during treaty negotiations in the North-West "aided the Government not a little in the good work of laying the foundations of law and order, in the North-West, in securing the good will of the Indian tribes, *and in establishing the prestige of the Dominion Government throughout that vast country* [emphasis added]." [15]

To emphasize the authority of the Dominion in the new province, the Militia lent gravitas to the latterly constituted political authority in Manitoba. While parliaments and legislatures in the British Empire during the late Victorian period were replete with iconic imperial symbolism, the embryonic provincial legislature in Manitoba was, in a word, rustic. The hyper-patriotic trappings that normally festooned these houses of imperial democracy were sorely wanting in Red River. Dr. John O'Donnell, who had moved to Red River from Ontario prior to 1869, and who would later become a member of Manitoba's short-lived upper house, the Legislative Council, recorded his observations of the new provincial legislature in 1870 as follows:

> when the first legislature met, it could not reasonably be expected that the same dignity and decorum, the same acquaintance with parliamentary methods or the same breadth of statesmanship would be manifested as in older lands. The appearance of the early House was peculiar and characteristic of a transition stage. I recall seeing in the old legislative chamber men clothed in the faultless Prince Albert black beside men in a curious compound of the old and the new, having the long hair of raven hue, wearing the moccasins to which they had always been accustomed and which certainly had the advantage of silence over creaky boots; coats open, displaying the colored flannel shirt without a collar, and across the waist, picturesquely slashed, the French belt or sash commonly worn on the prairies. [16]

It was to this example of frontier informality with traces of mature formality that the Militia was able to add a tinge of imperial symbolism, formality, and gravitas. During events of political and cultural significance, the soldiers of the Provisional Battalion or the Active Militia could be counted on to be present and lend an overt symbolic representation of Dominion and Imperial authority through the provision of guards of honour or gun salutes.

First, a word on what constitutes a guard of honour or a gun salute, and why they are symbolically important. Guards of honour are a military tradition, still very much in existence in modern armies, in which a military force is paraded before someone, normally a political, social, or cultural leader, in order to "honour" him or her. The force is normally attired in its most formal uniform and armed. The process is simple, contemporarily described in the *Regulations and Orders for the Active Militia* issued in 1870 as follows: "whenever called out for duty as a Guard of Honour, &c., the Militia are to receive His Excellency the Governor General with a general salute, Standards and Colours flying, Officers saluting, and Bands playing 'first part of a slow march.'" The *Regulations* also stipulated that similar guards of honour would be furnished to lieutenant-governors of provinces on the opening and closing of legislatures. The size of the guard of honor was directed to be one hundred rank and file, with a captain in command supported by two subalterns — junior officers such as lieutenants or second-lieutenants — with one carrying the regimental colours. Where possible, the Militia department dictated that the guards were to be augmented with a band.[17]

Artillery gun salutes were perhaps the most ostentatious of the symbolic uses of the Militia. The custom of discharging canon to honour a dignitary is an old one indeed. It originated at sea during the age of sail when muzzle-loaded canons were kept loaded for action — discharging the guns in salute and thus necessitating time-intensive and laborious reloading, was both a symbol of peaceful intent and an honorific. During the time it would take to reload, the ship was defenceless, thus symbolizing friendly intent. As time progressed, the use of canon to pay homage to distinguished persons become more formal.[18] In late nineteenth century Manitoba, they were used to reinforce the importance of a variety of events connected with the cultural transformation of Manitoba, from the visit of foreign and domestic dignitaries to the arrival of the first locomotive in Manitoba.

Artillery being a scientific and prohibitively expensive arm, the pomp of the uniformed gunners and the unmistakably conspicuous report of the gun when fired lent federal if not imperial gravitas to any situation.[19] Instructions for the provision of gun salutes were contained in *Regulations and Orders for the Active Militia, The Schools of Military Instruction, and the Reserve Militia* issued in 1870. Royal salutes consisted of the traditional twenty-one guns (the term refers to the number of rounds to be fired, not the number of actual guns) and were offered for the sovereign or any member of the royal family in the Dominion, as well as on the sovereign's birthday and Dominion Day. During the opening of Parliament in Ottawa, the Governor General was entitled to a salute of seventeen guns, and likewise the lieutenant-governors of the provinces were entitled to a salute of fifteen guns when provincial legislatures opened.[20]

This is not to say that the symbolic value of artillery was restricted to the forces of the Dominion or the Empire. Louis Riel, during his tenure as president of the Provisional Government of Assiniboia during the Red River Resistance, understood the symbolic value of the use of the canons of the Hudson's Bay Company when he installed his headquarters in Fort Garry during the 1869–70 Red River Resistance. Riel caused a salute of eighteen guns to be fired on Christmas Eve 1869, "thus ushering in Christmas in true military style." Likewise, he directed another salute of twenty-one guns to be fired June 17, 1870 upon the arrival of Archbishop Alexandre-Antonin Taché from his participation in the *Manitoba Act* negotiations in Ottawa, "announcing as it were, the success of his mission to Canada."[21] Later, the Hudson's Bay Company, having in its possession several field pieces, shook the inhabitants of Winnipeg awake on the morning of May 24, 1876, with an early morning gun salute fired in honour of the fifty-seventh birthday of Queen Victoria.[22]

The use of the Militia as symbolic representations of Imperial and Dominion authority in Manitoba began only a short time after Manitoba joined Confederation, in fact, before a legislature was even available for opening. On September 3, 1870, the new Lieutenant-Governor of Manitoba, Alexander Morris, only recently arrived in the province, held a levée at Hudson's Bay House in Fort Garry to meet with and speak to the local citizenry. After the levée, the lieutenant-governor conducted a review of a Guard of Honour furnished by the 1st Ontario Rifles who had assembled for inspection within the fort.[23] A short while later, at the opening of the very first legislative session in Manitoba, one hundred soldiers of the Ontario Rifles formed a guard of honor in front of A.G.B. Bannatyne's residence — the "best and most commodious building in Winnipeg"[24] — which was serving, in this instance, as the inaugural Legislative Building of the Province of Manitoba. Interestingly, waiting alongside the soldiers were two Canadian Militia veterans of the Red River Expedition who were the two newest officers of the legislature: Captain Villiers as the Gentleman Usher of the Blackrod, and Sergeant Louis Nathal De Plainval the Assembly's Sergeant-At-Arms. According to Begg and Nursey, the two veterans of the 2nd Quebec Rifles "shone in all the resplendence of their court uniforms."[25] If there were any doubt amongst the population that

Dominion authority had arrived in Fort Garry, it was quickly erased.

This scene was repeated often. In 1873, two guards of honor were employed to lend regal authority to the opening of the Legislature. First, in February 1873, the Legislature was opened with a guard of honor commanded by Captain Fletcher, while a battery of artillery under the command of Major Taschereau fired a fifteen-round salute. [26] Later that year, in November, the fourth session of the parliament was opened with the lieutenant-governor attending in person with a guard of honor furnished by the Provisional Battalion under the command of Captain Herchmer, Lieutenant Constantine, and Ensign Taliferro, lending pomp and circumstance to the proceedings.[27] Guards of honor were equally employed for the prorogation of the house as well, and in February 1876, Captain Herchmer of the Provisional Battalion marched a detachment of infantry from Fort Osborne to the Court House and presented-arms as the lieutenant-governor entered the building to assent to bills and prorogue the parliament. On this instance, the guard of honor was only one aspect of the patriotic trappings that lent regal authority to these proceedings, and in addition to the soldiers in their uniforms the *Free Press* reported that "the Court House was profusely decorated with flags, and drapery."[28]

Such displays were not reserved for the opening and closing of democratic institutions alone, even the arrival of a representative of the sovereign was cause for symbolic celebration. In 1876, when Lieutenant-Governor Morris returned from a trip to the east, the Dominion Artillery in garrison at Fort Garry deployed to the pier on the Red River and fired a fifteen-gun salute to herald his arrival by steamboat.[29] When the Governor-General, the Marquis of Lorne, visited Winnipeg in 1881 an even grander show was prepared. Upon his departure from the city, His Excellency was escorted from Silver Heights to the Point Douglas railway station by the Winnipeg Troop of Cavalry, where he was met by a guard of honor furnished by the St. Boniface Infantry Company, and the Winnipeg Field Battery fired a seventeen-gun salute.[30]

Foreign dignitaries were also recipients of these honors. General William Tecumseh Sherman, famed Union Army Commander of the US Civil War, paid a visit to Winnipeg on July 6, 1880, during a western inspection tour of US Army posts as Commanding General of the United States Army. Sherman received the compliment of a gun salute fired by the Winnipeg Field Battery and a guard of honor furnished by the Winnipeg Infantry Company.[31] Perhaps the most unique gun salute on record, however, must be that which was fired for the arrival of the first locomotive in Manitoba aboard the steamer *Selkirk* in October 1877. The *Manitoba Free Press* reported that when the steamer, with its precious cargo aboard, sailed past Fort Pembina it was saluted by the guns of the artillery.[32] Likewise, on July 1, 1886, when the first transcontinental train arrived in Winnipeg from Montreal, a salute was fired by the Winnipeg Field Battery and a *feu de joie* — the orderly discharge of small arms into the air by a battalion — was fired by the soldiers of the 90th Battalion. [33]

Splendid as they were, these salutes could be dangerous as well. The unfortunate Gunner Coleman of the Dominion Artillery was quite seriously burned during a royal salute on the sovereign's birthday in May 1874. Initially, his gun failed to fire, and when the crew was attempting to unload the barrel, the charge finally ignited. The unexpected flash caused a jet of flame to emanate from the vent hole, which was the hole at the top of the cannon barrel lead into the chamber of the cannon where the main propelling charge was held. The vent hole was filled with powder and when flame was applied to it, the powder ignited and flash travelled down the channel to the main propelling charge in the chamber, which would then ignite and discharge the projectile. The unexpected flash from the vent hole burned Gunner Coleman. The ramming pole, a pole with a bulbous end used to tap down the charge prior to loading the barrel with the projectile, was in the barrel at the time and the subsequent discharge of the gun launched it a good quarter mile distant. The quick wits at the *Manitoba Free Press*, despite the seriousness of the incident, remarked that when the burst occurred "a ramrod was observable to a quick eye, making excellent time in the direction of Little [Stony] Mountain." Fortunately, the soldier who was responsible for manning the ramming pole, who would normally have been standing directly in front of the barrel, had stepped clear just prior to the burst of the charge.[34] Additionally, only four months previous, one of Coleman's colleagues, Gunner Bight, suffered a fall when the carriage of his gun struck him while he and the remainder of the detachment were moving the gun to the firing point for a salute to mark the opening of the legislature. The unfortunate gunner was injured and suffered, what a local practitioner described to the board of inquiry as a cringe-inducing case of a "scrotal hernia" which laid the poor man up and for which he submitted a claim for compensation owing to his inability to work.[35]

A moment should be spared here to deal specifically with the arrival of proper uniforms for the Winnipeg Field Battery to coincide with the 1877 visit of the Governor General, Lord Dufferin. The Minister of Militia thought his visit was sufficient justification to complete the outfitting of the Winnipeg Field Battery with a full complement of tunics and trousers in order to present "a creditable turn-out to Lord Dufferin's visit."[36] It is important to note that for years previous, the calls to the Dominion government to redress the lamentable state of dress and equipment of the battery went unheeded — throughout all this time, however, the battery was still an operational unit. Like other Militia bodies, it was part of a security force to defend Manitoba, and Canada, from all manner of threats, both internal and external. The fact that it was only on the arrival of the Governor General that the powers that be at the Ministry of the Militia and Defence decided to deliver proper uniforms to the battery members indicates that perhaps the primary, although not exclusive, role of the battery may well have been symbolic, rather than operational. This is not unique — even today many countries have military organizations whose functions are exclusively symbolic in nature. Take, for example, the Canadian Armed Forces' Ceremonial Guard whose role is to "plan, prepare, and execute Public Duties in the Nation's Capital during the summer."[37] Perhaps more in line with the ceremonial duties of the Winnipeg Field Battery in the 1870s are the current duties of King's Troop, Royal Horse Artillery of the British Army whose duties include "the firing of Royal Salutes in Hyde Park and Green Park on Royal Anniversaries and State Occasions, providing a gun carriage and team of black horses for State and Military funerals and performing the world famous musical drive around the country."[38]

Taking the time to celebrate the anniversary of Confederation was another manner in which the connection between Manitoba and the Dominion was established. Once Manitoba entered Confederation, Dominion Day celebrations became important events in the annual calendar and the Militia, as an overt symbolic representation of federal authority, naturally played an important role in marking the birth of the country. Parades, gun salutes, and sporting events all found a place in these celebrations. On the tenth anniversary of Confederation, a larger-than-usual military celebration of Dominion Day took place in the young city in full view, and appreciation of, the public. The Winnipeg Field Battery paraded early in the morning, resplendent in their recently arrived uniforms and proudly displaying two fully kitted-out gun detachments, complete with harness and limber. The gunners were joined by the Winnipeg Infantry Company who put in three hours of drill practice and proceeded to the prairie beyond St. Mary's Church to conduct manoeuvres. At noon, the infantry and artillery joined up outside the Canada Pacific Hotel where the battery fired a royal salute of twenty-one guns, the infantry presented arms and the band played "God Save the Queen."[39] Additionally, as part of its summer practice in 1883, the Winnipeg Field Battery fired a gun salute on the 2nd of July in front of the penitentiary at Stony Mountain.[40]

SYMBOLS OF AUTHORITY AND THE INDIGENOUS TREATIES

A key step in achieving the goal to "occupy, possess and mold" the North-West was the conclusion of treaties with the indigenous peoples of the region to facilitate its settlement.[41] Dominion policy in the 1870s towards this end was one of negotiation with First Nations, and the creation of Indigenous reserves in order to free up lands for European settlement and cultivation.[42] Certainly, there had been negotiations, settlements, and treaties established between Imperial or Dominion authorities and indigenous peoples previously, but the negotiations in the North-West differed from those which took place in Central and Eastern Canada. As George F.G. Stanley observed the negotiations in the North-West were "more formal, ceremonious and imposing; the areas to be ceded were larger; and the number of [Indigenous persons] to be treated with more numerous and warlike."[43] As overt representations of Imperial authority and in consideration of the very high regard with which the Indigenous peoples of the North-West held the Queen, the Militia were critical strategic tools in the extinguishing of Indigenous land claim in the region.

The symbolic effect of the uniformed military on the Indigenous inhabitants of the North-West was identified early on. The original soldiers of the Red River Expeditionary Force being members of colonial *rifle* battalions they wore dark green uniforms rather than the familiar scarlet coat of British regiments. There is some debate, however, about just what colour of uniform the Militia did wear. According to orders, they were to be clothed as "rifle" battalions who wear dark green tunics. Shore states they wore blue serge uniforms, and he titled one of his chapters "Settlers in Blue Serge." Conversely, Joseph Tennant, who participated in the Wolseley Expedition as a private, recorded in his book *Rough Times* that the 60th Rifles and the Ontario and Quebec Rifles wore a black tunic with scarlet facings and black trousers with a red stripe.[44] Official correspondence from the adjutant-general indicates that they did in fact wear Rifle Green tunics, not the Blue Serge as indicated by Shore, or the black tunics as reported by Tennant. In preparation for the Wolseley Expedition, the adjutant-general directed that the expedition would be equipped as riflemen and every member would be issued with "1 Cloth (Rifle) Tunic."[45] "Rifle" tunics were dark green.

During his 1872 reconnaissance of the North-West, Robertson-Ross ascertained that the local Indigenous leaders did not care for the dark uniforms of the Militia, asking him "who are those soldiers at Red River wearing dark clothes? Our old brothers who formerly lived there [meaning the 6th Regiment stationed there previously, see Chapter 1] wore red coats ... we know that the soldiers of our great mother wear red coats."[46] Ross therefore directed that the Provisional Battalion in Manitoba change their uniform to the scarlet tunic. The order was recorded in a memorandum in which Robertson-Ross wrote that the uniforms were to change "under the provisions of an order in council dated 25 May 1873 ... [changing] uniforms from Rifles to Infantry [infantry regiments wore the red scarlet tunic.]"[47] He recorded his motivation in his Annual Report, stating that: "with a view, therefore of re-assuring the [Indigenous] mind ... I recommend a change in uniform ... the Militia on duty in Manitoba now wear red coats, and the matter apparently small in itself, will probably prove of great value and importance hereafter."[48] The change in hue seems to have made an impact, even on the non-Indigenous population. The *Manitoban and North-West Herald* reported in 1873 that "the Provisional Battalion was out in heavy marching order. In their handsome scarlet uniforms, and with the inspiring strains of their fine band, the force showed to great advantage."[49] Again, in March of 1875, the *Nor' Wester* beamed that the recent march out of the volunteers, in red serge tunic rather than winter overcoat, was a refreshing site.[50]

The symbolism behind the scarlet tunic is important. Associated as it was with the military and, later, the North-West Mounted Police which, despite its name, was originally a paramilitary force, it represented legal authority and the ability to enforce the law with force as required. It linked the military and police with greater British imperium and, inasmuch as it has been celebrated as a symbol of law and order, it was really more of a symbol of the great power that could be brought to bear in the face of resistance.[51]

The influence of the red tunic was profoundly evident during the North-West Rebellion in 1885 as well. Tasked to move the *Alberta Field Force* from Calgary to Edmonton with a goal to "overawe the Indians of the region"

General Thomas Bland Strange realized that the rifle green uniform of Montreal's 65th Battalion had failed to impress the Cree of the Battle River area. He therefore ordered Lieutenant-Colonel Osborne Smith's red-coated Winnipeg Light Infantry, who had been placed under his command, to march through the Indigenous reserve land "with bayonets fixed and rifles at the slope, with band playing and every weapon exposed to view." He reported that the Indigenous peoples were sufficiently impressed as they "gathered in the woods by the roadside and gazed wonderingly at the spectacle."[52] At least Strange *thought* it was the red-jacket that had made such an impression.

Notwithstanding these observations, perhaps the perceived impact of the red coat was more a projection of Anglo-Saxon tropes than Indigenous opinion. Desmond Morton wrote in the *Journal of Canadian Studies* that the idea of red coats, and the reason for their use with the North-West Mounted Police, was more sartorial than symbolic. He argued that the choice of the red serge for the Mounties was made by the Adjutant-General, Colonel Robertson-Ross, who he identified as "a noted devotee of military finery."[53] Was the red serge just a result of Imperial prudishness? It very well may have been, based on the report of Alexander Morris during his negotiations with the Cree near Forts Carlton and Pitt in August of 1876. As part of his negotiations, Say-Sway-Pus asked of Morris "If it is your intention to honour me with a Chief's clothing, I wish you would give me one that would correspond with the sky above." To which Morris steadfastly refused saying that "one of you made a request that if he were accepted as a Chief, he should have a blue coat ... red is the color all the Queen's Chiefs wear ... her soldiers and her officers wear red, and all the other Chiefs of the Queen wear the coats we have brought, and the good of this is that when the Chief is seen with his uniform and medal everyone knows he is an officer of hers."[54]

It seems, therefore, that Morton is right and that the psychological and symbolic impact of the red jacket on the Indigenous population was far less profound than is normally assumed, and far more of a projection by the English Protestant colonizers. However, the messages such as that above, and the use of the red jacket itself, were nonetheless an overt statement of Imperial and Dominion authority, linking as it did the federal dominion authority with the overarching British imperium. Even if the red serge did not overawe the Indigenous peoples as it was intended, it was nonetheless a reassurance to the culturally British population of Manitoba and the North-West.

Establishing the symbolic prestige over the North-West was one thing, following up with the actual legal imposition of authority over the region to facilitate settlement was something else. To accomplish this, after the creation of Manitoba and the culmination of the Red River Resistance, the Dominion Government set about negotiating treaties with the local Indigenous peoples. Seven numbered treaties were signed between commissioners representing the Dominion Government and Indigenous nations of the North-West during the 1870s, and the Militia was employed in many of these negotiations.[55]

There was precedence for the use of military forces during treaty negotiations in the North-West that stretched back to the 1850s. During the period of the Royal Canadian Rifles' sojourn to Fort Garry from 1857–61, the force was requested to provide military support by a local magistrate when a party of about twenty Sioux from Minnesota arrived at Fort Garry to conclude a peace treaty with Métis there. There was fear that violence might erupt during the negotiations, so a party of the Rifles consisting of its commander, Captain W. H. Sharpe, two subalterns, five sergeants, two buglers, and eighty-five rank and file, along with two three-pounder field guns, reported to the local courthouse where Sharpe found the Sioux surrounded by three hundred Métis and Saulteaux. Sharpe and his men escorted the Sioux away from the scene, positioning his force between the Sioux and the Saulteaux, avoiding any bloodshed.[56]

Use of the Militia during the negotiations of the numbered treaties in post-Confederation North-West began in July of 1871. Adams Archibald decided to bring a force of soldiers to the negotiations because "Military display has always a great effect on [Indigenous peoples], and the presence, even of a few troops, will have a good tendency."[57] Thus, a guard of forty soldiers led by Major A.G. Irvine departed Fort Garry by boat for the Lower Fort to be present at the negotiations of Treaties Number 1 and 2. Major Irvine was also a signatory of the treaty.[58] Treaty Number 3 was negotiated and signed during the fall of 1873 at the North-West Angle of Lake of the Woods. During these negotiations, the new Lieutenant-Governor of Manitoba, Alexander Morris, led a delegation to negotiate the treaty that included in its number a detachment of seventy-five men of the Provisional Battalion, complete with arms and supplies.[59] The Militia were added to the delegation in the hope that they would add imperial gravitas to the Dominion's offer, alongside other efforts to lend credibility to the negotiations: "everything that could be done to bring the matter to a conclusion has been done by the authorities. Ample provisions were sent out, presents were sent up from Canada, troops were sent out from Fort Garry to add to the pomp of the military display."[60] Beyond simply being there for show, an officer of the Militia also acted as a secretary and kept short-hand notes of the discussions.[61]

Similar use of the Militia as symbolic representation of imperial power occurred two years later during the Treaty 4 negotiations near Qu'Appelle in modern-day Saskatchewan, but on a much grander scale. The inclusion of a large Militia contingent in the Dominion delegation led the local military authorities to look at their participation much along the lines of an expeditionary mission. The 1874 annual report of Military District No. 10 includes an appendix describing the force's participation that reads like an exemplar of efficient military staff work.

The force marched out of Fort Garry on August 17, 1874 consisting of eight officers, 105 non-commissioned officers and men, and four mounted Métis scouts, complete with wagons for arms and provisions.[62] Osborne Smith led the force and decided to bring along one of the mountain howitzers that had been left behind by the Wolseley Expedition whose role, the *Free Press* assumed, was "to astonish the Indians."[63] The marching column was indeed impressive: twelve double wagons, fifteen carts, and forty-six horses. Additionally, a small drove of cattle accompanied the force to provide fresh meat on the march. The men's burden was lightened by placing equipment in the wagons, but nonetheless, the Militiamen were obliged to carry their rifle, waist belt, ammunition pouch with sixty rounds of ammunition, canteen, bayonet, and haversack. Osborne Smith's report indicated that the role of the Militia force was more than just symbolic and that some consternation about the outbreak of violence during the negotiations existed. Consequently, forty rounds of artillery shell were carried along for the mountain howitzer, suggesting its use beyond the firing of salutes was contemplated, and five thousand extra rounds of rifle ammunition were forwarded to Fort Ellice, near modern day St. Lazare, Manitoba, indicating the possibility of violent conflict was contemplated by negotiating authorities and military leadership.[64]

Negotiations were tense, particularly between two antagonistic First Nations, the Saulteaux and Cree. On one occasion the Saulteaux posted six warriors in the conference tent armed with muskets and pistols in what Morris perceived as an attempt to intimidate the commissioners and the

Cree negotiators. In response, Osborne Smith posted six armed Militiamen in the tent as well. Morris observed that "their presence exerted great moral influence, and, I am persuaded, prevented the jealousies and ancient feud between the Cree and Saulteaux culminating in acts of violence."[65] The Militia force was not mere bunting for the occasion, and the signatories of the treaty include a number of Militia officers including Lieutenant-Colonel Osborne Smith, Captain A. McDonald, Ensign G. Street, Surgeon A. Codd, Captain W. Herchmer, Ensign C. DeCazes, and Lieutenants J. Cotton and J. Allan.[66] The progress of the expedition was recorded by Osborne Smith and his officers in the most "scrupulously and careful manner" and a table of marching times and distances was maintained and published in the annual report, see figure xx.[67]

It's tempting to regard the symbolism of Militia participation in the Indigenous treaty negotiations as one-sided, namely the use of imperial and dominion regalia to overawe the Indigenous population and leverage their agreement to the treaties. Such a narrative is overly dismissive of the agency of the Indigenous peoples of the late nineteenth century and is an unfortunate infantilization of the Indigenous peoples. Quite the contrary, the use of the military regalia occurred in the context of a symbiotic exchange with Indigenous leaders who themselves had a strong ceremonial and symbolic culture. As Sarah Carter explained in the *Manitoba History Journal* the ceremonial aspects of the treaty negotiations were "rich hybrids of traditions, most of which were embedded in Aboriginal practice, and had developed through two centuries of fur trading with Europeans. Pipe ceremonies, welcoming salutes and escorts, parades, dances, enactments of bravery and oratory, all figured prominently in Plains diplomacy."[68] In this way, the presence of the Militia and the pomp and ceremony they exuded as a uniformed force helped to establish, at the very least, a theoretically level playing field for negotiations between what were ostensibly nation-to-nation, even if the Dominion Government representatives had a mindset that was more colonizer than colleague.

As Michael Walzer's statement at the beginning of this chapter reminds us, the modern nation state does not physically exist except in the tangible symbolic trappings that represent it such as flags, uniformed forces, and institutions. It is conceptual in nature and would be invisible if not for such physical manifestations. The Militia played a prominent role in establishing the symbolic linkage between Dominion authority and the role of the

Dominion in the wider British Empire. As a uniformed force, it was an overt manifestation of the Dominion authority in the new province, and its participation in public events, lent Imperial gravitas to them. While military forces are normally a world apart, cloistered, removed and independent, the Militia and the volunteers who comprised it in post-Confederation Manitoba were both citizens and soldiers. They were not just agents of societal change, but constituent members of the society as well.

5
SOCIETY

K. B. Wamsley observed in *Social History* that "while the British North America Act of 1867 provided a framework for the construction of a new federal administration in Canada, state formation was conducted, in part, through various ideological projects that were positioned to challenge the extant religious, cultural and regional differences across the country." He went on to note that one of the strategies that was used to remove these differences by what he terms the *dominant fundamental group,* was "the promotion of institutionalized social behaviour."[1] The Militia was a predominant tool in this strategy in early Manitoba.

Despite the unique nature of military life, and the somewhat naturally cloistered existence of a military garrison within a civilian society, the Militia was nevertheless intermingled with the society it served. In Eastern Canada, membership in the Militia was as much a social statement as a military one, aping the strictures of British Victorian society.[2] Canada could not directly replicate the British practice, where the officer class came almost exclusively from the aristocracy. Nonetheless, the officers of the Canadian Militia came from the middle- and upper-class bourgeois of nineteenth century Canadian society, and indeed the Militia was something of a tool of social organization. Writing in *Urban History Review,* Carmen Miller noted of the Militia in Montreal prior to the Great War that "not only was the Militia a social institution, but a socializing institution, one of a fascinating network of religious, occupational, recreational and fraternal associations, which facilitated the social adaptation of young, single males to middle class...urban life." [3]

This social stratification of the militia officer class in the established provinces of Canada was transferred to Manitoba in the 1870s by the officers of the militia garrison. Moreover, beyond simply imposing a ready-made officer class in the new province, the volunteers of the Provisional Battalion also played a significant role in recreating the British cultural norms of Ontario in the new province as well. This chapter will illustrate how the volunteers in the militia garrison served as agents of cultural transferral of the institutions, practices, and mores of nineteenth century Anglo-Protestant culture to Manitoba.

THE MILITIAMEN

Who, then, were the Militiamen? In 1870, the Provisional Battalion deposited a unique assortment of individuals into the middle of Manitoba society. A total of over 1,700 soldiers served in the permanent militia garrison between its arrival in 1870 and its eventual disbandment in 1877. The men comprising that force were not a particularly diverse lot, but that is not to say their cultural make-up was wholly monolithic. They originated, to a large degree, in Eastern Canada — 48 percent from Ontario, 36 percent from Quebec, 4 percent from New Brunswick and 3 percent from Nova Scotia. Some came from abroad — 8 percent originated from outside Canada altogether, consisting of about 5 percent from the British Isles with the remainder from continental Europe, including two intrepid chaps, one from Spain and one from Norway.[4] Despite the relatively balanced numbers between Ontario and Quebec, most of the Militia volunteers were Anglophones — 85.22 percent were English and 14.78 percent were French. They were all members of the Active Militia, meaning they weren't professional soldiers but had some sort of occupation besides the annual training in uniform. 28 percent were skilled labourers, 13 percent were general labourers, and 12 percent came from the service industry. Given that the government had hoped to convince a large portion of the volunteers to settle in agrarian Manitoba, surprisingly, only 12 percent were farmers.[5] 92 percent of them were single, only 7 percent were married, the remaining 1 percent were widowers or priests.[6] If the government had ever intended for the various Red River Expeditions to contribute new settlers to Manitoba with military experience, its level of success was decidedly lukewarm. Of the members of the original Red River Expedition, only 17 percent chose to take advantage of the land grants and settle in Manitoba. This small percentage may tempt readers to assume the Militia's cultural impact on Manitoba society was miniscule given the small number of volunteers who chose to remain in the North-West. Notwithstanding the relatively meagre number of soldiers who chose to stay in the province, the Militia was nonetheless a conspicuous presence in early Manitoba that left an indelible mark on provincial society during their deployment in the region.

It is perhaps unsurprising that the Militia would have a significant impact on the surrounding society in the early days of Manitoba. Historian Frank Howard Schofield gave Winnipeg's population in 1870 as 250 souls, growing to 1,467 in 1872.[7] The inundation of 800 Militiamen of the first Red River Expedition meant that for at least part of those two years of growth, there were more Militia volunteers in the area around Fort Garry than civilians. Even when the number of Militiamen decreased to 350 soldiers in 1871 after the reduction of forces upon the completion of the initial volunteers' terms of service, and the augmentation of the Second Expedition under Captain Scott, in 1872 the ratio of volunteers to citizens was approximately one-to-four, and this does not include members of the local active Militia corps. At such a ratio, one can assume with some confidence that the social impact of such a large component of soldiers was profound. Notwithstanding the mundane existence of the Militia, the soldiers still needed to eat, still drank in saloons, and still required the usual commercial support from the local economy that any large body of soldiers does. Fort Garry being the cultural, economic, and political hub of the province, the presence of the Militia would have been persistent and obvious — a composite element of the cultural mosaic of early Winnipeg.

Whereas the Dominion Forces in Manitoba would have stood out as a uniformed force, the local active Militia volunteer forces had a foot in both worlds. A review of two rolls of potential and actual Active Militia soldiers illustrates the makeup of the typical Militia Company in Manitoba. In April of 1877, after leaving the Provisional Battalion and taking up civil pursuits, Thomas Scott attempted to raise an Active Militia company in Winnipeg, and forwarded to Osborne Smith a roll of men who had professed to him a willingness to join his Active Militia corps. Today, enrolment in the Militia is very much centrally driven, with the Canadian Armed Forces spending

Age	'A' Company	'B' Company
Under 18	1	1
19-24	22	35
25-30	19	16
31-35	6	4
36-40	4	0
Over 40	1	1

significant amounts of money to attract and recruit potential soldiers, all coordinated by a centralized recruiting plan executed by the Canadian Forces Recruiting Group. In the late nineteenth century, conversely, local leaders, working under their own initiative would decide to raise a company, and then had to go about attracting and recruiting volunteers on their own. Prospective Militiamen would sign on a roll wherein they proclaimed something like the following, taken from Thomas Scott's proffered infantry company roll: "We the undersigned British subjects agree to serve in a volunteer Company to be formed under Capt. Thos. Scott and subject to the Militia Regulations of Canada."[8] Each of the men volunteering had to list their profession and we find that the fifty-four potential enrolees provided an interesting cross section of post-Confederation Manitoba society:

What this finding demonstrates is that the rank and file of the Active Militia corps in Manitoba were, as is to be expected, predominantly drawn from blue collar society, and are particularly reflective of the agrarian nature of the province. Many of the trades represented, such as teamsters, labourers, and blacksmiths, would all be very much engaged in the agricultural pursuits of the province.

A review of the pay rolls of two companies of the 90th Battalion from February 1884 provides another snapshot of the age of the average Militia volunteer in Manitoba. In A and B Companies, the ages of the members ranged from fourteen to forty-seven, distributed as per the graph above. The numbers indicate that the militia volunteer was generally in his mid- to late-twenties.[9]

MILITIA AS SOCIAL ELITE

While in the main the composition of the rank and file of the Volunteer Militia Corps were men of their mid-twenties belonging to blue-collar semi-skilled or skilled trades, the officer corps of the Militia was far more socially engaged and constituted an important part of the societal elite and bourgeoisie of early Winnipeg. This is perhaps because this elite class so closely mirrored the British cultural structure of the Militia writ large. As Don Nerbas pointed out in a revisionist analytical essay on Winnipeg's early business elite, wherein he questioned the narrative of the self-made frontier businessman, the Winnipeg bourgeoisie of the 1870s and 80s "formed a cohesive enclave in Winnipeg. They shared a common Anglo-Saxon Protestant background, they lived in common residential areas, they went to the same social and cultural clubs, and engaged in the same leisure activities, and they were a politically cohesive group." Further, in a reflection of the planter-like installation of British elite from Ontario, Nerbas also noted that "in a word, Winnipeg's elite shared a lot more in common with elites in other Canadian urban centres than they did with a substantial portion of the population in their own city."[10] These are all societal themes in which membership in the Active Militia in the late nineteenth century was an important part.

In nineteenth-century, Canada, a commission as an officer in the Militia was a symbol of social respectability, in fact Militia battalions were bulwarks of the social order.[11] For instance, in Wilfrid Laurier University's *Canadian Military History*, Robert Vineberg observed that the British Garrison in Montreal during the years 1830–50, provided a ready-made high society composed of the garrison's officer corps who came from British gentry and nobility. Vineberg noted that the presence of dozens of well-born English officers in the colonial town of Montreal established a social standard that "reinforced the imperial pretensions of Montreal society" especially amongst the Anglo-Gaelic protestants of the city.[12] Echoing Nerbas' conclusion, the garrison in Fort Garry, particular the permanent garrison provided by the Provisional Battalion, served to import the culture of Central Canada to the new province by grafting a ready-made officer corps, derived from the cultural pretensions of the late nineteenth century Canadian Militia, onto Red River

Trade	Number of Soldiers
Teamster	11
Labourer	5
Blacksmith	5
Harness Maker	4
Carriage Maker	4
Farmer	2
Shoe Maker	2
Clerk	2
Engine Driver	1
Carpenter	1
Butcher	1
Drugist	1
Molder	1
Baker	1
Storekeeper	1
Steward	1
Nil	1

society.

It's unsurprising, then, that prominent members of Manitoba society were prominent members of the Canadian Militia as well. The system of raising a local company, mentioned previously, necessitated that officers had to be drawn from the local social leadership if they were to be successful in enticing Militia volunteers to enrol in their proposed company. Consequently, the Captains of the local Active Militia companies were always prominent members of local society. For example, in response to the Fenian scare in the fall of 1871, the adjutant-general recommended the creation of two Militia Companies in Manitoba, suggesting as Commanding Officers Henry Joseph Clarke, who at the time was the Attorney General of Manitoba, and Joseph Dubuc, a Member of the Legislative Assembly and former member of the Provisional Government of Assiniboia.[13] Only two weeks previous, the Minister of Militia had authorized the creation of a Militia Company in South St. Andrews under John Schultz, who at the time was the Member of Parliament for Lisgar, having been elected in a by-election the previous March.[14]

The societal advantages to commanding a company of Militia meant that there was even competition for the right to raise volunteer companies. When Thomas Scott submitted his aforementioned proposal to raise his company of Active Militia in April of 1877, Osborne Smith was thrust on the horns of a dilemma, as George Frederick Carruthers — a Militia veteran of the Fenian Raids in Ontario, joint editor and proprietor of the *Manitoba Gazette*, and managing director of the Canada West Fire Insurance Company — had also requested permission to raise a company of Active Militia. Osborne Smith was compelled to forward both offers to the adjutant-general in Ottawa and had to offer a recommendation as to which offer of service should be accepted should Militia headquarters determine that two more infantry companies was too much of a good thing. He recommended Carruthers.[15]

The fact that holding an officer's position in the local Militia was socially beneficial meant that filling positions sometimes resulted in the overwhelming temptation to interfere in the process. As an illustration, in April of 1873, upon the death of Captain Gagnier due to indiscrete exposure in the winter (see Chapter 2) and the subsequent vacancy created in the position of Adjutant of the Provisional Battalion, Robertson-Ross was forced to pen a stern letter to John Haggart, Member of Parliament for Perth, Ontario, who had forwarded the name of Lieutenant Constantine, at the behest of Captain

Thomas Scott, to fill the empty post. Robertson-Ross assured Mr. Haggart that the good lieutenant's name, along with other officers, had been submitted for consideration and took the time to add that he "begs to state that it was not the duty of Captain Scott to interfere in the matter at all, his doing so, is highly prejudicial to discipline. [I desire] to point out that the position of adjutant in a Battalion is a strictly regimental one under the authority of the Commanding Officer of the Battalion ... it is undesirable that political considerations should prevail."[16] But, from time to time, prevail they did, and in a later letter to the Minister of Militia, Robertson-Ross recommended Ensign Street in glowing terms for the position of adjutant.[17] Despite this ringing endorsement, *Militia General Orders* of May 20, 1873 announced that Lieutenant Hayter Reed was gazetted as the new Adjutant of the Provisional Battalion.[18]

If the officers of the volunteer Militia companies needed to be prominent citizens, and active politically, William Nassau Kennedy stands as perhaps the greatest example. A soldier who came west with the First Red River Expeditionary Force, he was a ubiquitous member of the Militia in Manitoba, commanding at different times the Winnipeg Field Battery and the Winnipeg Light Infantry. In civilian life, he was prominent in business and civic governance. He was Winnipeg's second mayor, and a member of the first Council of the North-West Territory. He was a Freemason, a member of the Winnipeg Philharmonic Society, the Manitoba Bible Society, and the early Winnipeg YMCA. He served on the Board of Management of Wesley College, and on the Provincial School Board. He was involved in several cricket clubs, the first curling club in Manitoba and the Manitoba Rifle Association. As mentioned previously, he was also one of the original members of the Winnipeg Fire Brigade.[19]

Similarly engaged in both military and civic spheres was Captain Thomas Scott who came out with the first expeditionary force, and then returned as the commander of the second. Originally from Perth, Ontario he decided to stay on in Winnipeg and eventually became mayor of Winnipeg in 1877. He resigned his post as mayor and ran for the Legislative Assembly and won in both 1878 and 1879, and later represented Selkirk in the House of Commons from 1880.[20] Stewart Mulvey also came to Winnipeg with the original Expeditionary Force and decided to remain. He later became a city alderman and one of the original members of the Winnipeg Fire Brigade.[21] Sir

John A. Macdonald's only surviving son, Hugh John, came out to Fort Garry as a private with the Wolseley Expedition. He returned to Ontario thereafter but came back out west and permanently settled in Winnipeg in 1882, after which he became a lieutenant and then captain in the 90th Battalion. He went on to represent his Manitoba riding as a Member of Parliament, and later was the Premier of Manitoba. Likewise, William Nash of London, Ontario was a member of the First Expedition and returned to Manitoba in 1874 and raised the Emerson Infantry Company, later commanding a company during the North-West Rebellion. In political life he represented Emerson in the provincial legislature and also served as the town's mayor.[22] Although slightly outside the timeline on which this book is focussed, more evidence is found in *The Political Manual of the Province of Manitoba and the North-west Territories* published in 1887: The deputy Attorney General of Manitoba, Louise William Coutlee was also the Major Commanding the Winnipeg Field Battery; the Secretary and Stenographer in the Attorney General's office, Mr. George Broughall was also a lieutenant in the 90th Battalion of Rifles; and the member for St. Boniface, the Hon. Alphonse Alfred Clement LaRiviere was the captain of the Reserve Militia in Military District No. 10.

Some of these men may have acquired societal prominence, but that was no guarantor of military proficiency — in fact both Kennedy and Scott were not necessarily good soldiers. As Chapter 5 will illustrate, both men demonstrated particularly bad judgement, poor leadership and, in the case of Kennedy, borderline fraudulent activity. The fact that they were both politically and socially prominent, while also thoroughly engaged in the militia, reinforces the theory discussed above that the militia was more of a social club, or political ladder-climbing organization, than an efficient military force.

While many of Manitoba's preeminent citizens of the final three decades of the nineteenth century came west with the expeditionary force, many of those who were not original members of the expeditionary forces but played prominent roles in civic life can be found in the ranks of the military. For example, Richard Power came to the North-West in 1867, he later served as a lieutenant in the Winnipeg Troop of Cavalry, and also as the chief of the Manitoba Police.[23] Dr. John Schultz, whom has been mentioned previously, did not come to Manitoba with the Military but as a settler and became one of Riel's premiere antagonists during the Red River Resistance. Notwithstanding his failed attempt to raise a company under Osborne Smith, he was nonetheless a captain of the Saint Andrews Infantry Company, as well as a Member of Parliament, a senator and the Lieutenant-Governor of Manitoba. Indicative of the social value of Militia membership as opposed to the actual martial value, Schultz's role as captain of the St. Andrew's Company was criticized by Charles Allen in an open letter to the *Manitoba Free Press* wherein he complained that Schultz had resided in Winnipeg, not St. Andrew's, during his tenure despite the fact officers were expected to live in the locale of their corps, and he had never actually qualified to hold a commission.[24] The local active Militia corps were never numerous, so the inclusion of such luminaries in the ranks of the local corps speaks volumes to the social importance of Militia participation.

The social impact of the Militia went beyond the political and social leaders. In May of 1873 the editors at the *Manitoba and Northwest Herald* were excited at the prospect that Mr. James Gerard, of the Provisional Battalion, was contemplating staying in the province once his terms of service expired. His social value? He was a "capital florist and landscape gardener" who had been busy beautifying the living spaces of the Commanding Officer of the Battalion. The author expressed the hope Mr. Gerard would remain in Manitoba so that "many other gardens will follow suit. Kitchen gardening and landscape gardening have long been at a discount among us."[25] In addition to Mr. Gerard's green thumb, several local businesses were opened by Militia volunteers turned entrepreneurs. John Hackett of the 1st Ontario Rifles, for instance, opened the first bakeshop in Winnipeg on April 14, 1871, and Alexander Begg informs us that a mon-commissioned o fficer of the force became the city's first barber.[26] Likewise, Messrs. Hughes and Weddup, both formerly of the 1st Ontario Rifles, opened up a boot and shoemaker shop upon their discharge, a service the *Manitoba News Letter* reported as being much needed in the young city.[27]

THE CLUB

An important societal institution in Victorian Canada was the club or association, something that historian A. Milne Smith referred to as "an indispensable part of elite men's lives … an 'Eveless Eden' where upper-class men forged and cemented their class and gender identities."[28] Clubs were the natural habitat of the Victorian gentleman — indeed, American historian Peter Stansky joked in the pages of *English Literature in Translation* that "it is said that if three middle-class Englishmen found themselves on a desert island the first thing they would do would be to found a club, with one as the Hon. President, one as the Hon. Secretary and one as the Hon. Treasurer. "The Hon" emphasizes that they are English gentlemen and hence would be doing this on an amateur basis so nothing so vulgar as money would play a part of the story … they would be demonstrating their 'clubbable' qualities."[29] Naturally the elite of the planted British social leadership quickly imposed the Victorian club on Manitoba society, the Militia playing an important part in doing so. The exclusive Manitoba Club, which is still in operation today and refers to itself as "the original social network" opened its doors in 1874. Writing in the *Journal* of the Manitoba Historical Society, Don Nerbas reported that the Manitoba Club was "at the forefront of Winnipeg's elite social clubs." Nerbas also quotes historian W.L. Morton's observation that membership in the Manitoba club "was practically a certificate of leadership in the commercial community." Membership hinged on sponsorship by two members and approval by at least 80 percent of the members — a robust standard that ensured a high degree of exclusivity.[30] Unsurprisingly, the Manitoba Club's first president was none other than Military District No. 10's Deputy Adjutant-General Lieutenant-Colonel Osborne Smith. Osborne Smith, having been transferred from Montreal, was instrumental in importing this very British cultural institution, already much in vogue in Ontario and Quebec. Indeed, military members likely figured prominently in the early days of the Manitoba Club. The constitution specifically identified "Officers of H.M. Regular Forces or of the Dominion Militia on service in Manitoba or the North-West Territories" as "privileged members" and were to be "admissible without ballot."[31]

It may be tempting to consider this a lone example not indicative of a larger trend, but the truth is the idea of elite "clubs" for certain strata of society was not new in 1874. Several years previous, in 1872, a military institution was created with the lieutenant-governor as its patron, but it does not seem to have been very successful and little is heard of it after its initiation. Its successor, a Militia Institute created, again, by Osborne Smith in 1877 seems to have been far more successful. Indicative of the intermingling of the military and societal spheres, the inaugural meeting of the Militia Institute took place in the Manitoba Club. Osborne Smith hoped to create an institution, "on the club principle that will be an attractive resort of the volunteers of the city, where they can drop in to read the papers and periodicals, or to play a game of chess, draughts, or bagatelle."[32] Later, the meetings were held in Rocan's Block on Main Street, and then moved to West's boarding house where it found its long term situation. For the low price of a one-dollar entrance fee and fifty cents in monthly dues, bedrooms were available for rent by the members, and foils, single sticks and masks available for recreation. Honorary members, those who did not belong to the Militia, were required to pay a ten-dollar membership fee.[33] The Militia Institute seems to have been a success. A year after its creation, its quarters were newly papered and renovated, and a respectable married couple had been hired to keep it clean and comfortable. Bedrooms were furnished and were rented by tenants. There was a dearth of interesting literature available to the membership, and a call for donations of books from the public went out in the pages of the *Free Press*.[34]

PUBLIC ENTERTAINMENT

Entertainment was hard to come by in Fort Garry during the latter half of the nineteenth century. The small population and isolation from the rest of the country ensured that diversions in private time were few and far between. One citizen of Fort Garry opined that "among the unavoidable disadvantages of residence in so new a country as Manitoba is found the want of amusements of that class which persons of culture, accustomed to reside in or near large cities, have learned to appreciate so highly ... though Winnipeg is not to be classified among the places asserted to be 'at the ends of the world,' in one sense, at all events, her citizens find themselves beyond the *ultima thule* of civilization."[35]

That all changed with the arrival of the Militia in force in 1870. As in other corners of the Dominion, the Militia became a source of entertainment. Militia events were society events, and participation was socially critical for members of the upper strata of Manitoba society, thus competition to be involved in ceremonial events with limited space for attendance was high. For example, during the presentation of the regimental colours to the Provisional Battalion mentioned in Chapter 4, the *Nor' Wester* observed the ceremony was attended by "a number of the elite of the city who were fortunate in obtaining information of the event ahead of all their contemporaries."[36]

Militia events, such as the presentation of queen's and regimental colours, could be counted on to draw a large crowd, recall Sam Steele's recollection of

"Ladies' parades" referred to in Chapter 1. In another instance, the garrison organized snowshoe races on the Assiniboine River in February 1876 that became a local society event. The *Free Press* recounted that

> "in addition to the officers and men of the garrison, an unexpectedly large, as well as fashionable, gathering of ladies and gentlemen from the city were to be noticed. Among the visitors were his Honor the Lieutenant Governor, who, with the ladies of his family, remained until the programme was completed ... at the close of the proceedings a number of the ladies and gentlemen present were carried off to the officers' mess, and, after enjoying for some time the hospitalities of the Fort, the guests finally departed home highly delighted with the afternoon's enjoyment."[37]

The annual Militia training camp also became a society event, and many of the local populace made their way to the training grounds to observe the volunteers at work. During the Winnipeg Field Battery's annual camp held in September of 1877, for example, the *Manitoba Free Press* listed the following local luminaries as visitors to the scene: Lt. Col. Kennedy, Mr. Darby Taylor, the Mayor of Winnipeg, Mrs. Benson, Miss. Benson, Alderman Logan, and Mrs. W.N. Kennedy. The author also speculated that "there will doubtless be many present at the cricket match arranged for Saturday afternoon ... the church parade at 4 p.m. on Sunday is also sure to attract a large congregation." Indeed, both were well attended.[38] Standard military parades were entertainment as well.

The emerging British bourgeois of Winnipeg and Manitoba imitated the social customs and traditions of their places of origin so naturally, where the officers of the military were considered to be part of its *elite,* as it was in Great Britain and in Ontario, so too did the officers of the Militia in Manitoba, of both the Provisional Battalion and the Active Militia corps, naturally fill this role in the emergent British society of Manitoba. Take as an example the Benedict's Ball held in the ball room of the Canada Pacific Hotel in January of 1874. The *Manitoban and North-West Herald* reported it as "the most brilliant entertainment of the season" where 250 of the young city's bourgeois leaders gathered. The guest list was a veritable who's-who of Winnipeg's early political and commercial class, including the lieutenant-governor and his wife as well as the Bannatynes, the McMickens, the officers of the North-West Mounted Police, the officers of the Hudson's Bay Company and of course the officers of the Provisional Battalion. [39]

Perhaps more indicative of the importance of the Militia to public entertainment can be found in the realm of the arts, particularly in the theatre. The theatre was a vivacious element of Victorian society — one citizen going by the *nom de plume* of 'Private' wrote to the editors of the *Free Press* in 1874 to observe that "public amusements occupy at present a conspicuous position in moral recreation. Since civilization has advanced and enlightened popular opinions, the theatre above all, opens a means of pleasure, where young, old, and infirm can participate in the enjoyment of life."[40] Given the small population of the Red River Settlement in the years before Confederation, little in the way of theatrical amusement could be found. Some movement towards an established theatre in pre-Confederation Manitoba occurred when a small group of dramatic-minded inhabitants formed an amateur dramatic society in the fall of 1867. The troupe established themselves on the upper floor of a shop-building where applauding and foot-stomping was discouraged for fear the building's rustic construction would not withstand the reverberations. Eventually, the building burned to the ground in 1874.[41] Fortunately for this vanguard of dramatic arts, a large body of potential thespians could be found in the ranks of the Militia.

The monotony of life in Fort Garry was well articulated by members of the Provisional Battalion on service in Manitoba whose lives played out in a rote cycle of guard duties, training, and parades, exacerbated by homesickness and isolation. This was not an experience unique to the Militia in Manitoba — by 1870 the British Army had broad experience in garrisoning frontier regions of the expansive British Empire, and with that familiarity came certain cultural norms as well, in particular a strong tradition of amateur theatricals as a means to alleviate the tedium of colonial garrison duties.[42] Not long after the arrival of the first expedition and the subsequent departure of the British Regulars, when the Provisional Battalion had settled down to garrison Fort Garry, the Militiamen of the Ontario Rifles organized amateur dramatic performances to entertain both the garrison and the local population. December 16, 1870 was opening night of the Musical and Dramatic Association of the 1st Ontario Rifles at the Theatre Royal — the rear of Bannatyne's store on McDermot Street. The program included several dramatic presentations such as *The Child of Circumstances* and *The Long Lost Father.* The Militiamen were honoured with the patronage of the lieutenant-governor and his wife for the opening night.

The ennui expressed by the soldiers of the Provisional Battalion was not their lot alone to suffer — local settlers likewise found life in the isolated city somewhat tedious. The Militia therefore provided a welcome diversion to such monotonous existence, which the soldier-thespians were able to provide. The Theatre Royale could seat two hundred patrons who paid two shillings for box seats and one shilling for the pit. The troupe had a very successful run throughout the winter of 1870–71. When orders arrived to discharge the majority of the soldiers in 1871 the Militia dramatic society came to an end, and the last performance took place on April 24,1871. [43] The *Free Press* lamented the departure of the Musical and Dramatic Association stating that "during the past winter they have contributed no small share to the amusement of Winnipeg, in fact they formed the only public entertainment that our citizens had."[44] Fortunately, as the size of the garrison increased after the Fenian threat emerged in 1871, the tradition of military theatricals found new life. In early 1874, the Provisional Battalion was "seeking to relieve the monotony of their existence [formed] a dramatic company for the mutual improvement of both actors and audience."[45] And in 1875, the soldiers formed a Garrison Vocal and Literary Association "with a view to amusing their comrades and civilian friends during the winter."[46]

The construction of Fort Osborne in 1873–74 contributed mightily to the provision of theatrical entertainment to the growing city by providing space for the creation of the Garrison Theatre. Whereas previous theatres had to be found in the backs of shops, or on the unused floors of rickety buildings, a purpose-built theatre was included in the construction of the Fort Osborne Barracks. The theatricals were well received by the local populace and the demand for performances was high — sometimes up to three shows a month. For the troupe's second performance in early February 1874 the *Free Press* reported that "the house was full to overflowing; extra seats were procured, and still some could barely find standing room"[47] and for the third performance later that month the *Free Press* observed that "it would have been a difficult matter … to have crowded another person into the Garrison Theatre without producing an uncomfortable strain upon the walls"[48] The success enjoyed by the Amateur Dramatic Society paid dividends for the population in general, not just by providing much needed entertainment, but through charitable contributions as well. Sergeant Major Collins of the Provisional Battalion, and manager of the Amateur Dramatic Society, wrote to the *Free Press* in April 1874 to express his great thankfulness for the liberal patronage of the local population at the Garrison Theatre and to inform the *Free Press'* readership that all profits from ticket sales were to be "deposited in the Savings Bank for the benefit of charitable purposes."[49] That the proceeds were destined for charitable use is unsurprising, indeed the soldiers seemed to have a natural inclination to giving: in 1873, the men of the Dominion Artillery stationed in Winnipeg agreed to forgo their traditional Christmas dinner, and instead donated their portion of the canteen fund, sixty-six dollars, to the Winnipeg General Hospital.[50]

Its isolation meant that Fort Garry did not benefit from a ready supply of musical talent or even instruments. The fiddle, for the majority of the nineteenth century, was the predominant musical instrument in the North-West. The first piano arrived in Fort Garry around 1840 and around 1870, a surge in popularity of reed organs emerged in the village.[51] The arrival of the Red River Expedition in 1870 changed things dramatically. Amongst the ranks of the 1st Ontario Rifles was a military band — a critical component of Victorian armies.

The arrival of the regimental bands that accompanied the troops of the Wolseley Expedition brought a welcome source of entertainment to the Red River Settlement. Only days after the arrival of the First Red River Expedition, the *New Nation* proudly proclaimed that the band of the 60th Rifles was planning on holding a concert in Fort Garry in the late afternoon of August 27, 1870.[52] When the 60th departed, they arranged with the officers of the Ontario Rifles to leave their band instruments behind for use by the Manitoba Garrison.[53] Shortly thereafter, a Garrison Band was put together that made its first appearance during the aforementioned opening performance of the Musical and Dramatic Society on December 16, 1870. The band worked in tandem with the Dramatic Society and shared its success during the winter of 1870 and 1871. Like the Dramatic Society, the decision to reduce the garrison at Fort Garry spelled the end of Militia band, but the members were kind enough to leave their instruments behind for the use of a local civilian band when they departed.[54] As the size of the garrison grew with the arrival of subsequent expeditions, interest in revitalizing the military band increased.

In 1873, the Militiamen came together to create a band once again from amongst their number, which served to entertain both solider and citizen alike.[55]

In early 1873, the *Free Press happily* reported that "the dearth of amusement in our city this winter has stirred up the members of the Provisional Battalion Band and we are to have a minstrel performance" whose first performance was held in the immigrant sheds at the Forks in mid-February 1873.[56] The review of the performance was laudatory, the *Free Press* reporting that the Band of the Provisional Battalion "met with unprecedented success … the house having been crowded to its utmost capacity."[57]

The band became conspicuous in most social gatherings, and a review of Winnipeg's newspapers between 1870 and 1885 reveals a regularly recurring advertisement that various social gatherings would be entertained by a band of one of the Militia units *by the kind permission of the Officer Commanding*. The local residents saw the value in the musical talents of the soldiers, and the editors of the *Free Press* opined during the fall of 1875 that "music from the military band at Fort Osborne would be gratifying to the residents of the city, during the evenings."[58] Fortunately, formal military bands were a priority for the militia authorities of early Winnipeg, and when resources availed they were well subscribed and had a tremendous social impact on the young city. It was not hard to find musicians as bandsmen earned on average an extra twenty-five dollars per annum more than their less musically inclined colleagues.[59]

The events for which the military provided musical entertainment varied. For example, a Masquerade Carnival was scheduled for the Skating Rink on Thursday, January 28, 1875, and to entice attendees, the advertisement in the Free Press stated that the Military Band would be in attendance.[60] Even an outdoor charity picnic concert found the solider-bards entertaining their fellow citizens and during the summer of 1873 — the band managed to raise $270 in just such a pursuit. The good will evinced by the charitable act may have been immediately dispelled, however, when the band treasurer, Colour Sergeant Naylor, absconded with the money and made for Pembina where he was eventually caught and detained.[61]

The musical styling of the various bands, and the efforts of the amateur prairie thespians not only provided a welcome diversion to the monotony of life isolated on the marge of civilization, but it also provided an important psychological reassurance to the British inhabitants that they were, in fact, just like the cities back east. In one instance, during a concert performance of the Winnipeg Field Battery Band in September 1876, the *Free Press* noted that the city was "fortunate in obtaining the assistance of ladies whose musical talent would prove an attraction in any city in Canada."[62] Likewise, the editors at *The Manitoba and North-West Illustrated Quarterly* observed that "there is an impression both in the eastern limits of this continent and also in the old country, that because Winnipeg has sprung into existence, on ground which ten years ago was either open prairie, or at the best a collection of shanties, the inhabitants are of necessity rough pioneers, not versed in the arts or polished in the manners and customs of the civilized world. A greater mistake never prevailed, and we have only to point to our numerous and flourishing societies to prove the assertion false." The authors went on to state that the success of these amateur societies originated in 1870 with the Militia and the volunteers' desire to pass the time in their monotonous day, to the mutual benefit of soldier and citizen alike.[63] The explicit conclusion here being, Winnipeg was no longer a cultural backwater, and could attract and produce as talented a crop of musicians as any region in the Dominion.

SPORTING

Sporting pursuits in the late nineteenth century were more than just pass-times, but cultural exertions designed to imbue the Victorian traits of courage, fair-play, and above all masculinity in young men. Manly sports were viewed by Victorians in both Great Britain and Canada as a vehicle by which one could develop and maintain an appropriate level of virility and martial ardour. Such traits were considered desirable based upon the overarching societal assumption of a calamitous future conflict between competing nations and manly sports, it was believed, helped in some way to shape and mold the young boys of the Empire into stoic men and thus ensure their readiness for war.

Such an approach was decidedly British — one need only look at the *Free Press*' reprint of a column by *Blackwood Magazine* about the Governor General to see the linkage between his advocacy of manly sports and the connection with the British Empire: "the impetus he has given to the manly sports which has ever characterized Englishmen, and to the social amusements tending to bring classes and people together who might otherwise never meet, has produced a marked effect on Canadian society."[64] And, of course, one must recall the infamous remark attributed to the Duke of Wellington that *Waterloo was won on the playing fields of Eton*, a concept reinforced in 1898 by Captain William Wood, the Adjutant of the Royal Rifles, when he observed that "many men have unsuspected qualifications for the military calling: boxing, fencing, wheeling, athletics of every kind and every other form of manly sport are all real aids to training for war ... taking hockey and football teams through to victory, are no bad preparation for leading a company or a squadron." [65] Consequently, a cultural shift occurred in the latter nineteenth century in which sports came to dominate social life in British culture and even to eclipse the importance of more intellectual pursuits. Writing in *The Western Humanities Review*, Bruce Haley remarked that the literature of mid-nineteenth century Britain established a *zeitgeist* that "it was more important to behave courageously and fairly on the football field then to do well in Greek and Latin."[66]

Given the broad cultural importance of sports in British life, and its implicit connection with martial acumen, sports were enormously important to the society of early Manitoba. The local Militiamen, both of the Dominion forces and local Active Militia corps', formed teams to compete amongst themselves and against local civilian teams as well.[67] To illustrate, in 1876 the troops in garrison formed four baseball clubs, as well as football, and cricket clubs, all of which thrived.[68] The Prince Rupert's Lacrosse Club was organized by the Militia companies in August of 1871 and included amongst its executive committee were Sergeant Champion as president, Sergeant McGinn as vice-president, Colour-Sergeant Roberts as secretary-treasurer. Corporals Winters and Madigan rounded out the committee. Of interest, this was not an exclusively military sporting club, and civilians J. Thurston, William Yuill, William Williams, and R. Jackson were also members.[69] Sports were a critical element of the British cultural narrative and military games were often observed by the public with much enthusiasm. Celebrations of the Queen's birthday in 1873 included a series of military games such as races and single stick competitions — a sort of fencing with sticks — that were conducted on the prairie between Fort Garry and the town of Winnipeg, accompanied by the debut of the Winnipeg Brass Band, which managed to draw several hundred spectators.[70]

Perhaps the most blatant sporting pursuit to reinforce British culture in the province was cricket. Even today, the game, although immensely popular around the world, still maintains an air of distinct Britishness. The *Manitoba Free Press* enthusiastically exclaimed in 1873 that "the admirers of this fine old English game are making preparations for a vigorous campaign … we have a good many excellent cricketers in town, and trust that the meeting will be so fully attended as to lead to the formation of a club that will call it out, and afford many a pleasant afternoon's sport to those who admire this strictly British national game."[71] Cricket was slow to catch on in Manitoba, but it did take root and flourish in the late nineteenth century. Its popularity, however, had less to do with the actual fun found in the game, but in what the game itself represented. Morris Mott, writing in the *Journal of Sports History*, noted that cricket was one of a number of sporting pursuits considered "manly," along with lacrosse, baseball, soccer and rugby, and that "early Manitobans played and promoted manly games, not only because they were certain these activities revealed and nurtured many desirable qualities, but for another reason that was more distinctly Manitoban … this was the sense of duty they felt to establish and maintain British culture in their new, still only semi-civilized part of the world."[72]

The first cricket club in Manitoba, the North-West Cricket Club was founded in 1864, with the governor of Rupert's Land as its first president, although it went defunct the very next year. Cricket had been played prior to this date, however. Joseph James Hargrave recalled in his memoir of the years 1861–69 *Red River* that the occupants of Fort Garry had attempted of form cricket clubs and had even imported high-quality cricket equipment for the purpose. He recalled that so long as there was a military force stationed in Fort Garry, in this instance the Royal Canadian Rifles, the game enjoyed relative success. He noted, lamentably for the admirers of the game, that with the departure of the military garrison in 1861(see Chapter 2), the game languished until it was taken up again in 1864.[73]

Not only were military teams prominent, but military personnel themselves played a leading role in the cricket activities of the time. Of particular note, after the construction of Fort Osborne in 1874, the Fort's cricket ground became the ideal spot for matches, whether the military supplied a team or not, and thus it played a significant role in the promotion of the game.[74] The cricket matches became society events in themselves, attended by the cream of the upper class establishment, and aided no doubt by the frequent presence of a military band that enhanced the experience.[75] During one match in 1877 between a military team and a team representing the Province of Manitoba, the *Free Press* observed that "the ladies from Government House drove onto the ground and remained some time, and several other representatives of the fairer portion of humanity graced the scene with their presence."[76]

Initially, cricket teams were organized locally: the communities of Headingly and Selkirk figure prominently in the early years of cricket in Manitoba. By 1876, the interest in the sport had swelled throughout the small province, the rising popularity of this quintessentially British pastime was reflected by the organization of the Manitoba Cricket Club in March of that year.[77] Whilst most matches seem to have gone off in a gentlemanly manner, the rough edges of life in the North-West sometimes revealed themselves, such as in 1874 when the *Manitoban and North-West Herald* reported that "a very savory dispute is now going on between the military and civilian Cricket Clubs of the city: charges of moneyed interest in the result of the late match on the part of the military umpire, returned by counter charges of incivility and blackguardism from that side."[78]

Notwithstanding this hiccup, the popularity of cricket, and other sporting events continued. In 1876, the *Free Press* was happy to note the "revival of manly sports in Winnipeg this season … last year there could be hardly enough players drummed up to play any game excepting quoits, while this summer three cricket clubs, and two lacrosse clubs have been organized."[79] By 1884, cricket had become distinctly popular across the province. Minutes of the committee meeting of the Portage la Prairie Cricket Club held in June 1884 shed some light on the number of formal clubs existing at the time by listing the number of matches the Portage la Prairie team expected to play that season, which included matches against Brandon, Minnedosa, Stonewall, St. George's, and the Winnipeg Club.[80] By 1884, the Provisional Battalion had been disbanded for seven years, but the growth of the sport of cricket had been, if not sowed, certainly nurtured and propagated by the Militiamen who had come from Eastern Canada — interestingly, in the days after the Battle of Fish Creek during the North-West Rebellion, in late April 1885, the Winnipeg Field Battery and 'A' Battery, Royal Canadian Artillery engaged in a cricket match on the prairie using "cricket gear [that] was manufactured on the ground [which] had the merit of being unique."[81]

THE MANITOBA RIFLE ASSOCIATION

From a sporting perspective, perhaps the most obvious of the eastern Canadian cultural imports to Manitoba was the Manitoba Rifle Association, a branch of the Dominion Rifle Association. The cultural importance of the rifle association might seem odd to readers from the twenty-first century. It is likely the only familiarity many modern Canadians might have with a rifle association would be with the National Rifle Association in the United States and that familiarity, given the differing cultural approaches to gun ownership in Canada and the United States, is likely not a very amiable one. The situation was, however, quite different in the Dominion of Canada in the late nineteenth century. Competitive rifle shooting in pre-Confederation Canada was an extremely popular recreational activity, particularly amongst the upper strata of Canadian society. In 1865, in the Province of Canada alone, 23,301 men were involved in sport rifle-shooting.[82] With Confederation, the impetus to create a national network for such a popular sport was readily apparent. Consequently, the Dominion Rifle Association was formed relatively shortly after the birth of the country, in 1868, and was, in fact, the first federally funded national sport organization in Canada.[83]

Rifle shooting in Victorian Canada was, as one historian put it, "a politically charged leisure activity, enhanced by an integration of particular ideologies and practices."[84] The rifle associations were not only sporting pursuits, but served an important practical role as an activity that reinforced the *levée en masse* system of Militia organization by encouraging a familiarity and efficiency of arms amongst both the volunteer Militiamen and the general population which were liable to enlistment in the event of emergency. As the *Free Press* observed in 1878 "those who, being British subjects, learn to handle the national arm even in this way [rifle association practice] would be available for military duty."[85]

The rifle association was defined in society as a patriotic masculine duty in pursuance of imperial defence and was therefore an important element of the maintenance of masculinity and the Militia ethic amongst both the uniformed and civilian population. K.B. Wamsley, writing in *Social History*, observed that "successful shooters were celebrated as heroes … this activity refined the economic, gender and social order, and was suffused with the powerful patriotic metaphors reproducing a particular politics in society and the positions of individuals within the political process."[86] It's no surprise, then, that the patron of the Dominion of Canada Rifle Association was no less than the Governor General, and the patron of the Manitoba Rifle Association was the new province's own vice-regal representative, the lieutenant-governor. The Governors General and their provincial counterparts, along with local civic leaders such as mayors and members of parliament, also contributed to the rifle associations in material means, by donating prizes for champions in the form of cash, trophies, or gifts. For example, during the first annual competition of the Manitoba Rifle Association, the prize list included a solid silver plate valued at $100 and a cup of solid silver valued at $90 donated by the Hudson's Bay Company, a cash prize of $30 from R. Cunningham, a local Member of Parliament, a silver watch valued at $30 donated by Dr. Schultz the Member of Parliament for Lisgar, and a Martini-Henry rifle and five hundred rounds of ammunition provided by the Dominion of Canada Rifle Association. The latter prize was, amongst other prizes, donated to the Dominion Association for distribution to the various provincial associations by His Royal Highness, the Duke of Cambridge and the Right Honourable Lord Mayor of London as a gift to the Active Militia of the Dominion of Canada.[87]

The inclusion of such grand personages as benefactors and advocates valorised the rifle association and contributed to the establishment of a symbolic and patriotic imperial bond between Manitoba, Canada and the British Empire. In this regard, the witty remarks of the Governor General, Lord Dufferin, during his 1877 visit to Manitoba are particularly illustrative. During a dinner hosted by the Manitoba Rifle Association he proclaimed that he regarded "this Association as *one of those means which your Province possesses of connecting itself practically with the rest of Canada and the Mother Country.*" Adding that "though I am but imperfectly acquainted at present with that square which represents on the map the form of the Province, I shall not probably by far amiss if I come to regard it on further experience as the bull's eye of the Dominion [emphasis added]."[88]

The Manitoba Rifle Association began in 1872 and although it started out slowly, and struggled over time, it eventually became a successful sporting organization. Indicative of the mutual interest between civilian and military spheres, in 1873, the Council of the Manitoba Rifle Association consisted of Major Irvine, Major Kennedy, Mr. Brokovski, the Honorable Thomas Howard, Mr. G. McMicken and Dr. Bird.[89] Lest it be mistaken that even the preponderance of participants were military, at the annual meeting of the Dominion Rifle Association held in March 1873 in Ottawa, the Manitoba representatives were wholly civilian: Messrs. Bannatyne, Girard, Cunningham, Howard, and Royal, all local businessmen in Winnipeg, had made the trek to the nation's capital to represent their provincial association.[90] Likewise, the prize committee, formed to solicit the donation of prizes for the 1873 rifle competition was also wholly civilian, consisting of Messrs. Bannatyne, Spencer, and Howard.[91] It would be wrong, however, to conclude that the Militia did not play a large part in the Manitoba Rifle Association. On the contrary, at the annual meeting of the association in June 1873, it was resolved by the membership that the commanders of the volunteer corps and the deputy adjutant-general of Military District No. 10 would be *ex officio* members of the executive council of the Manitoba Rifle Association.[92]

The first rifle tournament was held in late September and early October 1873.[93] The ranges were constructed in St. Boniface in a location that some found a bit out of the way, an isolation that was necessitated by safety requirements. In fact, advance notices were printed in local papers asking the local populace to ensure that they, and their livestock, were well clear of the area during the competition. The *Manitoba Free Press* helpfully informed its readers how to locate the rifle range, stating that they need only "cross over the river at the Notre Dame street ferry and take the Dawson road, strike for the North-West Angle. Presently you come in sight of the rifle ranges ... down into a ravine, walking plank across the meandering Seine, uphill again and you are in the midst of a small village composed of a rough lumber office, the council tent, and a refreshment ranch."[94] Given these directions, it is likely that the first rifle ranges in Winnipeg were located in what is now the tiny neighbourhood of Tissot in St. Boniface. This being the first rifle competition held by the new provincial rifle association, it received the expected broad coverage in the local periodicals. To add an air of regality, and thus reinforce the imperial connection to this competition, the tournament was opened by Mrs. Morris, wife of the lieutenant-governor. Rifle competitions being new to the city and province, the *Free Press* took pains to describe the unique manner in which Mrs. Morris opened the competition:

> A rifle is secured upon two upright pieces of wood, and carefully aimed at the target. The piece is then loaded with a blank cartridge and a lanyard attached to the trigger. When all is ready the officiating body timidly takes hold of the rear

end of the lanyard, the piece is cocked, the lady administers a timid jerk — bang! And a little shriek, the marker signals a bull's eye, and the meeting is opened.[95]

The inaugural rifle competition seems to have been a success, even though the "diabolical weather" meant "spectators were rather scarce, nobody caring to shiver and freeze, just for the fun of looking at another shivering and freezing man trying to point an ungovernable gun at an almost obliterated target." [96] Nonetheless, the competition went on for five days. Since the inaugural annual rifle meeting in 1873, interest in competitive rifle shooting grew amongst the practitioners and the local businesses who contributed the prizes. By 1875, the overall purse of prizes was valued at a respectable $1,121.[97]

The rifle association was thus established and continued to operate rather successfully. Ranges in St. Boniface were administered by Captain Carruthers of the Provisional Battalion, who was also secretary of the rifle association, and for the cost of twelve and a half cents, members could use the range for practice. [98] It seems like the Association enjoyed broad support from all corners, although some concerned citizens wrote an open letter in the *Manitoba Free Press* in which they admonished the Rifle Association to refrain from its practice of having a liquor stand near the ranges. In the letter, the temperance-minded citizens called "upon the Council to shut down this thing at once, under pain of the Association losing its character, and its meetings to be frequented by only such as attend the lowest kind of revels."[99] Notwithstanding the risks referred to by the prohibitionist-inclined citizens, the Association enjoyed local success. By 1876, the success became international when one member, a Mr. Chambers, was chosen to represent the Association on the Dominion Rifle Association's team that was proceeding to Wimbledon, UK to participate in the National Rifle Association of the United Kingdom's annual competitive rifle shooting tournament.[100]

Despite early successes, eventually the association fell on hard times. Fortunately, by 1878, the deputy adjutant-general noted in his annual report that the association had thoroughly reorganized, the result of which, he observed, was a marked improvement in target practice returns for the volunteer Militia corps for that year.[101] The provincial rifle association was, therefore, not only a valuable tool in maintaining martial efficiency within the volunteer corps, but reinforced the overarching British narrative by strengthening the already robust bond between solider and citizen.

The various sporting pursuits enjoyed by the Militia volunteers provided an outlet for masculine prowess and, at least in the case of the Manitoba Rifle Association, contributed to the development of a more capable military force. The impact of the Militia involvement went far beyond the football pitch or the rifle range. The eager engagement of sporting pursuits by the Militia volunteers was a catalyst to the spread of sporting popularity throughout the general populace thus replicating the British cultural mores extant in the remainder of the Dominion and the British Empire. To paraphrase the Duke of Wellington's alleged comment mentioned above, modern Manitoba was made on the cricket ground of Fort Osborne.

CHURCH PARADE

Christian worship formed an integral part of British culture in the nineteenth century, a time when the importance of observing religious practices was far more in vogue than in our modern culture. The importance of not only attending church services but in properly observing the Sabbath is reinforced by a particular observance shared in the *Free Press* of November 1873 when it was noted that a citizen living in the neighbourhood of Post Office Street decided to haul in and unload three loads of hay on a Sunday. While today such an observance would not ruffle any feathers, the contemporary editors at the *Free Press* opined in response to this report that "a little administration of justice would now be in order."[102] The importance of the Sabbath in Victorian society thus meant that the "church parade" was itself a key pillar of society as well.

Church parades were more than simply the attendance of soldiers at church, more even than just the attendance of soldiers in uniform during the service. Indeed, church parades very much took on every aspect of a parade. In fact, in the British Army, the church parade was the ceremonial highlight of the week.[103] This tradition was adopted wholeheartedly in the Dominion and transferred to Manitoba upon its entry into Confederation. Joseph Tenant recalled that for the First Expedition church parade was strictly observed. The Anglican soldiers marched to St. John's Cathedral behind the regimental band, while the Catholic soldiers attended a chapel on Notre Dame Street.[104] Likewise, Reverend George Young, the Methodist minister who came to Manitoba in 1868, recounts in his memoir *Manitoba Memories,* that the men of the Red River Expedition were a religious lot, and brought a substantial increase to his flock. He recalled that "the arrival of a strong reinforcement of Methodistically-inclined soldiers resulted in a speedy augmentation of our congregations and membership." In fact, he went to great length to highlight the support of several officers of the force, specifically naming Kennedy, Mulvey, and Gardiner.[105] The men of the permanent garrison routinely attended church *en masse*. Mary FitzGibbon recalled in her memoir *A Trip to Manitoba* that she attended Holy Trinity Church, where "the choir was passable, and could boast of one thoroughly good tenor [and] an energetic clergyman preached an excellent sermon" and that "part of the church was occupied by the regiment of artillery quartered in Fort Osborne, a neat little barracks to the west."[106]

After the permanent garrison was disbanded, the Active Militia continued the practice. Take for example the combined infantry and artillery church parade that took place at Holy Trinity church in April of 1878. In this case, the Winnipeg Field Battery and Winnipeg Infantry Company assembled at the battery's headquarters, and then marched by Main Street to Holy Trinity Church. Indicative of the bond between the church and the military, the combined force had several rows of pews reserved for them which "until recently [had been] occupied by the defunct garrison [recall the Provisional Battalion had been disbanded the year previous]." The *Free Press* reported that it "seemed like old times to the congregation when martial music was heard approaching the sacred building, and the military presently filed in and took their accustomed seats."[107] A year later, the *Free Press* once again waxed nostalgic for the days of the Provisional Battalion at worship when the Winnipeg Field Battery and Winnipeg Cavalry Troop paraded to two different locations to attend divine worship — the former marching to the city hall behind the battery band and their commanding officer, Lieutenant-Colonel Kennedy, where a Presbyterian service was held and the latter lead by Captain Young to attend service at Holy Trinity Church.[108] By 1877, after the No. 1 Winnipeg Infantry Company was gazetted into existence, church parade for the company was a monthly affair, although the practice was discontinued for the winter in January 1878, resuming again in April.[109] When the Kildonan Infantry Company was gazetted, the *Free Press* reported that "last Sunday the company marched to church, a new sight in Kildonan to see the sons of the old settlers dressed in scarlet uniform; and it did not diminish the satisfaction of the congregation to know that, although there was war in other parts of the world, they could sit down quietly guarded by their own rather warlike sons."[110]

Church Parades were not restricted to the participation of local volunteer forces in the brick-and-mortar churches of early Winnipeg, but they were also organized for the volunteer Militia during their annual training camps, such as the September of 1876 annual training camp of the Winnipeg Field Battery at Little Stony Mountain. In this instance, a marquee tent that normally served as the officer's mess room and the battery recreation room, was used for the divine service officiated by the Reverend Mr. German of Grace Church.[111]

When it came to sermons, the messages often seemed designed to reinforce the British cultural network. This was readily apparent during the Winnipeg Infantry Company's Church Parade in October of 1877 when both the sermon delivered by the Reverend Mr. Bell, a former Militia volunteer, and the hymns chosen, had a "particular reference to the duty of the Christian soldier."[112] Patriotic tones and the reinforcement of the concept of the divine Queen crept in to the sermon, Reverend Bell articulating that membership in the military, like living a Christian life, has certain demands including "a conscious, intelligent presentation of the self to Christ; and, as the Queen of England, when she accepts a soldier, gives him a uniform and acknowledges him, so Christ gives to all who come to him the conscious assurance of this acceptance."[113]

THE LOCAL BOND

Unsurprisingly, given the profound connection between the civilian society and the Militia based on theatre, music, sports, and religious ceremonies, and the prominent roles certain Militia officers played in the civil life of the city, a great affinity emerged between the populace and the members of the Militia. Illustrative of this close connection, residents of St. Boniface, became quite smitten with Lieutenant Tasherau who had come to Winnipeg in command of the artillery troops of B Battery in the Third Expedition. The citizens wrote to *Le Métis* on the occasion of his promotion and transfer to Ottawa to say: "Nous félicitons M. Taschereau, et espérons que son mérite, ses qualités et ses travaux continueront d'être reconnus comme ils viennent de l'être par les autorités militaires à Ottawa."[114] Similarly, on the departure of another artillery officer for Kingston, the citizens of St. Boniface once again wrote to *Le Métis* to state "M. le Lieutenant Peters ... est un jeune officier qui, par ses qualités de gentilhomme, s'est [sic] attiré l'estime et les sympathies de tous durant le peu de temps qu'il a passé parmi nous."[115] On the departure of Major Acheson Irvine, who was returning to Quebec, the residents of Mapleton sent an open letter to the *Free Press* stating: *"Sir, we the undersigned residents of the Parish of Mapleton, in the County of Lisgar, and others have the honour to present to you our regret that circumstances have removed you from our midst, and to express our feelings of esteem and regard also that we did not learn in time of your departure to enable us to meet you at a social gathering. But yet we trust on your return to this Province that we may have that honour."[116]*

The arrival of such a large group of Anglo-Protestant young men was particularly welcome to the ascendant British stock in the province. George Young noted how beneficial the arrival of the Militia volunteers was to the local economy and society, writing "some of the many resultant benefits of the incoming of our troops and the deliverance effected thereby, soon appeared in the revival of business in the country, and the incoming of a *desirable class of settlers* [emphasis added]."[117]

The citizenry of the city stepped forward to try to make life in Winnipeg as comfortable as possible. Alexander Begg wrote to the *Manitoban and North-West Herald* in October 1870 to inform its readers that his firm would be purchasing twenty subscriptions for the first class newspapers in Canada to be furnished in the recreation rooms of the Ontario and Quebec volunteers, while also donating £5 for the purchase of books for a proper library in Fort Garry.[118] Likewise, when the Emerson company of volunteers was gazetted in 1877, the local citizenry pooled together to furnish a cash purse for marksmanship when the troops practiced at the rifle range.[119]

Perhaps the most poignant of the many statements of praise and affinity came from the *Free Press* upon learning of the decision to disband the Provisional Battalion in 1877:

> The garrison of Canadian regular Militia which has been maintained at Winnipeg for the past seven years was finally disbanded today, the term of service of the men composing it terminating ... even though they must admit the state of the country at the present time requires no exceptional provision for the preservation of order, *the citizens of Winnipeg and the people of Manitoba cannot but view with regret the abolition of*

the force serving here. Its mission may have been fulfilled; yet its absence will create a void which all will regret, more particularly as the draft recruited two years ago have by their soldier-like conduct and agreeable bearing towards the citizens established themselves very thoroughly in the good opinion of the public [emphasis added].[120]

The soldier's role in the erection of British cultural norms and society was profound. Their impact went far beyond simply providing security, as important as that was, but they also influenced local society as well. They contributed mightily to the erection of Anglo-Protestant tropes, institutions, practices, and norms of the eastern provinces in the newly created prairie province of Manitoba. The left an indelible impression with the local populace and in many cases these impressions were good — but that was not always the case. The effusive praise heaped on the soldiers and reported above emanated almost exclusively from the Anglo-Protestant element of Manitoba society, many of whom were staunch supporters of annexation to Canada from the outset, and newly arrived settlers looking to exploit the potential of the region. Not all residents shared these warm feelings concerning the troops who were sent to garrison the new province. Quite the contrary, many of the Francophone and Métis inhabitants of Manitoba suffered mightily at the hands of these soldiers, and saw them as petty tyrants, criminals, and murderers.

6

SKULLDUGGERY: INSOLENCE, INSUBORDINATION, AND INTIMIDATION

In many reports from leaders in the original Wolseley Expedition, and from the leaders of the Militia in Manitoba thereafter, the conduct of the Militiamen was consistently considered beyond reproach. As demonstrated in the previous chapter, the local citizenry often heaped praise upon the Militiamen for exemplary behaviour, supported them financially, and held them up as exemplars of discipline, dedication, and duty. The true record of the Militia's conduct is a much more sordid tale. Rather than scions of virtue, and notwithstanding the very important social contributions of the Militia heretofore demonstrated, the Militia were, to an uncomfortably large measure, undisciplined, violent, and prone to chicanery. The skullduggery of the Militiamen came in two flavours: general misbehaviour prejudicial to good order and discipline, and ethnically charged violence designed to intimidate Métis, French and Catholic citizens.

SOLDIERS BEHAVING BADLY

> A particularly scandalous Militia officer was one Captain Fletcher of the Provisional Battalion whose name was reported in the local newspapers several times, each for rather unsavoury

actions. In one case, Captain Fletcher was brought before a magistrate for assaulting Mr. Barton, the police clerk, and he was subsequently fined ten dollars. A year and a half later, the same Captain Fletcher was once again brought before the magistrate on a charge of indecent assault upon the person of Esther Cain, the wife of a private in the Provisional Battalion, whom he had propositioned while her husband was on duty.[1]

Captain Fletcher's indiscretions may have been rare, but they certainly weren't unique. In August of 1874, an officer of the garrison absconded with a horse from W.H. Carpenter & Co's stable and drove him hard enough to use up one of his legs. In another example of Militia miscreants, in 1875, the Commanding Officer was forced to take out a notice in the *Free Press* reminding local proprietors that the Crown and the Militia authorities bore no responsibility whatsoever for any debt incurred by soldiers of the Provisional Battalion with their businesses. This was in response to a number of applications to the commissary officer by local proprietors to make good on bills that soldiers of the Provisional Battalion couldn't, or wouldn't, pay.[2] Such minor ill-discipline is commonplace amongst military forces: large groups of unattached young men with plenty of time on their hands and too much alcohol are a dangerous mix. The monotony of garrison life in the North-West no doubt only exacerbated the situation. Of drink there was plenty available, and too many places to find it. W.F Butler recalled in *The great lone land: a narrative of travel and adventure in the North-West of America* that Winnipeg held "more saloons than any city of twice its size in the States could boast of. The vilest compounds of intoxicating liquors were sold indiscriminately to everyone."[3] Likewise, an officer of the British Regular battalion reported his observations when the men arrived in Fort Garry and were able to have their first drink since departing Toronto:

> It was so long since the men had tasted liquor that all who could, troops or voyageurs, went off to make up for lost time. Very little Winnipeg liquor is sufficient to overturn the strongest head and demoralize the steadiest legs-so that in a short time the streets were filled with recumbent figures. When a man fell, one side became a large cake of mud; when he picked himself up to fall on the other side he was sandwiched in Winnipeg earth, and the next morning was

encased in a thick, hard coating from which he was difficultly released. Pickets were sent out all through the evening to bring the men in; and the soldiers having had their one drink, have ceased to visit the liquor stores, and have settled down to their usual occupation.[4]

In such a spirited environment, charges against soldiers for drunkenness increased from 56 in 1870 to 470 in 1873, absence without leave increased five-fold from 99 to 500 in the same period, and the number of instances of involvement of Police or Civilians in occasions of military crime likewise increased from 29 to 112.[5]

The nature of the crimes committed by the Militiamen in Manitoba was broad. On Christmas Eve, 1873, Mr. J.J. Johnston was driving his cutter through the city when he was stopped by two soldiers, one of whom took hold of the horse while the other made to strike Mr. Johnston, presumably to steal the sleigh. Fortunately, a witness in a local saloon came to the man's rescue brandishing a unique type of sabre, a pool cue, and chased off the soldiers.[6]

A more nefarious example is the unfortunate case of the murder of James A. Brown in June of 1874. In the early morning hours of June 18, Brown's mutilated body was found prostrate in the middle of Portage Avenue just outside Holy Trinity Church. The *Manitoba Free Press* observed that "the appearance of the body is horrible in the extreme, being cut and slashed in a frightful way, and disfigured almost beyond recognition."[7] Indeed it must have been a grisly sight — Dr. Turvers testified at the coroner's inquest that the body had a total of thirty-three wounds, including three cuts to the throat and eight skull fractures, three of which were wounds that penetrated into the brain, and one lung was punctured. Suspected of the murder, or involvement in the act, four artillerymen of the Dominion Artillery were arrested at Fort Garry: Corporal Baker and Gunners Michaud, Marriage, and Bernier. Brown was a popular member of early Winnipeg society, so once word of his murder got out, and news that several Militiamen had been arrested in connection with it had been leaked, a large crowd gathered as the accused were transferred from Fort Osborne to the jail, and the prospect of lynching was openly discussed.[8]

The narrative of the event is disturbing. Gunner Michaud and Corporal Baker had gotten into an argument after a night of alcoholic excess and Brown had innocently stumbled upon them during their fisticuffs. Brown attempted to break up the fight, but Michaud turned on the unfortunate Good Samaritan and, as the description above attests, horribly murdered him, leaving him to die in the street. During the trial, Michaud was asked if he was guilty to which replied, "[Je suis] coupable dans mon cœur et je mérite la mort."[9] Michaud was sentenced to hang. Corporal Baker and Gunner Bernier were tried by Court Martial for "Breaking out of Barracks." The trial was presided over by Osborne Smith who found them both guilty. Gunner Marriage was found to not have been involved in the incident and was out of barracks on an authorized pass so he was released.[10]

Michaud's sentence was carried out in late August of 1874. The day previous, the necessary preparations were undertaken — namely the construction of the gallows. Since the macabre calculations determined the appropriate height of platform for an effective drop stood above the low walls of the prison, an enclosure of black curtain was constructed to obscure the view from the public. The test drop was carried out with two hundred pounds of cannon shot, doubtless borrowed from the garrison. At seven o'clock in the morning of the day of execution a black flag was hoisted over the Court House, and thereafter the Sherriff opened the courtroom to spectators, whose numbers were substantial. At 7:45, the bells of St. Boniface peeled the death knell, and the prisoner, having partaken of a final mass was led out to the scaffold followed by the Sherriff, two priests, and the masked hangman "dressed in a hideous suit of black."[11] Gunner Michaud's arms were bound with a belt, and he was instructed to kneel to receive a final blessing from his spiritual advisor. He then rose back to his feet and the noose was placed around his neck. At the Sherriff's signal, the hangman struck the bolt which released the trap door and ushered gunner Michaud into eternity. At approximately 8:20, his remains were lowered, the attendant physician declared him deceased, and the coroner's jury investigated the remains. Gunner Michaud was taken to St. Boniface cathedral where he was buried in sacred ground, the funeral attended by approximately thirty of his Militia brothers, many moved to tears.[12]

Michaud had prepared a final statement to read at the gallows, but understandably he could not deliver it, having become overcome with emotion. A copy was given to the reporter form the *Free Press* who subsequently printed it in the paper. In his statement, Michaud implored his colleagues to turn to a Christian life and avoid the vices of drink and poor companionship. He lamented that he had let his poor mother down and that he had "made the choice of evil companions; I indulged in drink and the disorders which follow drunkenness. I had of a Catholic only the name."[13] Temperance was the theme of Archbishop Taché's address during Gunner Michaud's funeral as well, and well it might be, as drunkenness seemed to be the root of many of the misfortunes of the force.

Inebriation and ill-discipline seemed to go hand in hand. Tenant recalls a brawl that broke out in a canteen erected on the Pembina Highway near the Boundary Line a few hundred yards south of the fort where the militiamen were stationed in 1870. Normally the soldiers patronizing the canteen would return to the fort upon hearing the bugle call, but in one instance three volunteers decided to prolong their stay. A mix up with inebriated Métis ensured, resulting in gunplay in which a volunteer named Sinclair was the intended target, but was saved by the intervention of another Métis, Gabriel Godon, who shielded him from the shot and was struck himself in the arm. The report of the pistol brought several volunteers streaming out of the fort resulting in a complete donnybrook that left the canteen a total wreck. Tenant recalls "the big fight at the canteen caused a number of the boys next morning to answer the defaulter's call, generally known as the Angel's whisper, and they were entertained for the next two weeks with pack drill [a punishment in which the defaulter is compelled to execute mundane drill whilst wearing equipment] in heavy marching order."[14]

Even when the over-consumption of spirits did not result in criminal conduct, they could nonetheless have wide ranging and lethal repercussions. Take for example the unfortunate Corporal Youngsteen of the Quebec Rifles. In early October 1870, the young corporal who was stationed in the Stone, or Lower, Fort escorted a squad of prisoners to Fort Garry and after delivering his charges, indulged a little too freely in intoxicating spirits — no doubt taking the opportunity to share some good cheer with colleagues in the comparatively cosmopolitan Fort Garry. He, with another private from the Ontario Rifles, tried to cross the Assiniboine in a small boat at a late hour, lost their balance and upset the boat. Corporal Youngsteen subsequently drowned, while his colleague from the Ontario Rifles managed to swim to safety. The *Manitoba News-Letter* lamented that "the untimely end of this promising young soldier is much to be regretted, and adds another instance to the long list of warnings to abstain from the soldiers' peculiar vice — rum."[15] This observation indicates that even at an early date, the negative influence of alcohol on the soldier's deportment was readily obvious to the civilian observers of the day.

In general terms, military justice is necessary for the maintenance of good order and discipline within a force. Punishments varied depending on the crime. Internal punishment was geared towards ensuring order and discipline through general deterrence — making an example of the offender *pour encourager les autres.* We've seen that the volunteers of the Ontario Rifles who were involved in the canteen brawl near Fort Pembina were subject to two weeks defaulters in the form of pack drill in heavy marching order. Joseph Tenant recalls his own punishment for being absent without leave with two colleagues due to overindulgence. In a humorous turn, as he was marched in front of Captain Cooke to receive his punishment, he looked pleadingly at Colour Sergeant Wilson standing behind the captain, hoping for an intervention. The colour sergeant had been subject to one of Tenant's practical jokes some time earlier and his response was not to intervene but instead he "quietly placed his thumb to his nose and extending his hand in the shape of a fan, gave a broad, mocking smile." This caused Tenant to explode into laughter, which only worsened the situation. "The dignity of the court was insulted" he recalled "the Captain, too, exploded, but with anger ... [I received] a month, confined to barracks." Tenant's colleagues got off easy with only two weeks' confinement.[16]

Another nefarious example was provided by an anonymous author in the pages of the magazine *Grip.* The raconteur recalled one of his colleagues in the Provisional Battalion presenting himself to First Nations and Métis inhabitants near Fort Garry as a doctor who charged substantially reduced rates for his services compared to the actual physicians in the settlement. When called for, he would report to his 'patient's' dwelling and conduct a thorough examination, studiously recording all the symptoms that had presented themselves, and then depart with a promise to deliver medicine the next day. The next morning, he would present himself to the regimental surgeon at sick parade complaining of the same maladies as he observed in his patient the day previous, the charade highlighted with a "furred" tongue compliments of canteen whiskey and a "most woe-begone and lugubrious visage" he would be detailed "sick in quarters" and issued the appropriate medication, free of charge. He would thereafter give the medication to a colleague who would then deliver to the unsuspecting patient. When he was finally found out, he was charged with malingering and at his court martial was awarded forty-two days' imprisonment with hard labour.[17]

Another example is given in the pages of the *Manitoba Free Press* of April 1874. In this case, Private Thomas Timoney of the Provisional Battalion was caught stealing socks and other items. He was punished with 168 days of detention and on completion of the punishment was "drummed out" of the regiment. In the drumming-out ceremony, the Provisional Battalion and Dominion Artillery were paraded in the square at Fort Garry and formed two parallel lines about twenty feet apart. The prisoner was marched out and met at the head of this column by Lieutenant-Colonel Osborne Smith. The adjutant read aloud Timoney's crime after which Osborne Smith upbraided him and declared him *persona non-grata* within the ranks. With that he was obliged to walk between the ranks, in front of his former peers and colleagues while the band played "Rogue's March", and out the north door of the Fort onto the prairie beyond, and into civilian life. Such a public and contemptuous manner of dismissal was meant to serve as a warning and deterrent to other Militiamen contemplating disobedience or disorderly conduct.[18]

The maintenance of discipline demanded rather severe punishments for transgressions. While Private Timoney was punished with 168 days of detention for theft, his colleague Gunner Vaughan of the Dominion Artillery received an even greater punishment for the very serious charge of desertion. In April of 1873, a court martial was convened by officers of the Provisional Battalion and Gunner Vaughan was found guilty and sentenced to thirty-six days of imprisonment with hard labour. As was the practice of the day, the findings of the court martial were forwarded to the adjutant-general of the Militia for endorsement. Colonel Robertson-Ross's response was that the punishment was insufficient and directed Osborne Smith to increase the punishment and include a forfeiture of the land grant promised to Gunner Vaughan as an Active Militia volunteer in Fort Garry.[19]

Gunner Vaughan's transgressions, while indicative of the lack of discipline amongst the force in Fort Garry, also hint at a more chronic problem — that of a lack of order and discipline amongst the officers and the non-commissioned officers of the force. In his report to the Adjutant-General of Militia, Osborne Smith added that upon his order to the officers convening the court martial to re-write the minutes of the court martial which he had found to be disorderly and incomplete, the officers refused. Upon learning of this disobedience, Robertson-Ross replied to Osborne Smith to state that he considers it "his duty to point out to these officers the impropriety of their conduct which could only be excused by their inexperience in matters of military discipline."[20] In fact, Robertson-Ross thought the ill-discipline displayed by the officers so profound, he went so far as to inform the Governor General of the situation. He also stated, in a letter he directed Osborne Smith to read to all the officers of the Militia in Fort Garry that "in the course of more than 25 years military service in various parts of the world, [I] have no recollection of seeing a more careless and slovenly written Court Martial." And later, in referring to the disobedience demonstrated by the officers, "in this instance certain officers of the Provisional Battalion of Militia serving at Fort Garry have failed in the most essential part of their duty and reflected injuriously upon the high character borne by the Militia of the Dominion for good conduct and discipline."[21]

It may be tempting to dismiss such actions as a rarity, or as Roberson Ross observed, a simple lack of experience. This was not the only such observation of a lack of leadership in Fort Garry commented upon by Militia Headquarters in Ottawa. A year previous, in response to the request for a leave of absence by Captain Thomas Scott, commander of the Second Red River Expedition, the adjutant-general refused the request observing that "it appears that the conduct of certain men in Captain Scott's company has recently been such as to render it indispensable that the officer should remain at his post until his company is reported to be in a proper state of discipline."[22] This illustrates not only a general lack of good order and discipline, but more importantly, a general inability of the officers, through incompetence or even collusion, to maintain such discipline. This situation came to a head most prominently several years after Captain Scott's request was denied when Osborne Smith felt compelled to write a memorandum to the General Officer Commanding the Canadian Militia in 1879, Major General Richard George Amherst Luard, to express what he felt was a steady decline in the efficiency of the Winnipeg Field Battery, notwithstanding the presence of the prolific Lieutenant-Colonel William Nassau Kennedy. In fact, Osborne Smith observed to the General Officer Commanding that "the entire lack of energy which characterizes Lt. Col. Kennedy has caused negligence in filling up the ranks and I am of opinion that there are practically not twenty efficient NCO and men in the Battery — a number of the men whose names are on the role being there simply for the object of prize shooting."[23]

The situation that drove Osborne Smith to send this memorandum to

Militia Headquarters was the poor response to a request for assistance to the civil power by the Battery. Recall in Chapter two that in 1879, in response to striking railway workers a force of Militia was sent to Cross Lake to subdue rioters. In anticipation of this request, Osborne Smith gathered the commanders of the Winnipeg Field Battery, Winnipeg Cavalry, and Winnipeg Infantry Company to determine how many men could be mustered in the event of a request for assistance. Kennedy responded that thirty men could be produced at short notice, while the officers commanding the other two corps replied that each could provide twenty men. When the time came, despite his assurances, Kennedy could only produce thirteen men, four of whom Kennedy had picked up that very morning and substituted for men who did not materialize! In response to the large number of men who had committed to parade but did not materialize when required, Osborne Smith wrote to the General that he "urged the necessity of making an example of some of the offenders, but [Kennedy did] not appear inclined to take proceedings."[24] Osborne Smith wrote that he hoped the return of Lieutenant Edward Worrell Jarvis from the School of Gunnery would result in a marked improvement in the discipline and efficiency of the Battery. Despite this optimism, quite the opposite occurred a little over a year later. Instead of being a source of calm and professionalism, in the early summer of 1880 Lieutenant Jarvis levelled serious allegations of fraudulent activity against Lieutenant-Colonel Kennedy.

In late June 1880, Jarvis submitted a memorandum to Osborne Smith alleging seven charges. Firstly, that pay was drawn for individuals not actually present at annual training. Secondly, he accused Kennedy of making false statements of the state of the battery. His third charge alleged that Kennedy produce false muster rolls, paylists and certificates of men and horses and retained pay for said documents. Fourthly, Jarvis alleged that Kennedy made false returns of government property, specifically the equipment of the battery. The fifth charge accused Kennedy of drawing pay for men belonging to other Militia corps while the sixth charge stated that Kennedy had allowed men to be absent from annual training to attend a celebration in uniform. Finally, the seventh charge alleged that Kennedy had enrolled men into the Battery who belonged to other corps.[25] Osborne Smith in turn duly reported the allegations to the Adjutant-General of the Canadian Militia who ordered him to convene an enquiry into the situation.

The enquiry took place at Fort Osborne on July 19, 1880, with Osborne

Smith presiding. Several witnesses were called to give evidence, with Captain Street acting as secretary. By July 22, the enquiry was complete, and Osborne Smith delivered his findings. Osborne Smith found that the first charge, that of the battery receiving pay for men who did not parade during annual drill, was proved in some instances, but not for all the names of the men which Jarvis had claimed pay was issued for despite their absence. Witnesses confirmed the presence of some of the men at annual training, while others were found to have been absent. The second charge was not proven, there being insufficient evidence to demonstrate that Kennedy knowingly made false statements about the state of the battery. The third charge of making false paylists and certificates was proven by evidence while the fourth charge concerning inaccurate returns concerning government property was not proven with sufficient evidence. The fifth charge, that several men of the Winnipeg Cavalry paraded with the Winnipeg Field Battery and had pay drawn by the Battery was proven, however, Osborne Smith also pointed out that the complainant, Lieutenant Jarvis, was present throughout the training camp, was aware that the men in question were not members of the Battery and took no steps to rectify the situation at the time. The sixth charge was proven, in that several men had left the site of the annual training camp to attend a celebration at Sturgeon Creek some six miles distant, a distance Kennedy argued was sufficiently close to be considered co-located with the training camp, a defence not accepted by Osborne Smith. On the final charge, of enrolling men of other corps, Osborne Smith concluded that several men were indeed improperly enrolled, but he found there was no evidence to prove that Kennedy was aware they belonged to another unit. In his summation, Osborne Smith concluded that the problems and issues that were proven in the enquiry had arisen due "carelessness" and a loose understanding of the "responsibilities of command" rather than from fraudulent behaviour.[26] In short, Kennedy was found to be incompetent, not criminal.

The ramifications of this enquiry were serious. Combined with the observations of the battery's efficiency submitted to the General Officer Commanding the Militia by Osborne Smith a year previous, the two incidents reflect a military force that was extremely poorly led and wholly unsuited for operations. Immediately after the enquiry ended, Osborne Smith and his staff conducted an exhaustive inspection of the stores and equipment of the Winnipeg Field Battery, the result of which revealed a corps whose administration and organization was a perfect shambles. This very conclusion was reached by the major general commanding the Militia who wrote, in response to Osborne Smith's enquiry and inspection, that the battery was in "a confused state … through negligence" and that "it is clear that the Winnipeg Field Battery is in a very unsatisfactory condition." Of greatest significance, however, was the suggestion by General Luard that the Battery be broken up.[27] The Acting Minister of Militia and Defence, Alexander Campbell, overruled the General Officer Commanding's conclusion on the future of the Winnipeg Field Battery.[28]

Did Kennedy's profound political connections save his position and the battery? Was he truly thoroughly incompetent, or was there some fraudulent skullduggery at play? It certainly seems that while Kennedy was given the benefit of the doubt by both Osborne Smith and the Acting Minister, his judgement and leadership skills were sorely lacking, and the suspicion of fraud never really dissipated. Considering the observations made against Kennedy, Scott, and the various other officers mentioned herein, one must conclude that throughout the period in question there were significant gaps in supervision and leadership amongst the Militia leaders.

To have such poor examples in the officer corps leads inevitably to poor discipline amongst the rank and file. The situation is equally disagreeable when the non-commissioned officers of the force are found wanting in their leadership skills. The corporals and sergeants of the Provisional Battalion and Militia Corps were meant to be the backbone of the Manitoba Militia force, but in many cases, like their officers, they were ineffectual.

Sam Steele recounts one example from when he was posted to No. 7 Company after his promotion to corporal. He found that in one room, "a number of the wild spirits were quartered" who were wholly undisciplined by the sergeant responsible. Steele recounts how one of the "toughs" became insubordinate after a night of drinking. Steel dutifully reported the situation to the sergeant, however Steele found that even though this man was "one of the greatest ruffians that [he had] ever seen out of gaol … our mild senior N.C.O. let him rave away in his drunkenness instead of letting him see the inside of the guardroom."[29]

This sort of lack of leadership resulted in ill-discipline, misuse of alcohol, and murderous violence. The latter was generally rare, while it seems low-level ill-discipline was rather prevalent. While the previous examples indicate what may be considered general disorder amongst the troops, the same lack of discipline presented itself in a far more unsavoury manner, one that was not wanton disobedience, but ethnically charged violence and intimidation that had the goal of dispersing the Métis of Red River to accommodate Canadian settlement.

THE PROCESS OF INTIMIDATION

Were the violence, riots, misbehaviour, and generally poor discipline exhibited by the Militia volunteers just a case of men with too much time on their hands, or was there an underlying *goal* behind some, or perhaps all, of it? Originally, an attempt was made to avoid sectional divisiveness in the composition of the Red River Expeditionary Force. When Lieutenant-General Lindsay provided his guidance to Wolseley prior to his departure, he expressly directed that

> it is most important that none of the persons who had during the last winter taken part in the troubles at Red River should accompany the Expedition, and you will do all that lays in your power to prevent them doing so. I have to recall to your memory that both in public and in private certain of those gentlemen have expressed themselves anxious to take the opportunity of the advance of the Expedition to pay off their scores. You will therefore discountenance them in a public manner should they attempt so to fasten themselves upon you.[30]

Despite this guidance, as Frederick Shore posits in his doctoral thesis for the University of Manitoba, many of the men who found their way into the ranks of the Red River Expeditions had ulterior motives.

From an official perspective, the Wolseley Expedition was intended to be a peacekeeping force. Contrarily, Shore concludes that amongst the Militia volunteers who filled the ranks of the Ontario and Quebec Battalions — particularly although not exclusively the former — there was an unofficial mission within the Red River Expeditionary Force to employ what Shore called a "Kansas-style influx of armed settlers whose purpose was to guarantee that the new Province of Manitoba assumed an Ontario image without the interference of the Métis."[31] He refers to this as *the process of intimidation.*[32]

One Militia volunteer confided in his memoirs that 90 percent of the volunteers joined to avenge the death of Thomas Scott.[33] As demonstrated in Chapter 2, Scott, an Orangeman, became a martyr to his confreres in the virulently Anglo-Protestant Orange Order when he was executed under the orders of Louis Riel, an act which became the *cassus belli* to many of the more violent volunteers. One of the soldiers of the expedition, Johnson E. Cooper, arrived in Fort Garry with the charter for the first Orange Lodge in the North-West in his knapsack. Nearly a month after the expedition arrived, Cooper, Thomas Hickey, and Captain Thomas Scott, were elected the first officers of Loyal Orange Lodge No. 1307 aboard the schooner Jesse McKinley which lay moored in the Assiniboine River. Only two months after the expedition arrived at Fort Garry, the Orange Lodge began recruiting members.[34]

A moment should be taken to consider Orangeism and its influence on the attitudes of those who counted themselves amongst its ranks and enrolled in the Red River Expeditionary Force. The Orange Order, which remains active to this day, is a fraternal organization dedicated to both the propagation of Protestant ideals and the British Empire. The modern incarnation in Canada fortunately bears little resemblance to the overtly antagonistic version of the late nineteenth century, or even their more pusillanimous cousins in Northern Ireland who make a point of marching through Catholic neighbourhoods every 12th of July. A visit to the website of the Grand Orange Lodge of Canada presents no overly objectionable terms. The Grand Orange Lodge describes itself as a "Christian, Patriotic, Benevolent and Protestant Society [whose] purpose is to: encourage its members to actively participate in a Protestant Church of their choice, participate in benevolent activities which will enrich our communities and our country, provide social activities which will enrich the lives of its members, actively support the Canadian System of Government, and anticipate Legislation and its impact on the civil and religious liberties of all Canadians."[35]

The modern Orange Lodge members' predecessors of the late nineteenth century were not nearly so agreeable in outlook. Although in the nineteenth century its tenets called for similar activities to improve one's local community, its oath of allegiance, written in 1869 and known as the *Obligation of an Orangeman* includes certain debatable elements. While it is not necessary to include the entire text of the oath here, there are tracts of it that are illustrative of the overarching goal of Orangeism in the nineteenth century, and which provide a valuable contextualization of Militia behaviour in Manitoba in the early 1870s. In particular, the Orange oath-taker commits to "steadily maintain the connection between the Colonies of British America and the mother country, and be ever ready to resist all attempts to weaken British influence or dismember the British Empire." It's not hard to see that members of this fraternal organization might easily but erroneously regard the resistance by Louis Riel and his supporters in Red River as an attempt to 'dismember the British Empire.' From a strictly cultural perspective, the oath-taker swears that he is "not now nor ever will be a Roman Catholic or Papist" and promises that he will not "educate [his] children, nor suffer them to be educated in the Roman Catholic faith."[36] Faced with the prospect of an upstart provisional government, led by predominantly French Roman Catholics who had recently executed a brother Orangeman, it is no surprise that the Orangemen's blood was up.

Militia members were active participants in the Orange Lodge in Ontario and later in Manitoba, indeed as we've seen the charter for the first Orange Lodge in the new province arrived in the kit of a member of the Wolseley Expedition. Militia volunteers in Manitoba held high offices in the Orange movement both in Ontario and in Manitoba. Stewart Mulvey, who came west as an Ensign in the 1st Ontario Rifles was the Grand Master of the Orange Lodge for ten years.[37] In 1875, the five-person executive of the District Orange Lodge in Winnipeg included two Militiamen: Brother Johnston Cooper, a Private of the Ontario Rifles originally from Toronto was the Worshipful Master and Captain Thomas Scott, who led the second Red River Expedition in 1871, was Deputy Master.[38] Even as late as 1883, when presumably tensions had abated to a degree, Scott, by then representing Winnipeg in the House of Commons, was called out in Parliament, along with other supporters of the Orange movement, for making belligerent comments at a recent rally. He was quoted as stating at a meeting of the Orange Lodge in Ottawa that the Orange Lodge in Manitoba had been organized by the officers and men of the 1st Ontario Rifles, and that "he believed that within the space of ten years, through the progress of the Anglo-Saxon race, that the French Language would become extinct in Manitoba."[39] Such comments are indicative of the ulterior motives pursued by the Orangemen of the various Red River Expeditions.

Even if not motivated by Orangeism, it wasn't hard to find hawkish opinions arguing for a punitive expedition to Red River at the outbreak of the resistance amongst the nineteenth century commentariat. In April of 1870, the

Volunteer Review and Military and Naval Gazette, a widely-read periodical on military affairs, published an editorial that observed "After what has occurred [in Red River] a peaceful solution is hardly possible, and the establishment of authority by force is the most certain as well as the most feasible plan … an expedition of sufficient force to render resistance impossible should be sent into the territory on the opening of navigation."[40] In addition, an even more hawkish approach was taken by a certain Korn Kobe, Jr (likely a pseudonym) in the very same edition of the *Review*. Kobe decided to vent his martial ardor in verse in his poem entitled "Canada's Battle Cry." Kobe wrote:

> To the West! To the West! Come ye Volunteers start;
> in this Red River drama you're playing a part.
> Rouse, rouse, to the breeze your banners unroll,
> Let your names be emblazoned on Victory's scroll;
> For the War note has sounded – blood! blood! Has been shed:
> Come avenge it, or fall by the grave of the dead!

And,

> Let the 'President' tremble with fear at the news;
> Let his centers and satellites shake in their shoes –
> We'll give their new Northern Republic a lift
> that will send all its friends and supporters adrift.
> At the old Royal beast they may rant and may rail.
> But they can't with impunity tread on his tail!
> Let them spout annexation, let them threaten repeal
> We'll give them a taste of Canadian made steel![41]

That such commentary as that mentioned above were included in its issues, it is a safe assumption to make that similar feelings were prevalent amongst the rank and file of the soldiers of the Red River Expeditionary Force.

Strong opinions both in support of the Métis and in support of the imposition of Imperial authority were shared in journals throughout Canada and around the world.[42] Notably, the hue and cry from English journals calling for vengeance was in turn remarked upon by the French-Canadian Press. Joseph Alfred Mousseau, an editor and contributor to the Montreal-based *l'Opinion Publique,* who later served as a cabinet minister under John A. Macdonald and the sixth premier of Quebec, observed of the anglophone media's commentary on the composition and goal of the Red River Expedition that "Le *Globe* n'y veut envoyer que des Anglais et des Haut-Canadiens; le *Telegraph* de Toronto, complétant probablement la pensée de son confrère, laisse clairement voir son désir sanguinaire — *qui est l'extermination des Métis français à la Rivière Rouge* [emphasis added]."[43]

While in Ontario their supporters were legion, the vengeance-minded volunteers also found willing accomplices amongst the population of Fort Garry, particularly amongst the so-called *Canada Party* led by the likes of Dr. John Schultz, and both groups seemed to feed off each other's imperialist zeal. Begg reported that pro-Canada elements of the settlement expressed their unambiguous anti-Métis beliefs when, during the resistance, they "declared that the half-breeds of Red River would have to give way before Canadians, and that the country would never succeed until they were displaced altogether."[44] As a consequence of this outlook, reinforced, literally, by the arrival of hundreds of soldiers sharing these sentiments meant the years between 1871 and 1873 were dark days for the Métis of Fort Garry. The Métis lived under a sustained atmosphere of violence and intimidation that even a newspaper in St. Paul, Minnesota referred to as a "reign of terror."[45] Brawls were commonplace between Militia Volunteers and Métis inhabitants as the former exerted pressure on the Métis to force them out of the settlement and establish British cultural dominance. The St. Paul *Daily Pioneer* quoted a Métis inhabitant of Fort Garry who lamented "our people cannot visit Winnipeg without being insulted if not personally abused by the soldier mob."[46]

Reports of poor behaviour amongst the soldiers arose quickly. Joseph Royale, a lieutenant of Riel's, wrote to the Quebec newspaper *Nouveau Monde* in February 1871, only six months after the arrival of the Red River Expeditionary Force, and shared that "all the evil disorders, the robberies, the personal armed attacks on the highways, have had for their authors, since the 23rd of August last, Messieurs the soldiers of the Ontario Battalion."[47] Royale's comments came on the heels of an extremely disagreeable turn of events in Fort Garry. In early February, a large group of soldiers went rogue, and busted up several businesses and pro-Métis newspaper offices crying "Death to the Pope! Death to Catholics! Death to the Half Breeds!" Royale stated that it was only due to the courage of the police who arrived under the command of Villiers and de Plainval, ironically late members of the expedition — although it should be noted they both came from the Quebec Rifles — and the organization of a small force of soldiers by Lieutenant-Colonel Jarvis, that the miscreants were stopped and eventually cajoled back into the fort.[48]

Later the same month, the *Volunteer Review* reported that Corporal John Hawman of No. 4 Company, 1st Ontario Rifles, was reported to police by a Métis citizen who suspected him of foul-play during a recent gambling event. Hawman was consequently arrested by members of the local constabulary and imprisoned. This resulted in a riot of 150 Militia volunteers who eventually broke into the jail and released their colleague. John Kerr, who was one of their number, recalled the event to his niece who captured it in his biography thusly:

> After parade, on the afternoon of the following day, a number of his comrades of No. 4 company, with others who belonged to the battalion, gathered and marched down to the police station, pushed aside the guards, and proceeded to knock the lock off the cell door and liberate [Hawman]. Not content with this, [they] smashed the lock from another cell door, and let another inmate, a civilian, free.[49]

The soldiers then proceeded to march to R. A. Davis' hotel where they freely imbibed in alcohol, mostly without paying, the proprietor being afraid of what actions might result from denying them drink. After they had consumed what they felt was a sufficient amount of intoxicants, or perhaps even drinking the saloon dry, they marched back to the barracks where they were confronted by Lieutenant-Colonel Jarvis and some other officers and the guard of the day. After some questioning, to which an intoxicated soldier named George Lee provide some rather curt answers, Jarvis ordered the guard to place the man under arrest. Lee, who stood six foot eight, patted the colonel on the head and uttered "you see, Colonel, your word don't go with this crowd" after which they resumed their march back to the barracks with Lee at the head of the mob. Needless to say, Lee was arrested later that night. The episode reveals the poor state of discipline amongst the soldiers of the battalion.[50]

While some supporters of the volunteers endeavoured to justify their actions on the tenuous argument that Corporal Hawman had been detained illegally, at least the writers at the *Volunteer Review* had the circumspection to observe that "the men who would set themselves above law and order could have little idea indeed of what military obedience meant, and the very act of opposing the constituted authorities showed that they would not obey their officers … whatever services the Ontario Rifles may have rendered the country they have been entirely obliterated by their own acts."[51] This is, perhaps, one of the first instances where the paradox of the Militia conduct in Manitoba is remarked upon. That is to say, the paradox arising from recognition of the benefits accrued by the presence of an armed force in assisting the establishment of a successful province in a vibrant liberal-democratic nation, versus disreputable and ethnically-charged blackguardism that left a permanent stain on Canadian and Manitoba history.

Indeed, it seems that when the soldiers got their backs up, and stiffened with drink, there was little that could be done to bring them to heel. The *Manitoban and North-West Herald* was effusive in its support of the creation of the North-West Mounted Police and when the paper learned that the force was *en route* to Fort Garry in 1873 the editors expressed their happiness at the impending arrival of a professional police force because "we have had various experiences with respect to our police. We have seen the whole police force when it was at its largest, not only threatened, but chased like prairie chickens by a crowd of Wolseley's heroes."[52]

The general atmosphere of the province after the arrival of the Red River Expeditionary Force was one of intense partisan apprehension. Modern Canadians, more progressive and accepting in their outlook, would likely be shocked to learn of the racial and religious tensions that pervaded nineteenth century Canadian society. These frictions were ubiquitous throughout the Dominion but were perhaps more acute in Manitoba during the 1870s because of the temporal proximity of the Red River Resistance. Indicative of such a mood, a celebration was held in Winnipeg on April 19, 1872, marked with an intense bonfire in which Louis Riel was burned in effigy. When, late in the evening, the Chief of Police arrived tried to pull down the smoldering figure, the *Manitoba Liberal* noted that "the crowd gathered around him, showing unmistakeable hostile intentions had he persevered, he made an apology for his unwarrantable interference, and left them masters of the situation."[53]

As a by-product of these partisan tensions, there were divergent opinions about the professionalism and conduct of the volunteers in Winnipeg. To illustrate, in 1875, the editorialists at the *Manitoba Free Press* dismissed their poor conduct with a *boys will be boys* attitude stating that "the conduct of the recruits since arrival has been excellent on the whole, but the first pay day did not pass by without a few inebriates falling into 'the hands of the Philistines.'"[54]

But the list of transgressions perpetrated by Militia volunteers against Métis in the first two years is long and too patently partisan in nature to casually dismiss as routine soldierly steam-venting. In a paper prepared for the Louis Riel Institute entitled "The Reign of Terror against the Métis of Red River," Lawrence Barkwell, the Coordinator of Métis History and Heritage Research, articulated a profoundly upsetting list of volunteer violence that clearly illustrates a partisan bias and targeting of Métis and their sympathisers. Moreover, Métis were not alone in suffering the intimidation of the volunteers — French Catholics, too, were considered legitimate targets of the miscreant soldiers. The list is too extensive to share in full here, but a sampling of the events will demonstrate the extent of volunteer intimidation. In many instances, the perpetrators were allegedly volunteers, and whether for a lack of vigour in the investigation, or perhaps a legitimate lack of evidence, many of the alleged perpetrators were never brought to justice.[55]

On August 24, 1870, a member of the Red River Expeditionary Force shot Father Kavanagh of White Horse Plains while a Métis named Wabishka Morin was also assaulted. In September of 1870, John Schultz, leader of the pro-Canada party during the Resistance, broke into the home of Thomas Spence the editor of the *New Nation*, a newspaper created by Louis Riel after he amalgamated the *Nor' Wester* and he *Red River Pioneer*, horsewhipped him, and then broke into his office, scattered his staff and destroyed the printing press. [56] In September of 1870, James Ross, who was representative of the English Métis was a member of the Provisional Government under Riel, had his home burnt to the ground in an act of arson. In November of 1870, a man named Landry was set upon by twelve to fifteen soldiers, had a rope tied around his neck and was dragged for about a hundred feet before the police were brought to the scene — the soldiers claiming they wanted revenge for the death of Thomas Scott.

John Schultz figured prominently in the process of intimidation. The enmity he held for French Catholics and Métis did not dissipate with the arrival of the Wolseley expedition, but rather it seemed to stoke the fires of his hate. His martial ardour that was so apparent during the resistance carried on throughout the years after Manitoba joined confederation. Indeed, his editorials, shared in his newspaper, in some cases crossed the boundaries of professional decency, even going so far as to encourage the Militia volunteers to engage in violence and intimidation. His role in this capacity was quite well known, enough that it caused several political commenters to express concern about his qualifications for office. Notwithstanding the jingoistic tone struck by the *Volunteer Review* at the outbreak of the Resistance, its columns were also replete with expressions of disgust at the volunteers' behaviour, and even at that of John Schultz. In one instance, upon learning of the appointment of William Nassau Kennedy and John Schultz to positions in the Active Militia, one "G.W." wrote anonymously the *Review* to express his extreme pleasure at the selection of Kennedy for the position. Schultz, however, was not as warmly received by G.W. Quite the contrary, G.W. observed that

> I should consider the appointment of Dr. John C. Shultz to a similar position, one of a very different character. His prominent position and the political influence which he has secured so entirely for ends of the most utter selfishness, doubtless designate him as a man not to be refused. I only trust that in a military position, he will acquire some slight knowledge of the requirements of military discipline, but I should think but little confidence can be felt in a man who could so far allow his selfish vanity to blind him to his plain public duty, as to prostitute the temporary prosperity he enjoyed to purposes of factious violence, and to do his best to bring disgrace on the military service of his country by tampering and causing his agents to tamper with the sense of military discipline of the men of the first Dominion expedition.[57]

With men like John Schultz in positions of power and influence, the process of intimidation grew exponentially. Unsurprisingly, Louis Riel and his family were specific targets of the volunteer intimidation. In December of 1871, a group of discharged soldiers of the first expedition burst into Riel's home claiming to have a warrant for his arrest. Riel was not present, so the brigands resorted to threatening the women by holding guns to their heads and demanding to know his whereabouts. One member vowed that Riel would be dead by the end of the evening. This act was disagreeable enough to motivate several citizens write a petition to the lieutenant-governor asking him to take steps to ensure such atrocities were not repeated.[58]

Perhaps most grievous was the assault and subsequent murder of Elzear

Goulet, a Métis who was involved in the execution of Thomas Scott. Goulet had been one of the staunchest supporters of Riel during the resistance which consequently made him one of the most despised inhabitants of Red River amongst the virulently pro-Canada partisans. While many of his colleagues fled after the arrival of Wolseley, Goulet chose to remain in Fort Garry. Of Goulet, Joseph Alfred Mousseau remarked in an October 1870 edition of *l'Opinion Publique,* that "depuis l'arrivée des troupes, il était resté au milieu des métis français, se gardant bien de s'aventurer sur le territoire ennemi. »[59] In September of 1870, Goulet reportedly accepted a job as a guide for a Mr. Cunningham from Toronto. He crossed the Red River from the parish of St. Boniface to the town of Winnipeg and was recognized by what Mousseau referred to as "un parent de l'un des prisonniers de Riel au Fort Garry."[60] He was then set upon by some volunteers — originating from *la vertueuse Province sœur,* as Mousseau sarcastically referred to Ontario, and fled his assaulters by bolting for St. Boniface.[61] He attempted to swim the Red River to evade his pursuers, but they pelted him with rocks as he swam, one rock striking him on the head, and he eventually drowned. No punishment was ever meted out to any of those involved.[62] Compounding the tragedy, his daughter, Laurette was allegedly raped by members of the Red River Expeditionary Force and died of her injuries.[63]

The story of the Goulet tragedy found its way into other major publications, for example the *Canadian Illustrated News* carried word of the murder which it called "a most unfortunate circumstance." The *Canadian Illustrated News* tried to strike a moral if not cultural balance and stated "While Riel, Lepine, O'Donoghue, Ross and others, ought to be tried for causing the death of Scott, so ought the two volunteers and the half dozen 'loyalists' who hunted poor Goulet into the river."[64]

Of course, there are differing recollections. Sam Steele recounted in his memoir that several Militia volunteers were on fatigue duty pulling boats out of the Assiniboine when two horsemen approached them and asked if they had seen Goulet. When the soldiers could produce no information, the horsemen rode into Winnipeg where they found him at the Davis House and then pursued him to the Red River where they took several shots at him as he tried to swim the river. According to Steele the horsemen had been followed to the riverbank by a crowd, amongst whom were two buglers from the force but no other soldiers. He admits "we had amongst us about a dozen very wild spirits, but they were kept in control by the strict discipline maintained in the regiment, and, what is sometimes better, the fear of the displeasure of their comrades." Steele also recounted that a strong party of military police were on duty and, in his opinion, "it is a certainty that they would be aware of any part taken by soldiers and would have arrested the delinquents on the spot."[65]

Notwithstanding Steele's optimistic tone and faith in the discipline of his colleagues, it is hard to accept the veracity of his account. He was inclined to accept that the wild spirits amongst the battalion were kept in check, but the list of transgressions indicates this is manifestly inaccurate. On the contrary, it seems like there was a singular lack of effective command and control in the battalion which only encouraged and enabled ill-discipline amongst these wild spirits. Even if Steele's recollection is accurate, it nonetheless reflects a very disagreeable state of ethnic violence in Winnipeg if a man could be chased and drowned with a large crowd looking on in silence. The only question that remains is whether Steele's account is deliberately inaccurate or simply naïve to the true nature of some of his colleagues.

Goulet's murder had strategic implications that reverberated well beyond the boundaries of the new province. He was an American citizen living in Manitoba, and his death piqued the interest of the United States counsel in Fort Garry, James Taylor. News of the murder of Goulet went as high as the Secretary of State in Washington who even penned a note to the Governor General asking him to furnish any information on the circumstances surrounding the death of Goulet. In his note to the Governor General, the Secretary of State even mentions that the President had been briefed on the subject.[66] This was not the only time that Volunteer violence resulted in strategic reverberations in the United States - in May of 1871, a drunken volunteer set upon Mr. Taylor and assaulted him, news of which was printed in no less than the *New York Times* under the heading "Military Reign of Terror in Manitoba."[67] The *New York Herald* also chimed in on the subject, adding that not only was the Consul assaulted, but the soldier also pulled down the American flag. The *Herald* reported that "the soldiers, generally... have created a reign of terror in the Territory. We advise them, however, to avoid American Consuls on the raiding expeditions."[68]

That the *New York Times* was carrying news of the situation in Winnipeg is not unique, indeed, word was spreading about the internecine conflict and racist violence in Fort Garry far beyond the borders of the tiny postage-stamp province. The outrages were widely reported in the St. Paul *Daily Pioneer*, no doubt reflecting the regional connection between Winnipeg and St. Paul. In fact, it was in the columns of the *Daily Pioneer* that the first use of the term "reign of terror" is found in October of 1870. At the same time, the *Telegraph* of Toronto announced that marauding gangs of volunteers were organizing to raid Métis houses in the settlement.[69]

Violent intimidation was an unsavoury tool in the establishment of a British society in Manitoba that, lamentably, enjoyed resounding success. The fact that both the established Anglo-protestant inhabitants, and the English Métis of Fort Garry, who were predominantly of Scottish ancestry, suffered no such oppression at the hands of the swelling British population illustrates that their cultural common ground allowed them to integrate and even assimilate with the emergent British cultural group. This conclusion is reinforced by the fact that between 1870 and 1886 the population of French Métis in Manitoba decreased by 24 percent, while the population of English Métis only dropped by 12 percent.[70] By 1885, two-thirds of the Manitoba's populace was Anglophone and Protestant.[71] In response to the influx of predominantly English Protestant British settlers and violent intimidation by the Militia volunteers, the Métis displaced westward into the St. Laurent Valley, and the cultural DNA of Manitoba changed forever.

Distance and time did nothing to assuage or redress the grievances of the Métis and First Nations peoples of the North-West as they were bullied out of their homes or sequestered on reserve lands. The peaceful prosperity of Winnipeg and Manitoba had as its foundation the partisan and racist intimidation and violence that marred the early years of the new province. As Manitoba swelled with immigrants, interest in the bountiful lands that lay west in what is now Saskatchewan and Alberta increased. Another clash of cultures, this one far more violent, was the result.

7

SUPPRESSION: THE NORTH-WEST REBELLION OF 1885

A small deputation of Métis from the North-West Territories consisting of Gabriel Dumont, Moise Ouellete, Michel Dumas, and James Isbister arrived in Montana in June of 1884. After fifteen years of Dominion intransigence, Dominion dubiousness in the Métis land claim agreement contained in the *Manitoba Act*, and in the face of increasing white settlement in the North-West, these emissaries travelled to St. Peter's Mission on the Sun River to plead with the erstwhile leader of the Métis, Louis Riel, to return to Canada. Since the arrival of the Red River Expedition, Louis Riel had been elected to parliament but denied permission to take his seat as a bounty was put on his head and a warrant for his arrest was issued. He decided to move beyond the reach of Canadian justice and settled with his family in Montana. Despite initial reticence, Riel agreed to return to the North-West. He packed up his wife and two kids and struck out for Batoche, a small settlement North-East of Saskatoon in modern Saskatchewan, the spiritual and cultural capital of the Métis people of the North-West, arriving there in early July. On July 8, 1885, he addressed the Métis concerning the way forward to establish and protect their rights.

At about the time that Riel was travelling to Batoche, a change in leadership of the Canadian Militia occurred miles to the east. A mere four days after Riel addressed his people upon his return to the Canadian prairies, the new British general officer commanding the Canadian Militia, Colonel Frederick Dobson

Middleton, who despite holding the rank of colonel was authorized to sport the local rank of major-general, was introduced to reporters at Quebec City. He was described by these journalists as "red-faced, very short, and friendly."[1]

As Riel pontificated to his people, and Middleton fielded questions from the press, somewhere in the middle, in Winnipeg, gunners of the Winnipeg Field Battery prepared for their annual summer camp. Only five days after Middleton's first exchange with the Dominion's fourth estate, and barely more than a week after Riel gave his remarks, the Winnipeg Field Battery paraded at Fort Osborne and then proceeded to conduct their training on the crest of a hill between the Fort and the Assiniboine River. The Field Battery was the only corps of the Active Militia in Military District No. 10 that went into camp that year, although the 90th Battalion and the Winnipeg Cavalry Troop paraded and were inspected later that fall.

These three events may seem to be disparate and unrelated, the only apparent commonality being that they occurred mere days apart, albeit hundreds of miles away from one another. It is very likely, given the pace that news spread at the time, that the people involved in each event knew very little about the other two. Despite this apparent randomness, and unbeknownst to all those participating, Middleton, the Militiamen, and the Métis shared one common destiny — ten months later Middleton and the Winnipeg gunners would be at war with many of those who gathered to listen to Louis Riel in Batoche.

The story of the North-West Rebellion, as the conflict in the spring and summer of 1885 has become known, is well trodden ground, but the level of involvement by the Militia units of Manitoba has had less historical rigour directed towards it. This is a lamentable gap in the historical narrative as the impact of the rebellion, by dint of sheer proximity, was more acute in Manitoba than it was in her sister provinces throughout the Dominion.

The Militia units of Manitoba figured prominently in the 1885 struggle in the North-West. Over 4,500 Canadian Militiamen joined the *North-West Field Force*, the task force created by the Dominion Government and placed under the command Major-General Middleton to suppress the rebellion. Of that number, 1,217, or approximately 27 percent of the force were raised in Manitoba.[2] This is a significant contribution, especially given that the Canadian population, as of the 1881 census, was approximately 4.3 million, and the population of Manitoba was only 65,954, or 1.5 percent of the national total.[3] Moreover, the *Militia Report* for 1884, the last calendar year before the Rebellion began, indicated that the Canadian Active Militia consisted of 37,036 total volunteers, of which only 607 were located in Military District No. 10, a ratio that is but 1.6 percent of the total number.[4] It is interesting to note, therefore, that the number of men raised for the North-West Field Force in Manitoba was actually double the number of men who were actually enrolled in the Manitoba Active Militia Corps' prior to hostilities. Viewed through this statistical lens, the Militia volunteers of Manitoba, and by extension the general population, were indeed decisively engaged in the Rebellion, so much so Lieutenant-Colonel Houghton was able to proudly claim in his Military District No. 10 Annual Report for 1885, which was completed after the hostilities ended, that "all the Corps in the District … were employed on active service in the North-West during the late rebellion."[5]

Much had changed in Manitoba in the fifteen years between the end of the Red River Resistance and the eruption of the North-West Rebellion. By 1885, Manitoba was no longer a tiny postage stamp province but instead it had grown substantially both in geographical size and in population. Of the former, in 1881, Manitoba's borders were extended westward to their present location significantly increasing Manitoba's share of the Dominion's territory. This increase in territorial size resulted in a substantial increase to the province's population to the number of about 16,000 souls. Most of these new Manitobans were Anglo-protestant settlers who, as their recently acquired provincial brethren had done when they arrived in Manitoba after the Red River Resistance in 1870, had transplanted their culture, institutions ,and traditions on their new home in the North-West.[6]

In previous chapters we have seen that, from a purely military perspective, between 1870 and 1885, the Militia in Manitoba was used as a military deterrent to American expansionism and Fenian incursions, albeit not a very intimidating one. This rather passive role changed completely in the spring of 1885. During the North-West Rebellion, the Canadian Militia units in Manitoba were employed in a strictly military-operational sense to achieve the same strategic ends that were so aptly articulated to the Governor General during his 1877 visit to Emerson, namely to occupy, possess and mold the

MILITARY DISTRICT NO. 10 ON THE EVE OF WAR

A review of the *Militia Report* for District No. 10 for calendar year 1884 provides a snapshot of the Militia in Manitoba on the eve of the rebellion. Houghton's report does not paint a flattering picture of the Manitoba Militia units in 1884, but instead reflects a force that is under-subscribed, ill-equipped, and poorly trained.

The *effective strength* of the Militia in Manitoba and the North-West, which is the number of men enrolled in Active Militia Corps, numbered a total of only 607 officers and men. Conversely, the *established strength,* which was the number of Militia volunteers that the district was authorized to have on its rolls, was 62 officers and 775 men based on a force of twelve Militia corps: a cavalry troop, an artillery battery, three companies of mounted rifles — two in Prince Albert and one in Duck Lake — and seven infantry corps: the 90th Battalion "city" corps of six companies, as well as individual "rural" corps of one company each in Kildonan, Emerson, St. Jean Baptiste, St. Boniface, Prince Albert and Battleford. Evidently, the Militia corps were not successful at filling their ranks, being 230 volunteers short of their authorized strength. Moreover, although the district was authorized to have 380 men conduct annual drill in the summer of 1884, only the Winnipeg Field Battery went into camp, while the 90th Battalion and the Winnipeg Cavalry Troop were inspected at their corps headquarters.

The importance of the annual camp cannot be overstated in terms of operational readiness, it being the only opportunity for Militia units to practice their martial skills for periods of time longer than a few hours, and on terrain likely to be used in combat, not on a parade square or in a drill hall. The fact that only one of the district's units conducted its annual drill is reflective of the level of amateurism amongst the Canadian Militia that would later become very evident during the rebellion.

While the district's overall enrolment numbers were down, that was not necessarily the case for all the individual units. In some cases, the unit staffing situation was rather good, while others lagged. As an illustration, the 90th Battalion was authorized 26 officers and 252 men, but paraded 23 officers and 262 men at its annual inspection on November 10. Conversely, the Winnipeg Cavalry Troop was authorized three officers and forty-two men, but could only muster three officers and thrity-one men at inspection, while the Winnipeg Field Battery was authorized six officers and seventy-nine men, but only paraded four officers and fifty-nine men at inspection.[7]

Perhaps due to their distance from the seat of population and power in the eastern provinces, and the attendant logistical challenges such a distance incurs, on the eve of the North-West Rebellion, the units of Militia District No. 10 remained woefully ill-equipped. Houghton noted during his inspection of the Winnipeg Field Battery that while their manoeuvres and drills were well done, the gunners had "a great deficiency in side arms and small stores ... [and] cannot properly be regarded as being in a state of efficiency."[8] Moreover, "the men's clothing was pretty well worn out, and [looked] exceedingly shabby," a state of affairs he attributed to the fact the battery had conducted five encampments in the four years that had passed since the issue of the battery's equipment and clothing.[9]

Despite the lack of proper equipment and accoutrements, the professionalism and competence of the Militia volunteers seemed to meet with Houghton's approval, at least for the Winnipeg Field Battery and the 90th Battalion. Of the former, we have observed that he was impressed with their manoeuvring during annual training and inspection, and of the latter, he remarked that during their annual inspection "the men moved with remarkable steadiness and precision, and all the Officers seemed well up in their work." He was particularly impressed with Major Boswell of the 90th Battalion who had "proved himself a most efficient and zealous Officer, having spared no pains, and been largely instrumental in conducing [the regiment] to such a satisfactory result."[10]

The rural corps of the district did not measure up to the high professional regard with which Houghton held the Winnipeg Field Battery and 90th Battalion. The Kildonan Infantry Company was practically extinct, and its commander had returned his arms and accoutrements into stores. It was a similar situation for the Emerson Infantry Company, despite the extensive efforts of its commander, Captain Nash, to keep it well established. For its part, 1884 was the third year in a row that the St. Boniface Infantry Company had not drilled. Houghton recommended to Militia Headquarters that all three of these corps be stricken from the rolls.[11]

Houghton reserved his most piquant criticism for the St. Jean Baptiste Infantry Company, which he regarded as "practically useless." Additionally,

Houghton went to the unusual step of singling out the Company's commander, Captain Thibault, as particularly unimpressive. He related to the adjutant-general that, despite having given Thibault enough time to prepare for an inspection by Houghton's delegate, Major Street, Thibault could only produce nine rifles for inspection, the remainder being in the possession of the volunteers who, being farmers, were scattered about the area. Major Street had to take a laboriously circuitous route to get to the Company's headquarters and arrived to find that the corps was completely unprepared for inspection, rendering his journey utterly profitless. As with the other three rural companies, Houghton recommended the abolishment of the St. Jean Baptiste Company.

In the place of the companies recommended for disbandment, Houghton suggested that another four companies should be created: one in Portage la Prairie, two in Brandon, and one in Indian Head in the North-West Territory. He felt that in these locations, recruitment would be more successful and the presence of a military force would be invaluable in the event of any martial contingency.[12] It should be noted that all of these locations lay along the Canadian Pacific Railway and his focus on establishing military forces astride its route reflects the strategic importance of the railway, and its allure to settlement and consequent concentration of the populace. The outbreak of the rebellion forestalled the pursuit of such a course of action, although in retrospect Houghton seemed to have understood the simmering tensions in the region.

The disparity between District No. 10's city and rural corps mirrored the experiences of the other districts across the Dominion. Historian Desmond Morton observed that while city battalions drilled regularly and participated in social and athletic activities that contributed to team cohesion, the rural corps were less homogenous and only drilled for twelve days every two years, or perhaps even more sporadically, as the District No. 10 *Militia Report* for 1884 indicated.[13] Houghton remarked that the rural corps of District No. 10 seemed to be at best ineffective, at worst completely useless. Perhaps this is the reason why Middleton, when he eventually realized that a substantial number of troops would be required to supress the Rebellion, sent a telegram to the Minister of Militia, Adolphe Caron on March 27, 1885 in which he stated, "matter getting serious, better send all Regular and *good City Regiments* [emphasis added]."[14]

Houghton concluded his 1884 annual report of Military District No. 10 with an observation that was indicative of the populace of Manitoba's latent fear of Indigenous uprisings, Fenian incursions, and the lawless Yankee malefactors who prowled the prairie in the mid-1880s. He lamented the fact that Manitoba stood isolated for seven months of the year — recall the admonition of the Manitoba Executive Council to the Secretary of State of Canada when discussions were afoot to disband the Active Militia garrison in Manitoba mentioned in the introductory chapter — with no reliable line of communication from the east to facilitate the concentration of reinforcing military forces should the need arise. Houghton concluded that Manitoba was "entirely dependent on its own internal resources for defence."[15] These resources, across a frontier of 1,260 miles, were limited to 607 Militiamen and, perhaps, a similar number of Mounted Police — a combined force he found wholly inadequate to the task. Curiously, although Houghton acknowledged the perceived threat posed by First Nations, he seemed to think the greatest threat came from the south. He admitted that while the Dominion had "no immediate reason for anticipating hostile action on the part of [its] neighbours … we cannot overlook the fact that we are still liable, as in the past to be subjected to the annoyance by a certain element to the south of us, which … Might, nevertheless, at any moment, compel us to stand on our defence."[16] This is an unsubtle reference to the pervading fear of Fenians, a fear that would manifest itself more acutely during the Rebellion. Unbeknownst to Houghton, the most prominent threat to the Dominion and his soldiers in Military District No. 10 was not south of the international boundary but brewing to the North-West.

DISCONTENT IN THE NORTH-WEST

What caused the conflagration in the North-West? What drove the Métis to reach out to their exiled leader and prophet to implore his return? The historical narrative of the years following the Red River Resistance — how the Métis were forced to migrate westward in the face of increasing white settlement, violence, and intimidation in Manitoba, and in pursuit of dwindling Bison herds, is well known. It is also a question of some detail that is beyond the scope of this book to investigate thoroughly, but a brief survey of the situation in the North-West between 1870 and the eruption of the North-West Rebellion in 1885 is advisable to contextualize the role of the Manitoba Militia units in the conflict.

The exodus of the Métis to the North-West began almost immediately after Manitoba and the North-West Territory entered Confederation at the culmination of the Red River Resistance. While most of the Métis at the time of Confederation lived in Red River and the territory that became the Province of Manitoba, they were also very familiar with the land of the North-West in what is now Saskatchewan and Alberta. For years the Métis had organized brigades of bison hunters who traversed the plains during the annual hunt. As the herds depleted and moved westward, the Métis followed them, the trails of their hunting brigades extending further and further towards the Rocky Mountains. As they roamed further and further west, the Métis latently conducted a sort of cultural reconnaissance of the region, growing familiar with the lay of the land, the run of the rivers and the location of potential future settlements. Many returned to Red River during the winter, while others over-wintered in the North-West.

Those who decided against returning to Red River during the winter and elected instead to over-winter in the unsettled areas of present-day Saskatchewan and Alberta, chose to stay in appropriate locations that were capable of sustaining them during the cold months of winter. They required locales with enough water to sustain life, and with sufficient wood nearby to construct and heat their shelter. These wintering settlements were prevalent throughout the region, focussed in the lower branches of the North and South Saskatchewan Rivers, and the Qu'Appelle Valley. Naturally as the Métis displaced to the North-West, they gravitated to these established settlements due to their familiarity with the locale, established kin and cultural connections, and the availability of resources necessary to support the re-establishment of their homes.[17]

There is an unfortunate belief in some historical circles that the North-West Rebellion of 1885 erupted out of nowhere. For example, Charles Pelham Mulvaney remarked in his book *The History of the North-West Rebellion* that "at eleven o'clock on the night of March the 27th the citizens of every city in Canada, from Halifax to Victoria, were startled by the tidings that armed rebellion had broken out in the Prince Albert region."[18] Even more prosaic, the gazette *The Riel Rebellion 1885* published by "Witness" Printing House in Montreal opined "no volcanic eruption ever broke out more unexpectedly than the rebellion in the North-West."[19] Nothing could be further from the truth. The eruption of violence came after a very long period of political intransigence, indifference, cruelty, and double-dealing on the part of the Dominion government towards the Métis and the First Nations people of the North-West. The fact the Métis and some First Nations of the North-West decided to take up arms in 1885 to redress the violation of their rights should not have surprised anyone.

A major source of discontent amongst the Métis was the ineffectual governance of the Territory. The first attempt to establish Canadian jurisdiction over the North-West occurred in 1869 with the passing of *An Act for the temporary Government of Rupert's Land and the North-Western Territory when united with Canada*. The provisions of this act were suspended on the outbreak of the Red River Resistance but were then re-enacted after royal assent was given to the *Manitoba Act*. Section 4 of the *Temporary Government of Rupert's Land Act* authorized the establishment of "a Council of not exceeding fifteen nor less than seven persons, to aid the Lieutenant-Governor [of Manitoba, *ex officio* lieutenant-governor of the North-West Territory] in the administration of affairs, with such powers as may be from time to time conferred upon them by Order in Council."[20] The council was not created until 1872, however, and even then, only on a temporary basis. Even when its status became more permanent, it lacked any real teeth and did very little to govern the territory. Consequently, while the *Manitoba Act* and the *Temporary Government of Rupert's Land Act* had solidified the political authority of the Dominion over Manitoba and the North-West Territories, in many ways, as far as those who lived in the North-West were concerned, they were governed by an absentee landlord: the Council of the North-West Territory may have acted as the *de jure* local government of the North-West Territories but it was essentially powerless, and the *de facto* political authority emanated from afar in Ottawa rather than Battleford, the original capital of the territory.

This resultant weak regional authority in the North-West Territory created a political vacuum that needed to be filled. The Métis' long association with the region through years of bison hunting, their kinship and connection with First Nations, and the complete lack of effectual federal authority prompted them to establish their own political control over the region which they saw as their patrimony. On December 10, 1883, at an assembly of Métis in St. Laurent, located in present day Saskatchewan, the Métis agreed to create a provisional government under the presidency of Gabriel Dumont. Of particular note, the Métis stressed that the creation of a provisional government was not meant to establish an independent state but, contrarily, as a regional authority of subjects, loyal and faithful to the Queen, who were willing to submit to the laws of the Dominion as soon as Canada was able to establish magistrates and a force capable of maintaining the authority of law in the region.[21] This Provisional Government thus became a voice for the Métis in redressing its grievances with the Dominion of Canada.

The Provisional Government sent several letters of complaint to Ottawa including, in March 1883, a list of fourteen demands which focused on an increase in French representation in government, a land grant to the Métis settlers, allowance of the Métis river-lot system and support for local schools.[22] The Dominion Government turned a deaf ear to their requests. Frustrated at Canadian intransigence and outright ignorance, the Métis turned to Louis Riel in Montana to help them in their remonstrations with the Dominion Government, causing him to return to Canada to lead his people once again.[23] Thereafter a series of warning signs emerged as temporal way markers from discontent to rebellion.

In the fall of 1884, events began that would eventually lead to conflict. Captain Samuel Steele of the North-West Mounted Police, at the time working to maintain order along the construction of the Canadian Pacific Railway line near the Alberta/British Columbia border, recounted in his autobiography *Forty Years in Canada,* that in September of 1884 reports emerged that there was a meeting of Métis and Indigenous in St Laurent "where a man called Jackson made and inflammatory speech, in which he said that the North-West Territory 'belonged to the Indians and not to the Dominion of Canada.'"[24] The next month, in October, presumably in response to the number of manifestations of the Métis and Indigenous persons, a Mounted Police post was established at Carlton, and the number of police in the region was increased to two hundred, deployed between Battleford, Carlton, Prince Albert, and Fort Pitt.[25] Over the winter of 1884–85, things seem to have remained relatively quiet. With the approach of spring, however, the situation began to sour.

The Métis Revolutionary Bill of Rights, passed on March 8, 1885 in St. Laurent, articulated the grievances of the Métis. Their key demands focused on equality of land grants, the creation of the provinces of Alberta and Saskatchewan with functioning legislatures for each, and improved provisions for indigenous persons.[26] On March 10, Superintendent Gagnon, the North-West Mounted Police officer commanding the police force at Fort Carlton located sixty-five kilometers north of Saskatoon, telegraphed to the North-West Mounted Police Commissioner, Acheson Irvine, formerly of the Wolseley Expedition and Military District No. 10, to state that his men had observed and heard reports of worrisome activity amongst the Métis. The next day Crozier telegrammed the Commissioner to request a seven-pounder gun and twenty-five men to reinforce Carlton from Battleford.[27]

Understanding that the situation was deteriorating, Colonel Irvine left Regina on March 18 with a force of four officers and eighty-six men to reinforce the northern area of Saskatchewan. On March 18 and 19, 1885, the Métis seized the church in Batoche where Riel thereafter established his headquarters. Irvine moved towards Batoche, but when he received reports of the large number of Métis situated there, he crossed the South Saskatchewan and made for Prince Albert, arriving there on March 24, and thence he proceeded to Fort Carlton. It was on this march to Fort Carlton that he received word of an event which would arguably be the catalyst of the conflict.

On March 26, 1885, a North-West Mounted Police patrol under the command of Major Leif Newry Fitzroy Crozier encountered a group of Métis outside Duck Lake in present-day Central Saskatchewan about ninety kilometres north of Saskatoon. The Mounties had travelled to Duck Lake to secure provisions from Hillyard Mitchell's general goods store. The Métis were under the command of Gabriel Dumont and had entrenched themselves on the road leading into Duck Lake. After a brief parley between Crozier and two Métis, nerves got the better of the men and gunfire erupted. What ensued, know to history as the Battle of Duck Lake, resulted in the death of twelve Mounties and five Métis, and the Mounties withdrawing from the field in defeat. Only the intervention of Louis Riel, who had had enough bloodshed for the day, kept Dumont and the Métis from pursuing the fleeing policemen and destroying them.[28] Crozier's superior, Colonel Irvine, was *en route* to reinforce him when the Battle of Duck Lake occurred. Irvine was thrust on the horns of a dilemma: should he withdraw his forces to the nearby town of Carlton, or return to Prince Albert. He concluded that Carlton was indefensible, and as Prince Albert was the most populous town in the region and almost completely defenceless, he determined to abandon Carlton and concentrate his forces in Prince Albert.[29]

News of the Métis victory at Duck Lake spread quickly throughout the region and, in an exemplar of the concept of *propaganda of the deed*, wherein bold actions serve as a catalyst to revolution, Dumont's victory galvanized several First Nations into action. Notwithstanding the important impact Dumont's victory had, the truth is that several tribes of Plains Indians had their own causes for redress with the Dominion Government and needed but little incentive to rise up in arms.

Like the Métis, the First Nations of the North-West were slowly pushed off the land they had lived on for centuries, and thence on to reservations. Once on the reservations, their problems were exacerbated by the arrival of drought and disease, and a general economic down-turn that resulted in a reduction of government-issued rations.[30] The First Nations found themselves confined, surrounded and starving. They were forced to adopt a sedentary, reservation-based lifestyle that was wholly at odds with their culture and history of a migratory existence. Like the Métis, their supplications to Ottawa fell on deaf ears. This was a time when the First Nations of the North-West were in desperate need of assistance but the government's policy of financial retrenchment only worsened the situation.[31] A key element of this problem lay in the Superintendent of Indian Affairs, Edgard Dewdney, whose parsimonious approach forced the Frist Nations to choose between starvation and violence.[32] The injustice of their suffering, coupled with the desperation that grew out of several years of drought, starvation and budgetary constraints, formed a combustible combination that was of immense concern to the federal authorities.

> While a Métis uprising made the federal government uncomfortable, the true fear in Ottawa was the potential for a broad indigenous uprising. Riel recognized that the Métis were unable to carry the day on their own, and desperately sought First Nations support dispatching Métis envoys amongst the First Nations to solicit their support. His strategy was militarily sound and was reinforced by sheer numbers. The eventual number of Métis insurgents in the North-West numbered only about 1,000 souls,[33] while the First Nations population of the North-West numbered some 26,000 in 1884.[34] The possibility of such a large number of First Nations

joining the rebellion was the single greatest threat to the establishment of Canadian authority in the North-West, the pre-emption of which was one of the critical objectives of the Dominion Government.

Despite Riel's efforts and Ottawa's fears, only a small number of the First Nations residents took arms against the federal government. [35] Riel's emissaries bringing enticements to rebellion, coupled with news of the Métis victory at Duck Lake, resulted in some discontented First Nation warriors willing to take up arms congregating at Battleford demanding provisions. When their demands were not met, the First Nations soldiers broke into the Hudson's Bay Company's stores and pillaged some local buildings while the terrified inhabitants fled to the sanctuary of the Mounted Police barracks. For the next month, the settlers in Battleford remained behind the ramparts of the barracks while the First Nations warriors occupied the town. As shocking as this development was, it paled in comparison to the event that would become known to history as the *Frog Lake Massacre*. [36]

Frog Lake sits in what is now the Province of Alberta, only a short distance west of the Alberta/Saskatchewan boundary and about fifty-five kilometres North-West of Fort Pitt. A Plains Cree band, under the leadership of their charismatic chief Big Bear had settled on a reservation near Frog Lake. The recent past had been hard on the band, exacerbated by the Dominion Government refusing to provide rations to the Cree followers of Big Bear due to his reticence to accept reservation life. All this led to an understandable enmity amongst a large portion of the Cree population, and on April 2, Indigenous warrior Wandering Spirit, who was often at odds with Big Bear, lead a Plains Cree party to Frog Lake where they shot and killed the federal Indian Agent Thomas Quinn, two priests, the government farming instructor, an independent trader, a miller and three other men.

Theresa Gowanlock was a recent settler from Southern Ontario whose husband, John Gowanlock had brought her out to Frog Lake after their wedding. Tragically for Theresa Gowanlock, he was one of the victims of the uprising in that locale, which she recorded emotionally in her memoir *Two*

> Mr. Williscroft, an old grey-headed man about seventy-five years of age came running by us, and an Indian shot at him and knocked his hat off, and he turned around and said, "Oh! Don't shoot! Don't shoot!" But they fired again, and he ran screaming and fell in some bushes. On seeing this I began crying, and my husband tried to comfort me, saying "my dear wife be brave to the end," and immediately an Indian behind us fired, and my husband fell beside me his arm pulling from mine. I tried to assist him from falling. He put out his arms for me and fell, and I fell down beside him and buried my face on his, while his life was ebbing away so quickly, and was prepared for the next shot myself, thinking I was going with him too. But death just then was not ordained for me. I had yet to live. An Indian came and took me away from my dying husband [sic] side, and I refused to leave ... but he took my arm and pulled me away.[37]

From Frog Lake the Cree war party moved south-east to Fort Pitt where the North-West Mounted Police garrison and the local citizenry abandoned the settlement and set out down the Saskatchewan River towards Battleford while behind them, their homes and buildings were set alight.[38]

The strategic situation in the North-West, from the Dominion's perspective at least, was concerning. In the space of seven days the government in Ottawa had been placed on the back foot. As historian George Stanley observed "by the end of April, Riel had met with success at every hand. At Duck Lake, Battleford, Frog Lake, Fort Pitt the Métis and the Indians had met and defeated the whites or compelled them to surrender."[39] What had initially been dismissed by authorities in Ottawa as Indigenous rabble-rousing had become a very successful insurrection. The Dominion response was swift.

CANADA AND MANITOBA RESPOND

While the focus of this work is on the contribution of the Manitoba Militia units in the conflict, it is important to provide a cursory review of the operational campaign of the North-West Field Force to contextualize what happened in Manitoba at the outset and throughout the conflict. Consequently, what follows in this section is a review of the whole of the North-West Campaign, highlighting where appropriate, the efforts of Manitoba Militia units in the overall operation.

Unlike the glacial pace of military preparations that accompanied the plans for the Red River Expedition of 1870, a temerity that was caused by the constant to-ing and fro-ing between Ottawa and London alongside much political handwringing and dithering, the Dominion exhibited much more martial resolve in 1885. Strategic guidance was issued almost immediately, on March 23, 1885, Middleton received his orders from the Minister of Militia Adolphe Caron to proceed immediately to the North-West. He received further strategic direction in a letter from Prime Minister Sir John A. Macdonald several days later, on March 29, 1885, in which the Macdonald wrote:

> Although quite inexperienced in military matters, it can do no harm for me to send you some of my crude ideas in the present trouble. The first thing to be done is to localize the insurrection. *The CPR must of course be guarded*, but besides that, parties should be sent to watch the people and stores coming in at Emerson by rail. The *different trails across the border should also be watched as closely as possible*. A force should be placed at Battleford, and, if possible, a line of communication from that place to the railway, should be watched *so as to prevent the flame from spreading westwards*.[40]

Macdonald's guidance is instructive in several ways. Firstly, it indicates that his greatest fear was the spread of the rebellion, and his guidance reflects the importance he placed on containing and isolating the conflict. Second, it seems he, like many others, regarded the threat of reinforcements, perhaps by Fenians or other Indigenous forces coming in from the United States, as a serious concern that needed to be addressed. As we shall see, Middleton's operational plan indicates that he took these suggestions seriously. Having received his military strategic guidance from Macdonald and Caron, Middleton departed Ottawa that very evening, joined by his *aide de camp* Captain Wise. To move more expeditiously, both officers travelled *incognito* via the United States.

Middleton was an atypical Victorian British officer. Not wealthy, and thus unable to purchase his promotions, which was a common practice of the era, he was forced to seek promotion through merit and professionalism rather than his bank account or pedigree. He had a unique career that oscillated around the globe from one colonial conflict to another culminating in a surprising affinity for Canada. He was born in Belfast in 1825 and was commissioned into the 58th Foot in 1842. Prior to his arrival in Canada, he gained experience in colonial confrontations in Australia where he was mentioned in dispatches for gallant conduct in operations against Maori rebels in 1845. He was promoted to lieutenant in 1848 and transferred to the 96th Foot in India where he fought during the Santal rebellion in 1855. He transferred again to the 29th Foot and served in Burma, only to be transferred to Calcutta in 1857 with the outbreak of the Indian Mutiny. Returning to England in 1859, he went on to occupy several staff positions until his regiment, still the 29th Foot, was transferred to Canada in 1867, although Middleton did not join it until 1868 after he had completed studies at the staff college. Once in Canada he became a unique British officer, going on half-pay to occupy staff positions that most traditionalist British officers would have spurned: Town Major in London, Ontario, acting assistant Quartermaster General in Montreal and temporary deputy adjutant and Quartermaster General at Militia headquarters.

Middleton returned to England in 1875 after having wed Eugenie Doucet of Montreal. While in England, he held several posts, including the Executive Officer of the Royal Military College at Sandhurst. Middleton actively sought a return posting to Canada, particularly the position of General Officer Commanding, and was assisted in this regard with the support of the Governor General and the Minister of Militia, indicating that he had robust political connections with the established Canadian authorities. Middleton arrived back in Canada in July 1884 to assume this position.[41]

Military District No. 10 became wrapped up in the Dominion response to the crisis at an early date. As early as March 22, even before the confrontation at Duck Lake, Militia Headquarters in Ottawa was investigating the possibility of military intervention in the crisis. On that date, the Adjutant-General Colonel W. Powell, telegraphed Houghton to inquire as to how soon the 90th Battalion and the Winnipeg Cavalry might be ready to deploy to the North-West.[42] Houghton replied that the 90th and half the Winnipeg Field Battery could be ready to move forward by March 25, 1885, but disparaged sending the Cavalry, stating they were "undesirable" lacking in horses and "shirking" their duty.[43] He consequently received orders to have the 90th Battalion and the Winnipeg Field Battery in readiness no later than the 25th. In response to these instructions, a general muster of the 90th Battalion was ordered, and at 8:30 a.m. on March 23, the Battalion gathered at its drill hall.

When the unit had assembled, Houghton and the battalion leadership put the 90th through some manoeuvres, after which Houghton addressed the volunteers, stating that "the present was the first serious difficulty that has arisen in this country, and he wanted Winnipeg to show what it could do." Shortly thereafter, Houghton and his staff posted the following formal orders for both the 90th Battalion and the Winnipeg Field Battery: "Orders having been this day received from [Militia] Headquarters to hold the Winnipeg Field Battery and 90th Battalion Winnipeg Rifles in readiness for immediate active service these corps are hereby notified to govern themselves accordingly. The officers commanding the above corps are requested to make the necessary arrangements to have the men under their command ready for embarkation for the Northwest Territories at any time that may be arranged on or after [March 24, 1885]."[44]

While Middleton was *en route* to Winnipeg, orders were issued to Houghton to begin raising further forces in Winnipeg. On March 26, two companies of the 90th Battalion, numbering 110 officers and men under the command of the regimental Adjutant Major Charles Musgrave Boswell, went west aboard a chartered train — a 'special' — bound for the station stop of Troy. On the special, along with the vanguard of the 90th Battalion, was Edgar Dewdney, a former Member of Parliament, and the Lieutenant-Governor of the North-West Territories. In addition to his vice-regal position, which was far more executive in nature than ceremonial due to the absence of a territorial legislature, Dewdney was also the Indian Commissioner for the Territory. The *Brandon Sun* speculated the rapid dispatch of the force to Troy was to deter an uprising by First Nations Chief Piapot and his band of Plains Cree who the North-West Mounted Police had settled near Indian Head, a small community near the modern Manitoba/Saskatchewan border.[45]

Despite the seemingly quick response by Houghton and the corps of District No. 10, their reaction time did not meet with approval from the Minister of Militia. When, on March 26, 1885, Houghton advised Caron that the main body would not be able to move out as their outfitting was not yet complete, and he asked for an advance of funds to purchase horses, he received several terse replies the very same day. The first rather blunt response was to "follow instructions and get horses and what is required for the force from the Hudson Bay [sic]." The second was even more blunt and curt: "Explain why instructions have not been carried out to forward troops as ordered — what is the reason they are awaiting [the] General? Instructions received must be carried out to the letter by you."[46]

Middleton and Wise arrived in Winnipeg on the morning of March 27.[47] At three o'clock that day, Middleton arrived at the drill shed where elements of the 90th Battalion and the Winnipeg Field Battery had been parading and inspected the men, after which he received an extremely patriotic address from several retired military officers. At 5:30 p.m. that evening, the vanguard of the 90th Battalion marched out of the drill shed to the railway depot to the strains of "The Girl I left Behind." According to the *Free Press* "the streets were lined with spectators, while hundreds of people followed the procession. Thousands of citizens assembled about the depot to give the boys a send-off." At eight o'clock that night the Battalion was joined by General Middleton, and the train pulled out of the station bound for Qu'Appelle or what would be referred to simply, over the coming weeks, as the 'front.'[48] In command of the 90th Battalion was Major Alfred Mackeand who was forced to assume the duties of Commanding Officer in the absence of Lieutenant-Colonel William Nassau Kennedy who was deployed to the Sudan in support of Lord Wolseley. Middleton had hoped to proceed with the 90th Battalion and the Winnipeg Field Battery, but despite the heightened war spirit he found a degree of reticence and perhaps of sluggishness amongst the Militia ranks. He later cabled to the Minister of Militia to report that when he had left Winnipeg "[he] had ordered the rest of the 90th and the Battery to go with [him] but they required a good deal of urging and beating up, and finally [he] only succeeded in getting the 90th off, leaving the artillery to come [the next day]."[49]

There were several reasons for the artillery's delay, the most pressing being a lack of horses.[50] The hippomobile artillery of the day was dependent upon the provision of horses from local farmers and ranchers, since the cost of maintaining dedicated horses for the Militia artillery, which were used only a handful of days per year, was prohibitively high. Consequently, the manoeuvres and training of the Winnipeg Field Battery were contingent on the availability of these horses for hire from local farmers, and thus their supply hinged on the local agricultural calendar as well. To illustrate, in the summer of 1884, when the Field Battery was contemplating the scheduling of its annual drill, the deputy adjutant-general decided to proceed with holding the Battery's practice camp in July despite the fact that the unit's commanding officer, Major Jarvis, was absent on leave in England because it was "deemed inexpedient to postpone the encampment until his return, owing to the anticipated difficulty of obtaining horses at a later period, when farming operations would be likely to interfere."[51]

As events progressed, the government realized that a more substantial force than the 90th Battalion and Winnipeg Field Battery was going to be required. The swirling rumours about the Duck Lake confrontation fed into the excitement with General Middleton telegraphing Caron undulating casualty reports ranging from an initial assessment of six civilian and two police deaths, to the later much more accurate report of eleven police deaths. In response, Middleton suggested to the Minister that the force would have to be at least 2,000 men strong.[52] There was no dithering from a strategic perspective. Whereas the Red River Resistance of 1870 was resolved by diplomacy in the form of the *Manitoba Act* in this instance it seems that from the very outset of the North-West troubles the Dominion Government was committed to solving this problem with the sword, not the pen.

After arriving at Troy, Middleton spent the next three days in operational preparations. This pause was particularly necessary for the 90th Battalion who, Middleton found, were not prepared for operations despite the high praise Houghton had bestowed on the battalion in his previous annual report. In fact, Middleton recorded in his official report that he took this operational pause in order to "enable the 90th Battalion to fire blank and ball ammunition as [he] found that many of the men had never pulled a trigger."[53] Not only was the 90th rusty in musketry, but it was not particularly well equipped, perhaps due to its rapid deployment. In fact, an historian of the 10th Royal Grenadiers who spent a lot of time alongside the 90th, recorded the poor state of the latter regiment's tentage and general stores, but their willingness to share nonetheless thusly:

> the good feeling displayed by the 90th to the Grenadiers was of the very warmest; the accommodation they themselves possessed in the way of tents, bedding and eating and drinking utensils was barely sufficient for their own needs and yet they 'shared and shared alike' with their comrades the Grenadiers. Imagine a small tent built to contain four, with seven sleeping

in it and not more than blankets enough for half of them. Tea had to be drunk out of wash bowls, empty meat tins, dippers which had 'once been new' and other miscellaneous articles. Of these very primitive utensils too there were only about half enough to go 'round.[54]

The 90th Battalion was the vanguard of the North-West Field Force and it would eventually play a major role in the campaign. Captain James of the Grenadiers recalled that "Of all the regiments engaged in the Northwest expedition I think the 90th "Winnipeg" Rifles can justly lay claim to having done more actual foot marching than any other."[55]

Qu'Appelle became Middleton's forward operational hub. Throughout the conflict, however, Winnipeg served as the strategic hub from which most, if not all, logistical and administrative support was coordinated. These efforts were undertaken by Lieutenant-Colonel William Hayes Jackson, Deputy Adjutant-General of Military District No. 1, who became the principal supply, pay and transport officer of the North-West Field Force. On March 29, 1885, while General Middleton was in Qu'Appelle organizing his operational campaign and the 90th were honing their musketry skills, Jackson received the following telegram at his district headquarters in London, Ontario from the Adjutant-General of the Canadian Militia: "proceed at once to Winnipeg in order that you may be available for duty required there; your instructions will be forwarded to Winnipeg from here."[56] Jackson took the first train he could and arrived in Winnipeg on April 2, 1885. As Jackson made his way over rail through the United States and north into Winnipeg the situation in the North-West became even graver.

News had not yet reached Winnipeg about the Frog Lake massacre when Lieutenant-Colonel Jackson arrived, but the rumours and stories of the uprising had worked the local populace into a frenzy. Unsurprisingly, when he detrained in Winnipeg, he found the city to be "filled with excited people."[57] From all corners of the province, local leaders sought assistance from the Dominion Government to protect them from the potential of Indigenous uprisings. On March 28, the Mayor of Winnipeg telegraphed to Caron and stated that he thought "it very necessary that City Police Force should be armed with rifles. Can you grant this and issue order to Officer here in charge?" The request was quickly refused.[58]

Being rebuffed by the Militia Department, the City of Winnipeg set about organizing their own defence. A group of concerned citizens met with the mayor and decided to form a home guard known as the *Winnipeg Guards.* The city was divided into five districts, each under the command of a captain who was responsible to enroll volunteers in his district. The districts approximated the city wards: District No. 1 was originally headquartered at Tessier's Hotel on River Avenue, later switched to a vacant house near the Osborne Bridge, next to the residence of Mr. McMicken who arranged for its use, and consisted of Ward 1, under the command of Captain Geoff Patterson. District No. 2 consisted of Wards 2 and 3, headquartered at the south fire hall under the command of Captain J.W. Kennedy, District No. 3 comprised Ward 4 under Captain G.D. McVicar headquartered at the Central Fire Hall. District No. 4 consisted of Ward 6, headquartered at the north Fire Hall under the command of Captain Alex Brown and finally, District No. 5 under Captain H.S. Crofty consisted of Ward 6 and was headquartered, fortuitously for Captain Crofty and his colleagues, at Drewry's Brewery. Alderman Carruthers was appointed Marshall in overall charge of the Winnipeg Guards, assisted by five Deputy Marshals.[59]

After the violence of late March and early April, requests for support in arms and men flowed quickly, and steps were taken to ensure home guards were enrolled to protect the settlements in the case of indigenous uprisings. Virden organized a home guard of fifty men on April 1 at town meeting "for the protection [of the settlement] in the event of an attack being made upon the town by the half-breeds and Indians in this vicinity."[60] The same day the Mayor of Rapid City telegraphed the Minister of Militia to state, rather forthrightly, that the "town council deem it absolutely necessary for safety of [the] town in view of the unsettled state of neighbouring Indians and by resolution ask me to urgently request that one hundred stand of arms and ammunition be forwarded immediately."[61] Likewise in Morris, the people of the settlement held a public meeting and unanimously adopted the palaverous proposition that: "considering the critical condition that affairs have assumed in the Northwest this meeting views with alarm this possible outcome and deem it wise for the better protection of ourselves and the rendering of assistance for the suppression of the present rebellion that the proper authorities be communicated with for instructions in regard to our organizing in such form as will best conduce to our protection, and the furtherance of support to the Government in the preservation of the peace."[62]

Although the crisis was unfolding to the North-West of the province, the latent fear of Indigenous violence knew no geographical limitation and even the town of Whitemouth, which lay to the north-east of Winnipeg, organized a home guard of twenty men on April 3, as did Rat Portage, now the City of Kenora in Northwestern Ontario, several days later.[63]

As the political leadership of the various settlements in Manitoba and the North-West Territory went about their preparations for their own defence, the military authorities continued to mobilize and deploy their forces. On March 27, 1885, Charles Boulton was authorized by the Militia authorities to enroll a company in the Shell River district comprising sixty soldiers, which he was easily able to fill with volunteers from Birtle and Russel, Manitoba.[64] In order to solicit permission to raise a corps of scouts, Boulton used his familiarity with General Middleton to request an audience when they were both in Winnipeg in late March. Middleton passed the request along to the minister in Ottawa by telegraph. Perhaps unbeknownst to both Middleton and Minister Caron, Boulton had already used his impressive political connections to telegraph Prime Minister Macdonald directly, offering his services in the troubles, on March 24, 1885.[65] Four days after his interview with Middleton, Boulton received a telegram from Caron directing him to "report [himself] to Gen. Middleton for services."[66]

Boulton was no stranger to friction with the Métis in the North-West. He had served in the British Army in the Royal Canadian Rifles, and retired in Southern Ontario, joining the ranks of the Active Militia. He first arrived in the North-West in 1869 as an employee with the Dominion surveyors whose indelicate approach to staking out farms was a major catalyst of the Red River Resistance. At the outbreak of hostilities, presumably given his military experience, he attempted to organize a military force to resist the forces of Riel but was instead captured, imprisoned in Fort Garry and even sentenced to death — a sentence that was eventually commuted by Riel.[67]

Boulton's force during the 1885 campaign was one of mounted infantry known as *Boulton's Scouts*. Leaders at every level of strategic command, including both the prime minister and the Minister of Militia, recognized the value of mounted infantry to combat operations on the prairie. Mounted infantry, it was thought, was the ideal force for the geographic region, and, moreover, the prairie men were considered far more apt for the job than their citified eastern brothers. Sir John A. Macdonald expressed as much when he wrote to General Middleton on March 29 to advise him to raise as many mounted soldiers from the North-West as possible, stating "if you can get men enough from the prairies, they would, of course, be much more serviceable than town bred men who compose our cavalry."[68]

Boulton's force consisted of two troops of cavalry, Troop Number 1 from Russell, Manitoba consisting of three officers and sixty-four men, and Troop Number 2 from Birtle, Manitoba consisting of two officers and fifty-four men.[69] It operated as a reconnaissance element of the North-West Field Force throughout the conflict and was thus destined to find itself at the centre of the action for most of the campaign. Boulton drew his recruits from the rural farmers of Western Manitoba, a practice that would no doubt have won the approval of the prime minister and Minister of Militia, given the high esteem in which they held prairie-bred mounted infantry units. He described his recruiting efforts in detail his memoir, *Reminisces of the North-West Rebellion* written shortly after the end of the conflict:

> Before leaving Winnipeg, I ordered from the Hudson's Bay Company my equipment of rifles, blankets, tents and saddlery. I came out by train to Moosomin, and drove north to Birtle, where I left notice with Mr. Pentland, land agent there, asking for thirty men and horses to be ready for inspection in two days. I then drove north to Russel, and there put up a similar notice. By the 6th of April, I returned to Moosomin, with sixty men and horses, besides officers, orderlies, cooks, etc. — in all eighty-two men, including six teams for transport of provisions, equipment and forage. I had travelled in the six days two hundred and twenty miles by rail and one hundred and forty miles by road. I purchased all my horses in the district, at an average of $165.00 a piece, giving orders on the Hudson's Bay Company posts, at Fort Ellice and Russell, which were duly honoured.[70]

At about the same time as Boulton was getting his scouts organized, the Minister of Militia gave direction to treble the number of infantry battalions raised in Manitoba: in addition to the 90th Battalion, two other infantry regiments were created, the 91st Winnipeg Battalion of Infantry and the 92nd Winnipeg Light Infantry.

Of the two regiments, the latter would be by far the most engaged of the pair. The 92nd Winnipeg Light Infantry was commanded by the redoubtable Lieutenant-Colonel William Osborne Smith who came out of retirement on the outbreak of the rebellion. Military and political leaders in both Ottawa and Winnipeg displayed a keen interest in returning Osborne Smith to active duty, for example, in the same letter to Middleton in which Sir John A. Macdonald provided his strategic direction, he also prompted the general to authorize Osborne Smith to raise a battalion.[71] Consequently, only days after Boulton received his authorization to enrol his company of sixty men, the *Free Press* reported to its readership that "the public will be glad to learn that in this grave emergency that has arisen, the services of Lieut.-Col. W. Osborne Smith, CMG, have been secured by the government. On Friday, General Middleton, having requested his presence at the Government House, asked him to immediately raise a battalion of infantry, and on Saturday, the request having been repeated in a telegram from the Minister of Militia, the Colonel consented to do so. The rolls of three companies are already reported full."[72]

Eventually the Winnipeg Light Infantry grew to include 28 officers and 298 men divided into a Headquarters Company and seven rifle companies lettered A through G. The companies were raised in and around Winnipeg, A Company being known as "A or Kildonan Company" although only sixteen of its forty-one men came from Kildonan. B through F Companies were recruited in Winnipeg, while G Company, with the exception of three men, was recruited exclusively from Minnedosa.[73] There is a single reference in the *Manitoba Free Press* to an Irish Company being part of the Winnipeg Light Infantry, but no further details about which company it might have been, or if it even was exclusively Irish, are available.[74]

While it certainly didn't take long for Osborne Smith to find recruits, the bureaucratic speed with which his command was set up in Ottawa was less inspiring. By the time his battalion was full, Osborne Smith had still not been gazetted into command, and consequently, could not legally move his battalion forward to the front. This disagreeable situation even drew the interest of Premier John Norquay, who telegrammed to Caron on March 29 writing that "Smith [is] embarrassed in consequence [of] not being gazetted; [he] has [a] good company already [and] should at once be placed on service"[75] and again on March 30 "Col Smith cannot get arms or clothes for his force as store keeper will not recognize his authority till gazetted. Cannot understand delay when so much depends on immediate action."[76] Further, on March

30, 1885, Osborne Smith telegraphed to the Minister of Militia directly to inform him that his battalion was full and that the local authorities wanted him to move out immediately, but he could not do so legally because, despite repeated prompts, he still hadn't been gazetted.[77] In fact, Osborne Smith's gazetting was not accomplished for another ten days until *Militia General Orders (8)* of April 10, 1885 were published in which his command, described simply as "a battalion at Winnipeg, Man. under command of Lt. Colonel Osborne Smith, C.M.G." was authorized.[78] On April 11, he was informed by Middleton that his battalion was destined to join the Alberta Field Force under General Strange, so he sent a telegram to his future commander stating "red tape detaining me and want of great coats. [I] Hope [to] start Monday…. [I] am telegraphing Ottawa savagely."[79] Despite having filled his battalion in late March, Osborne Smith and the Winnipeg Light Infantry did not move out of Winnipeg to the operational theatre until April 15. His final act before departing was to telegram to Caron to inform him that his regiment of 326 officers and men were moving out, "present and sober, all in good heart."[80] Osborne Smith *et al.* were seen off by a host of honourable delegates, including the lieutenant-governor and William Wagner, Member of the Legislative Assembly for Woodlands. The *Free Press* reported that the regiment marched along Main Street, which the paper described as being "lined with spectators" and further observed that "persons appeared at almost every window in the various buildings, all anxious to secure a farewell glimpse." Smith's battalion thereafter proceeded to the train depot where the "platform was packed with citizens and friends of the soldiers."[81]

Although full of zeal, it is important to note that almost the whole of the men of the Winnipeg Light Infantry were untrained in military affairs. There is no doubt that some of them had previous service in the Active Militia, and perhaps even with regular elements of the British Army, but in the main they were civilians whipped into a warlike frenzy by reports received from the front and wanting to get in on the fight. Major-General Thomas Bland Strange, who became Osborne Smith's superior officer, recalled in his memoir *Gunner Jingo's Jubilee* that the Winnipeg Light Infantry was "an entirely new Battalion raised on the present emergency by Osborne Smith … the physique of the men, mostly western working men, was far superior to that of a modern British Regular regiment, but the military training of officers and men, exclusive of the Colonel and two or three others, was *nil.* But they were willing and obedient and anxious to get to the front."[82]

Osborne Smith wasn't the only retired Militia officer to be reactivated into service. Thomas Scott, Member of Parliament, who led the Second Red River Expeditionary Force in 1871 and had made his home in Manitoba after his service with the Provisional Battalion, reactivated himself and raised the 91st Winnipeg Battalion of Infantry. Like Osborne Smith, he, too, had early success finding recruits, but despite the initial verve, the regiment would not leave Winnipeg for the front for about six weeks. Scott's regiment was headquartered in a musical pavilion on Lombard Street and consisted of a headquarters company and eight rifle companies that, like their sister battalion the 92nd, were recruited from around the province. A and E Companies were recruited in Winnipeg, B Company came for the most part from Brandon, although some members were from points outside the town, C Company came from Portage-la-Prairie, D Company from Stonewall and the surrounding area, F Company from Morden and Morris, and H Company came from Neepawa.[83] The *Free Press* was able to carry a description of their daily activities as they trained for operations: reveille at 6:30, parade 7:15, drill until 8:00, followed by breakfast, guard mounting at 9:00, morning parade at 10:00 and afternoon parade at 2:30. Curfew was 9:30 and lights out at 10:00. To one reporter, the Militia volunteers of the Battalion seemed "to entertain no thought of anything except going to the front shortly, and all would be disappointed beyond expression if they were excluded from the number thus honored."[84]

The 91st Battalion had auspicious beginnings, but disappointment was their destiny. The incredible success of Scott's recruiting drive was followed up with a lamentable pause before any movement towards the front took place. When they were finally authorized to move on April 16, 1885, it was indeed quite the spectacle. [85] The *Free Press* reported that as they mustered for review prior to departure "they presented a fine military appearance in their handsome scarlet tunics and blue and red touques." Not one to be accused of humility, Scott pronounced his regiment "the finest body of men in the Dominion."[86] Jackson, the Commissary officer, seemed to agree with the Scott's fawning review and wrote in his report on the rebellion that the regiment marched off as "432 officers and men, the strongest Corps on service, and in appearance all that could be desired."[87]

The battalion drew up at the corner of Portage and Main where they were addressed by the lieutenant-governor who complimented them on their turn out and, as it happens, exhibited some degree of clairvoyance and foreshadowing. He remarked that his "convictions were that there was but little fighting to be done … whether it be holding the fort in the far west, or on the way to the front, [he thought] the battalion would carry with them the sympathies of the people."[88] As it turns out, the 91st Battalion would spend the entirety of the campaign conducting garrison duty, a fact that would become a sore point amongst some of the ranks.

As the various corps from the east eventually arrived in Winnipeg, they would usually spend a day or two in the city and would then move forward to join one of the three columns of the North-West Field Force, or deploy into garrison positions further to the rear from which to protect the lines or communications. The fear amongst the populace in Winnipeg was somewhat assuaged by the presence of the various Militia units whilst they were in the city, but when the last of the corps from the east, the Halifax Battalion under Lieutenant-Colonel Jason Bremner, was called forward leaving Winnipeg without any soldiers to garrison it save for the staff officers operating the commissariat, the level of anxiety in Winnipeg increased dramatically. This concern was particularly poignant for those astute enough to observe that the magazine and military stores concentrated in the city presented a tempting target for rebel sympathisers and Fenians. Jackson reported that the only force available to protect these stores was a group of ten North-West Mounted Police recruits under the supervision of an Inspector Norman. Within the civilian populace "much anxiety [was] felt for their safety, the rumours of the intended seizing of these stores and firing the city still being in circulation."[89] Consequently, Jackson met with aldermen of the city and arranged for about forty citizens to mount a guard on Fort Osborne until a Home Guard could be enrolled, which occurred on May 6 when a guard of fifty men was detailed for nightly guard duty at Fort Osborne.[90] This guard was maintained until May 20, when the Montreal Brigade of Garrison Artillery arrived, went into camp near Fort Osborne, and assumed garrison duties for the city.[91]

THE CAMPAIGN

Qu'Appelle is a town on the Canadian Pacific Railway line. It was originally established as Troy Station in 1883, and it lay about fifty kilometres east of Regina in what is modern-day South Eastern Saskatchewan. It was from here that Middleton devised his operational plan to address the rebellion: he divided his force into three flying columns, one, the easternmost, under the command of Middleton himself, a second, in the center, under Lieutenant-

Colonel William Dillon Otter, and a third column, the Alberta Field Force out of Calgary, under Major General Thomas Bland Strange, formerly of the Royal Artillery.

In these latter two men, Middleton was joined by two experienced officers. Otter was a Permanent Force Canadian Militia officer and veteran of the Battle of Ridgeway during the 1866 Fenian incursion. He had originally enrolled in the Active Militia in 1864 and transferred to a Permanent corps in 1883. Several years prior to the rebellion, he compiled a tactical manual entitled *The Guide* which was eventually put into use by all the Canadian Militia Schools to instruct soldiers on contemporary drill and doctrine, thus he was instrumental in defining the tactical and operational art of the Canadian Militia at the outbreak of the Rebellion. At the commencement of hostilities, Otter was in command of one of the Canadian Army's Permanent Force units: "C" Company, Infantry School Corps which was stationed in Toronto. Otter's force was transported by rail to Swift Current from where it began its operations towards Battelford.

Strange was a former Major-General of the British Army and had taken his retirement in the North-West Territory to raise cavalry horses. He had extensive experience in the British military, but he had only limited prospects for advancement as a British Regular, so he accepted command of "B" Battery of the Canadian Permanent Force when it was created along with "A" Battery in 1871. Upon learning of the rebellion, he offered his services to the Dominion and the Minister of Militia gladly welcomed his participation and experience. Much of the third column under Strange were *ad hoc* corps raised in response to the rebellion, such as the 92nd Winnipeg Light Infantry, although eventually one Active Militia unit, the 65th Battalion from Montreal, was attached to it.

In addition to the three manoeuvre columns mentioned, many units were employed as line of communication troops. As Macdonald highlighted in his direction to Middleton there was concern about the prospects of the insurrection growing and attracting First Nations or Fenians from the United States as well as the need to secure the Canadian Pacific Railway line, the economic and political lifeline between Ottawa and the West. Consequently, Middleton could not afford to dedicate all of his Militia Corps solely to the three manoeuvre elements, and a number of units were tasked to maintain security along these vital lines of communication to interdict any forces looking to enter the fray from outside the region, monitor First Nations that might rise up, and ensure the free movement of sustainment supplies and communication.

Garrison duty was not glorious, but it was necessary to maintain a broad footprint throughout the region as a deterrent to potential indigenous uprisings. The fear of an Indigenous uprising was not the only concern pressing on the minds of the settlers in Manitoba and North-West. The old bogeyman of Fenian invasion once again reared its ugly green head in both the halls of Ottawa and in the North-West. As early as April 2, the *Brandon Sun* published some speculative journalism under the headline "A FENIAN INVASION! NOW ON THEIR WAY!" in which it claimed that the government had received reports that Fenians in New York and Chicago were "in a state of ferment, and not only intended to stir up the troubles in Canada but to take an active part in them also"[92] The *Sun* used some artistic licence to be sure, but their report wasn't wholly without merit: on March 30, 1885, a gentleman named H. Hughes sent a telegram to Caron advising him that he had received a letter from a friend in Chicago who informed him that Fenians were congregating there for a raid on Canada.[93] Meanwhile, a home guard organized in Emerson drew the attention of no less than the Premier of Manitoba, John Norquay who cabled Caron on behalf of the guard's commander, Captain Whitman, asking for the Dominion Government to provide arms because of reports that Fenians in Pembina, North Dakota were holding secret meetings in order to develop plans to exploit the troubles in the North-West.[94] The fear of Fenians exploiting the unrest in the North-West was pervasive throughout the conflict and was one of the direct causes of the large number of forces detailed to provide garrisons along the lines of communication. Obviously, this resulted in the number of forces being raised for service growing from Middleton's original estimate of 2,000 to over 4,500 men, almost all of who passed through Winnipeg at some point.

While Middleton and the 90th Battalion waited at Qu'Appelle, the Militia Department mobilized active service corps throughout the Dominion to deploy to the North-West. The deployment of forces started on March 27, unsurprisingly, with the full-time soldiers comprising the permanent corps of the Active Militia: 'A' and 'B' Batteries of the Canadian Artillery from Quebec City and Kingston, respectively, as well as C Company Infantry School Corps from Toronto. The same day, two Active Militia regiments from Toronto, the

2nd (Queen's Own Rifles) and 10th (Royal Grenadiers) Battalions, as well as the 65th Battalion from Montreal were also mobilized. On March 28, the Midland Battalion from Kingston was called out, followed on March 30 by the York and Simcoe Battalion, and the Governor General's Foot Guards. These forces were joined on March 31 by the 7th Battalion from London, Ontario, the 9th Battalion from Quebec City, the Halifax Provisional Battalion, and a day later the Governor General's bodyguard, a cavalry unit in Ottawa. Utilizing the nearly completed Canadian Pacific Railway, these corps passed through Winnipeg on their way to the theatre of operations between April 5 and 22. The table at right lists the corps that were assigned to each column and those detailed to provide security along important lines of communications.[95]

THE MIDDLETON COLUMN

On April 6, Middleton moved forward from Qu'Appelle with Winnipeg's 90th Battalion, half of the Winnipeg Field Battery, and some scouts, arriving in Humboldt, Saskatchewan on April 14. Continuing in a northwesterly direction towards Batoche, Middleton's column struck the South Saskatchewan River at Clark's Crossing, a ferry site about thirty kilometres North-East of Saskatoon, on April 17. He halted at the crossing for several days to repair the ferry scow and rope which crossed the river. On April 20, Middleton divided his column in two wings to advance northwards on each side of the South Saskatchewan River, floating the recently repaired scow along the river between the two wings for use if one element or the other required it to cross. The left column of Middleton's force was placed under the command of Lieutenant-Colonel Montizambert of the Royal Canadian Artillery and consisted of the Winnipeg Field Battery, the 10th Royal Grenadiers, and a force of scouts. Middleton remained on the right with A Battery, half of C Company Infantry School Corps, the 90th Battalion, and Boulton's Scouts.

The two wings moved in parallel down the river. On the right with Middleton, Boulton's Scouts, moved well in front of the force, followed three hundred yards behind by an advanced guard of the 90th Battalion, and then by the main body a further three hundred yards behind. During this part of the advance Middleton positioned himself well forward near the scouts, accompanied by Captain Hair, his assistant Quartermaster, and his two aides-de-camp. After the force had advanced for some distance it approached a series of forested bluffs on their left, whence several shots were fired. These shots

FIRST COLUMN Middleton	SECOND COLUMN Otter	THIRD COLUMN Strange
A Battery 90th Battalion Infantry School Corps (part) Boulton's Scouts 10th Battalion Royal Grenadiers Capt. French's Scouts Winnipeg Field Battery (part) Dennis' Surveyors' Scouts Midland Battalion	B Battery 2nd Battalion Queen's Own Infantry School Corps (part) Todd's Sharpshooters Winnipeg Field Battery (part) 35th Battalion (part)	65th Battalion Mount Royal Rifles 92nd Battalion Winnipeg Light Infantry Strange's Rangers Mounted Police

Line of Communication Troops		
Clarke's Crossing: 7th BattalionMidland Battalion	Touchwood: 2nd Company, 35th Battalion Quebec Cavalry School Winnipeg Troop Cavalry	Humboldt: Governor-General's Body Guard
Fort Qu'Appelle: 91st Battalion Winnipeg Infantry	Moose Jaw: 66th Battalion (part)	Medicine Hat: 66th Battalion (part)
Calgary-Ft. McLeod: 9th Battalion	Old Wives Lake: White's Scouts	Cypress Hills: Stewart's Rangers

were the opening salvoes of the confrontation that would become known as the Battle of Fish Creek, a hot affair that resulted in several casualties to the Dominion forces and was arguably one of the biggest reversals experienced by the Canadian Militia during the conflict.

After coming under fire, Middleton moved the main body forward, and a series of engagements between Dominion and Métis forces ensued, with the Dominion forces eventually advancing in columns from bluff to bluff, from time to time exchanging intense fire from the Métis defenders who had prepared well-constructed gun pits in defensive positions. Middleton even had a Métis bullet pass through his fur cap.

The Dominion forces carried the day, but at significant cost to the two Manitoba corps that were heavily engaged in the fighting, the 90th Battalion and Boulton's Scouts. The list of the wounded consisted of six killed in action, including four privates from the 90th Battalion, fourteen seriously wounded, including another four members of the 90th Battalion and five troopers of Boulton's Scouts, and twenty-nine lightly wounded, including twelve members of the 90th Battalion, and three members of Boulton's Scouts. Three of the wounded would eventually succumb to their injuries. Later, after the Battle of Batoche, Middleton and his men found papers indicating that the strength of the Métis at Fish Creek was 280 under the command of Gabriel Dumont, with eleven killed and eighteen wounded, or at least that is what Middleton reported.[96]

Gabriel Dumont tells a different story. Adolphe Ouimet, a Franco-Canadian lawyer in the North-West, compiled the oral biography of Dumont in his 1889 book *La vérité sur la question métisse au Nord-Ouest. Biographie et récit de Gabriel Dumont.* Dumont recounts that he and a band of approximately 130 men reconnoitred south from Batoche to survey the Militia column. Setting up camp near Fish Creek, at the farm of someone named Tourond, one of Dumont's scouts reported the advance of Middleton's column. Dumont and his men hid their horses in a bush and set up an ambush in a coulee into which Dumont intended to lure the Militiamen with an advance ambush of another twenty men who would force Middleton's force to stop to engage, after which the remainder would open fire from the flank once the Militia had entered an adjoining coulee. As Dumont put it, hearkening back to the days of Bison hunts on the plains "je voulais les traiter comme on traite les buffles."[97] Middleton's advance scouts discovered the ambush and when Middleton's men began engaging the Métis defensive position, Dumont relates that many of his men fled, leaving him only 47 of the original 130 to contend with the advancing Militiamen. Seeing that the wind was at his back, Dumont set a prairie fire in the hopes it would advance towards the enemy. In the end the fire was ineffectual, although he claims he caused the militia — erroneously identified as North-West Mounted Police — to withdraw, leaving a pile of baggage and even some medicinal supplies, including two bottles of *eau de vie,* behind in their haste. This aspect does not figure in Middleton's report. Despite being reinforced by his brother and eighty new horsemen from Batoche, Dumont, and his force collected their dead and wounded, and fell back towards Riel's headquarters. Dumont claims that his losses were far less than that reported by Middleton to Militia headquarters — four dead and two wounded. Dumont explained the conflicting numbers, chalking it up to Imperial incredulity: "Il est d'autant plus justifiable d'avoir cru ces exagérations, qu'il était difficile de croire, pour lui, plus que pour tout autre, qu'une poignée d'hommes mal armés, ait put, pendant toute une journée, tenir en échec et mettre en fuite, près de 1600 hommes armes de pied en cap et servis par l'artillerie. »[98]

Whatever the truth of the matter is, the fact is that Dumont and his force not only inflicted a blow on Middleton in terms of casualties, but they also imposed substantial delay on his advance, perhaps also sowing a seed of doubt and concern. After Fish Creek, Middleton tarried to allow his wounded to be evacuated and to bury his dead. Perhaps rattled by the engagement at Fish Creek, Middleton also paused to allow reinforcements to join him for the push on to Batoche, including the steamer *Northcote* which was bringing supplies and two companies of infantry from the Midland Battalion, as well as a Gatling Gun. The steamer was late, so Middleton directed that the wounded be evacuated by wagon. The *Northcote* finally arrived on May 5 and after outfitting it with metal walls as a defence against rifle fire and placing half of C Company Infantry School Corps aboard her, Middleton directed that she should proceed down the river until abreast the town of Batoche and create a diversion at approximately nine o'clock a.m. on May 9, hopefully also cutting the ferry wire across the South Saskatchewan.

Dumont anticipated the *Northcote* could cause a problem for the defence of Batoche and deployed approximately thirty men to guard his river-flank. As the steamer approached, this force engaged it in heavy fire and caused much damage, and while they were not capable of sinking her, the sharp fire delivered to the vessel rendered her *hors de combat* and she dropped anchor some distance below Batoche having not achieved Middleton's hoped-for diversion.

Middleton and his force moved out towards Batoche on May 7, his force now numbering approximately 850 men and comprising A Battery, one Gatling Gun under Captain Howard of the US Army, the Winnipeg Field Battery, half of C Company Infantry School Corps, 10th Royal Grenadiers, 90th Battalion Winnipeg Rifles, two companies of the Midland Battalion, Boulton's Scouts and French's Scouts.

The force arrived within 6 miles of the town on May 8, having moved to the east due to the poor state of the trails between Fish Creek and Batoche, picking up the trail running from Humboldt. Camping here, Middleton pushed some of Boulton's Scouts forward to reconnoitre the line of approach to Batoche. The scouts were able to advance to within four miles of the town without molestation, although they encountered a piquet of two of Riel's scouts who withdrew at their advance.

On the morning of May 9, Middleton advanced on Batoche, arriving within half a mile of a Catholic Church which stood on the eastern edge of the town. He brought up his Gatling Gun and artillery and engaged several men he had noticed around some houses surrounding the church, causing them to withdraw. Shortly thereafter a white flag was flown from a house, from which emerged several Catholic priests and nuns, as well as some women and children. Middleton advanced cautiously and was able to gain a foothold on a hill that dominated the whole of the village of Batoche, where he positioned some artillery and began to shell some of the houses in the town. Dumont estimates he had 175 men in the low ground on the other side of the hill, who began engaging the Militia and providing enough suppressive fire to cause Middleton to withdraw his artillery and the Gatling from the crest of the ridge. As the sun went down, Middleton withdrew his forces to a *laager*, pushed out picquets, and passed the night.

The next several days were generally a repeat of the first. The Militia would move forward and occupy ground along a ridge and exchange fire with the Métis who were well ensconced in their defensive positions around Batoche. In his report on the battle, Middleton made a point to remark how well positioned and prepared the Métis's rifle pits were, and to comment on their ingenious use of mannequins to deceive the Militia force as to their number and disposition.

On May 11, Middleton took a force of scouts and conducted a *reconnaissance in force* of an open stretch of prairie to the east of the village. Here he ran into a small force of Métis and exchanged some fire with them. Middleton credits this reconnaissance as a successful feint which drew off some of the Métis defenders from their own right flank, allowing some of his elements, namely the Midland Battalion, to push forward on his left flank, capturing a cemetery that had been used as a defensive position by some of Riel's men. This provided a position of fire from which Middleton was able to advance his artillery, specifically the Winnipeg Field Battery, to engage a house across the river flying what Middleton refers to as "Riel's white flag" and what Dumont calls the "drapeau de la Sainte Vierge." While Middleton claims that the firing did not do much damage, Dumont recalls that the house caught fire but "miraculously" extinguished. Luckily, it was so for an older deaf man was in the house and did not know he was being shelled until one artillery round went through one wall and out the other.

Charles Mulvaney relates in his history of the Rebellion the testimony of an anonymous member of Dennis's Surveyor Scouts concerning the Winnipeg Field Battery's engagement, which appears to have become something of an embarrassment for the professional standing of the Winnipeg gunners. The scout recounted that the Battery moved into position on the crest of a hill and began firing at the house across the river, drawing a few curious Militiamen to gather round to watch the display. The less than auspicious results were described as follows:

> we always had a sort of an idea that an artilleryman could hit his mark with much greater accuracy than we could with our rifles, for the muzzle of a nine-pounder is not so likely to describe figures in the air as a weapon whose holder feels a strong inclination to duck his head at the whizz of a passing ball. But from what we saw that day we think we could do better. How many shots were fired I do not like to say, but they went all round that house an apparently anywhere but through it until we got rather tired of the order 'Common shell, percussion fuze — load. [99]

The dawning of May 12 brought the decisive victory at Batoche that Middleton was looking for. The Métis were extremely low on ammunition, some resorting to firing pebbles from their rifles for want of bullets. Middleton once again took a strong force of mounted infantry, supported by a gun from "A" Battery and the Gatling, to his right flank near the open prairie where he had reconnoitred the day previous, and once again engaged the Métis rifle pits protecting this approach to the town. His intention, he claimed, was to have his other forces reoccupy their positions of the day previous on his left while he distracted the Métis on his right, but this was not done, owning, he states, to a misunderstanding of his orders. In his report he observed that this may have been fortuitous as he concluded the absence of any movement on his left reinforced in the minds of the defenders the assault would come from the prairie to the east.

After dinner, he ordered his men to reassume the previous day's positions, and after doing so, around two o'clock he advanced his left consisting of the Midland Battalion and Royal Grenadiers, supported by elements of Winnipeg's 90th Battalion who "dashed forward with a cheer and drove the enemy out of the pits." 100Reinforcing his success, Middleton then threw the Surveyors Scouts, Boulton's Scouts, and the remainder of the 90th into the assault on his right to extend his line. In a matter of moments, the Militia had swept forward and seized Batoche driving the Métis defenders out of their trenches, in some cases at the point of the bayonet. One morbidly interesting tale was shared by Surgeon G.S. Ryerson of the 10th Grenadiers who recalled that one soldier of the battalion attacked a rifle pit with his bayonet, lodging the weapon into the defender with such force that he was unable to withdraw it, and had to detach it from his rifle to continue the advance.101 With the onrush of the Militia, the survivors of Riel's force withdrew under pressure about a half mile to the rear. Dumont did his best to slow the advance of the Militiamen through harassing rifle fire from some high ground beyond the village, joined by six of his men. In his memoir, Dumont recalled the courage and commitment of one of his comrades, a man he referred to as the *vieux Ouellet*. Dumont remembered saying "Père, il nous faut reculer" to which the old man replied, "Arrête donc, je veux tuer encore un Anglais." Dumont said "C'est bien, mourons ici." Ouellet did, indeed, die on that hill. [102]

Middleton's recollection of the assault places a premium on the dash and courage of the Militia. In fact, he makes special mention of one young member of the 90th that left an indelible impression on him. He wrote in his report that "I cannot conclude without mentioning a little bugler of the 90th Regiment, named William Buchanan, who made himself particularly useful in carrying ammunition to the right front when the fire was very hot; this he did with peculiar nonchalance, walking calmly about crying : 'now boys, who's for cartridges?'"[103] Truth be told, the fact that the Métis defenders were mostly out of ammunition, heavily outnumbered and subject to effective artillery and Gatling fire is probably more likely the reason for the victory rather than the Militia's martial prowess. Dumont is firm in his conviction that the Métis defeat at Batoche was caused by his lack of ammunition and the fact that several traitors readily provided this information to the Militia.

His biographer records him saying :

> Nous avons tenu les ennemis trois jours en échec, et tous les soirs ils rentraient dans leurs trous. Et pendant ces trois jours, [Ils n'ont pas tué un seul homme]; ils n'ont touché que des mannequins que nous leur présentions et sur lesquels ils s'efforçaient de tirer … Nous l'avons appris de source certaine : Middleton, malgré qu'il eût reçu du renfort, désespérait nous réduire, quand des traîtres, que je ne veux pas nommer, lui ont fait connaître que nous n'avions plus de munitions, et que, à part quelques-uns, tous les Métis étaient découragés. Que d'ailleurs si les assiégeants ne se pressaient pas, des secours arriveraient bientôt pour renforcer les assiégés. Ces traîtres étaient continuellement en conversation avec l'ennemi et avec les nôtres qu'ils engageaient à déposer les armes en leur offrant des sauf-conduits.[104]

Although the Battle of Batoche did not end the rebellion, it was certainly the major event of the campaign. Batoche was the political and spiritual capital of the Métis nation in the North-West, and when it was lost there was no real hope for the rebellion afterwards. It is perhaps ironic that on May 12, 1885, the back of the rebellion was broken, fifteen years to the day after the Manitoba Act was passed in the House of Commons, ending the Red River Resistance. Even if there was the possibility of continuing the struggle after the fall of Batoche, any hope for the Métis cause was well and truly lost on May 15 when Louis Riel was captured and surrendered to Middleton.

After his victory at Batoche and subsequent capture of Riel, Middleton moved his force across the South Saskatchewan and then proceeded to Battleford, via Prince Albert. The threat of the Métis had been eliminated, but the First Nations that had risen in arms had yet to be defeated. The pursuit of Big Bear and the defeat of Poundmaker, the Cree Chief, was Middleton's next operational objective. It was on May 23 as Middleton moved towards Battleford that he received a note from Poundmaker indicating his willingness to surrender.

THE OTTER COLUMN

As these decisive actions were occurring in the Middleton column to the east, concurrent activity was occurring in the centre wing of Middleton's three flying columns, under the command of Lieutenant-Colonel Otter. The force congregated at Swift Current, having taken advantage of the Canadian Pacific Railway to position itself there. The apprehended threat to Battleford and its civilian population, it being the largest town in the region, caused Middleton to commit forces to securing the town. On April 11, Middleton telegrammed Otter and instructed him to proceed from Swift Current to Battleford, either by steamer or trail, with as little delay as possible.105 While the advance to, and battle of, Fish Creek played out to their east, Lieutenant-Colonel Otter marched his column of 543 soldiers and police out of Swift Current on April 13. Hindered by weather and a lack of steamers, the column was held up in crossing the Saskatchewan River. Otter finally got his column underway in earnest on April 18, arriving at Battleford on April 23. Upon their arrival, the First Nations forces who had invested the town exchanged a few shots with the lead elements of Otter's force and then withdrew after setting firing to the local magistrate's home. Otter and his troops entered the town unopposed.

On April 24, Otter assumed command of Battleford Garrison from North-West Mounted Police Inspector Dickens and set up his headquarters near Government House, which sat across the river from the town. The next several days were spent preparing and improving defensive works around Government house and the town, but despite the arrival of Otter's column, the citizens of Battleford were unwilling to return to their homes, considering the number of soldiers protecting the town to be insufficient.[106]

Otter received information that that the Cree leader Poundmaker and his followers were situated in the Cut Knife hills some thirty-five miles from Battleford. Poundmaker was dithering over whether or not to join the uprising and was waiting to see if he would receive any reinforcements from Big Bear before finalizing his decision. Otter thought it prudent to conduct what he would later describe as a *reconnaissance in force* to influence Poundmaker and pre-empt the congregation of indigenous forces. He marched his column out of Battleford on May 1 and advanced on the Cut Knife Hills.

The Battle of Cut Knife Creek was a complete reverse for the Dominion Forces. Otter and his men stumbled upon Poundmaker's forces in the early morning after conducting a night-time advance towards their camp. Otter had a substantial force at his disposal including considerable fire support in the form of two seven-pounder cannons that were part of his Mounted Police element as well as 'B' Battery and their nine-pounders. He also had forty-five men from C Company Infantry School Corps, a small detachment of Governor General's Foot Guards, sixty men from Toronto's Queen's Own Rifles, and forty-five men from the Battleford Rifles under Captain Nash. In addition, one of the two Gatling Guns acquired by the Dominion Government was also attached to his column. All in all, this was a force with considerable firepower.

Otter opened the action by placing his artillery and Gatling on the crest of the ridge overlooking the enemy. The seven pounders in use were older artillery pieces, indeed very likely the same guns carried to Fort Garry by the British artillery component of Wolseley's force in 1870. As the action increased and the guns fired more and more rounds, the trail of one gun broke, rendering it useless. After five hours of fighting, the trails on both guns had broken. The fact that both pieces suffered a similar fate speaks volumes to their advanced age.

The engagement did not proceed well for Otter. Suffering from loss of two guns out of action, albeit not from enemy fire, and placed in an untenable position, he ordered a withdrawal to Battleford, justifying his decision later when writing his report of the action that "the object of the reconnaissance had been accomplished." As he withdrew, First Nations forces attempted to maintain contact and pursued the withdrawing Militia and Mounted Police force. Otter was thus forced to cover his withdrawal with fire from a jury-rigged seven-pounder which was bound up with ropes and splints to hold it together. In the end, Poundmaker's warriors got the best of Otter and his column who lost four killed and twelve wounded. [107] Otter returned to Battleford where he ensconced himself in the fort and waited for the arrival of Middleton, who linked up with him on May 24, the day after receiving the communique from Poundmaker indicating his willingness to surrender. Two days later the Plains Cree leader met with Middleton and formally surrendered.

THE STRANGE COLUMN

During the weeks that Middleton and Otter were converging their forces towards Battleford, further to the west the Alberta Field Force under General Strange was focussed on bringing Big Bear to task. For the purposes of our inquiry here, the story of the Alberta Field Force is particularly important as the 92nd Winnipeg Light Infantry played a substantial role in its operations. In fact, besides the operations of Boulton's Scouts, the 90th Battalion and the Winnipeg Field Battery in Middleton's column, the 92nd Winnipeg Light Infantry under Osborne Smith was the only other Manitoba force that became decisively engaged with elements of Riel's forces. What follows here will be a brief survey of the Alberta Field Force operations with a particular focus on the 92nd Winnipeg Light Infantry.

On April 9, Strange received a telegram from Middleton in which the major general ordered him to assume command of the Alberta District and also directed him to proceed to Edmonton, and thence to Fort Pitt where he intended their forces to link up.[108] The state of fear amongst the settlers in Alberta was palpable after the events of Duck Lake, Frog Lake and Battleford, so when Strange became the face of the Dominion response to the Rebellion in Alberta, he was inundated with a plethora of requests from various locales to provide arms and men to protect them. Like Manitoba, however, he lacked enough resources to outfit every settlement with a home guard and a stand of arms.

The initial Alberta Field Force was comprised almost wholly of locally recruited forces and North-West Mounted Police officers. It originally consisted of a mounted rifle outfit styled the Alberta Mounted Rifles, a scout force of Mounties under the redoubtable Major Sam Steele, and another North-West Mounted Police outfit of picked men supported by a field gun. To this small force was added some Dominion muscle on April 12 with the arrival of the 65th Battalion of Voltigeurs from Quebec City.[109]

By mid-April, minor but dangerous uprisings occurred throughout south and central Alberta. First Nations raiders stole or scared off horses, took pot shots at the troops, and killed livestock. In one case local First Nations forces drove thirteen horses into a slough where they were drowned. Given the importance of the ranch industry to the region, Strange resolved to deploy Militia to guard certain areas against such raiding. This important, but not necessarily glorious, task fell to some companies of Osborne Smith's 92nd Winnipeg Light Infantry, who subsequently deployed a company under Major Lewis in the town of Gleichen about one hundred kilometres east of Calgary, while No. 6 Company under Captain Valency was sent to Fort McLeod to replace the detachment of Mounties who had joined Strange's column with the field gun.[110] These latter 45 Manitobans were well received by their hosts, the *Fort MacLeod Gazette* remarking that "the men are a fine, soldierly looking lot of fellows."[111] Osborne Smith and the remainder of the battalion arrived in Calgary on April 17.[112]

Strange decided to divide his force into three wings for the initial advance. The "Right Wing" consisting of 164 officers and men of the 65th Battalion and 73 men of the North-West Mounted Police left Calgary on April 20, followed on April 23 by the "Left Wing" of 148 men of the 65th Battalion and 25 Mounted Police. Strange left Osborne Smith in command of the forces remaining in Calgary which consisted of what remained of the 92nd Winnipeg Light Infantry and the Alberta Mounted Rifles. At this point the Alberta Mounted Rifles could not proceed because they had not yet received all their necessary equipment, in fact, the acquisition of proper saddlery was so hopelessly wrapped up in bureaucratic red tape, Strange went out and bought several saddles himself — only to have them seized by customs officials at Winnipeg.[113] Osborne Smith was instructed to remain in Calgary and then move the two units forward and join the main column when the equipment destined for the Mounted Rifles was finally received.

While Osborne Smith and the Alberta Force awaited saddles — any saddles — Strange's main body marched towards Edmonton, arriving there on May 5. Strange tarried in Edmonton in order, he reported, to test fire the twelve-year-old artillery ammunition he had been supplied with, and to allow the 65th Battalion the opportunity to conduct some musketry practice.

The movement of the Winnipeg Light Infantry and the Alberta Mounted Rifles from Calgary to Edmonton to link up with Strange's main column is an interesting aspect of the narrative, and a herculean effort in its own right, the march being a distance of some 320 kilometers. Osborne Smith's force finally moved out of Calgary on May 1 lead by fifty members of the Alberta Mounted Rifles under the command of Major Hatton, followed by the remaining four companies of the Winnipeg Light Infantry under the command of Major Thibodeau. The supply train of sixty horse teams carrying ammunition, provisions, and sundry sustainment items under the command of Captain Hamilton of the North-West Mounted Police pulled up the rear.[114]

After a little over a day of marching the force struck the Red Deer River, a major obstacle to their advance. The cable-ferry Osborne Smith intended to use was found to be out of service and repairs took over a day and a half to affect, imposing a significant delay on the force. After repairing the cable and slowly ferrying the force across the river, the column struck out once again, albeit with some trepidation as the remaining 175 kilometers of the route from the Red Deer River ferry to Edmonton passed through three First Nations reserves. Rumours, probably false and intensified by gossip mongers, were circulating that the chiefs of these bands and their people were leaning towards joining the rebellion and intended harm to the force. In the northernmost reserve, the Chief, Ermine Skin, was said to have three braves prepared to attack the column. Consequently, when Osborne Smith moved his column through this area, he ensured his men were postured more aggressively. The Mounted Rifles remained at the head of the force, followed by No. 1 Company of the Winnipeg Light Infantry with bayonets fixed and rifles at the slope, which is to say with the butt held in hand while the stock is rested on the shoulder. The supply train followed, flanked by Nos. 2 and 3 Company of the Light Infantry for protection, with the rearguard provided by No. 4 Company. As one soldier of the force described the scene in a letter home that was subsequently published by the *Free Press* "we all [had] our bayonets fixed and our pouches open, so as to be ready if they pounced down upon us."115 No violence was met, and Osborne Smith and his column were able to catch up with Strange and the main force in Edmonton on May 10.116

Only a few days after they had left Calgary, the three companies of the Winnipeg Light Infantry that had been detailed to garrison the ranching areas of Southern Alberta and Fort McLeod were relieved by elements of the 9th Battalion from Quebec, after which they hurried to join their comrades as they advanced on Edmonton.117 George Beauregard of No. 3 Company of the 9th Battalion recorded an interesting occurrence in early May in Calgary when he and his colleagues assumed the garrison duties from the Winnipeg Light Infantry. In this case, the soldiers of the 9th Battalion detained a member of the Winnipeg unit, a volunteer going by the name Ross, who had tried to shoot a cook of the 9th Battalion and was subsequently arrested by the Quebecois soldiers. Upon searching him, Beauregard *et al* found two or three watches, two chains, a medallion, and nearly a thousand dollars in counterfeit bank notes! [118]

Notwithstanding this miscreant, No. 6 Company of the Winnipeg Light Infantry who had garrisoned Fort MacLeod seems to have developed a strong bond with the folks thereabouts. Upon learning of their imminent departure, the *Fort MacLeod Gazette* remarked that "during their short stay here, officers and men made a most favourable impression, and we regret that the acquaintance could not have been prolonged." In keeping with their predecessors of the Provisional Battalion in Fort Garry, on the night of their departure No. 6 Company organized a concert for the benefit of the local citizens which included skits, songs, recitations and, unsurprisingly, a Red River jig performed by Constable Peasonell of the North-West Mounted Police and Private Gelder of the Winnipeg Light Infantry.[119]

The issues of the Winnipeg Light Infantry companies left behind to garrison the various locales around Calgary is an interesting one. It seems that Osborne Smith was not overly happy with the prospect of leaving so much of his force out of the fight. On April 25, 1885, he telegrammed directly to Caron to provide an update in which he not too subtly bemoaned the fact that leaving garrison companies would result in his "three Companies [of] my Regiment scattered at Calgary, Gleichen and MacLeod." This comment, of itself, is of little consequence but what followed is indicative of Osborne Smith's manipulation of his political connections. "Of course [I] must obey orders" he wrote magnanimously "unless counter-ordered." This latter statement certainly presents the appearance of a request for Ministerial intervention on his behalf. Perhaps it succeeded, given that his companies did rejoin him once relieved.[120]

While those three companies hustled to rejoin their colleagues, Osborne Smith and his column continued their advance towards Edmonton. While it is true that Osborne Smith and his force had the added benefit of following Strange's main body who had taken the time to detail pioneer teams to improve the trails and bridges along the way, it is nonetheless a complement to Osborne Smith and his men that the force was able to march the 320 kilometers in only eight and a half days, arriving in Edmonton in high spirits. [121] The march was certainly tough. One correspondent from the *Free Press* who accompanied the force reported that everyone on the force was terribly sunburnt and "in many places the skin is well peeled off faces." Three officers of the Light Infantry were so badly burned they sought out some Vaseline from the surgeon who erroneously provided them with carbolic acid instead. Carbolic acid is an antiseptic which can have caustic affects when applied in large amounts. This unfortunate mistake resulted in intense suffering amongst the officers who had erroneously applied it. [122]

Several days before the arrival of Osborne Smith's column, on May 8, Strange ordered the 65th Battalion to march out towards Fort Victoria, which sits on the Saskatchewan to the north-east of Edmonton, with the intent of having the remainder of his now-unified force move out shortly thereafter. He resolved to move the remainder of his force by scow down the Saskatchewan River. This caused a great deal of concern amongst members of his force who feared that the high banks of the river would be an excellent place for Métis or First Nations warriors to shoot down into an overloaded and defenceless vessel moving slowly down the river. Subsequently, Osborne Smith asked permission to convene a board to determine the advisability of this course of action. The irony of Osborne Smith lamenting "red tape" causing a delay in his deployment and later advocating for bureaucratic oversight to what was essentially a tactical decision appears lost on him.123

After conducting some tests to determine how many stacked flour sacks were required along the gunwales of the scow to prevent penetration by rifle fire, and further delay imposed by the onslaught of a spring storm, on May 14 the Winnipeg Light Infantry channeled the experiences of their forbears in the Red River Expeditions by becoming an amphibious force. Osborne Smith *et al* joined Strange, along with a nine-pounder gun and crew, aboard the flour-clad scows and descended the Saskatchewan River behind a force of scouts in canoes. The whole of Strange's force reunited in Fort Victoria, swapped roles and departed on May 20 with elements of the 65th Battalion aboard the river vessels and the Winnipeg Light Infantry, Steele's Cavalry and the artillery force moving by land.

The force arrived near Frog Lake on May 24 and the next day, May 25 celebrated Queen Victoria's birthday in the rain. Afterwards, some of the men wandered into the village where they found the victims of the massacre a month previous. The special correspondent to the *Free Press* took pains to describe the scene that the officers of the Winnipeg Light Infantry stumbled upon in a log cabin:

> In the cellar of the Parsonage, and guided there by the terrible smell, one of the most awful sights I ever saw was witnessed. Four dead bodies were found huddled together in a corner. Two of the bodies were Father Fafard and Father Lullac, another was that of the lay brother, and the fourth that of some one unknown. The corpses were horribly mangled. All four heads were charred beyond recognition, the four hearts had been torn out, wide incisions had been made in the lower parts of the stomach…and the feet and hands on some were

missing … It was a terrible ending for a Queen's birthday, and an ending no one present there will ever forget.[124]

The remains were removed for burial. Seven years later, Geoff Brooks recounted the experience in an article for *The Lake Magazine*: "it was no easy matter getting the bodies from the basement of the church to the surface, they were so much decomposed. With great trouble and after long working in a sickening atmosphere, it was at last accomplished by getting tarpaulins under each body."[125] A fatigue party was detailed to dig four graves and construct four caskets for the burial. By three o'clock a.m., the bodies were lowered into their graves. A funeral service was held for the deceased, the litany was read by Captain F. I. Clarke of No. 2 Company, Winnipeg Light Infantry as he was the only Roman Catholic officer in the regiment. The unidentified settler was given a Protestant service officiated by Osborne Smith.[126]

While engaged in this macabre task, reports came in from the advanced scouts that First Nations warriors were near Fort Pitt. Strange pushed off towards the redoubt at once, moving the 65th again by scow, and the cavalry by land with the Winnipeg Light Infantry following behind. Arriving in Fort Pitt, no First Nations forces could be found, so the Fort was put in a state of defence, and scouts were dispatched in every direction to reconnoitre and contact Big Bear's forces.

Steele and his scouts were part of this reconnaissance force and managed to contact the Big Bear's forces down the Saskatchewan River. Having made contact, Strange hurriedly cobbled his force together and on May 27, he marched towards the reported First Nations encampment, again separating his forces into land- and river-based columns, the Winnipeg Light Infantry being in the former, and the 65th Battalion the latter. Coming upon Big Bear's position, which was well prepared, Strange attacked immediately without waiting for the link-up with the 65th to occur, although the battalion immediately disembarked and proceeded to join the assault after they heard the outbreak of the firing. Strange's force carried the position and pursued the withdrawing First Nations forces until night fall, when he and his men bivouacked and passed a restless night without rations or great coats — all of which had been left in the wagons and boats.

On the twenty-eighth, Strange resumed his pursuit and engaged Big Bear in what was to become a rout of the militia force. Nearly lured into an ambush, Strange and his men exchanged fire for an extended duration with the First Nations defenders. He concluded, thanks to an attempted reconnaissance around the flank conducted by Steele and his cavalry, that turning the Indigenous position was impossible. Consequently, Strange ordered an ignominious withdrawal back to camp, and thence to Fort Pitt.

Returning to Fort Pitt, Strange dispatched messengers to request reinforcement from elements of the North-West Field Force at Battleford. Waiting in Fort Pitt, on June 1, Strange dispatched Steele's cavalry to reconnoitre Big Bear's position, which they found to be abandoned. Steele was ordered to pursue the withdrawing force the next day after a small element was able to liberate some of Big Bear's prisoners, one of whom was Theresa Gowanlock who was mentioned previously. Middleton's forces linked up with Strange on June 3 in Fort Pitt, after which Middleton took his force to follow Steele, linking up with him on June 5, while dispatching Strange to march towards Stoney Creek via Frog Lake. The forces merged again on June 15 at a Catholic Mission on the Beaver River.

Strange had dispatched Osborne Smith and the Winnipeg Light Infantry to move to Cold Lake to cut off Big Bear and his force as they withdrew north. Middleton's force linked up with Osborne Smith and the Winnipeg Light Infantry on June 17. It is here that Middleton seems to have concluded that he had sufficiently suppressed the rebellion that he could give up the pursuit of Big Bear, and so ordered his forces to return to Fort Pitt, from whence preparations for the disbandment of the North-West Field Force was begun. As Middleton reported "with Batoche taken and the prisoners there released, Riel and most of his councillors, and Poundmaker our prisoners, Big Bear and his band flying, disorganized and broken up, and all his prisoners released, I began to issue orders and make preparations for the breaking up of the whole Force, which had done its work so well, and by the 3rd of July, the last of the troops at Fort Pitt were embarked in the steamers for their homeward journey." [127]

In closing this narrative of the operational campaign and the role played by Manitoba's volunteers in it, we pause here to reflect on the activities of the 91st Battalion and the Winnipeg Troop of Cavalry. Recall from above the patriotic send-off of the 91st occasioned at the corner of Main and Portage in mid-April where Lieutenant-Colonel Scott proclaimed his men *the finest body of men in the Dominion*. Lamentably for the 91st Winnipeg Infantry Battalion and the

Winnipeg Cavalry Troop, their role in the campaign would be an important one, just not one in which much glory was to be found. For the entirely of the conflict, the two Manitoba corps provided Line of Communications security far away from the battlefields of Batoche and Fish Creek.

In a communique from the Battalion headquarters, likely drafted by one of Scott's staff officers and printed under the unfortunate byline of "Sojourning in Qu'Appelle" in the *Free Press,* it seems that the 91st received very warm greetings from towns in which they stopped while being transported by train from Winnipeg. In fact, Scott made the point of remarking on the good hospitality of the women of Portage la Prairie and Brandon. The battalion arrived at Qu'Appelle on April 18 and immediately went to work being drilled in skirmishing and field manoeuvres. The communique mentions that the battalion was "daily awaiting transportation facilities for a movement to the front" and, even at this early date was remarking on the lack of supplies and provisions, in particular a lack of fodder for horses.128

Regardless of the availability of transport, the lot of the 91st was to remain in garrison in Qu'Appelle, fighting boredom rather than rebels. In one letter to the editor of the *Free Press* dated May 5, a Mr. William Rowand wanted to express thanks to the people of Winnipeg who forwarded a bundle of books for the use of the men of the 91st in a reading room established by the local citizens of Qu'Appelle. In words perhaps unhelpful to the pride of the men of the 91st, Rowand reported that "the boys remain inactive in camp here, which they are very loath to do. They have considerable leisure for reading."129 In a letter home published in the *Brandon Sun* one teamster who had supported the columns that engaged Riel's forces, came across the 91st Battalion in Qu'Appelle when proceeding to the front and again when returning home. He recounted "when we arrived in the town the 91st battalion [sic] were quartered there, and very tired of the place they were, and most anxious to go to the front. Poor fellows! When we returned six weeks afterwards we found them at Fort Qu'Appelle, heartily sick of inaction, and praying for an Indian raid." [130]

Even as Middleton and his staff planned for the return of the troops, the 91st was ordered to languish in Qu'Appelle providing securing on the line of communication. By early July, it became obvious that the patience of the volunteers was wearing thin, so much so that two of them decided to write to the *Free Press* to lament their situation. One, going by the *nom de plume*

"Nemo" bemoaned the fact they were still being kept on in Qu'Appelle, writing "most of the volunteers of the 91st offered their services to the country when it was supposed to be in great danger, and at the time they did not expect to be away from their homes for more than five or six weeks. We are now going on four months away and at great personal loss … to a large number it is utter ruin to be kept on, our miserable pittance of 50 cents per diem does not half keep us in food."[131] Another, calling himself "One of the 91st Battalion" also wrote to the editor to complain that:

> the developments of the last two days seem to confirm the rumour in camp that the battalion had been offered for garrison duty, and as men who have left their work and homes to risk their lives in defence of law and order, and to protect the settlers of the Northwest, we protest against being kept for garrison duty, now, that the rebellion is quelled … if we are kept a few weeks longer and then discharged, how are we going to provide for the coming winter, as the season for remunerative employment will have gone by and we are not able to save much out of 50 cents per day when we have to pay for washing, blacking, pipe clay, soap, tobacco and other things."[132]

Finally, on July 21, telegraphs were received by the leadership of the 91st ordering them home. They entrained the next day, and arrived home early in the morning on July 23. Despite their lack of experience at the front, the citizens of Winnipeg nonetheless gave them a rousing reception, which included an address in front of city hall from the acting Mayor, Alderman Carruthers and the Honourable C.P. Brown.133 Between July 24 and 29, the companies were paid off and sent back to their corps headquarters.[134]

Despite early interest in getting the Winnipeg Troop of Cavalry into action, in the end the force found itself employed much the same as the 91st by providing line of communication garrison duties. The corps was commanded by the perfectly-named Captain Knight, and while it was one of the three corps in which the authorities expressed an interest in deploying early, being cavalry, it was difficult to fully equip, particularly with respect to proper mounts. As late as April 23, the *Manitoba Free Press* reported that while the Troop had been warned off to deploy shortly, it was only half equipped and had not yet received all the necessary horses due, the *Free Press* reported, to government refusal to purchase them.[135] In the intervening time, then, the Troop found itself doing rote duties in Winnipeg such as guard and fatigue duty at Fort Osborne.[136]

Eventually Knight and his men were able to move out and departed Winnipeg on April 24 for Fort Qu'Appelle, along with Quebec City's Cavalry School Corps under Lieutenant-Colonel Turnbull.137 There was some excitement in Fort Qu'Appelle, at least in early May, when a rash of horse thefts affected the force. These horse thieves employed audacity instead of cunning and actively engaged the Militiamen with rifle fire in attempting to steal horses, causing the whole of the Troop to deploy in a defensive position around midnight on May 5.138 About a week later, on May 14, the Winnipeg Cavalry and the Cavalry School Corps from Quebec City were dispatched to the Touchwood Hills, a region North-North-West of Qu'Appelle for garrison duties.139 They served in this region under the command of Colonel Turnbull until he and his Corps received orders to return to Quebec City in late June.140 Thereafter, the Winnipeg Troop of Cavalry remained in Touchwood until July 6 when they returned to Winnipeg where the *Free Press* reported that the men appeared "much browned by exposure to the weather, but [they seemed] to be well and hearty."141 One exception to this rather mundane deployment was the experience of Sergeant Back of the Cavalry who was tasked to act as General Middleton's orderly. He was bound for special recognition by the General, who reported that "he remained close to me through both the actions [Fish Creek and Batoche] where he was of assistance in carrying and transmitting orders, and also accompanied me on all my fatiguing and trying rides in pursuit of Big Bear."142

THE COMMISSARIAT AT WINNIPEG

It is impossible to consider Manitoba's role in the North-West Rebellion without considering the great importance the city played as the strategic sustainment hub for the entire force. It was from Winnipeg that the triumvirate of the Militia, the Hudson's Bay Company and the Canadian Pacific Railway worked to keep the North-West Field Force supplied, marching and fighting. Although the Dominion's response to the rebellion was in the main military, it is important to note that the Canadian Militia in 1885 had very little in the way of sustainment or support resources with which to keep an expeditionary force supplied in combat. There was no commissariat, no medical service, and no transport to support the expedition. Much of the responsibility for this fell to the Hudson's Bay Company, indeed, when surveying the state of sustainment resources in the Militia, the Company's Chief Commissioner observed that "all military supply organization seems to be miserably defective."143 Perhaps indicative of the inevitably close relationship between the Militia and the Hudson's Bay Company, Jackson was ordered by the adjutant-general to contact the Commissioner of the Hudson's Bay Company, J. Wrigley, upon his arrival in Winnipeg and, for the first few days after his arrival, Jackson even used rooms in the Company's offices to conduct his duties.144

From this, and subsequent, offices, Winnipeg became the logistical and sustainment heart of the North-West Field Force, from which every aspect of administrative support was provided. Even the mail service to the force emanated from Winnipeg, and an excellent job was done of it too. In his report, Middleton went to the length of singling out the efforts William Wallace Macleod, the Postal Inspector at Winnipeg, who he stated "took great trouble in maintaining our mail service."145

Medical support was of course of prime concern. Like many aspects of the nineteenth century Canadian Militia, its medical services were ill prepared for the conflict. The man assigned to the North-West Field Force as its Surgeon General, Dr. D. Bergin, described the woeful state of the Militia medical services in his report, stating "I was not blind to the difficulties of the situation. There were no fixed Departmental Medical Staff, no Field Hospital or Ambulance Service, no organized Corps of Nurses, no fixed method of recognizing such societies as the St. John's Hospital Aid Society, the Red Cross, and other similar charitable associations."146 The entire medical support infrastructure of the North-West Field Force would have to be developed from the ground up, and Manitoba played a large role in doing so.

The new Winnipeg General Hospital, located on what is now the Winnipeg Health Sciences Centre, was contracted with to provide accommodation for sick and wounded soldiers, at a *per diem* of one dollar and fifty cents per day, per bed. The head surgeon of the force, Major James Kerr, and Doctor Mewburn, were tasked to take control of the ward that was put aside for this task, and they were even able to incorporate four students from the Winnipeg School of Medicine into their team.147 The medical support in Winnipeg did not find favour in all its patients, however. At least one wounded soldier, a Private Cook who had been wounded through the arm, was not particularly happy with the medical service he received in Winnipeg. Charles Mulvaney, recalled the testament of Cook who had been evacuated to Saskatoon, and thence to Moose Jaw, and finally to Winnipeg to convalesce. Of Cook's experience in Winnipeg, Mulvaney plainly states "of their treatment at this place he does not speak with praise."148

Tactical-level supply depots were established throughout the North-West, but it was through Winnipeg that all operational and supply resources were funnelled: every solider from the East passed through the Manitoba capital, and most of the supply material was generated in the city. Even materiel purchased elsewhere, whether it was canned meat from Chicago, or horses from Morris, passed through Winnipeg.

Jackson's first few days in Winnipeg were indeed busy ones. He lamented in his report on the rebellion that he had no assistance whatsoever when he arrived in Winnipeg and he found himself "inundated with telegrams, contractors, and people from many parts of the country, who came to Winnipeg to urge the organization of local bodies, for home protection, or active service, as might be required."149

Since the transferral of Rupert's Land from the Hudson's Bay Company to the Dominion fifteen years previous, the company had diminished in stature, but it still maintained a large institutional footprint throughout the North-West which included a broad network of established trading forts. In fact, the first Lieutenant-Governor of Manitoba, Adams George Archibald, who was responsible for governing the North-West Territories, tried to establish a council for its governance representing "the three great interests of the West, the English, the French and the Hudson's Bay [Company]."150 Even by the mid-1880s the company still was one of the major "interests" of the region and at the time of the rebellion's outbreak, it still controlled one-twentieth of all the land south of the North Saskatchewan River.151 Through this presence, the Company of Adventures would prove invaluable to sustaining the North-West Field Force.

It must be said, however, that the Hudson's Bay Company shared some degree of culpability in setting the conditions that led to eruption of the rebellion in the first place. The lack of an effective central authority in the North-West Territories was a key element in the beginning of the rebellion. The diminishment of the Hudson's Bay Company's role as the legal government in the region since the transferral of the preponderance of its lands to Canada in 1870 left the North-West with no other established body to exercise authority.152 The political vacuum created by the waning of the Hudson's Bay Company's governing authority directly contributed to the rising caused by failing to provide a responsible, legitimate government to represent the will and needs of the Métis and settlers of the North-West.

In addition to the social and political presence that the Hudson's Bay Company maintained in the North-West, it also exercised a substantial trade in the region and thus, for purely selfish reasons, had a vested economic interest in seeing the rebellion suppressed as quickly as possible to avoid having its commercial interests suffer.[153] The Hudson's Bay Company posts that remained scattered about the region were tempting targets for the Métis and rebellious natives. Hudson's Bay Company officials knew it was in their best interest to induce the military and police forces in the region to use their posts as staging areas and thus provide some degree of security for the company's assets.154 An assessment conducted during the rebellion concluded that if the uprising managed to break the transportation network in the North-West, the fur trade upon which the Hudson's Bay Company so depended for its profits, could be interrupted for up to eighteen months resulting in the loss of revenue and profits.[155] Thus the impetus for the Hudson's Bay Company's faithful support to the Dominion Government may have laid more in its ledgers than in its patriotism.

Knowing the negative impact a rebellion in the North-West would have on its profits the Hudson's Bay Company put all of its resources at the disposal of the Dominion Government immediately after the Métis attack on Major Crozier's force at Duck Lake.[156] The proffered services were readily accepted by Minister Caron who knew that the military lacked sufficient sustainment and logistical capacity.[157] Upon his arrival in Winnipeg, Lieutenant-Colonel Jackson, who was tasked to create a commissariat corps to support the North-West Field Force, found that the only resource he had at his disposal were the Hudson's Bay Company facilities. The company's possession of an unrivalled number of posts and forts throughout the region, as well as its robust transportation network, meant the Hudson's Bay Company had just the logistical capabilities required to support the military force — available at a price.158 The Hudson's Bay Company became the *de facto* Quarter Master Service for the North-West Field Force. Middleton himself recounted that "our transport and stores, etc., were nearly all supplied through the Hudson Bay Company; Mr. Wrigley, their chief commissioner, being most indefatigable and successful in his endeavours to make things go smoothly."[159]

Although the Hudson's Bay Company certainly had its bottom-line in mind throughout the rebellion, excessive price gouging was not routine. Wrigley and his charges approached the supply of the North-West Field Force in a businesslike manner, but they recognized the need to expedite the suppression of the rebellion and therefore set prices accordingly.[160]

Despite the mutual interests and excellent support provided to the military by the Hudson's Bay Company, the relationship experienced some friction. Confusion arose during the rebellion as to where the proper delineation of responsibility between the military and company sustainment efforts should lie. Minister Caron's charge to the Hudson's Bay Company to supply the North-West Field Force, as well as the creation of a commissariat under Lieutenant-Colonel Jackson created two parallel, and in some cases overlapping, organizations that caused confusion. Where did one party's responsibility begin and the other's end? The situation was exacerbated when the question broadened from one of responsibility to one of liability. It was hard enough to determine who was responsible for the provision and movement of supply when faced with overlapping organizations, but even more problematic when consideration of liability arose for supplies such as food that may spoil if not properly cared for. An adequate structure was never arrived at.[161]

As a civilian, and with clout as Commissioner of the Hudson's Bay Company, Wrigley used his position to circumvent the chain of command when he saw fit. He did not allow mere staff officers to interfere with the execution of his duties. When Jackson arrived in Winnipeg, he informed Wrigley that he expected all requisitions to come through him, and he refused to authorize some of Wrigley's purchases since he had not received direction to do so from Ottawa. Wrigley went over Jackson's head directly to Caron to secure the authorization.[162] Of course such activity flew in the face of military protocol and subverted the chain of command that is so necessary for the efficient execution of military operations. *C'est la guerre.*

Having Jackson and his Commissariat Headquarters located in Winnipeg meant a number of local businesses were able to take advantage of Federal emergency funds. Local businesses certainly enjoyed the war economy the rebellion produced, and they and their proxies didn't hesitate to posture themselves to profit as much as possible. In one instance, the President of the Winnipeg Board of Trade, in an effort to convince the government to spend money in Winnipeg and thus assuage the negative impact the rebellion had imparted on business in Manitoba and the North-West, telegrammed directly to Prime Minister Macdonald stating "owing to the utter prostration of business in this country consequent on present trouble wholesale merchants wish [the government] to purchase commissariat supplies here as far as possible as stock are large and amply sufficient embracing provisions clothing blankets boots and shoes drugs wagons."[163]

Manitoba politicians and political hacks were unscrupulous in their pursuit of federal dollars. Both federal and provincial representatives waded into the fray to ensure their constituents had access to the Federal funds paying for the campaign. Joseph Royal, Conservative member for Provencher, telegrammed Caron to hint, not too subtly, that the Dominion Government should allow local businesses to wet their beaks, writing that "[there is] great dissatisfaction here because of Hudson Bay Co. having all [the] contracts to supply [the] troops."[164] On April 22, both David Howard Harrison, and Joseph Edward Woodworth cabled Caron to recommend that the soldiers of the North-West Field Force be concentrated in Brandon instead of Winnipeg, stating, magnanimously, that the former was drier and the water more pure. The pair's altruistic concern for the volunteers' health is suspect when one considers that Woodworth was the Conservative member for Brandon and Harrison was the Conservative member for Minnedosa — a rural riding that surrounded Brandon.[165]

Likewise, Amos Rowe, who was not a politician but rather the overtly conservative newspaper publisher of the *Winnipeg Times* with close connections to the Macdonald government, telegraphed the Minister of Customs (and future Prime Minister), Mackenzie Bowell to state that "[the] volunteers complain [they] are getting nothing but canned meat. [They] want fresh beef." Fortunately, he had the solution: "Gallagher & Son Winnipeg say [they] can furnish all [that is] required; [they] are good men [and] should get [the} contract."[166] Rowe was particularly active in securing business for his friends, and if previous telegram mentioned seemed non-partisan, a subsequently communication was blatantly politically motivated. He telegrammed Bowell again, and bluntly asked "will you request Minister Militia to instruct Wrigley to give contract for biscuits and bread to Thomas Chambers? He is good conservative and brother-in-law to Colonel [William Nassau] Kennedy. The man that has it now are [sic] Grits and bad ones at that." Partisanship and nepotism both in a single message.[167]

And well they should have agitated to secure business for their ridings and their friends, as the business was indeed lucrative. A large number of Winnipeg citizens profited from the rebellion, especially due to its selection as the commissariat headquarters of the entire force. A quick survey of the various expenditures included in the Dominion Government's official report on the rebellion indicates a substantial outlay of federal funds to Winnipeg business. These include, but are not limited to, the following: N. Bawlf received $63,830 for hay, oats, sacks, and cartage, John A. Tees earned $64,510 for the same, and Felide, Haffner & Co., McBean Brothers, E.A. Struthers and W. Shoutts, all of Winnipeg earned between $1,500 and $15,000 providing forage for the horses of the force. Amos Rowe obviously carried some influence in political circles and enjoyed some success due to his interventions as Gallagher & Sons made $25,000 selling beef and beef steak to the force. J. Hingston Smith & Co. only made $99, but the material this Winnipeg company provided was unique, including an Irish army revolver, handcuffs, a pair of leg irons and one ball and chain, amongst other items. Although the official report does not comment, perhaps these last items were secured for use with Louis Riel when he was brought back to Winnipeg after his capture near Batoche, as the *Manitoba Free Press* does report that he was shackled with an iron ball while incarcerated awaiting his execution.[168] The Hudson's Bay Company, scapegoat of the Winnipeg businessmen who envied their near-monopoly on the provision of stores, easily earned the lion's share of the money outlaid by the Dominion Government. The Company of Adventurers received a total of $1,025,852 from Ottawa during the rebellion divided between charges for supplies it produced directly, recouped funds paid out to subcontractors and, of course, a 5 percent commission. Of this amount, $538,996, was paid out in Winnipeg and doubtless materially benefitted the local economy.[169] From a purely economic perspective, the rebellion was a boon for Winnipeg.

PUBLIC SUPPORT

It wasn't dollars and cents that produced the patriotic fervour amongst the people of Manitoba. The citizenry of Winnipeg and all the major urban centres was effusive in its support of the soldiers, both those raised in Winnipeg and Manitoba, as well as those who came from the sister provinces to the east. As we've observed throughout this book, the Militia volunteers were always held in high esteem amongst the people of Manitoba. Certainly, there were some who, when the volunteers' behaviour was at its worst in the years immediately after 1870, were quick to point out their malfeasance. This notwithstanding, in the main, amongst the settler population in the west and the predominantly Anglo-protestant populations in the Eastern Provinces, Militia volunteers maintained an aura of patriotic glory. Such lionization was only enhanced with the eruption of the conflict.

The warm feeling evinced by the citizens of Winnipeg towards the Militia volunteers was recorded by a member of A Battery, Alexander Laidlaw, who had been dispatched from the Citadel in Quebec on March 27. He recounted the following about the battery's arrival in Winnipeg: "Here the scene beggars description; as we steamed alongside the platform cheer after cheer went up from thousands of throats. Disembarking from the car we deposited our arms and accoutrements in the large waiting room of the Canadian Pacific Railway depot and had a look round. The citizens brought us refreshments in the shape of coffee, sandwiches, lager beer, and so on.... Tobacco was also supplied to us from one of the Winnipeg firms, and in fact one and all vied with each other who should show us the greatest kindness."[170]

Winnipeg was a city of immigrants. As this book has illustrated, by 1885 its population was based to a very large degree on immigration of Anglo-Protestant settlers from the eastern provinces and Great Britain, but there were smaller pluralistic groups of settlers who also found their way to the city. Consequently, diasporic communities in Winnipeg turned out in strength to welcome their newly-arrived soldier-friends from the various corners of the Dominion when they arrived in the North-West. Robert A. Sherlock, who accompanied the Halifax Battalion to the North-West, recalled that when they reached Winnipeg on Wednesday, April 22, they were "met by a delegation of Nova Scotians, who welcomed us in the name of the resident Bluenoses of that city." And later he added "[they] were entertained in Selkirk Hall by the Winnipeg Nova Scotians; and when I call it an entertainment I simply nickname it. It was beyond an entertainment, something which language fails me to describe." [171]

The French population of the city were eager to see their confreres from the east as well. Take, for example, the observances of Charles Daoust, who came to the North-West with the 65th Regiment, Montreal's Mount Royal Rifles. He recalled in his memoir *Cent-Vingt Jours de Service Actif* about the role of the regiment in the North-West Rebellion, the following concerning the warm welcome the regiment received upon its arrival: "enfin, quelques minutes avant sept heures, les premières maisons de Winnipeg parûrent dans le lointain et fûrent saluées par des cris de joie. Bientôt le train entra dans la gare. La ville avait revêtue sa toilette de fête; les pavillons flottaient partout, et les jeunes filles avaient mis leurs robes de dimanche pour recevoir le bâtaillon."[172]

Additionally, *Le Manitoba* recorded that "depuis quelques semaines Winnipeg a vu défiler plusieurs bâtaillons venus de l'Est en destination pour l'Ouest ... On a pu admirer ces différents corps; mais pour nous, il nous fallait voir le 65eme de Montréal et le 9eme de Québec. Enfin vendredi matin on apprend que le 65eme était à Winnipeg depuis six heures. Aussitôt presque tout Saint-Boniface se rend à la gare : les uns pour y rencontrer de leurs parents, d'autres des amis, les autres pour voir des Canadiens d'en bas."[173]

Not all encounters were friendly. George Beauregard of the 9th Battalion from Quebec City recalled in his memoir, *Le 9me Battalion au Nord-Ouest* that he and his colleagues enjoyed running the streets of Winnipeg and speaking "aux jolies anglaises de Winnipeg" but the well-established Anglo-Protestant disdain for the French remained present in Winnipeg, even against those soldiers, loyal to Queen and country, who volunteered to suppress the rebellion. Beauregard recounted one particularly unfortunate incident: "À six heures et demie nous avons quitté Winnipeg. À notre départ de l'hôtel, un individu bien mis, ayant assez l'apparence d'un homme bien élevé, probablement le sang échauffé parce qu'il n'avait pas mis d'eau dans son vin, s'approcha de nous et commença à nous insulter. Il a voulu porter l'enthousiasme jusqu'à frapper un de nos officiers. Mais on l'a prévenu, un sergent lui a appliqué un coup de poing dont il se souviendra longtemps. Voilà ce qu'il a dû appeler, dans sa langue maternelle, *short and sweet*."[174]

Religious organizations were quick to offer their support as well. The president of the Bible Society in Winnipeg received a telegram from his counterpart in Toronto in early April stating that they were forwarding five hundred bibles to be issued to the Toronto volunteers. In a rather unthankful response, W.R. Mulock replied "send one thousand more for men here." The

Toronto Bible Society replied it was unfortunately short of testaments but had arranged for the 1,500 to be shipped from New York.175 Likewise, The Sisters of St. Boniface offered to nurse the sick and wounded.[176]

But perhaps the best indicator of public support for the Militia volunteers was the way their deaths were publicly mourned. Canadian military history is, in the main, a narrative of Canadians fighting abroad. The North-West Rebellion forms one of a very small number of conflicts in Canadian military history after Confederation in which the fighting occurred *in* Canada. Consequently, the deaths and casualties that resulted from the conflict were not buried or treated on the other side of the ocean, but rather at home and in full view of the Canadian public. Moreover, the substantial number of volunteer mortal casualties that originated in Manitoba combined with the fact all casualties moved through Winnipeg *en route* to their homes in the east combined to form a very emotional atmosphere in Winnipeg during the conflict. The result was that the funerals of those killed in action drew substantial public support and participation. Jackson relates the story of the burial of the first two soldiers killed during the conflict in his report:

> the remains of Lieutenant Charles Swinford and Private A.W. Ferguson, of the 90th Battalion, the first wounded and subsequently died, and the other killed at Fish Creek, having been sent to their friends in Winnipeg were buried today. His Honor the Lieutenant Governor and his Ministers, all the military officers in the city, the Municipal Council, and many thousands of people, attended, thus sympathizing with the friends and showing respect to the deceased, who had sacrificed their lives assisting in the maintenance of law and order. All business was suspended and the people appeared to be in deep mourning.[177]

Later, when word of the deaths of Corporal Code, and Privates Hardisty and Fraser, all of the 90th Battalion, was received, the mayor met with local military officers to arrange the details for a military funeral. The Montreal Garrison Artillery, which had been left behind to garrison Winnipeg, provided the band and a firing party.[178] A funeral service was held for all three in Grace Church and the public turnout was large enough, if the *Free Press* is to be believed, to warrant the observation that "no such gathering has ever before been seen in Winnipeg or in the Northwest."[179] After the funeral the remains of all three were conveyed to St. John Cemetery in a procession led by the clergy — no less than six men of the cloth — followed by the city police, the fire brigade, and the firing party and guard of honor from the Montreal Garrison Artillery. Again, the *Free Press* remarked the "procession was the largest and most imposing ever seen in the city." Upon reaching the cemetery, the remains were interred near the resting place of Lieutenant Swinford and Private Ferguson on a plot of ground donated by the Bishop of Rupert's Land expressly for the burial of volunteers during the rebellion.[180]

On July 5, the funeral of Privates Wheeler and Ennis, both of the 90th Battalion, was conducted at Holy Trinity Church and their remains were interred next to those of their five colleagues. A heavy rain prevented a very large gathering of the public in this instance, but the procession was, as was the case with their colleagues, well represented by city police, the fire brigade, and various other organizations.[181]

Victory in the West: Homecomings and Celebrations.

With the rebellion over, celebrations were in order. The citizens of Winnipeg and Manitoba had lived *in* the war, not *through* it. Living on the frontier of the Dominion, the rebellion was fought, in many ways, on their doorsteps, in their backyards and in their neighbourhoods. Manitoba's fathers, sons, and brothers, from a *per capita* perspective, fought the rebellion in far greater number than any other region of the country. Winnipeg was the conduit through which the *entire* North-West Field Force flowed into the theatre of operations and also, for the majority of the regiments, back home – including every casket of a fallen volunteer.

One cannot overstate the emotional impact the rebellion had on Manitobans. Families and friends of Manitoba volunteers paid a high price for their patriotism: a total of twenty-six Militiamen killed, and 103 wounded during the campaign, Manitoba volunteers accounted for eleven dead and thirty-two wounded, 42 percent and 31 percent respectively. This from a province that represented but 1.5 percent of the national population. Retrospect obscures contemporary reality, and while we have seen that a number of Manitoba's corps were relegated to relatively safe Line of Communication garrison duties, there was no way for the men thus deployed to be confident of their security at the time. While references were constantly made to the "front" in newspaper columns and official correspondence, in reality a rebellion or an insurgency is amorphous, decentralized and non-linear. However much a corps' deployment may appear "safe" from an historical perspective to the volunteers the threat was ever present and all around. However far away the "front" was, the perceived threat to Manitoba and North-West settlers was ubiquitous.

Victory celebrations were thus as much an expressive emotional outlet for the citizens of Manitoba as a commemoration of the actions of the volunteers. If there is one constant theme throughout the period in discussion in this book, it is the Anglo-Protestant proclivity to lionize the valour and dedication of the Canadian Militia volunteer. Guided by this spirit, in Winnipeg plans to celebrate the military's victory in the North-West began well before hostilities ended. The acting mayor of Winnipeg, Alderman Carruthers, even reached out to the Minister of Militia by telegram on June 26, 1885 asking, "Would it be possible to have troops go East via Winnipeg[?] Citizens anxious to do them honors."[182] Sadly, Middleton could not make it happen. He replied to Caron: "For many and obvious reasons it is not advisable and I have declined; but [the] 9th [Regiment], part of the 65th, and Halifax [Provisional Battalion] being on line of railway must go via Winnipeg; the Seventh, York & Simcoe regiments must also go via Winnipeg as they must strike the Railway to get home ... I fear I must keep 91st and 92nd Regiments for duty a little while longer."[183] While not all regiments passed directly through Winnipeg, a very large proportion did due to its strategic location on the railway line. Winnipeg would have its chance to honor the volunteers.

The Winnipeg City Council formed a Reception Committee to plan a proper welcome for the returning warriors. It held its first meeting on July 8 under the direction of Alderman Carruthers, himself late of the Militia, where it was decided that a victory arch would be erected on Main Street, positioned so that it could be seen from both directions. In the Market Square, a platform would be erected where the assembled dignitaries would express their gratitude to the volunteers, although surprisingly the plan for speeches was kept short as "it [was] thought the men will be anxious to disperse and meet their friends as soon as possible." The platform would transform into a grand promenade in the evening, and it was requested that "the people turn out *en masse*, on the arrival of the troops."[184] The city even dedicated the Council Chambers to act as the Committee Room and Office of the Winnipeg Volunteers' Aid and

Relief Committee.[185]

The first units to return to Winnipeg were those who came overland by train. The 9th Battalion, fresh from garrison duties in and around Calgary, arrived in Winnipeg on July 11 and were met by a large reception. After enjoying a dinner provided by the depot restaurant, the French-Canadian regiment marched to St. Boniface where they set up camp in front of St. Boniface College.[186]

While the railway was the primary means of transporting troops between the theatre of operations in the North-West and Winnipeg, as so many of the battalions had marched north from the railhead to conduct operations in areas such as Batoche, and were thus some distance from rail transport, upon the cessation of operations Middleton took advantage of the availability of river transport. Many of the soldiers were transported from the theatre of operations on steamships, via the Saskatchewan River and Lake Winnipeg to Selkirk, Manitoba. The plan had a number of battalions departing by rail directly from East Selkirk back to their homes in the east while the others would move down to Winnipeg for the victory celebrations, and thence back home. The reception committee asked Colonel E.A. Whitehead to rendezvous with General Middleton when he arrived at Selkirk, and when the expected arrival of the battalions destined for Winnipeg was known, Colonel Whitehead was to release a number of homing pigeons who would bring the glad tidings of the return of the troops to the citizens in Winnipeg.[187]

The flotilla of steamships arrived in Selkirk on July 15 to a very warm welcome reception, complete with quarts of strawberries and, of more interest to the soldiers, quarts of lager. This latter addition, while no doubt a welcome sight to the weary volunteers, led to the unsurprising result of a bunch of intoxicated miscreants arguing, fighting, and generally behaving badly in the streets of Selkirk. Thomas Champion recorded the event in his history of the 10th Royal Grenadiers with an unsurprised tone, writing matter-of-factly that "about fifteen miles up [the Red River] we reached Selkirk, landed, and had a lunch that was prepared for us; the Midland [Battalion] got drunk and began to fight about three o'clock."[188] The nonchalance with which he describes the Midland Battalion's actions leaves the definite impression this sort of behaviour was unsurprising. As Middleton had informed the Minister, the Midland and 65th Battalions were ferried to East Selkirk and thence by train homeward so they were unable to enjoy the welcome awaiting them in

Winnipeg — perhaps a blessing in disguise given the Midland's proclivity for inebriation. As for the other battalions, the 90th Winnipeg Rifles, the Queen's Own Rifles, the 10th Royal Grenadiers and the Ottawa Sharpshooters were bound for Winnipeg on a train which pulled out of Selkirk in the late afternoon, arriving in Winnipeg a short while after six o'clock p.m.

Word arrived to the citizens of Winnipeg that the troops were on their way via messenger pigeon and telegram. A flurry of activity erupted as the citizens redoubled their efforts to prepare for the troop's reception. Throughout the downtown area of Winnipeg, streets and windows were adorned with patriotic flags and bunting. At about one o'clock, the York and Simcoe Battalion arrived in the Winnipeg Depot, having taken a train from the west. To their chagrin, the Southern Ontario lads were obliged to wait at the depot until the remainder of the battalions who were *en route* from Selkirk arrived in the city.[189]

At about seven o'clock that night, the training bringing the troops from Selkirk arrived at the depot in Winnipeg to an immense cheer from the large crowd that had gathered. After detraining, the brigaded regiments marched along Main Street from the train depot, arriving at City Hall where the awaiting crowd was so dense it was difficult to find sufficient space to form the battalions into a square. Eventually, with enough pushing and shoving and manipulating, the returned volunteers were formed into a three-sided square facing city hall. The officers, mounted on horses in front of their troops, were presented with wreaths from local citizens. Afterwards came the expected laudatory speeches from important personages such as General Middleton, the lieutenant-governor, the premier and the mayor. The citizens of Winnipeg had done splendid work ensuring the city was properly adorned for so patriotic an event, the *Free Press* opining that "it is safe to say that the city never presented a more attractive appearance."[190]

But this welcome alone was not sufficient. The regiments were marched off to their encampments for an evening's respite and perhaps some celebrations amongst friends and colleagues. More celebrations were scheduled for July 16, but foul weather caused them to be postponed for twenty-four hours. The skies cleared in the late afternoon, however, just in time for the arrival of the Winnipeg Field Battery at the train depot at 6:20 p.m. The cleared skies meant that many admiring citizens dutifully reported to the station to celebrate the arrival of the Battery. When the Battery Commander, Major Jarvis, emerged from the depot he was immediately grabbed by the crowd and hoisted on the shoulders of several citizens who paraded him around like a war trophy. Some sort of order was eventually established, and a more dignified military air was presented when the Battery formed into columns outside the station. The Battery proceeded to march down Main Street following the band and a guard from the 90th Battalion and the Winnipeg Fire Brigade who escorted them along. Crowds lined the streets to welcome them home, and, according to the *Free Press*, the "young girls waved their handkerchiefs about their heads as though intoxicated with delight" and "Old men threw away their canes and joined with the younger element in welcoming home the battery." The Battery was marched to their drill shed where they were dismissed for the evening.[191]

It was July 17 that presented the biggest celebration, in fact the *Free Press* pulled no punches calling it "the biggest day Winnipeg has ever seen." The twenty-four-hour postponement of the grand celebration meant that several of the eastern regiments were forced to depart by train before they could participate in Winnipeg's victory festivities. The grand finale was a torchlight procession through downtown Winnipeg that incorporated the remaining militia corps in the city and many city organizations such as the boys' brigade, the Fire Brigade, the Police Force, and the St. Albert Society. As much of the city-wide decorations were flags and evergreen boughs, several caught fire when a careless torch was passed too close, including the impressive arch erected across Main Street to welcome the volunteers. Fortunately, all conflagrations were caught and extinguished in sufficient time to avoid any major mishaps. The usual marching tunes were played, augmented by a new tune entitled "We will hang Louis Riel to a sour apple tree" which was highlighted with an effigy of the captured Métis leader hung from the Main Street arch and filled with firework powder which, when lit, sent the effigy into the air and "in the course of time he descended in fragments amid the yells of the excited crowd." There was certainly no magnanimity in the victory celebrations. The procession broke up late in the evening when all participants went off to celebrate and "paint the town until a late hour — very late indeed."[192]

Over the course of the next several weeks the remaining corps arrived in Winnipeg and the men were eventually released back to their civilian occupations. Victory celebrations having ended, the memorializing of the rebellion began in earnest. Notwithstanding the large-scale outpouring of the civic pride in the volunteers, perhaps the most enduring symbol of the public lionization of the volunteers was the creation of the volunteer memorial to commemorate the casualties of the conflict which remains standing today.

Plans for the memorial began in early June of 1885 but, curiously, despite the obvious public support for the volunteers, the committee organizing the erection of the memorial had difficulties raising the necessary funds. The committee's June 16 meeting adjourned for a week with no action taken as only $1,000 of the anticipated $5,000 cost had been received. The following week's meeting likewise revealed a deficit of subscriptions for the memorial.[193]

If there was a shortage of people willing to contribute monetarily to the erection of the memorial, such was not the case for people willing to build one. The committee received plans from no less than eleven individuals and companies interested in designing and building the memorial.[194] The mayor called a public meeting in late June to discuss the question of financing the memorial, to which attendance was disappointingly low. The *Free Press* reported that "it looks as if there [is] a chance of the monument falling through if citizens do not take more interest in the matter."[195] Even by the end of July 1885 the amount raised for the memorial was only half of what was required.[196] By the end of August , the committee's treasurer, F. H. Mathewson reported that the funds received stood at $4,900, only one hundred dollars shy of the committee's goal of $5,000.[197] Despite this welcome news, it was not until mid-November 1885 that the committee put out a call for tenders to erect the memorial.[198]

In September of 1886, the monument to the volunteers was unveiled in a large ceremony held in front of City Hall on Main Street, an appropriate location given that it was there that so many of the volunteers were both sent off to the front and welcomed home. Surprisingly, the monument was dedicated solely to the 90th Battalion Winnipeg Rifles, seemingly ignorant of the efforts of the various other corps who participated in the rebellion. It must be said that the 90th Battalion was at the tip of the spear for the two most significant clashes of the campaign, at Fish Creek and Batoche. And, of all the corps engaged, including those from Central Canada, the 90th Battalion with nine fatalities paid the largest price of any single regiment in the conflict.

At the very least, the other corps of the Militia were invited to participate in the solemn ceremony that revealed the monument to the citizens. At the unveiling, while the 90th Battalion was presented front and center, the Winnipeg Troop of Cavalry and the Winnipeg Field Battery participated in the ceremony by furnishing marching components, as well as the men of the Infantry School Corps which had been created in District No. 10 after the conflict. The ceremony was unremarkable for its expected lionization of the volunteers and its lamentations for the fallen, expressed by the usual cast of personages: the mayor, the premier, and the lieutenant-governor. One comment, however, by the Mayor Henry Westbrook is interesting and nicely captures the emotion and connection of Winnipeg and Manitoba to the rebellion:

> I was compelled to listen to the remarks of one of the officers of an eastern battalion and my heart was stirred within me when I heard him say that the people in the city were little less than rebels in that they did not treat those from the east with more consideration, especially when they had come so far to defend them. And I can assure you fellow citizens my blood boiled when I replied to him that the trouble was none of our making and that we were quite able to quell any rebellion in this country without assistance. And, said I, 'you boast of sending men here to defend us, and still the city you represent, although larger than our own has sent less than 500 men to help quell the trouble you have caused, while we, though innocent, for the sake of our beloved country, have now nearly 1,500 good and true men at the front, and could still at an hour's notice have another battalion ready if required.'[199]

The North-West Rebellion was, in many ways, Manitoba's war and its importance to Canadian and Manitoba history cannot be overstated. In many ways the victory of the Dominion Forces in the North-West was the culmination of Dominion strategic efforts that had begun in 1870 and became finally manifested in the consolidation of Dominion authority throughout the region. This authority was established at the expense of the Métis and the Indigenous peoples, whose unsuccessful attempts to peacefully redress their legitimate grievances forced them to pursue violence in what would eventually be a fruitless endeavour to maintain their culture and way of life. In this light, perhaps the best way to close this chapter is with the words of Gabriel Dumont in conversation with Louis Riel after their defeat at Batoche:

> J'ai été ensuite rejoins par un groupe de nos amis qui s'étaient

réugiés dans un grand bois où Riel les encourageait à se battre. Celui-ci, en me voyant, me dit; qu'allons-nous faire, nous sommes vaincus. Je lui ai dit : il faut périr; vous deviez savoir qu'en prenant les armes, nous serions vaincus.[200]

CONCLUSION

The Manitoba Militia underwent a sort of crucible in 1885. In one form or another, every single corps of Military District No. 10 had been involved in the conflict in the North-West in some way, even if not every single volunteer had. The influx of funds for equipment and uniforms that had accompanied the emergency, even if wholly inadequate, abated shortly after the conflict ended and the familiar paradigm of federal neglect of the western militia units settled back in. Despite, and in many ways because, of their recent operations, the corps of Military District No. 10 were in a very sorry state.

In his report for 1885, Houghton noted that in the Winnipeg Field Battery "the carriages and limbers are much in need of repair, and some of the wheels are deficient, they having been lost or gone astray by some means during the North-West campaign."[1] Amongst the 90th Battalion, Houghton noted that "their old [uniforms] being completely worn out on service and long since discarded, [the men] have been obliged to confine themselves to night drills in plain clothes" presumably to evade observation and embarrassment by the general public.[2]

At least there was some glimmers of optimism. The Winnipeg Troop of Cavalry happily received new uniforms in time for the arrival of the Governor General, who was returning from a trip to British Columbia on October 21, 1885. The troopers formed a Vice-Regal escort in which the *Free Press* described the corps thusly: "the boys looked resplendent in their new uniforms and were well mounted on somewhat wild and handsome steeds."[3] The very next day a new Drill Shed was officially opened by the Governor General.[4]

Much had changed in the previous fifteen years. A pluralistic yet isolated and rustic settlement had been replaced by a thriving city connected by railway and telegraph lines to the outer world. Where cart trails had run through thick prairie mud, streets were paved. Where scattered wood frame buildings, shanties and tents had broken the horizon, brick and mortar edifices of numerous floors cast long shadows. The interminable squeal of the Red River Cart had been replaced by the horn of the locomotive and the spark of the electric streetcar. Instead of waiting for months if not years for news from the outside world, near-instantaneous communication by telegraph had been established. The chrysalis of Confederation had produced a Manitoba whose infrastructure had changed dramatically.

If Manitoba's exoskeleton had morphed, so too did its cultural soul. The French and English Métis, Hudson Bay Company men, Selkirk Settlers and the small number of Anglo-Protestant settlers who had huddled around the confluence of the Red and Assiniboine Rivers had been replaced by a thriving city whose social and political direction were guided by an Anglo-Protestant elite. The institutions, mores and practices of Ontario had been transplanted in Manitoba by a decade and a half of immigration that emanated, predominantly, from Southern Ontario and Great Britain. The Winnipeg of 1885 was nearly as different from the Winnipeg of 1869, as the latter was from Toronto.

Too often the Militiamen in Manitoba from 1870|85 are regarded one-dimensional and their influence on the socio-cultural evolution of Manitoba and the North-West marginalized or outright ignored. These men had a far broader cultural influence than the prevailing narrative allows: they were citizens, settlers, soldiers, and scoundrels whose impact went far beyond the barracks and battlefields. Like the throngs of British settlers from the east who installed their familiar political, economic, religious, and social practices and institutions on their new home, for good or ill, the Militia enabled the cultural transmogrification of Manitoba.

This book has illustrated that the Militia's impact in contributing to the establishment a common cultural norm in Manitoba that was consistent with the hegemonic Anglo-Protestant culture of late nineteenth century Canada was profound. The Militia provided the security to protect the growing settlements from exterior threats, even the perceived yet unfounded threat from

First Nations peoples. The Militia also provided a valuable force to maintain peace, order, and good government within the province through the provision of aid to the civil power, thus facilitating Manitoba's growth and evolution. Additionally, the Militia provided a tangible and overt representation of both the Dominion and British Empires through the provision of guards of honour, the firing of gun salutes, and its participation during treaty negotiations with First Nations. Such symbolic efforts served to reinforce the wider cultural linkage between Manitoba, Canada and British Empire. While providing this valuable symbolism, the Militia became a bulwark of the emergent Anglo-Protestant society, aping the social role of the Militia in the older provinces of the Dominion, mores inherited from Great Britain and the legacy of British colonialism in North America. Eminent members of early Winnipeg society sought membership in the ranks of the local Militia corps, the bands played concerts and dramatic companies entertained soldier and citizen alike. This all served to recreate the social structure extant in Manitoba's sister provinces to the east and direct the social cohesion within Winnipeg and Manitoba. Most unfortunately, the Militia employed ethnically charged violence to intimidate the Métis and their supporters in Manitoba to encourage them to displace, with a view to accommodating the emergent Anglo-Protestant cultural hegemon in the new province and set the conditions for settlement.

Finally, when the Métis and Indigenous Peoples of the North-West understandably took arms to address the many injustices imposed upon them by an indifferent and cruel absentee landlord in Ottawa, the Militiamen of Manitoba played a disproportionately large role in the military response to the North-West Rebellion. As historian Desmond Morton put it, 1885 heard the last war drum beaten. In Fish Creek, Batoche and the Cut Knife Hills the destiny of Manitoba, the North-West and Canada was, for good or ill, confirmed.

This book does not pretend to endorse or condemn the actions of the Militia or argue the propriety of the cultural upheaval it enabled, it simply tells a story, one that is too often overlooked. There is plenty to critique in the way the Militia behaved and the colonization of the North-West writ large. The Militiamen of Manitoba were culpable for enabling what would come to be an oppressive and cruel treatment of Canada's Indigenous peoples. This cannot be denied.

There is a paradox in modern Canada. Despite tragic mistakes of the past, there is still much to be proud of in the modern Province of Manitoba and Canada. We are a successful liberal democracy that cherishes and protects human rights and freedoms. We have positively influenced the world and have established peaceful and productive communities. We are trying to atone for the past and provide a better future. Much of what is good and successful about modern Manitoba is thanks to the dedication, sacrifice and efforts of the men who served their nation in uniform during war and peace. The legacy of their efforts resonates to this day. The Militia's socio-cultural influence in the creation of modern Manitoba, the good parts and the very, very bad ones, was far more profound than it has been given credit for. I hope this book has in some small way addressed that deficiency.

EPILOGUE

There is a quote that is widely accredited to Winston Churchill, perhaps apocryphally, that the reservist is "twice the citizen." Even if the great statesman and orator never did utter the phrase, it has nonetheless been established in rhetorical annals as representative of the dual nature of the army reservist as both solider and citizen. In fact, the phrase was even adopted by the United States Army Reserve for the title of its official history: *Twice The Citizen: A History of the United States Army Reserve, 1908-1995* and it is the motto of the United States Army Reserve Command.[1]

Much about the Canadian Militiamen serving in Winnipeg has changed since the arrival of the Wolseley Expedition in 1870, the one constant being an unbroken stream of Canadian Militia presence in Winnipeg and Manitoba. Since the moment the first member of the 1st Ontario Rifles disembarked his canoe near Fort Garry in August 1870, not a day has gone by that a Militia volunteer could not be found in Winnipeg. A full history of the military in Manitoba is a question of some detail that is too broad for inclusion here, but there are certainly several important evolutions worthy of brief mention.

Military District No. 10 remained generally intact until 1946, although as provinces were created in the North-West new districts were created to administer the militia therein. In 1915, Military District No. 13 was created to administer Alberta, and in 1916 Military District No. 12 was created to administer Saskatchewan. In 1946, the entire Canadian Army underwent a comprehensive organizational change. General Order Number 21/1946, dated January 28, 1946, authorized the creation of five *Commands* which did away with the long-standing districts. Under this scheme Military District No. 10 was lumped it in with District No. 12 and fell under the authority of Prairie Command, which included all Militia units in Saskatchewan, Manitoba and Northwestern Ontario. This was changed again in 1968 with the creation of *Areas* and the return of districts, as subordinate commands. In the *Prairie Militia Area* five districts were created: Northern Alberta Militia District, Southern Alberta Militia District, Saskatchewan Militia District, Thunder Bay Militia District, and Manitoba Militia District. Another reorganization occurred in 1991 although "Areas" were kept as superior formations with the additional title of "Land Forces." Manitoba Militiamen thereafter found themselves members of the *Manitoba-Lakehead District* of *Land Forces Western Area* which consisted of all Canadian Army units, regular or reserve, south of the Yukon and Northwest Territories, between Vancouver Island and Thunder Bay. In 1997, the districts were replaced with *Brigade Groups* and in 2014 the Land Force Areas adopted Divisional nomenclature. The modern Canadian Militia in Manitoba exists as 38th Canadian Brigade Group. It is headquartered in Winnipeg and includes all Militia units in Saskatchewan, Manitoba, and Northwestern Ontario. The 38th Canadian Brigade Group is a formation of the 3rd Canadian Division, headquartered in Edmonton, Alberta.[2]

Despite the many name changes over the years, the echoes of the early Militia in Manitoba still reverberate. Much has changed in the size, nature, and professionalism of the Militia in Manitoba over the years, but a linear connection still exists. For example, in a small armoury tucked away north of the main street in Portage la Prairie, 13th Field Battery of the 26th Field Artillery Regiment, which is headquartered in Brandon, still parades. 13th Field Battery is the original Winnipeg Field Battery, gazetted into existence in 1871 in response to the threat of Fenian Invasion. It has existed consistently since those days long ago, even if the evolving organizational nature of the Canadian Militia has bestowed upon it a different name and a designating number. Likewise, the 90th Battalion, created under the auspices of the second Deputy Adjutant-General of Military District Number No. 10, Lieutenant-Colonel C.F. Houghton in 1883, is perpetuated by the Royal Winnipeg Rifles which continues to parade this very day in Minto Armouries in Winnipeg.

As Chapter 6 illustrated, the 90th Battalion and the Winnipeg Field Battery both participated in the North-West Rebellion. During the Great War, both generated troops for service in the Canadian Expeditionary Force, although due to the Minister of Militia's decision to ignore the established mobilization plans and create a new force from scratch, neither of the two units deployed to Europe. It should be noted that at the time of the Great War, Military District Number No. 10 was under the command of no less a personage than the indefatigable Lieutenant-Colonel Sam Steele.

Manitoba Militia units only generated forces for the Canadian Expeditionary Force during the Great War, and did not participate themselves, but that was not the case in the Second World War. The 13th (Winnipeg) Field Battery, direct descendent of the Winnipeg Field Battery, served in the 6th Field Regiment, Royal Canadian Artillery supporting the 2nd Canadian Division. The Royal Winnipeg Rifles, descendants of the 90th Battalion, constituted one of the infantry battalions of 5th Canadian Infantry Brigade of 3rd Canadian Division. The Rifles were even one of the assaulting battalions that landed on Juno Beach in Normandy on D-Day, June 6, 1944. These are but two examples of the still existent spirit and tradition of the original Militia that helped to shape Manitoba into what it is today.

Names, uniforms, and equipment have changed, but what has remained consistent throughout was the presence and participation of men, and now women, who are the "bone and sinew' of the North-West in the ranks of these units. They are not a force apart, they are shopkeepers, police officers, students, teachers, mothers, fathers, brothers, sisters, neighbours, and friends. They are the person next to you on the bus, at the neighbouring table in the restaurant, or sitting next to you in your classroom. As they were in the 1870s, they are integral members of the cultural mosaic of Manitoba and in their own way, continue to help Manitoba society evolve with changing times and changing attitudes. While doing so they continue to stand, fight and sacrifice for the freedoms, rights and privileges we Canadians cherish, in 2006 Corporal Anthony Boneca of the Lake Superior Scottish Regiment in Thunder Bay was killed on duty in Afghanistan.

It is perhaps fitting, then, to close this book with the motto of 38th Canadian Brigade Group: *Progredere ne regredere* — Ever forward never back.

ABOVE: General Garnet J. Wolseley. As a Colonel, Wolseley led the 1870 joint Anglo-Canadian Red River Expeditionary Force dispatched to Fort Garry, ostensibly as a peacekeeping force, in response to the Red River Resistance. He went on to great success and became a Field Marshall in the British Army. His aggressive overtones towards Riel and the Metis leadership likely contributed to the levels pf violence and intimidation exercised by many of the soldiers who remained in the area. (Library and Archives Canada)

ABOVE: Louis Riel was a Metis leader who was elected as the President of the Legislative Assembly of Assiniboia in 1870, the representative government of the people of the North West who negotiated the entrance of Manitoba in to Confederation. He was elected as a Member of the Canadian Parliament, but was never allowed to take his seat. He later led the North West Rebellion of 1885. He has been recognized as a Father of Confederation by the Canadian Government, and recently recognized as the first Premier of Manitoba by the Manitoba Government. (Library and Archives Canada)

ABOVE: William Nassau Kennedy epitomized the societal role senior officers of the Canadian Militia played. Not only a prominent member of the Militia, but he was also a prominent member of Manitoba society, even serving as the Mayor of Winnipeg. (City of Winnipeg Archives)

ABOVE: Major General Frederick Dobson Middleton was the British Army officer who commanded the North West Field Force, the Canadian Militia organization dispatched to the North West in response to the 1885 North West Rebellion. (Library and Archives Canada/Topley Studio)

ABOVE: Fort Garry was the political, economic and social epicenter of the Red River Settlement in the second half of the nineteenth century (Library and Archives Canada/James Lockhart collection)

BELOW: Reminiscences of the Red River Expedition by a Volunteer of the Ontario Battalion. (Library and Archives Canada/Peter Winkworth collection)

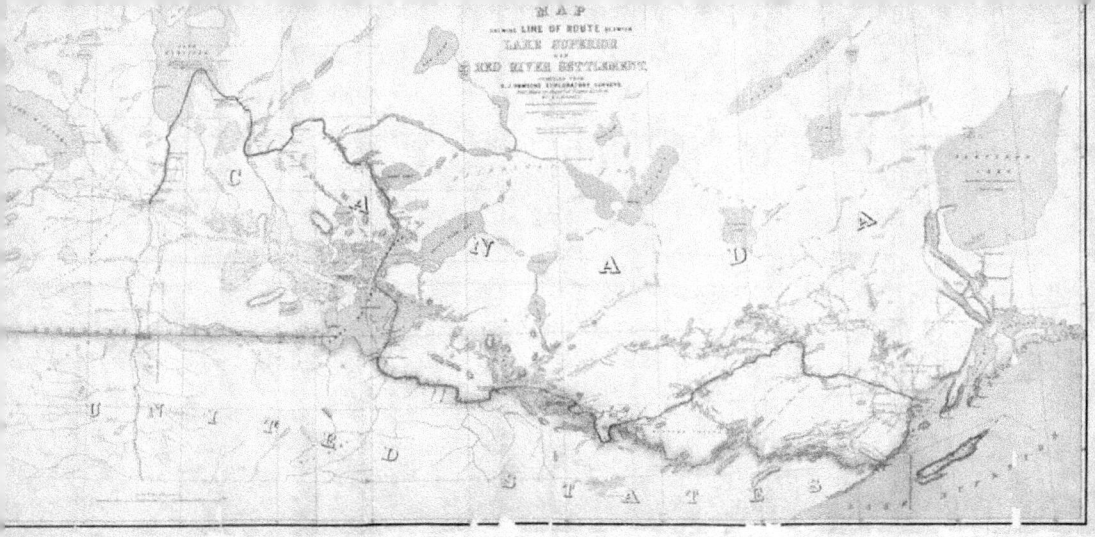

ABOVE: Map showing the route between Lake Superior and the Red River Settlement, compiled from S.J. Dawson's exploratory surveys. (Library and Archives Canada)

BELOW: Map showing the City of Winnipeg and parts of the parishes of St. Boniface and St. John in the Province of Manitoba. From actual surveys by G. McPhillip.

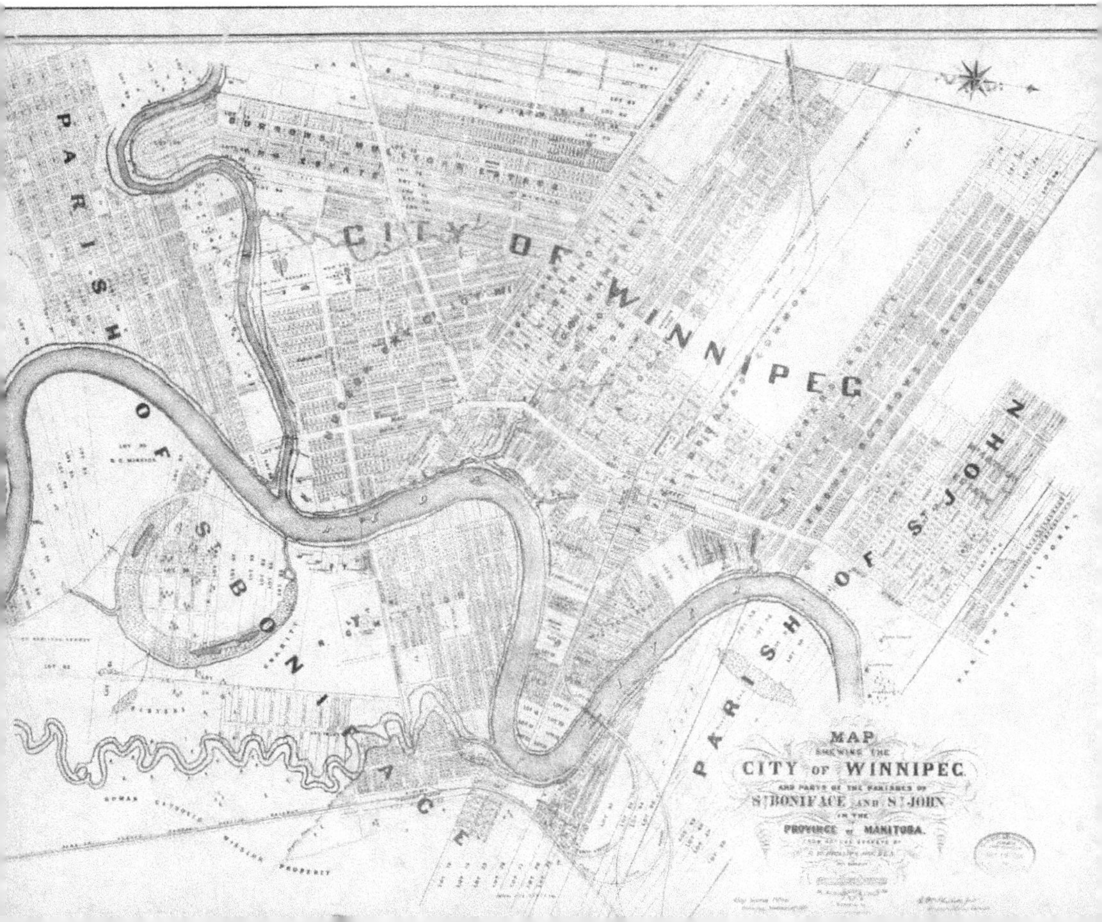

ABOVE: Sketch of Upper Fort Garry with Militia Parading outside the walls.
(City of Winnipeg Archives)
BELOW: Plan of the Government Reserve, Winnipeg, showing Fort Osborne.
(Library and Archives Canada/Department of Public Works)

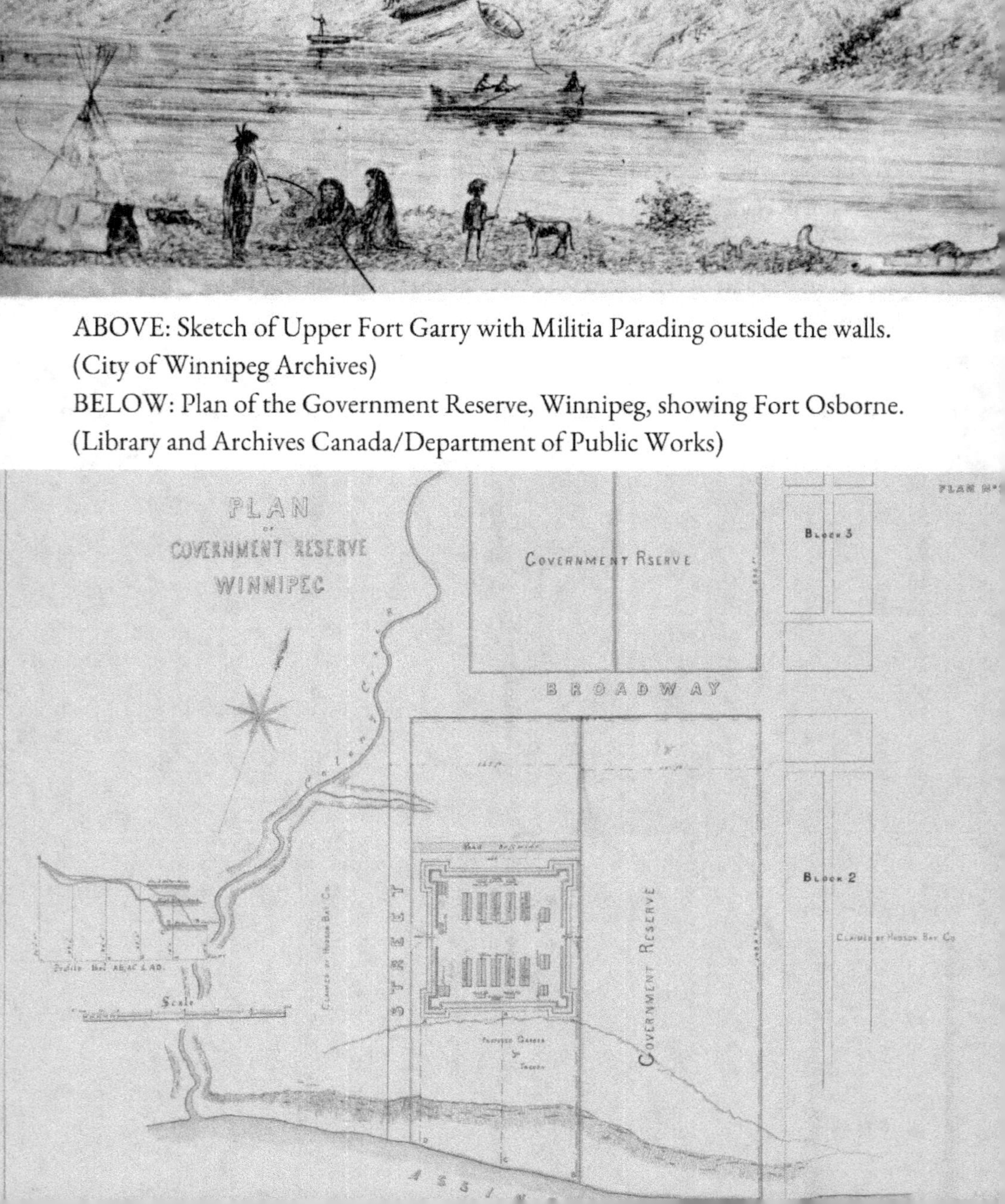

ABOVE: The Manitoba Indian Treaty. Note the presence of Militia officers observing the proceedings. (Library and Archives Canada/Peter Winkworth collection)
BELOW: A famous depiction of the Capture of Batoche by F.W. Curzon. (Library and Archives Canada)

ABOVE: Unveiling of the North West Rebellion Memorial in the city of Winnipeg, 1886. (City of Winnipeg Archives)
BELOW: Louis Riel and other leaders during Red River Resistance. (City of Winnipeg Archives)

ENDNOTES

INTRODUCTION

1   W.L. Morton, Manitoba: A History, (Toronto: University of Toronto Press, 1957), p. 199.
2   George Bryce, Manitoba: Its Infancy, Growth and Present Condition, (London: Sampson Low, Marston, Searle and Rivington, 1882), p. 358.
3   Alfred Burrows, "Civic Meeting" in Manitoba Free Press, 24 December 1875, p. 4.
4   Alexander Begg, Walter R. Nursey, Ten Years in Winnipeg. A Narration of the Principal Events in the History of the City of Winnipeg from 1870 to 1879 inclusive. (Winnipeg: Times Printing and Publishing, 1879), p. 225. The population of 100 souls referred to by Begg is almost certainly inaccurate, although it is likely that he limited his reference to what was considered to be the city itself, not the entire Red River Settlement which was significantly larger in population.
5   Gerhard J. Ens, Homeland to Hinterland. The Changing Worlds of the Red River Métis in the Nineteenth Century. (Toronto: University of Toronto Press, 1996), p.140; Gerald Friesen, The Canadian Prairies. A History. (Toronto: University of Toronto Press, 1987), p. 202. The differing population levels between Ens and Begg is explained by the latter's focus on the population of the village of Winnipeg, not the entire Red River Settlement, which is the focus of Ens' numbers.
6   Friesen, The Canadian Prairies..., p. 202.

CHAPTER 1

1   Manitoba Free Press, "The Viceregal Visit" 11 August 1877, p. 3
2   Early Canadiana Online Website, Report of resolutions adopted at a conference of delegates from the provinces of Canada, Nova Scotia, and New Brunswick, and the colonies of Newfoundland and Prince Edward Island : held at the city of Quebec,

October 10, 1864, as the basis of a proposed confederation of those provinces and colonies, p. 2, http://www.canadiana.ca/view/oocihm.9_01325/1?r=0&s=1, accessed 3 December 2019.

3   Early Canadiana Online Website, Resolutions adopted at a Conference of Delegates from the Provinces of Canada, Nova Scotia, and New Brunswick, held at the Westminster Palace Hotel, London, December 4, 1866, http://www.canadiana.ca/view/oocihm.9_01325/1?r=0&s=1 , p. 2, accessed 3 December 2019.

4   Early Canadiana Online Website, The British North America act, 1867 and amending acts, pp. 68-69, http://www.canadiana.ca/view/oocihm.9_04236/69?r=0&s=1, accessed 3 December 2019.

5   K.B. Wamsley, "Cultural signification and national ideologies: rifle shooting in late nineteenth-century Canada" in Social History, Vol. 20, No. 1, 1995, p. 63.

6   Morris Zaslow, The Opening of the Canadian North: 1870-1914, (Toronto: McClelland and Stewart, 1971), 14.

7   Morris Mott, "The British Protestant Pioneers and the Establishment of Manly Sports in Manitoba, 1870-1886" in Journal of Sports History, Vol. 7, No. 3, (Winter, 1980), p1.

8   For the purposes of this article, the term British will be used to denote a cultural block consisting of Canadian-born or immigrant persons with European heritage, predominantly Protestant and predominantly originating in the British Isles including Scotland, England, Wales and Northern Ireland.

9   Andrew Smith, "Patriotism, Self-Interest and the 'Empire Effect': Britishness and British Decisions to Invest in Canada, 1867-1914" in The Journal of Imperial and Commonwealth History, Vol. 41, No. 1, p. 59.

10   Jeffrey Gee, A Sketch of Both Sides of Manitoba, (Nelsonville: Manitoba Mountaineer Book and Job Printing Establishment, 1881), p. 6.

11   Kurt Korneski, "Brtishness, Canadianness, Class, Race: Winnipeg and the British World, 1880s-1910s" in Journal of Canadian Studies, Vol. 41, No. 2, Spring 2007, p. 167.

12   CP Champion, The Strange Demise of British Canada. The Liberals And Canadian Nationalism, 1964-1968, (Montreal: McGill-Queens University Press, 2010), pp. 10-11.

13   Korneski, "Britishness....", p. 165.

14   Chamption, The Strange Demise...., p. 46.

15   Public Archives Manitoba, Sessional Journal of the Legislative Assembly of Assiniboia, "Legislative Assembly of Assiniboia First Session," https://www.gov.mb.ca/chc/archives/leg_assembly/pdf/leg_assembly_transcript.pdf last accessed 30 June 2017.

16   Korneski, "Britishness....", p.166.

17   Granville to Young, 30 November 1869, Correspondences connected with Recent Occurrences in the North-West Territories, 1870, p. 139.

18   D.M. Schreuder, "The Cultural Factor in Victorian Imperialism: A Case-Study of the British 'Civilising Mission'" in The Journal of Imperial and Commonwealth History, $: 3, 1976, pp. 285.

19   Fritz Pannekoek, "A Little Britain in the Wilderness" in A Snug Little Flock. The Social Origins of the Riel Resistance 1869-70, (Winnipeg: Watson & Dwyer Publishing, 1991), pp. 79-96.

20   Macdougall's Guide to Manitoba and the North-West, (Winnipeg: W.B. Macdougall, 1880), p. 60.
21   Ibid.
22   The Volunteer Review, Vol. 7, No. 24, 17 June 1873, p. 8.
23   Korneski, "Britishness...", p. 164.
24   Geoff Read and Todd Webb, "The Catholic Mhadi of the North-West: Louis Riel and the Métis Resistance in Transatlantic and Imperial Context" in Canadian Historical Review 93, 2, June 2012, p. 177.

CHAPTER 2

1   Oxford Dictionary, English, https://en.oxforddictionaries.com/definition/Militia, last accessed 21 December 2016.
2   The Armed Forces of Canada, Lieutenant-Colonel D.J. Goodspeed, Ed. (Ottawa: Directorate of History and Heritage, 1967), p. 269.
3   National Defence and the Canadian Armed Forces website, Archived – The Reserve Force and Reserve Classes of Service http://www.forces.gc.ca/en/news/article.page?doc=the-reserve-force-and-reserve-classes-of-service/hnmx1bib, last accessed 10 August 2017.
4   C.P. Stacey, Canada and the Age of Conflict, Volume 1: 1867-1921, (Toronto: University of Toronto Press, 1984, o.p. 1977), p. 10.
5   Lieutenant-Colonel D.J. Goodspeed (ed), "A Fighting Heritage" in The Armed Forces of Canada 1867-1967. A Century of Achievement, (Ottawa: Directorate of History and Heritage, 1967), pp. 1-10
6   Ibid.
7   Department of Militia and Defence, Report of the State of the Militia of the Dominion of Canada [hereafter Militia Report] for the year 1870, (Ottawa: LB Taylor, 1871),p. 10.
8   Ibid, p. 10.
9   Department of National Defence, Department of History and Heritage, The Canadian Militia 1867-1900. A Political and Social Institution, https://www.canada.ca/content/dam/themes/defence/caf/militaryhistory/dhh/reports/ahq-reports/ahq102-1.pdf, p. 9
10   Ibid, p. 8.
11   Ibid, p. 9.
12   Department of Militia and Defence, Report of the State of the Militia of the Dominion of Canada [hereafter Militia Report] for the year 1870, (Ottawa: LB Taylor, 1871),p. 10., pp.10-11.
13   The Canadian Militia...p. 8.
14   Militia Act, 31 Victoria, c. 40 (Canada), s. 1&2 (1868).
15   Militia Report 1870, p. 11.
16   The Canadian Militia..., p. 10
17   Harris, Canadian Brass, p. 47. The term "gazetted" refers to having ones promotion, appointment, commissioning published in the Canada Gazette. This was often the only way such events were propagated to the wider public. It was also in the Canada Gazette that Militia units were added to the rolls or stricken from them – essentially announcing whether or not they exist.

18   George F.G. Stanley, Canada's Soldiers: A military history of an unmilitary people, 3rd ed. (Toronto: Macmillan of Canada, 1974, o.p. 1954), p. 260.
19   Militia Act (1868), s. 12.
20   The Canadian Militia…p. 10.
21   Ibid, p. 9
22   Ibid, p. 11.
23   Fritz Pannekoek, A Snug Little Flock. The Social Origins of the Riel Resistance 1869-70, (Winnipeg: Watson & Dwyer Publishing, 1991), p. 91.
24   Pannekoek, A Snug Little Flock…, p. 97.
25   Naval & Military Gazette, 27 June 1846, p. 3.
26   "The Oregon Expedition" Evening Telegram, 19 October 1846, p. 1; Naval & Military Gazette, 21 November 1856, p. 4.
27   Naval & Military Gazette, 13 June 1846, p. 1; "The Oregon Expedition" Evening Telegram, 19 October 1846, p. 1.
28   Naval & Military Gazette, 21 November 1856, p. 4.
29   "The Army" London Magnet, 8 May 1848, p. 6.
30   "Royal Canadian Rifles in Fort Garry. (1857-1861). Directorate of History and Heritage Archives.
31   Royal Canadian Rifles in Fort Garry. (1857-1861). Directorate of History and Heritage Archives; George F. G. Stanley, Toil and Trouble. Military Expeditions to Red River. (Toronto: Dundurn Press, 1989), pp. 19-52.
32   United Kingdom, Copy or Extracts of Correspondence between the Colonial Office, the Government of the Canadian Dominion, and the Hudson's Bay Company, relating to the surrender of Rupert's Land by the Hudson's Bay Company, and for the Admission Thereof into the Dominion of Canada, (London: Colonial Office, 1869), pp. 1-2.
33   Ibid, pp. 1-11.
34   Edwin A. Pridham, "The Title to Land in Manitoba" in MHS Transactions, http://www.mhs.mb.ca/docs/transactions/3/landtitles.shtml, (accessed 14 March 2019).
35   Alexander Begg, The Creation of Manitoba; or, A History of the Red River Troubles, (Toronto: Hunter, Rose & Co., 1871), p. 24-25.
36   Ibid, p. 26.
37   Ibid, p. 22.
38   Ibid, p. 28.
39   "Memorandum of Facts and Circumstances connected with the active Opposition by the French Half-Breeds in the Settlement to the prosecution of the Government Surveys" in Correspondence Relative to the Recent Disturbances in the Red River Settlement, (London: Her Majesty's Stationary Office", p. 5.
40   Begg, Creation of Manitoba…, p. 34.
41   Memorandum of Facts and Circumstances connected with the active Opposition by the French Half-Breeds in the Settlement to the prosecution of the Government Surveys" in Correspondence Relative to the Recent Disturbances in the Red River Settlement, (London: Her Majesty's Stationary Office",, p. 8.
42   For a fascinating and chilling account of the execution of Thomas Scott and the mystery surrounding the condition and final resting place of his remains, see J.M. Bumsted's Thomas Scott's Body and Other Essays on Early Manitoba History

(Winnipeg, The University of Manitoba Press, 2000).

43 'Copy of a letter from Sir Frederick Rogers, Bart., KCMG to the Right Hon. Sir Staffor H. Northcote, Bart., MP' dated 8 January 1870, in Correspondence Relative to the Recent Disturbances in the Red River Settlement, (London: William Clowes & Sons, 1870), p. 189.

44 The Canadian illustrated News, Vol. 1, no. 24 (Apr. 16, 1870), p. 374.

45 The volunteer review and military and naval gazette : Vol. 4, no. 16 (Apr. 18, 1870), p. 25.

46 Correspondence James Lindsay, p.1.

47 Sir John A. Macdonald, Parliamentary debates, Dominion of Canada, third session, 33 Victoriae, 1870, (Ottawa : Ottawa Times Print. & Pub. Co., 1870), p. 902.

48 "From Montreal" Volunteer Review, Vol. 4, No. 15, 11 April 1870, p. 230.

49 Early Canadiana Website, The War Office to Lieutenant-General the Honourable James Lindsay, pp. 10-11, http://eco.canadiana.ca/view/oocihm.91209/2?r=0&s=1 (accessed 20 February 2019).

50 Correspondence James Lindsay, p.1.

51 Heritage Website, "Outline Plan for Sand An Armed Force to Red River" in Governor General Numbered Files, http://heritage.canadiana.ca/view/oocihm.lac_reel_t184/1712?r=1&s=6 , accessed 14 December 2019.

52 Early Canadiana Website, The War Office to Lieutenant-General the Honourable James Lindsay, pp. 8-11, http://eco.canadiana.ca/view/oocihm.91209/2?r=0&s=1 (accessed 20 February 2019).

53 Ibid, pp. 13-14

54 Ibid, pp. 13-14.

55 The Canadian illustrated News, Vol. 1, no. 24 (Apr. 16, 1870), p. 374.

56 Early Canadiana Website, The War Office to Lieutenant-General the Honourable James Lindsay, pp. 12, http://eco.canadiana.ca/view/oocihm.91209/2?r=0&s=1 (accessed 20 February 2019).

57 "Lieutenant-General the Honourable James Lindsay to His Excellency the Governor-General" in Correspondence relative to the Recent Expedition to the Red River Settlement with Journal of Operations, (London: Harrison and Sons, 1871), p. 14.

58 Early Canadiana Website, The War Office to Lieutenant-General the Honourable James Lindsay, pp. 19, http://eco.canadiana.ca/view/oocihm.91209/2?r=0&s=1 (accessed 20 February 2019).

59 Ibid, p. 19.

60 Ibid, p. 6.

61 Sir Alexander Campbell, Parliamentary debates, Dominion of Canada, third session, 33 Victoriae, 1870, (Ottawa : Ottawa Times Print. & Pub. Co., 1870), p. 1184.

62 Sir John A. Macdonald, Parliamentary debates, Dominion of Canada, third session, 33 Victoriae, 1870, (Ottawa : Ottawa Times Print. & Pub. Co., 1870), p. 1294.

63 The Canadian illustrated News, Vol. 1, no. 24 (Apr. 16, 1870), p. 374..

64 See the author's "Rowboat Diplomacy: The Dominion of Canada's Whole of Government Approach to The Red River Rebellion" in Canadian Military Journal,

Vol. 13, No. 3, Summer 2013, pp. 57-66.

65   Samuel Steele, Forty Years in Canada, (London: London and Norwich Press, 1914), pp. 11-12; Canadiana Online, 'The War Office to Lieutenant-General the Honourable James Lindsay' dated 5 May 1870 in http://online.canadiana.ca/view/oocihm.91209/2?r=0&s=1, (accessed 9 February 2019), p. 7..

66   Government of Canada, "Militia Report 1870" in Sessional Papers of the Dominion of Canada, Vol. 4, 4th Session of 1st Parliament, 1871, p. 7-4

67   Canadiana Online Website, "Telegram from the Adjutant General to the Minister of Militia dated 15 April 1870" in 'The War Office to Lieutenant-General the Honourable James Lindsay' dated 5 May 1870 in http://online.canadiana.ca/view/oocihm.91209/2?r=0&s=1, (accessed 14 March 2019).

68   George F.G. Stanley, Toil and Trouble. Military Expeditions to Red River. (Toronto: Dundurn Press, 1989), p. 92; Frederick John Shore, "The Canadians and the Métis: The Re-Creation of Manitoba, 1858-1872" (unpublished doctoral thesis, University of Manitoba, 1991), pp. 179-182.

69   "Lieutenant-General the Honourable James Lindsay to the War Office" in Correspondence relative to the Recent Expedition to the Red River Settlement with Journal of Operations, (London: Harrison and Sons, 1871), p.5.

70   LAC, Records relating to the North-West Rebellion, 1880-1885 – 10393, RG9 II A3, Memo from Military Secretary to the Governor General, dated 1 June 1870.

71   "Lieutenant-General the Honourable James Lindsay to the War Office" in Correspondence relative to the Recent Expedition to the Red River Settlement with Journal of Operations, (London: Harrison and Sons, 1871),, p. 5.

72   "From Montreal" in The Volunteer Review, Vol IV, No. 20, p. 6.

73   Frederick Shore, The Canadians and the Metis: The Re-creation of Manitoba, 1858-1872. (Doctoral Thesis, University of Manitoba, 1991), p. 180.

74   Simon Dawson, Report of the Red River Expedition of 1870 [hereafter Dawson Report] (Ottawa: Times Printing and Publishing, 1871), p. 14, p. 5-6

75   Ibid, p. 6.

76   Dominion of Canada, Correspondence Connected with Recent Occurrences in the North-West Territories, (Ottawa: I.B. Taylor, 1870), p. 143.

77   Ibid, p. 143.

78   Dawson Report, p. 6.

79   Heritage Canadiana Website, Department of Militia and Defence : Records relating to the North-West Rebellion, 1880-85 Letter Wolseley to Mil Sec 16 July 1870, http://heritage.canadiana.ca/view/oocihm.lac_reel_t10393/598?r=0&s=1 (accessed 9 February 2019).

80   Willoughby, p. 7; 'The Red River Expedition' in Canadian Illustrated News, (1) no. 28, 14 May 1870, p. 435

81   Simon Dawson, Report of the Red River Expedition of 1870 (Ottawa: Times Printing and Publishing, 1871), p. 14.

82   This company never reached Fort Garry, and returned to Quebec after the British Regulars passed through when returning to Ontario from the North-West.

83   Rat Portage (now Kenora) derived its name from the relatively short isthmus over which travelers could portage from Lake of the Woods to the Winnipeg River, instead of venturing further eastward to the mouth of the river which added time to the journey. Muskrats were plentiful at this portage site thus it became known as

the Rat Portage. In 1908 the Maple Leaf Flour Company decided against opening a factory in Rat Portage because it didn't want to have the word "Rat" printed on its sacks of flour for obvious reasons. The civic leadership decided to change the name of the town to Kenora. This name was arrived at by taking the first two letters from the names of the three settlements that had developed in the area: Keewatin, Norman, and Rat Portage.

84   Willoughby Wallace, The Rebellion in the Red River Settlement, 1869-70, its causes and suppression. A Lecture delivered at Clifton, October 25th, 1871, (Barnstaple: Henry T. Cook, 1872), p. 9.

85   Garnet Wolseley, "Narrative of the Red River Expedition" in Travel Adventure and Sport from Blackwoods Magazine, (New York: White and Allen, 1871), p. 244.

86   See Huyshe, The Red River Expedition (Uckfield, The Naval and Military press, o.p. 1871), George F.G. Stanley, Toil and Trouble, Samuel Steele, Forty Years in Canada, (London: London and Norwich Press, 1914), Willoughby Wallace, The Rebellion in the Red River Settlement, 1869-70, its causes and suppression. A Lecture delivered at Clifton, October 25th, 1871, (Barnstaple: Henry T. Cook, 1872).

87   "Official Journal of Operations" in Correspondence relative to the Recent Expedition to the Red River Settlement with Journal of Operations, (London: Harrison and Sons, 1871), p.92.

88   Capt G.L. Huyshe, The Red River Expedition, (London: Macmillan and Co., 1871), pp. 195-197.

89   "The Red River Troubles" in Boston Globe, 9 June 1870, p. 2.

90   "The Winnipeg War" in Buffalo Express, 7 June 1870, p. 2

91   "Canada" in Fort Wayne Daily Gazette, 8 June 1870, p. 1.

92   E. Lugard, The War Officer to Lieutenant-General the Honourable James Lindsay, dated 5 May 70, last accessed 22 December 2016.

93   C.P. Stacey, "Cardwell Cuts the Gordion Knot" in Canada and the British Army 1846-1871, rev. ed. (Toronto: University of Toronto Press, 1936), pp. 204-229.

94   Militia General Orders (26) No. 1 dated 26 August 1870.

95   Militia Report 1870, p. 17, 30.

96   Samuel Steele, Forty years…, p. 27, 33.

97   See Shore "The Process of Intimidation" in The Canadians and the Métis: The Re-Creation of Manitoba, 1858-1872, pp. 217-299.

98   Militia Report, 1870, p. 31.

99   Ibid, p.38.

100   Ibid, p. 32.

101   Manitoba News Letter, "Discharge of Volunteers", 27 May 1871, p, 2.

102   Militia Report, 1871, p. 37-38.

103   LAC, Correspondence Sir John A Macdonald, 13 October 1871, MG26-A. Volume/box number: 61.

104   "Militia General Orders (23) dated 16 October 1871 in The Canada Gazette, Vol. V, No. 17, dated 21 October 1871.

105   Militia Report, 1871, "Militia District No. 10 (Manitoba)" p. 40.

106   Ibid, p. 44.

107   C.P. Stacy, "The Second Red River Expedition, 1871", Directorate of History and Heritage Archives, The Northwest Rebellion 1885, 500.009 (D32), p. 7.

108   Ibid, p. 7.
109   Manitoba Liberal, "Arrival of the Troops" 19 Nov 71, p. 3; Justus Griffin, From Toronto to Fort Garry. An account of the Second Expedition to Red River. Diary of a Private Solider. (Hamilton: Evening Times, 1893, p.53.
110   Militia Report, 1871, p. 40.
111   The original name was the Provisional Battalion of Rifles, but was renamed to the Provisional Battalion of Infantry.
112   Justus Griffin, From Toronto to Fort Garry an account of the Second Expedition to Red River. Diary of a Private Solider. (Hamilton: Evening Times, 1893), p. 44.
113   Justus Griffin, From Toronto to Fort Garry an account of the Second Expedition to Red River. Diary of a Private Solider. (Hamilton: Evening Times, 1893) p. 49.
114   Ibid, p. 50.
115   "Memorable Manitobans: William Osborne Smith (1831-1887), Manitoba Historical Society website, http://www.mhs.mb.ca/docs/people/smith_wo.shtml, last accessed 10 March 2017; "Smith, William Osborne" in Dictionary of Canadian Biography website, http://www.biographi.ca/en/bio.php?BioId=39963, last accessed 10 March 2017.
116   Letter from the Adjutant General of Militia to the Deputy Adjutant General of Military District No. 10, DATED 10 March 1872, LAC, RG 9, II B1, Volume 518.
117   Letter from Adjutant General of Militia to all Deputy Adjutant Generals, dated 6 September 1872, LAC, RG 9, II B1, Volume 518.
118   Letter from Adjutant General of Militia to Deputy Adjutant General of Military District 7 dated 6 September 1872, LAC, RG 9, II B1, Volume 518; Government of Canada, "Militia Report 1873" in Sessional Papers of the Dominion of Canada, Vol. 5, 1st Session of 2nd Parliament, 1873, p. 9-XX.
119   Government of Canada, "Militia Report 1872" in Sessional Papers of the Dominion of Canada, Vol. 5, 1st Session of 2nd Parliament, 1873, p. 9-XX
120   Militia General Orders (25) No. 1 dated 11 October 1872.
121   Journal of the Provisional Battalion of Rifles at Fort Garry, 1871 in James Taylor Collection: "Provisional Battalion Canadian Light Infantry & Artillery 1871-1877", Public Archives Manitoba, MG6, B5. The journal erroneously only refers to the 184 volunteers who were destined to join the Provisional Battalion of Rifles, and leaves out the 24 artillerymen from B Battery who formed the Dominion Artillery on Service in Manitoba.
122   Letter from Adjutant General of Militia to all Deputy Adjutant Generals, dated 6 September 1872, LAC, RG 9, II B1, Volume 518.
123   Joseph Ford Arel, Montreal to Fort Garry. Journal of a Private in Third Expedition, (Fort Garry, n.p, 1874), p.41.
124   Ibid, p. 42.
125   Anon., 'Dawson Route Military Expedition' in The Manitoban, Vol 1, No. 4, March 1892.
126   Militia General Orders (11) No. 1 dated 23 May 1873.
127   Militia General Orders (10) No. 1 dated 16 May 1873.
128   Ibid.

129   Manitoba Free Press, "Local and Provincial", 12 July 1873, p. 5.
130   Ibid.
131   Militia General Orders (13) dated 2 June 1874.
132   Manitoba Free Press, "Military Here to Be Reduced", 4 November 1874, p.1.
133   Militia Report 1874, p. 51.
134   Militia Report 1873, and Militia Report 1874.
135   Manitoba Free Press, "Volunteer Land Warrants," 29 July 1876, p. 2.
136   Manitoba Newsletter, "How is this for High in Military Jurisprudence" 10 May 1817, p. 2.
137   Manitoba Free Press, "Dominion Forces in the North-West," 20 July 1876.
138   Manitoba Free Press, 'Local and Provincial', 4 August 1877, p. 4.
139   Militia General Orders (18), dated 13 October 1876.
140   Manitoba Free Press, "Expected Abolition of the Garrison," 26 May 1877, p.4.
141   Abstract from the minutes of Council held on 31st day of May 1877 at Government House Fort Garry, LAC, RG9-II-A-1. Volume/box number: 85. File number: 3723
142   Militia Report, 1882, p.44.
143   Militia Report, 1883, p. 57.
144   Samuel Steele, Forty Years in Canada, (London: London and Norwich Press, 1914), p. 39.
145   Ibid, p. 39.
146   Ibid, p. 40.
147   Manitoban and Northwest Herald, "To Arms!", 29 October 1870, p. 2.
148   Manitoban and Northwest Herald, "That Evening Gun" 17 May 1873, p. 3
149   Manitoba Free Press, "Excitement at Fort Garry," 18 Jan 73, p.5
150   Constance Kerr Soissons, John Kerr, (Toronto, Oxford university press, 1946), p. 55.
151   Steele, Forty Years…, p. 45.
152   Soissons, John Kerr…, p. 55.
153   Manitoba News-Letter, 22 October 1870, p. 4.
154   Soissons, John Kerr… p. 55.
155   Manitoba Liberal, 8 March 72, p. 2.
156   Tennant, Rough Times…, p. 76.
157   Journal of the Provisional Battalion of Rifles at Fort Garry, 1871.
158   Tennant, Rough Times…, pp. 86-87.
159   Manitoba Free Press, "Death By Lightning" 4 July 1874, p. 5.
160   Colonel Robertson Ross, Militia Report 1872, p. cx.
161   Ibid, p. cx.
162   Steele, 40 Years…, p. 29; Anon., "Dawson Route Military Expeditions" in The Manitoban, Vol. I, No. 7, June 1892.
163   Tenant, Rough Times…, p. 78.
164   Militia Report 1872, (Ottawa: LB Taylor, 1873), p. cx
165   Justus Griffin, From Toronto to Fort Garry an account of the Second Expedition to Red River. Diary of a Private Solider. (Hamilton: Evening Times, 1893) p. 53, 56-60)
166   Ibid, p. 62.

167   Steele, Forty Years…p. 40.
168   Ibid, p. 39.
169   Griffin, From Toronto to Fort Garry….p. 60.
170   Tennant, Rough Times…, p. 78
171   Ibid, p. 79.
172   Griffin, From Toronto to Fort Garry ….p. 62.
173   Ibid, p. 61.
174   Manitoban and Northwest Herald, 25 April 1874, p. 3.
175   Manitoba Free Press, "Dominion Forces in the North-West", by "An Ex Sergeant," 20 July 1876, p. 2
176   Ibid.
177   LAC, Letter from Adjutant General of Militia to Minister of Milita and Defence dated 29 April 1873, Reel T-287, 133544, RG 9 II B 1.
178   Manitoba Free Press, "Emancipation", 3 May 1873.
179   Robertson Ross, Militia Report 1872, p. cx.
180   Telegraph Gilbert McMicken to John A. Macdonald dated 19 April 1873, Heritage Canadiana Website, https://www.bac-lac.gc.ca/eng/CollectionSearch/Pages/record.aspx?app=fonandcol&IdNumber=553229&new=-8585915800611045399, last accessed 8 January 2021.
181   Manitoba Free Press, "The Barracks", 13 September 1873, p. 5.
182   Manitoban and Northwest Herald, 20 September 1873, p. 3.
183   Manitoban and Northwest Herald, 'Our Public Buildings', 23 August 1873, p. 2; Manitoba Free Press, 'The Barracks ', 13 September 1873, p. 5; Manitoban and Northwest Herald, 20 September 1873, p.3; Journal of the Provisional Battalion of Rifles at Fort Garry, 1871.
184   Militia Report 1874, pp. 282-291.
185   Manitoba Free Press, "Dominion Forces in the North-West", 20 July 1876, p. 2.
186   Militia Report 1881, pp. 56-57.
187   Adjutant General of Militia - (373) - Forwards letter of Lt. Col. W.O. Smith, recommending that a name be given to the new Barracks at Winnipeg. LAC, RG9-II-A-1. Volume/box number: 71. File number: 1248.
188   J.C. Hamilton, The Prairie Province; Sketches of Travel from Lake Ontario to Lake Winnipeg, (Toronto: Belford Brothers, 1876), p. 38.
189   Militia Report 1879, p. 84.
190   "Pats to Parade" Winnipeg Free Press, 16 May 1973, p. 3.
191   Militia Act 1868, s.44-51.
192   Manitoba Free Press, "Winnipeg Field Battery" 9 September, 1876, p.8.
193   Manitoba Free Press, 'Local and Provincial', 16 June 1877, p.5
194   Manitoba Free Press, "Annual Drill of the Militia", 2 June 1877, p.7.
195   Manitoba Free Press, "Manitoba Militia", 17 July 1875, p.2
196   Manitoba Free Press, "A Wail From Winnipeg", 26 February 1876, p.6.
197   LCol Davis, The Canadian Militia! Its Organization and present condition, (Caledonia: William T. Sawle, 1873), p. 5.
198   Manitoba Free Press, "Winnipeg Field Battery", 5 December 1874, p. 3; Manitoba Free Press, "Emerson", 23 December 1876, p. 2; Manitoba Free Press, "The Volunteer Militia", 15 September 1877, p. 3.

199   Militia Report 1881, p. 54.
200   "City and Province", Manitoba Free Press, 26 January 1884, p. 4; James. B. Hartman, "The Churches of Early Winnipeg" in Manitoba History, Number 45, Spring/Summer 2003.
201   "City and Provincial" in Manitoba Free Press, 2 May 1884, p. 4.
202   Militia Report1879, p. 76.
203   Manitoba Free Press, 'Winnipeg Field Battery', 3 November 1877, p. 3
204   Manitoba Free Press, "City Council," 19 May 1877, p. 1.
205   Manitoba Free Press, "City Council," 8 December 1877, p. 5.
206   Manitoba Free Press, 'Local and Provincial', 16 March 1878, p. 1; Manitoba Free Press, 'Local and Provincial', 20 April 1878, p. 1.
207   Memorandum of facts and suggestions relating to the present position of the Winnipeg Field Battery and the three Infantry companies in the Province of Manitoba, compiled from notes taken at a Conference of the officers of the several corps, held at Winnipeg, March 22nd, 1878, LAC, RG9-II-A-I Vol 88 File 4332
208   Ibid.
209   Ibid.

CHAPTER 3

1   Paul Phillips, "The National Policy Revisited" Journal of Canadian Studies, Vol. 14, No. 3 (Autumn 1979), p. 3. For another excellent historical summary of how the established provinces of the Dominion of Canada treated the North-West as a colony with natural-resources to exploit, see Mary Janigan's Let the Eastern Bastards Freeze in the Dark: The West versus the Rest since Confederation, (Toronto: Knopf, 2012).
2   Greg Marquis, "The 'Irish Model' and Nineteenth-Century Canadian Policing" in The Journal of Imperial and Commonwealth History, Vol 25, No. 2, May 1997, p. 208.
3   Peter Burroughs, "Imperial defence and the Victorian army" in The Journal of Imperial and Commonwealth History, Vol 15, No. 1, July 1986), p. 65.
4   Ibid, p. 58.
5   The Volunteer Review, Vol. 5, No. 4, 23 Jan 1871, p.1.
6   Russell W. Fridley, "When Minnesota Coveted Canada" in Minnesota History, Summer 1968, 76.
7   George F.G. Stanley, Canada's Soldiers. The Military History of an Unmilitary People. 3rd ed., (Toronto: Macmillan, 1974 o.p. 1954), pp. 272-273.
8   George F.G. Stanley, The Birth of Western Canada, A History of the Riel Rebellions (Toronto: University of Toronto Press, 1960), 24.
9   "the Northwest" in The volunteer review and military and naval gazette, Vol. 1, No. 45, 11 November 1867, p. 10.
10   Arthur S. Morton, A history of the Canadian West to 1870-71: being a history of Rupert's Land (the Hudson's Bay company's territory) and of the North-west territory (including the Pacific slope), (London: T. Nelson & Sons, 1939), 853.
11   Ibid, 854.
12   Ibid, 854.
13   J. Wesley Bond, Minnesota and its resources; to which are appended camp-fire sketches or notes of a trip from St. Paul to Pembina and Selkirk settlement on the

Red River of the North, (New York: Redfield, 1854), 243-245.
14   Ibid, p. 246.
15   Morton, A history of the Canadian West…, 696.
16   Charles P. Stacey, Canada and the age of conflict: a history of Canadian external policies. Vol. 1. (Toronto: Univ. of Toronto Press, 1989), 29.
17   David Orchard, The Fight for Canada: four centuries of resistance to American expansionism. (Westmount: Robert Davies Multimedia Pub., 1999), 49.
18   C.P Stacey, Canada and the Age of Conflict…,29
19   Thomas D'Arcy McGee, Parliamentary debates on the subject of the confederation of the British North American provinces, 3rd session, 8th Provincial Parliament of Canada (Quebec: Hunter, Rose & Co., 1865), p. 132.
20   Stacey, Canada and the age of conflict…p 5.
21   "Red River" New York Herald, 26 July 1870, p.8.
22   Stanley, Toil and Trouble…, p. 74.
23   Extract from a letter of Sir John A. Macdonald, January 26th, 1870, quoted in Stanley, The Birth of Western Canada…, p. 129.
24   Charles P. Stacey, "The Military Aspect of Canada's Winning of the West, 1870-1885" in The Canadian Historical Review, Vol. XXI, No. 1, 1940, pp. 6-7.
25   "Militia General Orders (19) dated 1 September 1871" in The Canada Gazette, Volume 10, No. V, 2 September 1871, p. "Militia General Orders (19) dated 1 September 1871"
26   "Militia General Orders (22)" dated 13 October 1871 in The Canada Gazette, Vol. V, No. 16, dated 14 October 1871.
27   Militia Report 1876, p.49.
28   Militia Report, 1871, "Statement shewing the strength of Companies, &c., which enrolled in accordance with Proclamation issued by Lieut-Governor, 3rd October 1871", p. 39.
29   Ex. C.S. "Correspondence" Volunteer Review, Vol. 5, No. 43, 23 October 1871, p. 3.
30   See Hon. Gilbert McMicken, "The Abortive Fenian Raid on Manitoba" Manitoba Historical Society Transactions, Series 1, No. 32, 11 May 1888.
31   Manitoba Liberal, 16 February 1872, p. 1.
32   Manitoba Liberal, "Correspondence" 13 January 1872, p. 1.
33   Ibid.
34   Manitoba Free Press, "Proclamation" 13 January 1877, p. 7.
35   Colonel Robertson-Ross, Canada, Dept of Militia and Defence, Militia Report 1872, (Ottawa: LB Taylor, 1873),p. cvii
36   Ibid, p. cxi
37   Colonel Patrick Robertson-Ross, Report of Colonel Robertson-Ross, Adjt.-General of Militia, on the North-West Provinces and Territories of the Dominion, (Ottawa: Dominion of Canada, 1872), p. 26.
38   "Extract of a letter from Archibald McDonald, Esq., Chief Trader, addressed to D.A. Smith, dated 11 February, 1873, from Fort Ellice" in Annual Report on Indian Affairs for the yearending June 20 1872, Canada Sessional Papers, Volume 5, 1st Session, p. 17.
39   "Sioux Indians" in Manitoba Fre Press, 15 March 1873, p. 5.
40   Letter from the Adjutant General of Manitoba to the Acting Minister of Militia

and Defence dated 22 March 1873, LAC, RG 9, II B1, Volume 518.

41   Letter from Adjutant General of Militia to Acting Minister of Militia and Defence dated 25 March 1873, LAC, RG 9, II B1, Volume 518.

42   See Manitoba Free Press, "The Indian Humbug" 3 May 1873, p. 5.

43   LAC, Correspondence of the General Officer Commanding of the Canadian Militia and His Predecessor the Adjutant General, RG 9 II B 1, 133544, Letter from Adjutant General of Militia to Donald A. Smith, MP dated 30 April 1873.

44   Manitoba Free Press, "The Indian Humbug" 3 May 1873, p. 5.

45   Manitoba and Northwest Herald, "Indian Hostilities" 17 May 1873, p. 2

46   Manitoba Free Press, "The Indian Humbug" 3 May 1873, p. 5.

47   The Great Sioux War was an attempt by the US Government to pacify the Indigenous tribes of the norther mid-west, specifically the Black Hills region of modern South Dakota and Wyoming.

48   Winnipeg Free Press, "Dominion Forces in the North-West," 17 July 76, p. 2.

49   Debates and proceedings of the Senate of Canada: [Debates of the Senate of the Dominion of Canada : fifth session, third Parliament, 27 March 1878, p. 304.

50   LAC, RG 9 II A1, Volume 86, Docket 3791, Memo DAG MD 10 to Major General Commanding.

51   Lieutenant-General Edward Selby-Smith, Canada, Dept of Militia and Defence, Report of the State of the Militia of the Dominion of Canada for the year 1879, (Ottawa: LB Taylor, 1880), p. li.

52   Militia Report 1883, p. 58.

53   Portage la Prairie Weekly Tribune, "Editorial Notes", 25 April 1884, p. 4.

54   Militia Act 1868, s. 27.

55   Desmond Morton, "Aid to the Civil Power: The Canadian Militia in Support of Social Order, 1867-1914" in The Canadian Historical Review, Vol. LI, No. 4, December 1970, p. 407.

56   Manitoba Free Press, "Winnipeg Field Battery," 3 November 1877, p. 3

57   Benjamin Sulte, Histoire de la Milice Canadienne-Francaise, (Montréal : Desbarats & Co., 1897), p. 88

58   Huyshe, p. 222.

59   Morton, "Aid to the Civil Power", p. 407.

60   Archibald Adams, Copy of Letter to LCol Jarvis dated 20 September 1870, LAC, Adjutant General Correspondence, RG 9, II, A 1 Vol. 24, File 3930.

61   Instructions for the officer in command of a company of the Ontario Rifles dispatched to the neighborhood of Pembina in compliance with a requisition for such aid to the Civil Power by the Lieut. Governor of Manitoba of this date. LAC, Adjutant General Correspondence, RG 9, II, A 1 Vol. 24, File 3930.

62   Ibid.

63   Robertson Ross, Militia Report 1872, p. cx.

64   Samuel Steele, Forty Years in Canada, (London: The London and Norwich Press, 1914), p. 45.

65   Journal of the Provisional Battalion of Rifles at Fort Garry, 1871.

66   Alexander Begg and Walter R Nursey, Ten Years in Winnipeg. A Narration of the Principal Events in the History of the City of Winnipeg from the Year A.D. 1870 to the year A.D. 1879, Inclusive, (Winnipeg: Times Printing and Publishing House, 1879), p. 80.

67   Osborne-Smith, Militia Report 1873, (Ottawa: LB Taylor, 1874),p. 36; Journal of the Provisional Battalion of Rifles at Fort Garry, 1871.
68   Manitoba Free Press, 'Arrests by the Military', 5 July 1873, p, 5; Journal of the Provisional Battalion of Rifles at Fort Garry, 1871.
69   Militia Report 1873, p.36; J.L. Johnston, "Lord Gordon Gordon" in Manitoba Historical Society Transactions, Series 3, 1950-51, http://www.mhs.mb.ca/docs/transactions/3/lordgordongordon.shtml, last accessed 5 January 2019.
70   Journal of the Provisional Battalion of Rifles in Fort Garry, 1871.
71   Carman Miller, "The Montreal Militia as a Social Institution Before World War I" in Urban History Review, Vol. 19, No. 1, 1990, p.63.
72   Library and Archives Canada, Department of Militia and Defence, Accounts and Pay Branch, Nominal Rolls and Pay lists for the Volunteer Militia, 1855-1914, RG 9 II-F-6 p. 219.
73   Begg & Nursey, Ten Years in Winnipeg...,p. 217
74   Lieutenant General Edward Selby-Smith, Militia Report 1879, (Ottawa: LB Taylor, 1880), p. xxvii
75   "The Lash" in Manitoba Free Press, 31 October 1884, p. 4.
76   "The Lash" in Manitoba Free Press, 1 November 1884, p. 4.
77   "Miller's Mistake" in Manitoba Free Press, 1 November 1884, p. 4.
78   Militia Report 1884, p. 46.
79   "Miller's Mistake" in Manitoba Free Press, 1 November 1884, p. 4.
80   "Military Called Out" in Manitoba Free Press, 3 November 1884, p. 4.
81   Ibid.
82   Ibid.
83   Begg & Nursey, Ten Years in Winnipeg, ...p. 15; Shore, "The Canadians and the Métis...", p. 170.
84   "Montreal," Volunteer Review, Vol. 6, No. 47, 18 September 1872, p. 9.
85   Anne M. Collier, A History of Portage la Prairie and Surrounding District, (Portage la Prairie: City of Portage la Prairie, 1970), p. 314.
86   Letter from the Adjutant General of Militia to Captain Armstrong dated 21 February 1872, LAC, RG 9, II B1, Volume 518; MHS Website, Memorable Manitobans: Edward Armstrong, http://www.mhs.mb.ca/docs/people/armstrong_e. shtml last accessed 27 July 2017.
87   Manitoba Free Press, "Court of Queen's Bench Friday," 25 January 1873, p. 5.
88   Manitoba Liberal, "The Police", 16 July 1871, p. 3.
89   Manitoba Historical Society website, Memorable Manitobans: Louis Fasse Plainval, http://www.mhs.mb.ca/docs/people/plainval_ln.shtml last accessed 21 January 2017; Manitoba Free Press, "Local and Provincial", 5 August 1876, p. 2.
90   Manitoba Free Press, "Local and Provincial" 2 Sep 1876, p. 5
91   Ernest Chambers, The Royal North-West Mounted Police. A Corps History. (Montreal: The Mortimer Press, 1896), pp. 19, 160.
92   Victoria Daily British Colonist, "Dominion Mail Summary" 26 October 1873, p. 3.
93   Letter from LCol W.O. Smith to Mr. W.E. Parker dated 10 December 1873, Commissioner's Office Letter Box, LAC, RG 18, B3, Volume 2184.
94   Letter from LCol W.O. Smith to the North-West Council dated 10 December 1873, Commissioner's Office Letter Box, LAC, RG 18, B3, Volume 2184.

95   Commissioner's Office Letter Box, LAC, RG 18, B3, Volume 2184.
96   Manitoban and Northwest Herald, 15 March 1873, p. 2
97   Begg, Ten Years in Winnipeg…., p. 93.
98   Manitoban and Northwest Herald, "Disastrous Fire, Burning of the Parliament Buildings!" 6 Dec 73, p. 2.
99   Manitoba Free Press, "Fire! Fort Garry the Victim This Time", 17 January 1874, p. 5.
100   Journal of the Provisional Battalion.
101   Ibid.
102   Manitoba and Northwest Herald, "The Late Fire at Fort Garry", 7 February, 1874, p. 2.
103   Fire Fighters Museum of Winnipeg, Manitoba, "Archives", http://www.winnipegfiremuseum.ca/archives/archives01.htm last accessed 21 January 2017.
104   Daily Free Press, "City Council", 28 December 1875, p. 3.
105   For an excellent review of the impact of the 1870 smallpox epidemic in the North-West see James Daschuk's chapter "Canada, the Northwest, and the Treaty Period, 1869-1876" in Clearing the Plains. Disease, Politics of Starvation, and the loss of aboriginal life (Regina; University of Regina Press, 2013).
106   Father Albert Lacombe, "Manitoba" The Volunteer Review, Vol 4, No. 47, 21 November, 1870. p. 10.
107   WF Bulter, Report by Lt Butler (69th Regt) of his journey from Fort Garry to Rocky Mountain House and Back: Under Instructions from the Lieut. Governor of Manitoba, during the Winter of 1870-71, (Ottawa: Times Printing and Publishing Co., 1871), p. 12.
108   Manitoba News Letter, "Small Pox", 8 October 1870, p.1.
109   Manitoba and Northwest Herald, "The Board of Health", 15 October 1870, p. 2.
110   Sessional Papers, Volume 4, Fourth Session of 1st Parliament, 1871, "Return: Instructions to the Honorable A. Archibald" p. 67
111   Manitoban and Northwest Herald, "Departure of Capt. MacDonald", 29 October 1870, p. 2.
112   Dominion of Canada, Report of the Select Standing Committee on Immigration and Colonization, (Ottawa: Maclean Roger & Co., 1877), p. 5.
113   "The Smallpox Epidemic of 1876-1877 in the Icelandic Settlements" in Manitoba Pageant, Autumn 1973, Volume 19, Number 1, Manitoba Historical Society website, http://www.mhs.mb.ca/docs/pageant/19/smallpox.shtml, last accessed 21 March 2017.
114   Begg and Nursey, Ten Years…, p. 142.
115   Manitoba Free Press, 'The Small-Pox News from the North' 2 Dec 76, p. 5
116   Manitoba Free Press, 'Local and Provincial' 30 Dec 76, p. 2
117   Militia Report 1876, p. 51.
118   Manitoba Free Press, 'Local and Provincial' 28 Jul 77, p. 2
119   Manitoba Free Press, 'Local and Provincial – Gun Accident', 13 Jan 77, p. 8
120   An Act Respecting the North-West Territory to create a separate territory out of part thereof, 39 Victoria, C 21.
121   Although the name of the town of Rat Portage originates from a reference to Muskrats, not sewer dwelling vermin, it nonetheless had an unpleasant ring to one's

ear. As the town grew and local authorities intended to amalgamate three near-lying towns into a single city, they thought it wise, for esthetic reasons, to rename the town and took the first two letters from the three townships: KE for Keewatin, NO for Norman, and RA for Rat Portage, hence, Kenora.

122   "The Rat Portage War", Winnipeg Police Service Website, http://www.winnipeg.ca/police/history/story13.stm, last accessed 17 March 2017.
123   Militia Report 1883, p. 55.
124   "The Rat Portage War", Winnipeg Police Service Website, http://www.winnipeg.ca/police/history/story13.stm, last accessed 17 March 2017.

CHAPTER 4

1   Michael Walzer, "On the Role of Symbolism in Political Thought," Political Science Quarterly, 82 (1967), 194 quoted in Alistair B. Fraser "A Canadian Flag for Canada" in Raven, Vol. 1, 1994, pp. 30–40.
2   Dictionary of Canadian Biography Website, Fletcher, Henry Charles, http://www.biographi.ca/en/bio/fletcher_henry_charles_10E.html, (last accessed 13 May 2019); Lieutenant-Colonel H.C. Fletcher, Memorandum on the Militia System of Canada, (Ottawa: Citizen Printing Company, 1873), p. 5.
3   Sarah Carter, "Your Great Mother Across the Salt Sea: Prairie First Nations, the British Monarchy and the Vice Regal Connection to 1900" in Manitoba History, Number 48, Autumn/Winter 2004-2005.
4   Ibid.
5   Peter G. Goheen, "Symbols in the Streets: Parades in Victorian Urban Canada" in Urban History Review, Vol. XVIII, No. 3 (February 1990), p. 237.
6   Nor'Wester, 'Presentation of Colors to Provisional Battalion' 19 October, 1874, p. 3;
7   E.C. Russell, Customs and Traditions of the Canadian Armed Forces, (Ottawa: Deneau&Greenberg Publishers, 1980), p. 170.
8   Ibid, p. 170.
9   Nor'Wester, 'Presentation of Colors to Provisional Battalion' 19 October, 1874, p. 3; Francis J. Dunbar, Joseph H. Harper, Old Colours Never Die. A Record of Colours and Military Flags of Canada, (Ottawa: Department of National Defence, 1992), p.38,42.
10   Manitoba Free Press, "Colors of Early Years," 19 June 1879, p.3.
11   Manitoba Free Press, "Local and Provincial," 24 October 1874, p. 5.
12   Letter from Lieutenant-Colonel Osborne Smith to Adjutant General of Militia dated 22 August 1877, LAC RG 9 II A1 Volume 86, Docket 03851.
13   Francis Dunbar and Joseph Harper, Old Colours Never Die: A Record of Colours and Military Flags in Canada, (Ottawa: Directorate of History and Heritage, 1992), p. 42.
14   Correspondence author and Gwen Lowes, administrative assistant of Holy Trinity Church.
15   Alexander Morris, The Treaties of Canada with the Indians of Manitoba and the North-West Territories including the negotiations on which they were based, and other information relating thereto, (Toronto: Belfords, Clarke, & Co., 1880), p. 78.
16   Roderick MacBeth, The Making of the Canadian West: being the reminiscences

of an eye-witness, (Toronto: Brigg, 1898), p. 96.

17   Canada, Department of Militia and Defence, Regulations and Orders for the Active Militia, (Ottawa: Queen's Printer, 1870), p. 6, 10.
18   Russell, Customs and Traditions …p. 9.
19   See the author's, The Guns of Manitoba. How Canon Shaped the Keystone Province – xxxx to 1885, (Manitoba Journal).
20   Canada, Regulations and Orders for the Active Militia, The Schools of Military Instruction, and the Reserve Militia, (Ottawa, Queen's Printer, 1870), p. 14.
21   Alexander Begg, The Creation of Manitoba; or, a history of the Red River Troubles, (Toronto: Hunter, Rose & Co., 1871), p. 197, 378.
22   Manitoba Free Press, "The Queen's Birthday" 25 May 1876, p. 7.
23   Manitoba News-Letter, "Lieut.-Governor Archibald's Levee" 13 September 1870, p. 1.
24   Alexander Begg and Walter Nursey, Ten Years in Winnipeg. A narration of the principal events in the history of the city of Winnipeg from 1870 to 1879 inclusive. (Winnipeg: Times Printing and Publishing House, 1879), 20.
25   Ibid, 25.
26   Le Métis, "Legislature de Manitoba," 8 February 1873, p 2.
27   Manitoba Free Press, "Provincial Parliament Opening of Fourth Session," 15 November 1873, p. 7.
28   Manitoba Free Press, "Manitoba Legislature", 5 February 1876, p.5
29   Manitoba Free Press, "City and Provincial News", 6 May 1876, p. 9.
30   Manitoba Free Press, "Militia Orders", 4 Aug 1881, p. 1
31   LAC, RG 9 II-F-6, Volume 239, 13th Field Battery, Winnipeg, 1871-1892, p. 208.
32   Manitoba Free Press, "The First Locomotive", 13 Oct 77, p.2.
33   W.J. Healey, Winnipeg's Early Days, (Winnipeg: Stovel Company, Limited, 1927), p. 30.
34   Manitoba and Northwest Herald, "Accident" 30 May 1874, p. 3; Manitoba Free Press, "Queen's Birthday" 30 May 74, p. 5
35   LAC, RG 9 II A1 Vol 86, Docket 3928, Gunner Bight Injury Claim.
36   Manitoba Free Press, "Local and Provincial" 19 May 77, p. 2
37   Government of Canada Website, "Ceremonial Guard," http://www.army-armee.forces.gc.ca/en/ceremonial-guard/index.page, last accessed 25 June 2017.
38   Government of the United Kingdom Website, "The King's Troop Royal Horse Artillery," http://www.army.mod.uk/artillery/regiments/24679.aspx, last accessed 25 June 2017.
39   Manitoba Free Press, "Celebration of Dominion Day", 7 July 1877"
40   Militia Report 1883, p. 55.
41   James Daschuk, Clearing the Plains. Disease, Politicis of Starvation, and the loss of Aboriginal Life, (Regina: University of Regina Press, 2013), Kindle Edition, Chapter 6.
42   George F.G. Stanley, The Birth of Western Canada. A History of the Riel Rebellions. (Toronto, University of Toronto Press, 1960, first published 1936), p. 195.
43   Ibid,p. 207.
44   Joseph Tennant, Rough Times, (n.p., 1920), p. 22.

45   LAC, Correspondence of the General Officer Commanding (GOC) of the Canadian Militia and his predecessor, the Adjutant General, RG 9 II B 1, 133544, Reel T284, Memorandum for Dept. Adj. General.
46   Colonel Robertson-Ross, Militia Report 1872,p. cxi.
47   LAC, Correspondence of the General Officer Commanding (GOC) of the Canadian Militia and his predecessor, the Adjutant General, RG 9 II B 1, 133544, Reel T287, Memorandum, dated June 1873.
48   Ibid, p. cxi.
49   Manitoban and Northwest Herald, 3 May 1873, p. 3.
50   Nor'Wester, "City and Vicinity", 15 March 1875, p. 3.
51   Walter Hildebrandt, Views from Fort Battleford. Constructed Visions of an Anglo-Canadian West. (Regina: AU Press, 2008), 1.
52   Jack Dunn, The Alberta Field Force of 1885, (Calgary: Jack Dunn, 1994), p. 92.
53   Desmond Morton, "Cavalry or police: keeping the peace on two adjacent frontiers, 1870-1900" in Journal of Canadian Studies, Vol. 12, No. 2 (April, 1977), p. 30.
54   Alexander Morris, The Treaties of Canada with the Indians of Manitoba and the North-West Territories, (Toronto: Belfords, Clarke & Co., 1880), p. 226.
55   David Laird, "The North-West Indian Treaties" in Manitoba Historical Society Transaction, Series 1, No. 67, 1905 located at http://www.mhs.mb.ca/docs/transactions/1/treaties.shtml last accessed 16 February 2017.
56   "Royal Canadian Rifles at Fort Garry 1857-1861," Directorate of History and Heritage Archives. MORE
57   Adams Archibald letter to The Secretary of State for the Provinces dated 22 July 1871, in The Treaties of Canada with the Indians of Manitoba and the North-West Territories, (Toronto: Belfords, Clarke & Co., 1880), p. 32.
58   Manitoba Liberal, 26 July 1871, p. 3.
59   Manitoba and Northwest Herald, 20 September1873, p. 3.
60   Manitoba Free Press, "The Indian Treaty", 18 October 1873, p. 7.
61   Alexander Morris, The Treaties of Canada with the Indians of Manitoba and the North-West Territories, (Toronto: Belfords, Clarke & Co., 1880), p. 45.
62   Lieutenant-Colonel Osborne Smith, Militia Report 1874, p. 52.
63   Manitoba Free Press, "Little Steps. Departure of the Qu'Appelle Guard of Honor", 22 August 1874, p. 6.
64   Militia Report 1874, p. 52.
65   Morris, The Treaties…, p. 82.
66   Manitoba Free Press, "Qu'Appelle. Full Text of the Treaty", 28 September 1874, p.4
67   Militia Report 1874, p.53.
68   Carter, "Your great mother…"

CHAPTER 5

1   K.B. Wamsley, "Cultural signification and national ideologies: rifle-shooting in late nineteenth-century Canada." In Social History, Vol. 20, No. 1, January 1995, p. 63.

2   Ibid, p. 57.

3   Carmen Miller, "The Montreal Militia as a Social Institution Before World War I" in Urban History Review, Vol. 19, No. 1/2 (June 1990 / October 1990), pp. 57-64.

4   Shore, The Métis and the Canadians..., p. 183.

5   Shore, The Métis and the Canadians..., p. 191.

6   Ibid, p. 184.

7   Frank Howard Schofield, The Story of Manitoba, Volume 1, (Winnipeg, The S. J. Clarke Publishing Company, 1913), p. 318.

8   LAC, RG 0 II A1 Volume 84, Docket 03525, Captain Scott Proposes to Form a Volunteer Company at Winnipeg, 3 April 1877.

9   LAC RG 9 II B1 Volume 61, Docket 04670, Service Rolls of A and B Company, 90th Battalion of Rifles.

10   Don Nerbas, "Wealth and Privilege: An Analysis of Winnipeg's Early Business Elite" in Manitoba History, Number 47, Spring/Summer 2004, http://www.mhs. mb.ca/docs/mb_history/47/winnipegbusinesselite.shtml, last accessed 11 August 2017.

11   Morton, "Aid to the Civil Power", p.416, 420.

12   Robert Vineberg, "The British Garrison and Montreal Society, 1830-1850" in Canadian Military History, Volume 21, Number 1, Winter 2012, pp. 3-16.

13   LAC, Correspondence of the General Officer Commanding (GOC) of the Canadian Militia and his predecessor, the Adjutant General, RG 9, B 1, 133544, Reel T-286, Letter from Adjutant General of Militia to Minister of Militia and Defence Recommending the formation of two companies of rifles, dated 13 September 1871.

14   LAC, Correspondence of the General Officer Commanding (GOC) of the Canadian Militia and his predecessor, the Adjutant General, RG 9, B 1, 133544, Reel T-286, Letter from Militia Headquarters to Dr. John Schultz dated 1 September 1871.

15   LAC, RG 0 II A1 Volume 84, Docket 03525, Captain Scott Proposes to Form a Volunteer Company at Winnipeg, 3 April 1877.

16   LAC, Correspondence of the General Officer Commanding (GOC) of the Canadian Militia and his predecessor, the Adjutant General, RG 9, B 1, 133544, Reel T-287, Letter Adjutant General of Militia to John Haggart, MP dated 8 April 1873.

17   Ibid.

18   Canada Gazette, "Militia General Orders" Number 48, Volume 6, p. 4.

19   Morris Mott, "The British Protestant Pioneers and the Establishment of Manly Sports in Manitoba, 1870-1886" in Journal of Sports History, Vol. 7, No. 3, (Winter, 1980), p 32

20   J.A. Gemmill, Ed., The Canadian Parliamentary Companion, [Ottawa: J. Dubie & Son, 1885]p. 159

21   http://www.mhs.mb.ca/docs/people/mulvey_s.shtml

22   Militia Report 1883, p. 57; Manitoba Historical Society Website "Memorable Manitobans: William Hill Nash (1846-1917)" http://www.mhs.mb.ca/docs/people/ nash_wh.shtml, (accessed 14 February 2020).

23   Manitoba Historical Society Website "Memorable Manitobans: Richard Power (c1851-1880)" http://www.mhs.mb.ca/docs/people/power_r.shtml, (accessed 14

February 2020).

24   Charles William Allen, "Non-Effective Militia Companies in Manitoba" in, Manitoba Free Press, 13 August 1878, p.2.

25   Manitoba and Northwest Herald, 3 May 1873, p. 2.

26   Edith Paterson, Tales of Early Manitoba from the Winnipeg Free Press, (Winnipeg: The Winnipeg Free Press, 1976, p. 85); Begg, Ten Years…, p. 21.

27   "Into Business" Manitoba News-Letter, 3 June 1871, p. 1.

28   A. Milne-Smith, London Clubland, A Cultural History of Gender and Class in Late Victorian Britain, (XXX), p. 1.

29   Peter Stansky, "The Victorian Club" in English Literature in Translation Vol. 57, Issue 3, 2014, p. 60.

30   Don Nerbas, "Wealth and Privilege: An Analysis of Winnipeg's Early Business Elite" in Manitoba History, Number 47, Spring/Summer 2004.

31   Constitution and by-laws of the Manitoba Club, (Winnipeg: Nor-Wester Print, 1874), p. 7

32   Manitoba Free Press, "Proposed Militia Institute," 3 November 1877, p. 3.

33   Le Métis, 'Association Militaire', 14 Aug 72, p.2; Manitoba Free Press, Militia Institute of Manitoba, 1 December 1877, p. 5; Manitoba Free Press, 'Local and Provincial', 26 Jan 78, p. 5; Manitoba Free Press, 'The Canadian Militia', 11 May 1878, p.7

34   Manitoba Free Press, "The Canadian Militia", 11 May 1878, p. 7.

35   Manitoba Free Press, "Music Hath Charms" 19 August 1876, p. 5.

36   Nor'Wester, 'Presentation of Colors to Provisional Battalion' 19 October, 1874, p. 3

37   Manitoba Free Press, "The Snowshoe Races" 21 February 1876, p. 3.

38   "Winnipeg Field Battery Camp", Manitoba Free Press, 8 September 1877, p. 2.

39   Manitoban and Northwest Herald, "Benedict's Ball" 31 January 1874, p. 2.

40   Manitoba Free Press, "The Amateur Theatricals" 7 February 1874, p. 7.

41   James B. Hartman, "On Stage: Theatre and Theatres in Early Winnipeg" in Manitoba History, Number 43, Spring/Summer 2002.

42   Ibid.

43   Ibid.

44   Manitoba News-Letter, "Farewell Entertainment", 22 April 1872, p. 1.

45   Manitoba Free Press, 'Amateur Theatricals' 7 February 1874, p. 8

46   Manitoba Free Press, "Amusement", 6 December 1875

47   Manitoba Free Press, "Garrison Theatricals", 14 February 1874, p. 5.

48   Manitoba Free Press, "Garrison Theatricals", 28 February 1874, p. 5.

49   William Collins, Manitoba Free Press, "The Garrison Theatricals," 18 April 1874, p. 5.

50   Manitoba Free Press, "Local and Provincial," 27 December 1873, p. 5

51   James B. Hartman, "The Growth of Music in Early Winnipeg to 1920" in Manitoba History, Number 40, Autumn/Winter 2000-2001.

52   New Nation, "The Band of the 60th", 27 August 1870, p. 2.

53   New Nation, "The Band", 3 September 1870, p. 2.

54   James B. Hartman, "The Growth of Music in Early Winnipeg to 1920" in Manitoba History, Number 40, Autumn/Winter 2000-2001.

55   Manitoba Free Press, 'Minstrels' 22 February 1873, p. 5

56   Manitoba Free Press, "Minstrels" 22 February 1873, p. 5.
57   Manitoba Free Press, 'Local and Provincial', 1 March 1873, p. 5
58   Manitoba Free Press,4 September 1875, p3
59   Miller, "The Montreal Militia as a Social Institution Before World War I", p.60.
60   Manitoba Free Press, "Masquerade Carnival" 13 January 1875
61   Manitoba and Northwest Herald, 'Misplaced Confidence', 9 August 1873
62   Manitoba Free Press, "Winnipeg Field Battery Concert" 23 September 1876, p. 5.
63   The Manitoba and North-West Illustrated Quarterly, "Sports and Pastimes" Vol. 1, No. 1, Christmas 1883, p. 14.
64   Manitoba Free Press, "Canada and Lord Dufferin", 21 August 1875, p. 3.
65   Captain William Wood, "In Case of War" in The Canadian Magazine, Vol. XI, No. 2, June 1898, p. 99.
66   Bruce Haley, "Sports and the Victorian World" in The Western Humanities Review, Volume 22, Number 2, Spring 1968.
67   Manitoba Free Press, "Cricket. Military vs. Headingly", 20 July 1874
68   Manitoba Free Press, "City and Provincial News," 3 May 1876, p. 3
69   Manitoba Liberal, 30 August 1871, p. 2.
70   "Military Games" in Manitoba Free Press, 31 May 1873, p. 5.
71   "Cricket" in Manitoban and Northwest Herald, 3 May 1872, p. 3.
72   Mott, "The British Protestant Pioneers and the Establishment of Manly Sports in Manitoba," p. 29.
73   James Joseph Hargrave, Red River, (Montreal: John Lovell, 1871), p. 341.
74   William Weighton, "The Story of 100 Years of Cricket" in Manitoba Pageant, (Autumn 1974, Volume 20, No. 1).
75   Ibid.
76   "Local and Provincial. Cricket" in Manitoba Free Press, 24 June 1876, p. 3.
77   "Manitoba Cricket Club" in Manitoba Free Press, 18 March 1876, p. 2.
78   "Local and Provincial Items" in Manitoba and Northwest Herald, 8 August 1874, p. 3.
79   "Local and Provincial" in Manitoba Free Press, 6 May 1876, p. 2.
80   "Local News" in Portage la Prairie Weekly Tribune, 13 June 1884, p. 8.
81   Alexander Laidlaw, From the St. Lawrence to the North Saskatchewan, (Halifax, n.p., 1885), p. 27.
82   Wamsley, "Cultural signification and national ideologies...", p. 66.
83   Ibid, p. 63.
84   Wamsley, "Cultural signification and national ideologies...", p. 63.
85   "Government Rifles and the Deer-Hunters," Manitoba Free Press, 16 Jan 1878, p;. 1.
86   Wamsley, "Cultural signification and national ideologies...", p. 64.
87   The Rifle Tournament. The Prize List" in Manitoba Free Press, 4 October 1873, p. 5.
88   Manitoba Provincial Rifle Association webpage, "History", http://www.manitobarifle.ca/history/, last accessed 21 March 2017.
89   "Manitoba Rifle Association" in Manitoban and Northwest Herald, 21 June 1873, p.2
90   "Dominion Rifle Association" Manitoba and Northwest Herald, 29 March

1873, p. 3

91   "Manitoba Rifel Association" in Manitoba Free Press, 23 August 1873, p. 5.

92   "Manitoba Rifle Association" in Manitoban and Northwest Herald, 21 June 1873, p.2

93   "Rifle Tournament of the Manitoba Rifle Association" in Manitoban and Northwest Herald, 4 October 1873, p.2.

94   "The Rifle Tournament" Manitoba Free Press, 27 September 1873, p. 5.

95   "Ibid, p. 5.

96   "The Rifle Tournament. The Prize List" in Manitoba Free Press, 4 October 1873, p. 5.

97   "M.R.A. Prize Presentation, Manitoba Free Press, 11 September 1875, p. 5.

98   "Manitoba Rifle Association", Manitoba Free Press, 21 Aug 74, p. 3.

99   "A Reproach" Manitoba Free Press, 1 September 1875, p. 3

100   "Manitoba to be Represented at Wimbledon," Manitoba Free Press, 25 April 1876, p. 7.

101   Militia Report 1878, p. 76.

102   Manitoba Free Press, Local and Provincial", 29 November 1873, p. 5.

103   J.M. Bereton, quoted by Jeremy A. Crang in "The Abolition of Compulsory Church Parades" in The Journal of Ecclesiastical History, Vol. 56, No. 1, January 2005, p. 92.

104   Tenant, Rough Times…, p. 71.

105   George Young, Manitoba Memories. Leaves from my life in the prairie province., 1868-1884, (Toronto: William Briggs, 1897), pp. 193-195.

106   Mary FitzGibbon, A Trip to Manitoba, (London: Richard Bentley and Son, 1880), 39.

107   Manitoba Free Press, "Church Parade at Holy Trinity", 22 April 1878, p. 1.

108   Manitoba Free Press, "Citizen Soldiers. Church Parade Yesterday", 14 July 1879, p. 1.

109   Manitoba Free Press, "Military Service at Grace Church", 20 October 1877, p. 6; Manitoba Free Press, "City and Provincial News", 11 January 1878, p. 1.

110   Manitoba Free Press, 'Local and Provincial', 16 June 1877, p.5

111   Manitoba Free Press, "Winnipeg Field Battery", 11 September 1876, p. 3.

112   Manitoba Free Press, "Military Service at Grace Church", 20 October 1877, p. 6.

113   Ibid.

114   Le Métis « Une Bonne Promotion », 12 July 73, p.2

115   Le Métis, 11 October 1873, p. 2

116   Manitoba Free Press, "Presentation to Major Irvine", 27 November 1874, p. 3. The signatories of the open letter included SL Bedson, Thomas Bunn, James Green Stewart, AGB Bannatyne, WJ Piton, Thomas Sinclair, AJ Peers, Robert McBeth, JR Bunn, Thomas Taylor, J. McLeod, George Calder, Thomas Lyons, William Buchanan, William Flett, R Hamilton, GS Davidson, RH Hunter, Alex Dahl, Thomas Fidler, Robert Black, George Black, Thomas Black, and George West.

117   Young, Manitoba Memories, 192-193.

118   Manitoban and Northwest Herald, "The Volunteer Banquet", 22 October 1870, p. 2.

119   Manitoba Free Press, "Emerson," 27 October 1877, p. 3.

120   Manitoba Free Press, 'Disbandment of the Garrison' 11 August 1877, p. 2.

CHAPTER 6

1   Manitoba Free Press, 'Police Court' 4 January 1873, p.5; Manitoban and Northwest Herald, 'City Police Court', 12 September 1874, p, 2
2   Winnipeg Free Press, "City and Provincial News," 28 August, 1874,p.3; WFP, 12 January 1875, p. 7
3   W.F. Butler, The great lone land : a narrative of travel and adventure in the North-West of America (London: S. Low, Marston, Low & Searle, 1872), p. 192.
4   "At Fort Garry" in Southern Reporter and Cork Commercial Courier, 7 October 1870, p. 3.
5   Shore, p. 287.
6   Manitoba Free Press, 27 December 1873, p. 5.
7   Manitoba Free Press, "Murder!", 20 June 1874, p. 5.
8   Ibid.
9   Nor'Wester, "The Execution" 31 August 1874, p. 1.
10   Letter from Lieutenant Colonel Osborne Smith to Lieutenant Colonel Powell dated 27 June 1874, LAC, RG9-II-A-1. Volume/box number: 64. File number: 9934.
11   Nor'Wester, "The Execution" 31 August 1874, p. 1.
12   Ibid; Manitoba Free Press, "Michaud's Execution" 29 August 1874, p. 7.
13   Manitoba Free Press, "Michaud's Execution" 29 August 1874, p. 7.
14   Tenant, Rough Times…, pp. 80-81.
15   Manitoba News-Letter, 8 October 1870, p. 1.
16   Tenant, Rough Times…, p. 88.
17   "Touchstone Talk" in Grip, (20), no. 2, 5 May 1883, p. 6.
18   Manitoba Free Press, "Drummed Out", 25 April 1874, p. 5.
19   Memorandum on the Proceedings of the Garrison Court Martial assembled at Fort Garry on the 17th April 1873 for the Trial of No. 24 Gunner Vaughan of the Artillery Detachment Now on Duty at Fort Garry, To be Read to the Officers Composing the Court, the presences of the Officer Commanding the Provisional battalion, by the Officer Commanding the Militia, LAC, RG 9, II B1, Volume 520.
20   Memorandum in the Case of No. 24 Gunner Vaughan, LAC, RG 9, II B1, Volume 520.
21   Memorandum on the Proceedings of the Garrison Court Martial assembled at Fort Garry on the 17th April 1873 for the Trial of No. 24 Gunner Vaughan of the Artillery Detachment Now on Duty at Fort Garry, To be Read to the Officers Composing the Court, the presences of the Officer Commanding the Provisional battalion, by the Officer Commanding the Militia, LAC, RG 9, II B1, Volume 520.
22   Memorandum from the Adjutant General of Militia to the Minister of Militia and Defence dated 2 March 1872, LAC, RG 9, II B1, Volume 518.
23   Memorandum from LCol Osborne Smith to the General Officer Commanding dated 19 May 1879, LAC, RG9-II-A-1. Volume/box number: 105. File number: 6780
24   Ibid.
25   Findings of an Enquiry held at Fort Osborne on the nineteenth day of July

1880 by Lt.Col Osborne Smith DAG No. 10 Military District by order of the Adjutant General of Militia dated the 6th of July 1880. LAC, RG9-II-A-1. Volume/box number: 105. File number: 6780.

26   Ibid.

27   Memorandum Major General Luard to Lieutenant Colonel Osborne Smith dated 7 September 1880. LAC, RG9-II-A-1. Volume/box number: 105. File number: 6780.

28   Memorandum on the matter of the charges preferred by Lieutenant E.W. Jarvis against Lt.Col W.N. Kennedy, commanding the Winnipeg Field Battery, dated 12 November 1880. LAC, RG9-II-A-1. Volume/box number: 105. File number: 6780.

29   Steele, Forty years…p. 38.

30   Lieutenant General James Lindsay, "Instructions for the guidance of Colonel Wolseley" in The War Office to Lieutenant General James Lindsay, p. 22.

31   Shore, The Canadians and the Métis…., p. 217.

32   Ibid, p. 217-218.

33   Jim McKillip "Emboldened by Bad Behaviour: The Conduct of the Canadian Army in the Northwest, 1870 to 1873" in The Apathetic and the Defiant: Case Studies of Canadian Mutiny and Disobedience (Kingston: Canadian Defence Academy Press, 2007), p. 153.

34   Ibid, p. 156; "Thomas Scott" Perth Historical Society Website, http://www.perthhs.org/documents/thomas-scott-shaw.pdf (accessed 4 February 2019).

35   Grand Orange Lodge of Canada Website, "About" http://grandorangelodge.ca/about/, last accessed 1 July 2017.

36   The Canadian Monthly and National Review, "Current Events", Vol. 3, No. 4, April, 1873, p. 335.

37   Manitoba Historical Society, Memorable Manitobans: Stewart Mulvey (1834-1908), http://www.mhs.mb.ca/docs/people/mulvey_s.shtml, last accessed 1 July 2017.

38   Manitoba Free Press, "District LOL" 15 January 1875, p. 2.

39   Canada, Official Reports of the Debates of the House of Commons of the Dominion of Canada: First Session Fifth Parliament, Volume XIV, (Ottawa: Maclean, Roger & Co, 1883) , p. 1170.

40   The Volunteer Review and Military and Naval Gazette, Vol IV, No. 16, 18 April 1870

41   Korn Kobe, "Canada's Battle Cry" The Volunteer Review and Military and Naval Gazette, Vol IV, No. 16, 18 April 1870

42   See Geoff Read and Todd Webb, "'The Catholic Mahdi of the North-West': Louis Riel and the Métis Resistance in Transatlantic and Imperial Context" in The Canadian Historical Review, 93, 2, June 2012.

43   Joseph Alfred Mousseau, "La Paix ou La Guerre" in l'Opinion Publique, Vol 1, No. 17, 28 April 1870, p. 2.

44   Alexander Begg, The Creation of Manitoba: Or, a History of the Red River Troubles (Toronto: A. H. Hovey, 1871), 23.

45   Shore, The Canadians and the Métis…, p. 230.

46   Ibid, p. 247.

47   Manitoba Newsletter, "Lies from Manitoba", 18 February 1871, p. 2.

48   Ibid.

49   Constance Kerr Sissons, John Kerr, (Toronto: Oxford University Press, 1946), pp. 57-58

50   Ibid, p. 58.

51   Volunteer Review, Volume V, No. 12, 20 March 1871, p. 185.

52   Manitoban and Northwest Herald, "The Mounted Police Force", 4 October 1873, p. 2.

53   Manitoba Liberal, "Public Rejoicings", 20 April 1872, p. 1.

54   Manitoba Free Press, "Reorganization of the Military at Fort Osborne" 11 September 1875, p. 2.

55   See Lawrence Barkwell, "The Reign of Terror Against the Métis of Red River", (Winnipeg: The Louis Riel Institute, 2008). http://www.metismuseum.ca/resource.php/07260 last accessed 12 June 2017

56   John W. Dafoe, "Early Winnipeg Newspapers: The Last 70 Years of Journalism at Fort Garry and Winnipeg" in MHS Transactions, Series 3, 1956-57 season, http://www.mhs.mb.ca/docs/transactions/3/earlywinnipegnewspapers.shtml last accessed 12 June 2017.

57   G.W. "Notes and Queries" by The Volunteer Review, Vol. 5, No.39, 25 Sept 1871, p. 12.

58   PAM, Lieutenant Governor's Papers, Pierre Parenteau et al to Archibald, December 9, 1871.

59   J.A. Mousseau, "Goulet" in L'Opinion Publique, Vol. 1, No 41, 13 October 1870, p. 2

60   Ibid, p. 2.

61   Ibid, p. 2

62   Shore, The Canadians and the Métis…,. 230-232.

63   Lawrence Barkwell, "The Reign of Terror Against the Métis of Red River", (Winnipeg: The Louis Riel Institute, 2008), p.12. http://www.metismuseum.ca/resource.php/07260 last accessed 15 June 2018..

64   The Canadian Illustrated News, "Affairs in Manitoba", Volume II, No. 16, 15 October 1870, p. 1.

65   Steele, Forty years…p. 34.

66   LAC, Department of Militia and Defence, Records Relating to the North-West Rebellion, 1880-1885, RG9 11A3 Vol 2

67   Lawrence Barkwell, "The Reign of Terror Against the Métis of Red River", (Winnipeg: The Louis Riel Institute, 2008), p.9. http://www.metismuseum.ca/resource.php/07260 last accessed 12 June 2017

68   New York Herald, 12 June 1872, p. 4.

69   Barkwell, "The Reign of Terror… p. 4.

70   McKillip "Emboldened by Bad Behaviour...", p. 162.

71   Mott, "The British Protestant Pioneers….", p.26.

CHAPTER 7

1   Desmond Morton, "Sir Frederick Dobson Middleton, Dictionary of Canadian Biography Website, http://www.biographi.ca/en/bio/middleton_frederick_dobson_12E.html, last accessed 24 April 2018.

2   Canada. Department of Militia and Defence. Report of Lieutenant-Colonel

W.H. Jackson on Matters in Connection with the Suppression of the Rebellion in the North-West Territories in 1885 (Ottawa: McLean, Roger & Co., 1887), p. 15.

3   Canada. Departure of Agriculture. Statistical Abstract and Record. (Ottawa: Maclean, Rogers & Co., 1886), p. 22.

4   Militia Report 1884, p. 246.

5   Militia Report 1885, p. 49.

6   Ken Coates, "Western Manitoba and the 1885 Rebellion" in Manitoba History, Number 20, Autumn 1990, http://www.mhs.mb.ca/docs/mb_history/20/1885rebellion.shtml#10, last accessed 25 March 2018.

7   Militia Report 1884, p 134.

8   Ibid, p. 46.

9   Ibid, p. 46.

10   Ibid, p. 47.

11   Ibid, pp. 47-48.

12   Ibid, pp. 48-49.

13   Desmond Morton, "Sir Frederick Dobson Middleton, Dictionary of Canadian Biography   Website,   http://www.biographi.ca/en/bio/middleton_frederick_dobson_12E.html, last accessed 24 April 2018

14   LAC, "Telegram from Middleton to Caron dated 27 March 1885" in Caron Papers, c1654, image 19.

15   Militia Report 1884, p. 49.

16   Ibid, pp. 50-51.

17   Stanley, The Birth of Western Canada…, 177-179.

18   Mulvaney, The History of the North-West Rebellion…p. 17.

19   The Riel Rebellion 1885, (Montreal: Witness Printing House, 1885), p. 1.

20   Canada, An Act for the temporary Government of Rupert's Land, and the North-Western Territory when united with Canada, 22 June 1869.

21   Stanley, The Birth of Western Canada…, p. 180.

22   Thomas Flanagan. Riel and the Rebellion: 1885 Reconsidered. (Toronto: University of Toronto Press, 2000), 10.

23   Charles Pelham Mulvaney, The North-West Rebellion of 1885 Including a History of the Indian Tribes of North-Western Canada. (Toronto: A.H. Hovey & Co., 1885), 24.

24   Samuel Steele, Forty Years in Canada, (Toronto: McClelland, Goodchild & Stewart, 1915), p. 201.

25   Ibid, p. 201.

26   Inter.Canada: The Canadian Constitution and Unity Group. "The Métis List of Rights," last accessed 4 March 2013, http://www3.sympatico.ca/rd.fournier/inter.canada/doc/metis1.htm. The Metis List of Rights can be found at Annex A.

27   Steele, Forty Years…, p. 202.

28   Stanley, Canada's Soldiers…, p. 252

29   Ibid, p. 252.

30   Stanley, The Birth of Western Canada… , 285.

31   Ibid, 269.

32   J.E. Rea, "The Hudson's Bay Company and the North-West Rebellion" in The Beaver. Summer 1982, 43.

33   Stanley, The Birth of Western Canada…, 353.

34   Desmond Morton. The Last War Drum: The North-West Campaign of 1885. (Toronto: A.M Hakkert, Ltd, 1972), 16.
35   Blair Stonechild and Bill Waiser. Loyal till Death: Indians and the North-West Rebellion. (Calgary: Fifth House Ltd., 1997), 240.
36   Richard Gwyn. Nation Maker, Sir John A. Macdonald: His Life, Our Times Volume Two: 1867-1891. (Toronto: Random House of Canada Limited, 2011), 450.
37   Theresa Gowanlock, Two Months in the Camp of Big Bear. The Life and Adventures of Theresa Gowanlock and Theressa Delaney. Part I. (Parkdale: The Times, 1885), pp. 24-25
38   Stanley, Canada's Soldiers…, p. 254
39   Ibid, p. 254.
40   Letter Macdonald to Middleton dated 29 March, Extracts from Correspondence of Sir John Macdonald Bearing on the North-West Rebellion, in "North-West Rebellion 1885", Directorate of History and Heritage Archives, 500.009, D32.
41   Desmond Morton, "Sir Frederick Dobson Middleton, Dictionary of Canadian Biography   Website,   http://www.biographi.ca/en/bio/middleton_frederick_ dobson_12E.html, last accessed 24 April 2018
42   Telegraph Powell to Houghton dated 22 March, Caron Papers, LAC.
43   LAC, Caron Papers, Telegraph Houghton to Caron dated 23 March 1885.
44   "Riel's Rebels" in Manitoba Free Press, 24 March 1885, p. 4.
45   "Bound for Troy" in Brandon Sun, 26 March 1885, p. 9.
46   LAC, Caron Papers, Telegram Houghton to Caron dated 26 March 1885, Telegram Caron to Houghton dated 26 March 1885; Telegram Caron to Houghton dated 26 March 1885, C1654, Image 14.
47   Frederick Middlleton, "Special Report by Major-General Sir Frederick Middleton, KCMG, CB, Commanding the Militia of Canada Upon the Military Operations in the Northwest Territories, in 1885" in Report Upon the Suppression of the Rebellion in the North-West Territories, and Matters in Connection Therewith, in 1885, (Ottawa: 1886), p. 2.
48   "Bloodshed" in Manitoba Free Press, 28 March 1885, p. 1.
49   LAC, Caron Papers, Telegram Middleton to Caron dated 3 April 1885, C1654, image 134-135
50   LAC, Caron Papers, Telegram Houghton to Caron dated 26 March 1885, C1654, image 14.
51   Militia Report 1884, p. 46.
52   Telegram Middleton to Caron dated 27 March 1885 image 19.
53   Middleton, Report…, p. 2.
54   Thomas Edward Champion, History of the 10th Royals and of the Royal Grenadiers from the formation of the regiment until 1896, (Toronto: The Hunter Rose Company, 1896), p. 134.
55   Captain James Mason, No. 2 Company Royal Grenadiers, "Homeward Bound" in Manitoba Free Press, 8 Jjuly 1885, p. 1.
56   W.H. Jackson, Report of Lieutenant-Colonel W.H. Jackson on Matters in Connection with the Suppression of the Rebellion in the North-West Territories in 1885 (Ottawa: McLean, Roger & Co., 1887), p. 5.
57   Jackson, Report…., p. 5.
58   LAC, Caron Papers, Telegram from C.E. Hamilton to Caron dated 28 March

1885.

59   "About Town" in Manitoba Free Press, 1 April 1885, p. 1.

60   "Virden's Valor" in Manitoba Free Press, 2 April 1885, p. 1.

61   LAC, Caron Papers, Telegraph to Caron dated 1 April, image 163.

62   "Morris Military" Manitoba Free Press, 2 April 1885, p. 1.

63   "Whitemouth Warriors" in Manitoba Free Press, 4 April 1885, p. 1; "Local Notes" Manitoba Free Press, 6 April 1885, p. 4.

64   Ken Coates, "Western Manitoba and the 1885 Rebellion" in Manitoba History, Number 20, Autumn 1990, http://www.mhs.mb.ca/docs/mb_history/20/1885rebellion.shtml#10, last accessed 25 March 2018.

65   LAC, Caron Papers telegram from Boulton to Macdonald dated 24 March 1885, C1654, image 7.

66   LAC, Caron Papers telegram from Boulton to Macdonald dated 28 March 1885, C1654, image 25.

67   Manitoba Historical Society Website, "Memorable Manitobans: Charles Arkoll Boulton (1841-1899)" http://www.mhs.mb.ca/docs/people/boulton_ca.shtml, last accessed 30 March 2018.

68   Letter Macdonald to Middleton dated 29 March, Extracts from Correspondence of Sir John Macdonald Bearing on the North-West Rebellion, in "North-West Rebellion 1885", Directorate of History and Heritage Archives, 500.009, D32.

69   Services in the North-West in 1885 of units organized for the campaign, other than provisional units, made up of quotas from existing Militia regiments in "North-West Rebellion 1885", Directorate of History and Heritage Archives, 500.009, D32.

70   Chalres Boulton, Reminiscences of the North-West Rebellions, (Toronto: Grip Printing and Publishing, 1886), p. 203.

71   Letter Macdonald to Middleton dated 29 March, Extracts from Correspondence of Sir John Macdonald Bearing on the North-West Rebellion, in "North-West Rebellion 1885", Directorate of History and Heritage Archives, 500.009, D32.

72   "Col Osborne Smith" in Manitoba Free Press, 30 March 1885, p. 1.

73   Services in the North-West in 1885 of units organized for the campaign, other than provisional units, made up of quotas from existing Militia regiments in "North-West Rebellion 1885", Directorate of History and Heritage Archives, 500.009, D32.

74   "The Irish Company" in Manitoba Free Press, 1 April 1885, p. 1.

75   LAC, Caron Papers telegram Norquay to Caron, 29 March, 1654, image 54

76   LAC, Caron Papers telegram Norquay to Caron, 30 March, 1654, image 63.

77   LAC, Caron Papers, telegram Osborne Smith to Caron, 30 March, 1654, image 54.

78   "Militia General Orders (8) dated 10 April 1885" in Canada Gazette No. 41, Volume XVIII, 11 April 1885.

79   Strange, "Telegram Osborne Smith to General Strange dated 11 April" in Gunner Jingo's Jubilee…, p. 417.

80   LAC, Caron Papers, telegram Osborne Smith to Caron, 30 March, 1654, image 282.

81   "To the Front" in Manitoba Free Press, 16 April 1885, p. 1.

82   Thomas Bland Strange, Gunner Jingo's Jubilee, (London: Remington & Co. Ltd., 1893), p. 417.

83   Services in the North-West in 1885 of units organized for the campaign, other

than provisional units, made up of quotas from existing Militia regiments in "North-West Rebellion 1885", Directorate of History and Heritage Archives, 500.009, D32.

84   "The 91st Battalion" in Manitoba Free Press, 9 April 1885, p. 1.
85   "The 91st" in Manitoba Free Press, 13 May 1885, p 1.
86   91st Battalion" in Manitoba Free Press, 17 April 1885, p. 1.
87   Jackson, Report…, p. 22.
88   "91st Battalion" in Manitoba Free Press, 17 April 1885, p. 1.
89   Jackson, Report…, p. 26.
90   Ibid, p. 28.
91   Ibid, p. 30.
92   A Fenian Invasion" Brandon Sun, 2 April 1885, p. 16.
93   LAC, Caron Papers, C1654, image 57.
94   Telegram 3 April 1885, C1654, image 140.
95   "The North-West Field Forces", Report on the Suppression…., frontispiece.
96   Frederick Middleton, "Appendix A to the Report of the Major General Commanding" in Report on the Suppression…., pp. 17-21.
97   B. A. T. de Montigny, Adolphe Ouimet, La verite sur la question metisse au nord-ouest. Biographie et recit de gabriel dumont sur les evenements de 1885 (Montreal : n.p. 1889), p. 132.
98   Ibid, pp. 132-134.
99   Mulvaney The North-West Rebellion…, p. 255.
100   Middleton, "Appendix C. To the Report of the Major General Commanding" in Report on the Suppression…p. 32.
101   G.S. Ryerson, History of the 10th Royals and the Royal Grenadiers, (Toronto: The Hunter Rose Company, 1896), p. 149.
102   Ibid, p. 139.
103   Middleton, Report… p. 20.
104   Ouimet, La verite sur le question…, p. 138.
105   "Appendix E. To the Report of the Major General Commanding" in Report on the Suppression…., p. 45.
106   Ibid, pp. 45-46.
107   "Appendix B. To the Report of the Major General Commanding" in Report on the Suppression…, p. 24
108   Frederick Middleton, "Appendix No. 1 Special Report by Major General Sir Frederick D. Middleton" in Report on the Suppression…, p. 2
109   Thomas Bland Strange, "Appendix G To the Report of the Major General Commanding" in Report on the Suppression…, pp. 51-52.
110   Strange, Gunner Jingo's Jubilee…p. 435.
111   "Volunteers Arrived" in Fort MacLeod Gazette, 25 Apr 1885, p. 3.
112   Strange, "Appendix G To the Report of the Major General Commanding" in Report on the Suppression…, p. 52.
113   Strange, Gunner Jingo's Jubilee…p. 429.
114   "The Edmonton Column" in Manitoba Free Press, 20 May 1885, p. 1.
115   "The March to Edmonton" in Manitoba Free Press, 20 May 1885, p. 4.
116   "The Edmonton Column" in Manitoba Free Press, 20 May 1885, p. 1.
117   "From Calgary" in Manitoba Free Press, 5 May 1885, p. 1.
118   Beauregard, 9me Battalion…, p. 34.

119   "Departure of the W.L.I." and "Impromptu Concert" in Fort MacLeod Gazette, 9 May 1885, p. 3.
120   LAC, Caron Papers, Telegram Osborne Smith to Caron dated 25 April, 1885.
121   Strange, Gunner Jingo's Jubilee...p. 448.
122   "The Edmonton Column" in Manitoba Free Press, 20 May 1885, p. 1.
123   Strange, Gunner Jingo's Jubilee...p. 453.
124   "With Gen. Strange's Column" in Manitoba Free Press, 8 June 1885, p. 1.
125   Geoff Brooks, "A Horrible Night. An Historical Sketch of the North-West Rebellion" in The Lake Magazine, 1, No. 3, October 1892, 165-168.
126   Ibid.
127   Middleton, Report on the suppression..., p. 12.
128   "From Qu'Appelle" in Manitoba Free Press, 23 April 1885, p. 1.
129   Wm. L.H. Rowand, "Reading Matter for the 91st" in Manitoba Free Press, 8 May 1885, p. 1.
130   "Some Notes by a Teamster With the North-West Field Force" in Brandon Sun, 2 July 1885, p. 11.
131   Nemo, "The 91st" in Manitoba Free Press, 10 July 1885, p. 2.
132   One of the 91st Battalion, "The 91st" in Manitoba Free Press, 10 July 1885, p. 2.
133   "Home Sweet Home" in Manitoba Free Press, 24 July 1885, p. 4.
134   Jackson, Report..., p. 34.
135   "Ordered Out" in Manitoba Free Press, 23 April 1885, p. 1; "The Body Guards" in Manitoba Free Press, 24 April 1885, p. 1.
136   Jackson, Report..., p. 6.
137   Ibid, p. 15, 26.
138   "Sentries Fired On" in Manitoba Free Press, 7 May 1885, p. 1.
139   "Movement of Troops" in Manitoba Free Press, 14 May 1885, p. 1.
140   Jackson, Report..., p. 34.
141   "The Cavalry" in Manitoba Free Press, 7 July 1885, p. 1.
142   Middleton, Report...p. 15.
143   Ibid, 49-50.
144   Jackson, Report..., p. 6.
145   Middleton, Report..., p. 14.
146   D. Bergin "Report of the Surgeon General" in Sessional Papers of the Dominion of Canada: Volume 5, Foruth Session of the Fifht Parliament, Session 1886, (Ottawa: MacLean, Roger & Co., 1886), p. 327.
147   James Kerr, « Report of Surgeon Major James Kerr" in Report Upon the Suppression of the Rebellion in the North-West Territories, and Matters in Connection Therewith, in 1885, (Ottawa: 1886), p. 360.
148   Charles Pelham Mulvaney, The History of the North-West Rebellion of 1885 Including a History of the Indian Tribes of North-Western Canada, Toronto: A. H. Hovey & Co, 1885, p. 293.
149   Jackson, Report...., p. 6.
150   Stanley, The Birth of Western Canada..., p. 191.
151   Ibid , p. 189.
152   Ibid, 190.
153   J.E. Rea, "The Hudson's Bay Company and the North-West Rebellion" in The

Beaver. Summer 1982, 44.

154   Ibid, 46.

155   Ibid, 46.

156   Ibid, 44.

157   Gordon E. Tolton, Prairie Warships: River Navigation in the Northwest Rebellion. (Vancouver: Heritage House, 2007), 78.

158   Morton, The Last War Drum…, 45.

159   -Major-General Frederick Middleton, Suppression of the Rebellion in the North-West Territories

160   Tolton, Prairie Warships…, 78.

161   Rea, "The Hudson's Bay Company…", 47.

162   Morton, The Last War Drum…, 46.

163   T10394, image 28.

164   Telegram royal/caron 6 April 1885, c1654, iamge 177.

165   LAC, Caron Papers, Telegram from Joseph Edward Woodworth to Adolphe Caron, dated 22 April 1885.

166   LAC, Caron Papers, "Telegram Rowe to Powell" dated 7 April 1885.

167   LAC, Caron Papers, "Telegram Rowe to Powell" dated 13 April 1885, c1654, image 270.

168   "Some Other Day" in Manitoba Free Press, 14 November 1885, p. 1.

169   "Details of Expenditures" in Report Upon the Suppression of the Rebellion in the North-West Territories, and Matters in Connection Therewith, in 1885, (Ottawa: 1886), pp. 457-502.

170   Alexander Laidlaw, From the St. Lawrence to the North Saskatchewan, being some incidents connected with the Detachment of A Battery, Regt. Canadian Artillery, who composed part of the North-West Field Force, in the Rebellion of 1885, (Halifax, n.p., 1885), p. 14.

171   Robert A. Sherlock, Experiences of the Halifax Battalion in the North-West, (Halifax: Jas. W. Doley, 1885), p. 9.

172   Charles R. Daoust, Cent-Vingt Jours de Service Actif. Recit Historique Tres Complet de la campagne du 65eme au Nord-Ouest, (Montreal : Eusebe Senecal & Fils, 1886), p. 33.

173   « Les Volontaires Canadiens » in Le Manitoba, 16 April 1885, p. 2.

174   George Beauregard, Le 9me Battalion au Nord-Ouest, (Quebec : Jos.-G. Giingraas & Cie., 1886), pp. 26-27.

175   "Bible Society and Volunteers" in Manitoba Free Press, 4 April 1884, p. 1.

176   Dr. Sullivan, "Report of the Purveyor-General, Hon. Dr. Sullivan." in Report Upon the Suppression of the Rebellion in the North-West Territories, and Matters in Connection Therewith, in 1885, (Ottawa: 1886), p. 377

177   Jackson, Report…, p. 28.

178   "A Military Funeral" in Manitoba Free Press, 21 May 1885, p. 1.

179   "Toll for the Brave" in Manitoba Free Press, 23 May 1885, p. 4.

180   Ibid.

181   "Military Funeral" in Manitoba Free Press, 6 July 1885, p. 4.

182   LAC, Caron Papers, "Telegram from C. Carruthers (Alderman and Acting Mayor) to Caron" dated 26 June 1885

183   LAC, Caron Papers, "Telegram Middleton to Caron" dated 29 June 1885.

184 "Our Noble Defenders" Manitoba Free Press, 9 July 1885, p. 4.
185 "Notice!" in Manitoba Free Press, 10 July 1885, p. 2.
186 Beauregard, 9me Battalion…, p. 88.
187 Jack Dunn, "The Biggest Day Winnipeg Has Ever Seen: The Northwest Field Force Returns From the Front" in Manitoba History, Number 43, Summer 2002, http://www.mhs.mb.ca/docs/mb_history/43/fieldforcereturns.shtml, last accessed 19 September 2018..
188 Champion, History of the 10th…, p. 191.
189 "The Welcome Home" in Manitoba Free Press, 16 July 1885, p. 3.
190 Ibid.
191 "End of the War" in Manitoba Free Press, 17 July 1885, p. 1.
192 "The Agony Over" in Manitoba Free Press, 18 July 1865, p. 4.
193 "Volunteer Memorial" in Manitoba Free Press, 16 June 1885, p. 4; "City and Province" in Manitoba Free Press, 23 June 1885, p. 4
194 "Volunteer Memorial" in Manitoba Free Press, 16 June 1885, p. 4.
195 "City and Province" in Manitoba Free Press, 30 June 1885, p. 4.
196 "City and Province" in Manitoba Free Press, 29 July 1885, p. 4.
197 "City and Province" in Manitoba Free Press, 31 August 1885, p. 4.
198 "City and Province" in Manitoba Free Press, 14 November 1885, p. 4.
199 Mayor Henry Shaver Westbrook, "In Memoriam" Manitoba Free Press, 29 September 1886, p. 8.
200 de Montigny, La verite sur la question metisse…p. 139.

Conclusion

Epilogue

1 Militia Report 1885, p. 50.
2 Ibid, P. 51.
3 "Our Guest" in Manitoba Free Press, 22 October 1885, p. 4.
4 "Our Guest" in Manitoba Free Press, 22 October 1885, p. 4.
1 James T. Currie and Richard B. Crossland, Twice The Citizen: A History of the United States Army Reserve, 1908–1995 (2nd ed), (Washington: Office of the Chief, Army Reserve ,1997); United States Army Reserve Command homepage, http://www.usar.army.mil last accessed 22 February 2017.

2 Canadian Soldiers Website, "Domestic Military Organization 1900-1999", https://www.canadiansoldiers.com/organization/districts.htm, last accessed 18 September 2018.

SELECT BIBLIOGRAPHY

BOOKS

Arel, Jospeh Ford. Montreal to Fort Garry. Journal of a Private in Third Expedition, Fort Garry, n.p, 1874.

Begg, Alexander. The Creation of Manitoba; or, a history of the Red River Troubles, (Toronto: Hunter, Rose & Co., 1871.

Begg, Alexander and Nursey, Walter, Ten Years in Winnipeg. A Narration of the Principal Events in the History of the City of Winnipeg from 1870 to 1879 inclusive. Winnipeg: Times Printing and Publishing, 1879.

Beauregard, George Le 9me Battalion au Nord-Ouest, Quebec : Jos.-G. Gingras & Cie., 1886.

Boulton, Charles A. I fought Riel. A military memoir. Toronto, James Lorimer & Company, 1985.

Bryce, George. Manitoba: It's Infancy, Growth and Present Condition, London, Samspon Low, Marston, Searle and Rivington, 1882.\

Chambers, Ernest. The Royal North-West Mounted Police. A Corps History. Montreal: The Mortimer Press, 1896.

Champion, CP. The Strange Demise of British Canada. The Liberals and Canadian Nationalism, 1964-1968, Montreal: McGill-Queens University Press, 2010.

Champion, Thomas Edward History of the 10th Royals and of the Royal Grenadiers from the formation of the regiment until 1896. Toronto: The Hunter Rose Company, 1896.

Collier, Anne M. A History of Portage la Prairie and Surrounding District,

Portage la Prairie: City of Portage la Prairie, 1970.

Currie, James T. and Crossland, Richard B. Twice The Citizen: A History of the United States Army Reserve, 1908–1995 (2nd ed), Washington: Office of the Chief, Army Reserve ,1997.

Daschuk, James Clearing the Plains. Disease, Politics of Starvation, and the loss of aboriginal life Regina; University of Regina Press, 2013.

Dunbar, Francis J. and Harper, Joseph H. Old Colours Never Die. A Record of Colours and Military Flags of Canada. Ottawa: Department of National Defence, 1992.

Ens, Gerhard J. Homeland to Hinterland. The Changing Worlds of the Red River Métis in the Nineteenth Century. Toronto: University of Toronto Press, 1996.

Fletcher, Lieutenant-Colonel. Memorandum on the Militia System of Canada. Ottawa: Citizen Printing Company, 1873.

Friesen, The Canadian Prairies: A History, Toronto: University of Toronto Press, 1987.

Gee, Jeffrey A Sketch of Both Sides of Manitoba, Nelsonville: Manitoba Mountaineer Book and Job Printing Establishment, 1881.

Goodspeed, Lieutenant-Colonel D.J. (ed), The Armed Forces of Canada 1867-1967. A Century of Achievement, Ottawa: Directorate of History and Heritage, 1967.

Gowanlock, Theresa and Delaney, Theresa, Two Months in the Camp of Big Bear. The Life and Adventures of Theresa Gowanlock and Theressa Delaney. Part I. Parkdale: The Times, 1885.

Griffin, Justus. From Toronto to Fort Garry an account of the Second Expedition to Red River. Diary of a Private Solider. Hamilton: Evening Times, 1893.

Harris, Stephen J. Canadian Brass. The Making of a Professional Army 1860-1939, Toronto: University of Toronto Press, 1988.

Hamilton, J.C. The Prairie Province; Sketches of Travel from Lake Ontario to Lake Winnipeg, Toronto: Belford Brothers, 1876.

Healey, W.J. Winnipeg's Early Days, Winnipeg: Stovel Company, Limited, 1927.

Hildebrandt, Walter. Views from Fort Battleford. Constructed Visions of an Anglo-Canadian West. Regina: AU Press, 2008.

Hoare, Quentin and Nowell, Smith, Geoffrey (eds.), Selections from the Prison Notebooks, New York: 1971.

Huyshe, Captain G.L. The Red River Expedition. Woolwich: The Naval and Military Press, Ltd, o.p. 1871.

Laidlaw, Alexander From the St. Lawrence to the North Saskatchewan. Being some incidents connected with the Detachment of "A" Battery, Regt. Canadian Artillery who composed part of the North-West Field Force in the Rebellion of 1885, Halifax, n.p., 1885.

Manitoba Club. Constitution and by-laws of the Manitoba Club, Winnipeg: Nor-Wester Print, 1874.

McKillip Jim. "Emboldened by Bad Behaviour: The Conduct of the Canadian Army in the Northwest, 1870 to 1873" in The Apathetic and the Defiant: Case Studies of Canadian Mutiny and Disobedience Kingston: Canadian Defence Academy Press, 2007.

MacBeth, Roderick George. The Making of the Canadian West: being the reminiscences of an eye-witness. Toronto: Brigg, 1898.

MacDougall, W.B. (Ed), MacDougall's Guide to Manitoba and the North-West, Winnipeg, W.B. MacDougall, Publisher, 1880.

Morton, Arthur S. A history of the Canadian West to 1870-71: being a history of Rupert's Land (the Hudson's Bay company's territory) and of the North-west territory (including the Pacific slope), London: T. Nelson & Sons, 1939.

Morton, WL, Manitoba: A History, Toronto, University of Toronto Press, 1997.

Orchard, David. The Fight for Canada: four centuries of resistance to American expansionism. Westmount: Robert Davies Multimedia Pub., 1999.

Pannekoek, Fritz. A Snug Little Flock. The Social Origins of the Riel Resistance 1869-70. Winnipeg, Watson & Dwyer Publishing, 1991.

Paterson, Edith. Tales of Early Manitoba from the Winnipeg Free Press, Winnipeg: The Winnipeg Free Press, 1976.

Robertson-Ross, Patrick. Report of Colonel Robertson-Ross, Adjt.-General of Militia, on the North-West Provinces and Territories of the Dominion, Ottawa: Dominion of Canada, 1872.

Russell, E.C. Customs and Traditions of the Canadian Armed Forces, Ottawa: Deneau & Greenberg Publishers, 1980.

Schofield, Frank Howard. The Story of Manitoba, Volume 1, Winnipeg, The S. J. Clarke Publishing Company, 1913.

Sherlock, Robert A. Experiences of the Halifax Battalion in the North-West, (Halifax: Jas. W. Doley, 1885.

Stacey, Charles P. Canada and the age of conflict: a history of Canadian external policies. Vol. 1. Toronto : University of Toronto Press, 1989.

------------- Canada and the British Army 1846-1871, Rev. Ed. Toronto: University of Toronto Press, 1936.

Stanley, George F.G. The Birth of Western Canada. A history of the Riel Rebellions. Toronto: University of Toronto Press, 1936.

------------ Canada's Soldiers. The Military History of an Unmilitary People. 3rd ed., Toronto: Macmillan, 1974 o.p. 1954.

-----------Toil and Trouble. Military Expeditions to Red River. Toronto: Dundurn Press, 1989.

Strange, Thomas Bland. Gunner Jingo's Jubilee, London: Remington & Co. Ltd., 1893.

Sulte, Benjamin. Histoire de la Milice Canadienne-Française, Montréal : Desbarats & Co., 1897.

Tennant, Joseph. Rough Times, A Souvenir of the 50th Anniversary of the Red River Expedition and the Formation of the Province of Manitoba (n.p., 1920).

Young, George. Manitoba Memories.

JOURNAL ARTICLES

Artibise, Alan F.J. "Winnipeg, 1874-1914" in Urban History Review, Number 1, June 1875, pp. 43-50.

Berry, John W. "Immigration, Acculturation, and Adaptation" in Applied Psychology: An international review, Vol 46, No. 1, 1997.

Brooks, Geoff. "A Horrible Night. An Historical Sketch of the North-West Rebellion" in The Lake Magazine, 1, No. 3, October 1892, 165-168.

Burroughs, Peter. "Imperial defence and the Victorian army" in The Journal of Imperial and Commonwealth History, Vol 15, No. 1, July 2008.

Carter, Sarah. "Your Great Mother Across the Salt Sea: Prairie First Nations, the British Monarchy and the Vice Regal Connection to 1900" in Manitoba History, Number 48, Autumn/Winter 2004-2005.

Conway, Shannon. "George Bryce and Anglo-Canadian Identity, 1880s to 1910s" in Manitoba History, No. 86, Spring 2018.

Crang, Jeremy A. "The Abolition of Compulsory Church Parades" in The Journal of Ecclesiastical History, Vol. 56, No. 1, January 2005.

Dafoe, John W. "Early Winnipeg Newspapers: The Last 70 Years of Journalism at Fort Garry and Winnipeg" in MHS Transactions, Series 3, 1956-57

Fridley, Russell W. "When Minnesota Coveted Canada" in Minnesota History, Summer 1968

Glueck, Alvin C. "The Riel Rebellion and Canadian-American Relations." In The Canadian Historical Review, Vol. XXXVI, no. 3, Sept, 1955.

Goheen, Peter G. "Symbols in the Streets: Parades in Victorian Urban Canada" in Urban History Review, Vol. XVIII, No. 3 (February 1990),

Grebstad, David. "Rowboat Diplomacy: The Dominion of Canada's Whole of Government Approach to The Red River Rebellion" in Canadian Military Journal, Vol. 13, No. 3, Summer 2013.

Haley, Bruce. "Sports and the Victorian World" in The Western Humanities Review, Volume 22, Number 2, Spring 1968

Hartman, James B. "The Growth of Music in Early Winnipeg to 1920" in Manitoba History, Number 40, Autumn/Winter 2000-2001.

Korneski, Kurt. "Brtishness, Canadianness, Class, Race: Winnipeg and the British World, 1880s-1910s" in Journal of Canadian Studies, Vol. 41, No. 2, Spring 2007

Lears, T.J. Jackson "The Concept of Cultural Hegemony: Problems and Possibilities" in The American Historical Review, vol. 90, no. 3 (June 1985).

Macdougall, Brenda and St-Onge, Nicole "Rooted in Mobility: Métis Buffalo-Hunting Brigades" in Manitoba History, Number 71, Winter 2013.

Marquis, Greg. "The 'Irish Model' and Nineteenth-Century Canadian Policing" in The Journal of Imperial and Commonwealth History, Vol 25, No. 2, May 1997.

McMicken, Gilbert. "The Abortive Fenian Raid on Manitoba" Manitoba Historical Society Transactions, Series 1, No. 32, 11 May 1888.

Miller, Carman. "The Montreal Militia as a Social Institution Before World War I" in Urban History Review, Vol. 19, No. 1, 1990.

Morton, Desmond. "Aid to the Civil Power: The Canadian Militia in Support of Social Order, 1867-1914" in The Canadian Historical Review, Vol. LI, No. 4, December 1970.

----------Cavalry or police: keeping the peace on two adjacent frontiers, 1870-1900" in Journal of Canadian Studies, Vol. 12, No. 2 , April, 1977.

Mott, Morris "The British Protestant Pioneers and the Establishment of Manly Sports in Manitoba, 1870-1886" in Journal of Sports History, Vol. 7, No. 3, (Winter, 1980).

Nerbas, Don. "Wealth and Privilege: An Analysis of Winnipeg's Early Business Elite" in Manitoba History, Number 47, Spring/Summer 2004.

Phillips, Paul. "The National Policy Revisited" Journal of Canadian Studies, Vol. 14, No. 3 Autumn 1979.

Read, Geoff and Webb, Todd. "The Catholic Mhadi of the North-West: Louis Riel and the Métis Resistance in Transatlantic and Imperial Context" in Canadian Historical Review 93, 2, June 2012.

Schreuder, D.M. "The Cultural Factor in Victorian Imperialism: A Case-Study of the British 'Civilising Mission'" in The Journal of Imperial and

Commonwealth History, $: 3, 1976, pp. 283-1317.

Smith, Andrew. "Patriotism, Self-Interest and the 'Empire Effect': Britishness and British Decisions to Invest in Canada, 1867-1914" in The Journal of Imperial and Commonwealth History, Vol. 41, No. 1, pp. 59-80.

Stacey, Charles P. "The Military Aspect of Canada's Winning of the West, 1870-1885" in The Canadian Historical Review, Vol. XXI, No. 1, 1940, pp 1-24.

----------"The Second Red River Expedition" Directorate of History and Heritage Archives, 500.009 (D32).

Stansky, Peter. "The Victorian Club" in English Literature in Translation Vol. 57, Issue 3, 2014.

Vineberg, Robert. "The British Garrison and Montreal Society, 1830-1850" in Canadian Military History, Volume 21, Number 1, Winter 2012

Wamsley, K.B. "Cultural signification and national ideologies: rifle shooting in late nineteenth-century Canada" in Social History, Vol. 20, No. 1, 1995.

Walzer, Michael. "On the Role of Symbolism in Political Thought," Political Science Quarterly, 82 (1967).

PERIODICALS

Le Métis.

The Manitoba Free Press.

Manitoba Liberal.

The Manitoba Newsletter.

Manitoba and Northwest Herald.

L'Opinion Publique.

Portage la Prairie Weekly Tribune.

The Volunteer Review and Military and Naval Gazette.

Governmental Primary Sources

Assiniboia. Sessional Journal of the Legislative Assembly of Assiniboia.

Bulter, WF. Report by Lt Butler (69th Regt) of his journey from Fort Garry to Rocky Mountain House and Back: Under Instructions from the Lieut. Governor of Manitoba, during the Winter of 1870-71, (Ottawa: Times Printing and Publishing Co., 1871.

Canada. Correspondence Relative to the Recent Disturbances in the Red River Settlement, London: Her Majesty's Stationary Office (1870).

Canada. Correspondence and papers connected with recent occurrences in the North-West Territories. Ottawa: I.B. Taylor, 1870.

Canada, Department of Militia and Defence, Regulations and Orders for the

Active Militia. Ottawa: Queen's Printer, 1870.

Canada. Report of the State of the Militia in the Dominion of Canada. (1870-1885). Canada. National Defence. Directorate of History and Heritage.

Morris, Alexander. The Treaties of Canada with the Indians of Manitoba and the North-West Territories including the negotiations on which they were based, and other information relating thereto. Toronto: Belfords, Clarke, & Co., 1880.

United Kingdom, Copy or Extracts of Correspondence between the Colonial Office, the Government of the Canadian Dominion, and the Hudson's Bay Company, relating to the surrender of Rupert's Land by the Hudson's Bay Company, and for the Admission Thereof into the Dominion of Canada, London: Colonial Office, 1869.

United Kingdom. Correspondence relative to the recent disturbances in the Red River Settlement, London: William Clowes & Sons, 1870.

United Kingdom, The War Office to Lieutenant-General the Honourable James Lindsay, London, 1870.

UNPUBLISHED THESES

Hogarth, GM. The Canadian Military Tradition in Western Canada 1870-1900, Master of Arts Thesis, Royal Military College of Canada, 1973.

Shore, Frederick. The Canadians and the Métis: The Re-creation of Manitoba, 1858-1872. Doctoral Thesis, University of Manitoba, 1991.

Public Archives

Journal of the Provisional Battalion of Rifles at Fort Garry, 1871 in James Taylor Collection: "Provisional Battalion Canadian Light Infantry & Artillery 1871-1877", Public Archives Manitoba, MG6, B5.

"The Royal Canadian Rifles at Fort Garry 1857-1861" in History of the Royal Canadian Rifle Regiment, Department of National Defence Directorate of History and Heritage Archives, 504.013 (D2).

Websites

Archives 1873-1899 - The Fire Fighters Museum - Winnipeg, Manitoba, Canada. Accessed September 29, 2017. http://winnipegfiremuseum.ca/archives.htm.

"Gabriel Dumont Institute of Native Studies and Applied Research Virtual Museum of Métis History and Culture." The Virtual Museum of Métis History and Culture. September 11, 2013. Accessed September 29, 2017. http://www.metismuseum.ca/resource.php/07260.

"Manitoba Historical Society" Accessed September 29, 2017. http://www.

mhs.mb.ca/.

INDEX

Manitoba Rifle Association: 142, 155-160.
McDougall, William: 30, 31, 32.
Middleton, Major-General Frederick Dobson: 24, 190, 194, 203, 204, 205, 206-208, 210-213, 216-228, 234, 236, 237, 238, 241, 248-250.
Military Districts (General): 25, 38.
    Number 1: 38, 53, 208.
    Number 2: 38, 53.
    Number 3: 38, 53.
    Number 4: 38, 53,
    Number 5: 38, 49, 53.
    Number 6: 38, 53.
    Number 7: 38, 53.
    Number 10: v, 48, 49, 53, 54, 56, 59, 87, 94, 95, 108, 132, 143, 145, 158, 190-195, 198, 204, 255, 259-261.
    Number 11: 53,
    Number 12: 259.
    Number 13: 259.
Military Units:
    1st Battalion, 60th Rifles: 39, 40, 45, 86, 129, 150.
    1st Ontario Rifles: 1, 40, 44, 48 57 63 64 66, 99, 105, 111, 121, 124, 144, 148-150, 169-170, 178-179, 182, 259.
    2nd Quebec Rifles: 40, 44, 48, 61, 65, 87, 105, 111, 125, 129, 169, 181.
    9th Battalion: 218, 230, 245, 248, 249.
    65th Battalion: 130, 216, 218, 228, 229, 232, 233, 245, 248, 250.
    91st Winnipeg Battalion of Infantry: 212, 214, 215, 235, 236, 248,
    92nd Winnipeg Light Infantry: 53, 130, 142, 212-214, 216, 228-234, 248.
    'A' Battery: 53, 56, 156, 218.
    Alberta Field Force: 130, 213, 216, 227, 228.
    Alberta Mounted Rifles: 228, 229.
    'B' Battery: 53, 54, 56, 218, 227.
    Boulton's Scouts: 210, 211, 218, 220, 222, 224, 228.
    Governor General's Foot Guards: 218, 227.
    Halifax Provisional Battalion: 215, 216, 245, 248.
    Midland Battalion: 218, 221, 222, 223, 224, 250.
    Montreal Garrison Artillery: 215, 247.
    North-West Field Force: iv, 190, 191, 202, 208, 211, 215, 234, 238, 240, 241, 242, 247.

318 | David W. Grebstad

ABOUT THE AUTHOR

David Grebstad, a proud Red River Métis, is deeply passionate about Manitoba's rich history and cultural legacy. With over thirty years of distinguished service in the Canadian Armed Forces, he brings a unique perspective to his writing. His previous works include *A Confluence of Destinies: The Winnipeg Falcons 1920 Gold Medal Olympic Victory in Ice Hockey* and *Iron Indignation: The Evolution of Canadian Artillery Tactics and the Victory at Vimy Ridge*, both of which explore pivotal moments in Canada's history. David now resides in Ottawa with his wife, Colleen, where he continues to explore his Métis heritage and love of Manitoba history.

DOUBLE‡DAGGER
— www.doubledagger.ca —

DOUBLE DAGGER BOOKS is Canada's only military-focused publisher. Conflict and warfare have shaped human history since before we began to record it. The earliest stories that we know of, passed on as oral tradition, speak of war, and more importantly, the essential elements of the human condition that are revealed under its pressure.

We are dedicated to publishing material that, while rooted in conflict, transcend the idea of "war" as merely a genre. Fiction, non-fiction, and stuff that defies categorization, we want to read it all.

Because if you want peace, study war.